Understanding Kristeva, Understanding Modernism

The aim of each volume in **Understanding Philosophy, Understanding Modernism** is to understand a philosophical thinker more fully through literary and cultural modernism and consequently to understand literary modernism better through a key philosophical figure. In this way, the series also rethinks the limits of modernism, calling attention to lacunae in modernist studies and sometimes in the philosophical work under examination.

Series Editors:
Paul Ardoin, S. E. Gontarski, and Laci Mattison

Volumes in the Series:
Understanding Bergson, Understanding Modernism
Edited by Paul Ardoin, S. E. Gontarski, and Laci Mattison
Understanding Deleuze, Understanding Modernism
Edited by S. E. Gontarski, Paul Ardoin and Laci Mattison
Understanding Wittgenstein, Understanding Modernism
Edited by Anat Matar
Understanding Foucault, Understanding Modernism
Edited by David Scott
Understanding James, Understanding Modernism
Edited by David H. Evans
Understanding Rancière, Understanding Modernism
Edited by Patrick M. Bray
Understanding Blanchot, Understanding Modernism
Edited by Christopher Langlois
Understanding Merleau-Ponty, Understanding Modernism
Edited by Ariane Mildenberg
Understanding Nietzsche, Understanding Modernism
Edited by Douglas Burnham and Brian Pines
Understanding Derrida, Understanding Modernism
Edited by Jean-Michel Rabaté
Understanding Adorno, Understanding Modernism
Edited by Robin Truth Goodman

Understanding Flusser, Understanding Modernism
Edited by Aaron Jaffe, Rodrigo Martini, and Michael F. Miller
Understanding Marx, Understanding Modernism
Edited by Mark Steven
Understanding Barthes, Understanding Modernism
Edited by Jeffrey R. Di Leo and Zahi Zalloua
Understanding Kristeva, Understanding Modernism
Edited by Maria Margaroni
Understanding Bakhtin, Understanding Modernism (forthcoming)
Edited by Philippe Birgy
Understanding Badiou, Understanding Modernism (forthcoming)
Edited by Arka Chattopadhyay and Arthur Rose
Understanding Žižek, Understanding Modernism (forthcoming)
Edited by Jeffrey R. Di Leo and Zahi Zalloua
Understanding Nancy, Understanding Modernism (forthcoming)
Edited by Cosmin Toma
Understanding Cavell, Understanding Modernism (forthcoming)
Edited by Paola Marrati

Understanding Kristeva, Understanding Modernism

Edited by
Maria Margaroni

BLOOMSBURY ACADEMIC
NEW YORK • LONDON • OXFORD • NEW DELHI • SYDNEY

BLOOMSBURY ACADEMIC
Bloomsbury Publishing Inc
1385 Broadway, New York, NY 10018, USA
50 Bedford Square, London, WC1B 3DP, UK
29 Earlsfort Terrace, Dublin 2, Ireland

BLOOMSBURY, BLOOMSBURY ACADEMIC and the Diana logo are
trademarks of Bloomsbury Publishing Plc

First published in the United States of America 2023
This paperback edition published 2024

Copyright © Maria Margaroni, 2023

Each chapter copyright © by the contributor, 2023

Cover image © JR Korpa / Unsplash.com

All rights reserved. No part of this publication may be reproduced or transmitted in any form or by any means, electronic or mechanical, including photocopying, recording, or any information storage or retrieval system, without prior permission in writing from the publishers.

Bloomsbury Publishing Inc does not have any control over, or responsibility for, any third-party websites referred to or in this book. All internet addresses given in this book were correct at the time of going to press. The author and publisher regret any inconvenience caused if addresses have changed or sites have ceased to exist, but can accept no responsibility for any such changes.

Library of Congress Cataloging-in-Publication Data
Names: Margaroni, Maria, editor.
Title: Understanding Kristeva, understanding modernism / edited by Maria Margaroni.
Description: New York : Bloomsbury Academic, 2023. | Series: Understanding philosophy, understanding modernism | Includes bibliographical references and index. | Summary: "Explores and illuminates Kristeva's profound impact on our understanding of literary modernism"– Provided by publisher.
Identifiers: LCCN 2022028632 (print) | LCCN 2022028633 (ebook) | ISBN 9781501362354 (hardback) | ISBN 9798765102169 (paperback) | ISBN 9781501362361 (epub) | ISBN 9781501362378 (pdf) | ISBN 9781501362385 (ebook other)
Subjects: LCSH: Kristeva, Julia, 1941- | Modernism (Literature) | LCGFT: Essays.
Classification: LCC B2430.K7544 U53 2023 (print) | LCC B2430.K7544 (ebook) | DDC 194–dc23/eng/20220819
LC record available at https://lccn.loc.gov/2022028632
LC ebook record available at https://lccn.loc.gov/2022028633

ISBN:	HB:	978-1-5013-6235-4
	PB:	979-8-7651-0216-9
	ePDF:	978-1-5013-6237-8
	eBook:	978-1-5013-6236-1

Series: Understanding Philosophy, Understanding Modernism

Typeset by Integra Software Services Pvt. Ltd.

To find out more about our authors and books visit www.bloomsbury.com and sign up for our newsletters.

CONTENTS

Notes on contributors ix
Series preface xiv
Acknowledgements xvi
List of abbreviations xvii

Introduction: Kristeva at the bleeding edge of modernism
Maria Margaroni 1

Part 1 Conceptualizing Kristeva 13

1 Kristeva telle quelle: A seductive encounter *Danielle Marx-Scouras* 15

2 Julia Kristeva: *Chora*, infinity, modernism *John Lechte* 37

3 Indifferent feminine: Kristeva and the avant-garde *Miglena Nikolchina* 57

4 Modernist trajectories in time: Kristeva's *The Enchanted Clock* *Carol Mastrangelo Bové* 75

5 Sanctity and scandal: Teresa and the challenge of nineteenth-century 'false mysticism' *Martha J. Reineke* 93

6 Kristeva's traumatic real: Securing the symbolic nation through the law of the veil *Tina Chanter* 109

7 Kristeva on Arendt: Politics and the subject *Robin Truth Goodman* 129

Part 2 Kristeva and aesthetics 147

8   Modernism unleashed and restrained: Joyce, Céline and Arendt in Kristeva's tale of the century
    Marios Constantinou 149

9   The fabric of gothic modernism: Powers of horror in M. R. James' 'Oh, Whistle, and I'll Come to You, My Lad'
    Nicholas Chare 179

10 The impact of Kristeva's theory of abjection on modernist art *Rina Arya* 197

11 Androgynous and a foreigner: Orlando's revolt
    Christina Kkona 213

12 'Let it end, this cold insanity. Let it happen.' Kristeva's melancholic modernism and the Parisian novels of Jean Rhys *Rossitsa Terzieva-Artemis* 231

13 The mirror before the mirror: Reflections on Kristeva and Martha Graham's *Hérodiade* *Robert R. Shane* 251

Part 3 Glossary 267

14 Abjection *Dawid Kołoszyc* 269

15 Avant-garde *Christos Hadjiyiannis* 277

16 Female genius *Elisabetta Convento* 287

17 Intertextuality *Gertrude Postl* 297

18 Intimate revolt *Gertrude Postl* 305

19 Spirituality *Alison Jasper* 313

20 Subject in process/on trial *Esther Hutfless and Elisabeth Schäfer* 321

21 The semiotic/The symbolic *Dawid Kołoszyc* 329

Index 337

CONTRIBUTORS

Rina Arya is a Professor at the University of Huddersfield. She is interested in the visual and material culture of religion. Author *of Francis Bacon: Painting in a Godless World* (2012) and *Abjection and Representation* (2014), she is currently working on a study of cultural appropriation in a Hindu context.

Carol Mastrangelo Bové is Teaching Professor in English/Gender, Sexuality, and Women's Studies at the University of Pittsburgh and Professor Emerita in French at Westminster College, Pennsylvania. She is the author of two books on Kristeva, *Language and Politics in Julia Kristeva: Literature, Art, Therapy* (SUNY Press, 2006) and *Kristeva in America: Re-imagining the Exceptional* (Palgrave Macmillan, 2020). Her other publications include many articles on twentieth- and twenty-first-century literature, film and literary translation. She has translated Hélène Cixous, Luce Irigaray and Julia Kristeva. A book on Colette as well as a new translation of her *La Maison de Claudine* is in the works.

Tina Chanter has published on contemporary French philosophy, drawing inspiration from a range of sources, including feminist theory, race theory, psychoanalysis, art, politics, film and tragedy. Her most recent books are *Whose Antigone? The Tragic Marginalisation of Slavery* and *Art; Politics and Rancière: Broken Perceptions*. She taught in the United States, most recently in Chicago, before returning to the UK, where she worked and taught in Bristol and London before joining Newcastle University.

Nicholas Chare is Professor of Art History in the Department of History of Art and Film Studies at the Université de Montréal. He is the author of *After Francis Bacon* (2012) and the co-editor (with Valérie Bienvenue) of *Animals, Plants and Afterimages* (2022) and (with Ersy Contogouris) *On the Nude* (2022). His work has appeared in journals including *Angelaki*, *Art History*, *Cultural Critique*, *Paragraph*, *parallax* and *symplokē*.

Marios Constantinou received his PhD from the New School for Social Research. He is the editor of *Badiou and the Political Condition* (EUP), as well as of special issues on *Space and Event* (*Environment and Planning D: Society and Space*) and *Imperial Affect* (*Parallax*). His writings and essays appeared in *Third Text, Parrhesia, The Year's Work in Critical and Cultural Theory, Angelaki, Parallax, Thesis Eleven, Postcolonial Studies* and elsewhere. They all attempt from different angles to retrieve the counter-imperial truth of the political from the grip of contemporary norms of biopower.

Elisabetta Convento (MA University of Padova, MA Purdue University, PhD University of Trento and Paris 8) is Director of Boston University Padova programme and Professor of Italian Studies. For Boston University she recently taught *Contemporary Italian Literature* and *The Intersection of Gender, Race, Media and Covid 19*. She has published in the fields of linguistics, women studies and Italian studies. Among other works, she is the translator and editor of Julia Kristeva's *Il rischio del pensare* (Il Melangolo, 2006) and editor of a *Twentieth-Century Literary Criticism* volume devoted to Dino Buzzati (Gale, 2021).

Robin Truth Goodman is Professor of English at Florida State University. Her published works include: *Gender Commodity: Marketing Feminist Identities and the Promise of Security; Understanding Adorno, Understanding Modernism; The Bloomsbury Handbook of 21st Century Feminist Theory; Promissory Notes: On the Literary Conditions of Debt; Gender for the Warfare State: Literature of Women in Combat; Literature and the Development of Feminist Theory; Gender Work: Feminism After Neoliberalism; Feminist Theory in Pursuit of the Public: Women and the 'Re-Privatization' of Labor; Policing Narratives and the State of Terror; World, Class, Women: Global Literature, Education, and Feminism; Strange Love, or How We Learn to Stop Worrying and Love the Market;* and *Infertilities: Exploring Fictions of Barren Bodies*. She has recently edited *Feminism as World Literature* (forthcoming from Bloomsbury, 2023).

Christos Hadjiyiannis is a research fellow at the Centre for Medieval Arts and Rituals at the University of Cyprus. He has published widely on twentieth-century literature and art, and is the author of *Conservative Modernists: Literature and Tory Politics in Britain, 1900–1920* (Cambridge University Press, 2018). He is also the editor, with Rachel Potter, of *The Cambridge Companion to Twentieth-Century Literature and Politics* (2020).

Esther Hutfless is a philosopher and psychoanalyst in Vienna, Austria. Her main teaching and research areas include: deconstruction, psychoanalysis, feminist philosophy, Écriture féminine and queer theory. Her recent publications include essays on the case of Dora, a 'Freuderridian' approach to a non-normative psychoanalysis and on Jean Laplanche and Queer Theory. She has co-edited a book on queer theory and psychoanalysis with Barbara Zach, and the German translations of Hélène Cixous' *The Laugh of the Medusa* (with Elisabeth Schäfer and Gertrude Postl) and *Writing Blind* (with Elisabeth Schäfer).

Alison Jasper was, until recently, Senior Lecturer in Religion and Gender at the University of Stirling in Scotland, where she was instrumental in setting up its masters programme in gender studies. She is a founder member of the Critical Religion Association (https://criticalreligion.org/).

Christina Kkona is currently a Marie Curie fellow at Bordeaux-Montaigne University. She has previously been a COFUND fellow/associate professor at Aarhus Institute of Advanced Studies, Aarhus University. After receiving her PhD in History and Semiotics of Text and Image from Paris 7-Diderot University, she taught cultural and literary theory at American Hellenic University of Athens for seven years. Her articles and reviews in English and French have been published in international journals and conference proceedings. Recent publications include *Women of Science Fiction and Horror in Their Own Words*, co-authored with Seb Doubinsky and forthcoming from Bloomsbury (2023); *Migrating Minds. Theories and Practices of Cultural Cosmopolitanism*, co-edited with Didier Coste and Nicoletta Pireddu, forthcoming from Routledge (2022).

Dawid Kołoszyc is Professor of Humanities, Philosophy and Religion at Vanier College. His doctoral work explored the relationship between literary, psychoanalytic and religious language in Julia Kristeva's examinations of the crisis of meaning in late modern culture. He lives in Montreal.

John Lechte is Emeritus Professor of Sociology at Macquarie University in Sydney. His most recent book is *The Human: Bare Life and Ways of Life* (Bloomsbury, 2018). He also authored (with Saul Newman) *Agamben and the Politics of Human Rights: Statelessness, Images, Violence* (Edinburgh, 2015, pbk) and *Genealogy and Ontology of the Western Image* (Routledge, 2012). His doctorate on Rousseau's fiction was supervised by Julia Kristeva and he has published numerous essays on her work. He has also published widely in European philosophy and theory, especially on the work of Agamben, Arendt, Bataille, Derrida and Levinas.

Maria Margaroni is Associate Professor of Literary Theory and Feminist Thought at the University of Cyprus. She has held visiting fellowships at the Institute for Advanced Studies in the Humanities (University of Edinburgh) and the Centre for Cultural Analysis, Theory and History (University of Leeds). She has published extensively on the work of Julia Kristeva in peer-reviewed journals and collected volumes. She is the co-author of *Julia Kristeva: Live Theory* (with John Lechte, Continuum, 2004). Other publications include three edited volumes, most recently *Arts of Healing: Cultural Narratives of Trauma* (with Arleen Ionescu, Rowman and Littlefield, 2020), and two special issues (in *The European Journal of English Studies* and *Philosophy Today*).

Danielle Marx-Scouras, Professor of French at the Ohio State University (Columbus, Ohio), works in contemporary French and Francophone literatures, theory, intellectual history and popular music. She is the author of *La France de Zebda 1981–2004, Faire de la musique, un acte politique* (Editions Autrement, 2005) and *The Cultural Politics of Tel Quel: Literature and the Left in the Wake of Engagement* (Penn State University Press, 1996). She guest-edited a special issue of *Research in African Literatures* on 'Dissident Algeria' in 1999 and has published numerous articles and book chapters on authors and topics such as Albert Camus, women and the Algerian war, French and Maghrebian (North African) theory, Leïla Sebbar, Elio Vittorini's Politecnico, Jean Sénac, Driss Chraïbi, Hélé Béji and French popular music.

Miglena Nikolchina is Professor at the Department of Theory of Literature at the University of Sofia, Bulgaria. She is a poet, writer and theoretician whose research interests involve the interactions of literature, philosophy, political studies and feminist theory. In English, her publications include numerous articles on Kristeva's work as well as the books *Matricide in Language: Writing Theory in Kristeva and Woolf* (2004) and *Lost Unicorns of the Velvet Revolutions: Heterotopias of the Seminar* (2013).

Gertrude Postl is Professor of Philosophy and Women's and Gender Studies at Suffolk County Community College, Selden, New York, USA. She currently serves on the Executive Committee of the Association for Philosophy and Literature (APL). Her research interests are focused on feminist philosophy, especially the intersection between body, language and representation (Luce Irigaray, Julia Kristeva, Hélène Cixous), and issues of reading/writing, author and text (Roland Barthes and Jacques Derrida). Her recent publications include: *Hélène Cixous. Das Lachen der Medusa zusammen mit aktuellen Beiträgen* (co-editor with Esther Hutfless and Elisabeth Schäfer, Vienna: Passagen, 2013); 'Kristeva's Revolt, Illusion, and the Feminine', in Maria Margaroni et al. (eds.), *Textual Layering: Contact, Historicity, Critique* (Lexington Books, 2017); entry on 'Language, Writing, and Difference', *The Routledge Companion to Feminist Philosophy* (2017).

Martha J. Reineke (PhD Vanderbilt University) is Professor in the Department of Philosophy and World Religions at the University of Northern Iowa. Her areas of teaching and research expertise include psychoanalytic theory, religion and society, and Existentialism. She is the author of *Sacrificed*

Lives: Kristeva on Women and Violence (Indiana University Press, 1997) and *Intimate Domain: Desire, Trauma, and Mimetic Theory* (Michigan State University Press, 2014). She is the editor, with David Goodman, of *Ana-María Rizzuto and the Psychoanalysis of Religion: The Road to the Living God* (Lexington Books, 2017). She also serves as Executive Secretary of the Colloquium on Violence and Religion.

Elisabeth Schäfer is a philosopher at the Department of Philosophy at the University of Vienna, where she has been teaching since 2010. Her areas of research and teaching include deconstruction, queer feminist philosophy, Écriture féminine, writing as artistic research and performance philosophy. She gives lectures and lecture performances on a regular basis, also participates in conferences and symposia, makes interventions and so on. She is the co-editor of the first German translation of Hélène Cixous' *Le Rire de la Méduse* (Passagen, 2013), as well as author of several essays and book chapters, most recently in Ruth Mateus-Berr and Richard Jochum (eds.), *Teaching Artistic Research. Conversations across Cultures* (De Gruyter 2020), and in Laura Cull Ó Maoilearca, Alice Lagaay (ed.), *The Routledge Companion to Performance Philosophy* (2020).

Robert R. Shane is an independent art historian, critic and curator. He received his PhD in Art History and Criticism from Stony Brook University. He is a curatorial consultant to the University Art Museum at the University at Albany, New York; gallery programme coordinator at Collar Works, Troy, New York; and a frequent contributor to *The Brooklyn Rail*. His scholarly work has been published in *Hypatia*. His research work on art and dance has been published in the journals *Art Criticism* and *theory@buffalo*, as well as the book *Seeing Whole: Toward an Ethics and Ecology of Sight*, eds. Mark Ledbetter and Asbjørn Grønstad. Dr Shane has presented this research at the Society of Dance History Scholars, the Kristeva Circle and the College Art Association.

Rossitsa Terzieva-Artemis is Professor of Literature in the Department of Languages and Literature at the University of Nicosia, Cyprus, and works in the fields of modern British, American and Anglophone literatures, continental philosophy and cultural studies. She holds an MA in English Language and Literature, an MPhil in Gender Studies and an MPhil and a PhD in the Human Sciences with a specialization in literature, philosophy and psychoanalysis. She is the author of the book *Stories of the Unconscious: Sub-Versions in Freud, Lacan, and Kristeva*, as well as the editor of special issues on Iris Murdoch and Julia Kristeva of the journal *Studies in the Literary Imagination* and a volume of essays on Ford Madox Ford's novel *The Good Soldier*.

SERIES PREFACE

Sometime in the late twentieth century, modernism, like philosophy itself, underwent something of an unmooring from (at least) linear literary history in favour of the multi-perspectival history implicit in 'new historicism' or, say, varieties of 'presentism'. Amid current reassessments of modernism and modernity, critics have posited various 'new' or alternative modernisms – postcolonial, cosmopolitan, transatlantic, transnational, geomodernism or even 'bad' modernisms. In doing so, they have not only reassessed modernism as a category but also, more broadly, rethought epistemology and ontology, aesthetics, metaphysics, materialism, history and being itself, opening possibilities of rethinking not only which texts we read as modernist but also how we read those texts. Much of this new conversation constitutes something of a critique of the periodization of modernism or modernist studies in favour of modernism as mode (or mode of production) or concept. Understanding Philosophy, Understanding Modernism situates itself amid the plurality of discourses, offering collections focused on key philosophical thinkers influential both to the moment of modernism and to our current understanding of that moment's genealogy, archaeology and becomings. Such critiques of modernism(s) and modernity afford opportunities to rethink and reassess the overlaps, folds, interrelationships, interleavings or cross-pollinations of modernism and philosophy. Our goal in each volume of the series is to understand literary modernism better through philosophy as we also better understand a philosopher through literary modernism. The first two volumes of the series, those on Henri Bergson and Gilles Deleuze, have established a tripartite structure that serves to offer accessibility both to the philosopher's principal texts and to current new research. Each volume opens with a section focused on 'conceptualizing' the philosopher through close readings of seminal texts in the thinker's oeuvre. A second section, on aesthetics, maps connections between modernist works and the philosophical figure, often surveying key modernist trends and shedding new light on authors and texts. The final section of each volume serves as an extended glossary of principal terms in the philosopher's work, each treated at length, allowing a fuller engagement with and examination of the many, sometimes contradictory ways terms are deployed. The series is thus designed both to introduce philosophers and to rethink their relationship to modernist studies, revising our understandings of both modernism and philosophy, and offering resources that will be of use across disciplines, from philosophy, theory and literature to religion, the visual and performing arts, and often to the sciences as well.

ACKNOWLEDGEMENTS

I am grateful to Robin Truth Goodman and Paul Ardoin for their initial advice and encouragement to pursue this project. I am also indebted to the commissioning and production team at Bloomsbury, especially Haaris Naqvi, who has been very supportive throughout. I would also like to thank the series editors for their appreciation of the different perspectives presented in this volume and helpful feedback. Immense thanks are due to the contributors of the volume who sustained their enthusiasm and commitment during the lengthy editorial process and at a time which turned out to be a challenge for many of us.

As ever, the book is dedicated to Ellipolis, *ma joueuse/joyeuse.*

ABBREVIATIONS

ACW	*About Chinese Women*, trans. A. Barrows, New York: Urizen Books, 1977.
BS	*Black Sun: Depression and Melancholia*, trans. Leon S. Roudiez, New York: Columbia University Press, 1989.
C	*Colette,* trans. Jean Marie Todd, New York: Columbia University Press, 2004.
CES	*Crisis of the European Subject*, trans. Susan Fairfield, New York: Other Press, 2000.
DL	*Desire in Language: A Semiotic Approach to Literature and Art*, ed. Leon S. Roudiez, trans. Thomas Gora, Alice Jardine and Leon S. Roudiez, New York: Columbia University Press, 1980.
E	*Étrangers à nous-mêmes*, Paris: Gallimard, 1988.
EC	*The Enchanted Clock*, trans. Armine Kotin Mortimer, New York: Columbia University Press, 2017.
EPE	'Experiencing the Phallus as Extraneous, or Women's Twofold Oedipus Complex', *Parallax*, 4 (3) (2005): 29–41.
FS	(with C. Clément). *The Feminine and the Sacred*, trans. Jane Marie Todd, Basingstoke: Palgrave, 2001.
HA	*Hannah Arendt*, trans. Ross Guberman, New York: Columbia University Press, 2001.
HDA	*Histoires d'amour*, Paris: Denöel, 1983.
HE	*L' Horloge enchantée*, Paris: Fayard, 2015.
HF	*Hatred and Forgiveness*, trans. Jeanine Herman, New York: Columbia University Press, 2010.
HP	*La haine et le pardon: Pouvoirs et limites de la psychanalyse*, III, Paris: Fayard, 2005.

I	*Interviews*, ed. Ross Mitchell Guberman, New York: Columbia University Press, 1996.
INB	*This Incredible Need to Believe*, trans. Beverley Bie Brahic, New York: Columbia University Press, 2009.
IR	*Intimate Revolt: The Powers and Limits of Psychoanalysis*, II, trans. Jeanine Herman, New York: Columbia University Press, 2002.
JMV	*Je me voyage. Mémoires. Entretiens avec Samuel Dock*, Paris: Fayard, 2016.
KCR	*The Kristeva Critical Reader*, ed. John Lechte and Mary Zournazi, Edinburgh: Edinburgh University Press, 2003.
KR	*The Kristeva Reader*, ed. Toril Moi, Oxford: Blackwell, 1986.
MB	*Murder in Byzantium*, trans. C. Jon Delogu, New York: Columbia University Press, 2006.
MK	*Melanie Klein*, trans. R. Guberman, New York: Columbia University Press, 2002.
NMS	*New Maladies of the Soul*, trans. Ross Guberman, New York: Columbia University Press, 1995.
ND	'"Nous deux" or a (Hi)story of Intertextuality', *The Romanic Review*, 93 (1–2) (2002): 7–13.
NFR	'New Forms of Revolt', *Journal of French and Francophone Philosophy – Revue de la philosophie française et de langue française*, 22 (2) (2014): 1–19.
NWN	*Nations Without Nationalism*, trans. L. S. Roudiez, New York: Columbia University Press, 1993.
OMW	*The Old Man and the Wolves*, trans. Barbara Bray, New York: Columbia University Press, 1994.
OPD	'Oscillation between Power and Denial', in Elaine Marks and Isabelle de Courtivron (eds), *New French Feminisms*, 165–7, New York: Schocken Books, 1981.
P	*Possessions*, trans. Barbara Bray, New York: Columbia University Press, 1998.
PH	*Powers of Horror: An Essay on Abjection*, trans. Leon S. Roudiez, New York: Columbia University Press, 1982.
PK	*The Portable Kristeva*, ed. Kelly Oliver, New York: Columbia University Press, 1997.

PL	*Polylogue*, Paris: Seuil, 1977.
PSF	*In the Beginning Was Love – Psychoanalysis and Faith*, trans. A. Goldhammer, New York: Columbia University Press, 1987.
PST	*Proust and the Sense of Time*, trans. Stephen Bann, London: Faber and Faber, 1993.
PT	*Passions of Our Time*, ed. Lawrence D. Kritzman, trans. Constance Borde and Sheila Malovany-Chevallier, New York: Columbia University Press, 2018.
R	'Reliance, or Maternal Eroticism', *Journal of the American Psychoanalytic Association*, 62 (1) (2014): 69–85.
RI	*La révolte intime: discours direct (Pouvoirs et limites de la psychanalyse, II)*, Paris: Fayard, 1997.
RLP	*La Révolution du langage poétique. L'avant-garde à la fin du XIXe siècle: Lautréamont et Mallarmé*, Paris: Seuil, 1974.
RPL	*Revolution in Poetic Language*, trans. Margaret Waller, New York: Columbia University Press, 1984.
S	*Σημειωτική [Séméiotiké]: Recherches pour une sémanalyse*, Paris: Seuil, 1969.
SA	*The Samurai: A Novel*, trans. B. Bray, New York: Columbia University Press, 1992.
SH	*The Severed Head: Capital Visions*, trans. Jody Gladding, New York: Columbia University Press, 2012.
SM	'Stabat Mater', in Toril Moi (ed.), *The Kristeva Reader*, 160–86, Oxford: Blackwell, 1986.
SNS	*The Sense and Non-Sense of Revolt: The Powers and Limits of Psychoanalysis*, I, trans. Jeanine Herman, New York: Columbia University Press, 2000.
SO	*Strangers to Ourselves*, trans. Leon S. Roudiez, New York: Columbia University Press, 1991.
SP	'The Subject in Process', in Patrick ffrench and Roland-François Lack (eds), *The Tel Quel Reader*, 133–78, London: Routledge, 1998.
SUF	*Seule une femme*, Paris: Éditions de l'Aube, 2007.
TAS	*Time and Sense: Proust and the Experience of Literature*, trans. Ross Guberman, New York: Columbia University Press, 1996.

TL   *Tales of Love*, trans. Leon S. Roudiez, New York: Columbia University Press, 1987.

TML   *Teresa, My Love: An Imagined Life of the Saint of Avila*, trans. L. S. Fox, New York: Columbia University Press, 2014.

TR   *Le Texte du roman: approche sémiologique d'une structure discursive transformationnelle*, Paris: Mouton, 1970.

TSP   'Towards a Semiology of Paragrams', in Patrick ffrench and Roland-François Lack (eds), *The Tel Quel Reader*, 25–49, London: Routledge, 1998.

VC   *Visions capitales*, Paris: Réunion des musées nationaux, catalogue of an exhibition held at the Musée du Louvre, Paris, 27 April–3 November 1998.

WND   'Woman Can Never Be Defined', trans. Marilyn A. August, in Elaine Marks and Isabelle de Courtivron (eds), *New French Feminisms*, 137–41, New York: Schocken Books, 1981.

WT   'Women's Time', in Kelly Oliver (ed.), *French Feminism Reader*, 181–200, Lanham, MD: Rowman and Littlefield, 2000.

Introduction: Kristeva at the bleeding edge of modernism

Maria Margaroni

Julia Kristeva's contribution to the theorization of the European avant-gardes from the end of the nineteenth century to the Second World War has widely been acknowledged and continues to be the focus of much critical debate. Equipped with a solid knowledge in a variety of fields (i.e. continental philosophy, linguistics, European literature and aesthetics, Russian avant-gardism and Poetics, Marxist political theory, anthropology, psychoanalysis), Kristeva has revolutionized the study of modernism by developing a theoretical approach that is uniquely attuned to the dynamic interplay between, on the one hand, linguistic and formal experimentation, and on the other hand, subjective crisis and socio-political upheaval. Inspired by the contestatory spirit of the late 1960s in which she emerged as a theorist, Kristeva has defended the project of the European avant-gardes and has systematically attempted to reclaim their legacy in the new societal structures produced by a global, spectacle-dominated capitalism. Although her reading of this legacy changes in response to the different challenges her generation faces from the Cold War climate of the 1960s and 1970s to the fall of the Berlin wall in 1989 and the new terror-haunted landscape of the twenty-first century, Kristeva's allegiance to avant-garde thought never wavers and continues to inform her more recent reflections on a politics of permanent conflictuality.[1]

As a number of commentators have argued, her early work (*Semiotiké, Le texte du roman*) already contains the seeds of what will be recognized as a groundbreaking theory of avant-garde writing.[2] It is, however, *La révolution du langage poétique* (1974) that establishes Kristeva as one of the major theoretical voices in the literary field, introducing some of the concepts that remain touchstones in the analysis of key modernist figures, from Mallarmé and Lautréamont to Bataille, Artaud, Joyce, Woolf, Colette, Céline, Celan, Proust and Aragon (among others). Focusing on the nineteenth-century post-Symbolist avant-garde generation, Kristeva's main concern in this book is to theorize a process of signification that exceeds and disrupts codified communicative operations. Produced by the movement of instinctual matter, this process which she prefers to call *signifiance* forces us, according to her, to reconceptualize not only the object defined by our philosophies of language and the phenomenological subject they presuppose but also 'literature' as the realm of the beautiful, divorced from sociohistorical formations and material operations. What she calls 'poetic language' is not (as some commentators have thought)[3] a language *other* than ordinary language but a signifying practice that infinitizes both meaning and the subject, remaining always at work within and against semantic, pragmatic, syntactic as well as grammatical constraints. Because of its antagonistic function, its basis in the movement of instinctual matter, poetic language is by definition revolutionary and, *under specific sociohistorical conditions*, can bring about the subject's rebirth as much as the community's renewal. In *La révolution du langage poétique* Kristeva seeks to understand the distinct contexts (e.g. the Franco-Prussian war, the emergence of nationalism, the Paris Commune of 1871) that have made possible at the end of the nineteenth century the eruption of a writing at the underbelly of beautiful language, unfolding as an exploration of psychic and societal crisis. Thus, in her theorization of avant-garde literature as a radical form of textuality, Kristeva insists on both its sociohistorical basis and its sociohistorical effects. The key question for her in the 1970s concerns less the introduction of a metalanguage that can do justice to formal innovation than the development of a practice-oriented theory[4] committed to translating the negativity at work in avant-garde writing in terms comprehensible to 'the subjects transforming the process of history' (SP 173).

This task is most important for Kristeva at a time when Jean-Paul Sartre's approach to literature as 'engagement' seems to fall short of the socio-political challenges faced by the post-war generation. As a prominent member of *Tel Quel*, an avant-garde theory journal in France which aimed at defining itself as the continuation of early twentieth-century literary modernism (especially, surrealism and the transgressive aesthetics of Bataille and Artaud),[5] Kristeva devotes herself to the formalization of an avant-garde 'terrorist aesthetics' (Sjöholm 2005: 3), taking up the modernist legacy while acknowledging and seeking to move beyond the political impasses that lie at the heart of this legacy.

Although, as has been argued, her work reinscribes many of the myths associated with the late nineteenth- and early twentieth-century avant-gardes,[6] this reinscription is far from uncritical (especially as her thinking develops from the 1960s to the present), seeking to transform the myths into wagers, the 'sweeping claims' of a revolutionary enthusiasm into problems of a theoretical discourse that is materialist in its approach and aims at social transformation (Cavanagh 1993: 286). Thus, she never assumes a mirror-relation between aesthetic and political revolution, yet she is reluctant to abandon the challenge of reconceptualizing their complex interplay. What is at issue is how this interplay gets mobilized in distinct historical periods; how it develops or is prevented from developing; how it inspires subjects posited at diverse nodes of the historical unfolding; how it is used to serve antagonistic historical ends, to prevent or empower particular historical possibilities.

If she, like other thinkers of her generation, has foregrounded the role of language in this interplay between the aesthetic and the political that constitutes the source of attraction and the site of a crisis within the history of the avant-gardes, this is not out of a (predictably postmodern) conviction that 'there is no World', as Cavanagh assumes (1993: 297), but precisely because our relation to and interpretations of the world are negotiated through language, the nature and function of which cannot be taken for granted.[7] According to Kristeva, this is, indeed, where the value of avant-garde writing lies: that is, in its exploration of 'the resources of the *word* – what to say? how to say it? what does "say" mean? to make and unmake sense?' (SNS 107; emphasis in the original). What the avant-gardes teach us is that – although aesthetic and political transformations are inevitably born on the level of material existence: an existence circumscribed by biological and social constraints, experienced by subjects pulled in different directions and split apart by ambivalent interests or desires – they are also the product of an (always discursively formed) imaginary, where the subjective and communal crises brought about by material constraints are turned into deadly or regenerative encounters with what Kristeva calls 'the impossible': the death drive, the 'impasses of consciousness', the breaking down of sense, the loss of borders (SNS 107). Such encounters with the impossible constitute the source of the negativity Kristeva theorizes at the heart of both the process of historical change and the workings of the avant-garde text. As she argues, this negativity is the critical force that needs to be preserved from the avant-garde project and transposed into the present.[8]

Despite her appreciation of 'the culture of revolt' that is part of the legacy of avant-garde thought, Kristeva remains sensitive to the dangers inherent in it (SNS 6–9). In 'The Subject in Process' she focuses on the experience of limits performed in the controversial writings of Antonin Artaud and traces 'the surplus of pleasure' produced by the expulsion of heterogeneous matter as it disrupts symbolic and social safeguards, musicating the phonemic, morphological and syntactic levels of the conventional grammatical sentence (146). At the same time, she insists that this expulsion which is 'a passage outside meaning, the shadow of non-sense through sense' can be 'murderous for the subject and his readers' (161–2). In 'The Novel as Polylogue', reading Philippe Sollers' *H*, she notes that the joy experienced in the avant-garde text is 'ripped with pain' as the collision between semiotic or material functions and symbolic operations dissolves subjective, sexual, familial and transfamilial borders (DL 174, 184). The impasses and risks of avant-garde literary practice are even more pronounced in her analyses of Louis Aragon and Louis-Ferdinand Céline, which are paradigmatic in this respect, exposing the 'tragic dimension' of modernist writers' heroic attempt to confront the unthinkable of historical or psychic violence and articulate a revolutionary agenda at 'the razor's edge between poetry and reality' (SNS 115–16). More particularly, in her reflections on Aragon and surrealism in *The Sense and Non-Sense of Revolt*, Kristeva points to the difficulty and risks of the desire to realize in the world 'the extravagant logic' of poetic experience (114). She also points to the 'trap' of investing in dangerous political utopias, as Aragon did, when confronted with the failure to turn the avant-garde work into a transformative, miraculous event (115). By contrast, the trap for Céline, a radical non-believer, was abjection, an overwhelming and fascinated revulsion at the nihilistic collapse of all borders, values or meaning. Kristeva's analysis of Céline epitomizes her key argument regarding the production of twentieth-century literature at 'the fragile limits of the speaking being' where subject and object, self and other, pure and impure, organic and inorganic 'push each other away, confront each other, collapse, and start again' (PH 18). She situates Céline in 'a black lineage' of writers who dare tackle the inhuman within the human: i.e. 'horror, death, madness, orgy, ... disgust and fright' (PH 137). What these inventors of an impossible, unpalatable aesthetics share is a black '*piercing laughter*', a 'laughter without complacency yet complicitous' (PH 133; emphasis in the original), an 'apocalyptic laughter' (PH 204). As she describes it, this 'bare, anguished' 'gushing forth' becomes the index of the negativity of material operations, the pulverization of both sign and subject (PH 206); the uncontrollable and contagious denial of all forms of mastery and the 'One' (one meaning, one identity, one logic, etc.); the symptom of godless, nihilistic horror; the madness of 'a-thought' (SNS 113), the ecstatic burst of nothingness and death at the heart of being.[9]

As a theorist of literature, Kristeva posits herself at what I call *the bleeding edge of modernism*. This does not refer simply to the forefront of the movement, the cutting edge of formal, linguistic and ideological innovation. It also invokes the high stakes, the trials and errors, the controversial ends and precarious beginnings that have marked the history of modernism, for the bleeding edge is the liminal space where dreams are fleshed out and sometimes turn into totalitarian, murderous nightmares. To her credit, Kristeva does not refrain from forcing us to confront and acknowledge these nightmares. She guides our fingers to the open sore of the 'suffering-horror' that anchors modernist literature in the psychic territory she calls abjection, enabling us to experience through 'body and tongue' the 'moral, political and stylistic revulsion that brands our time' (PH 23, 141).

As a *woman*-philosopher, Kristeva has also been particularly keen on reclaiming the role of the body in the workings of poetic language, paying close attention to the rhythmic and sonorous intensities of bodily operations as they infiltrate the verbal function and to the pulse of sensation invading the unfolding of sense. Of equal importance is her rehabilitation of the significance of the maternal feminine not merely as a corporeal memory transferred through the semiotic modality of signification but also as part of the avant-garde psychic imaginary. This is a consistent thread in her work from *La révolution du langage poétique* and her theorization of the maternally connoted semiotic *chora* to her later exploration of melancholia in *Black Sun* and the experience of abjection in *Powers of Horror*, where all writing is conceptualized as the confrontation with an archaic maternal authority 'on the nether side of the proper Name' (75). In the *Sense and Non-Sense of Revolt* she posits 'the translation of the feminine' (119) at the heart of all three stages she identifies in the development of the avant-garde in France, namely, the period of Rimbaud, Lautréamont and Mallarmé, the period of surrealism and, finally, that of *Tel Quel* (107). Indeed, the avant-garde artist's changing relation to, on the one hand, the maternal feminine and, on the other hand, what Nikolchina in this volume calls the 'indifferent feminine' have been discussed as a catalyst in Kristeva's gradual turn away from a transgressive model of avant-garde writing or, as Nikolchina puts it, 'a modernist aesthetics of "pulverization"' to a model based on transubstantiation.[10] In 'The *Vital Legacy of the Novel and Julia Kristeva's Fictional Revolt*' I have argued that her growing interest in the novel post-1990s shows an increasing dissatisfaction with what she has called in an interview 'the sacred puritanism' of an overwhelmingly male-dominated avant-garde (SUF 138). It points to a concern on her part with defining 'an avant-garde in the feminine', which no longer centres on the son's erotic struggle with the archaic maternal feminine but on the '*other*' woman' (the daughter aspiring to become a writer herself), which this struggle leaves out (Margaroni 2013: 156, 164).

Finally, as 'a monster of the crossroads' (to recall one of her favourite descriptions of herself; CES 167), an immigrant from Bulgaria who has experienced both the pain and the gifts of displacement, Kristeva has been able to do justice to a recurrent concern in modernist writing, namely, the concern with exile, alienation and the status of the foreigner.[11] This, according to Roland Barthes, is her distinct mark as a theorist who has refused to occupy a position of universality or neutrality, grounding her thought in her own subjective experience of crisis (KCR 11–14). As she puts it in 'The Subject in Process', the theorist needs to remain capable of putting herself on trial in order to 'utter the logic of' a process which is 'suffered if not understood' (133).

The aim of the volume is to bring together essays that take up all the above threads in Kristeva's analyses of the avant-garde, seeking to offer an appreciation of her overall contribution and the intellectual-cum-political horizon within which she has produced her seminal works, as well as of the blind spots that need to be recognized in any contemporary examination of her insights. The many faces of modernism, as Kristeva has theorized it from the 1960s to the present, emerge: a *revolutionary modernism* that offers an outlet to a crisis already at work within society and the unitary subject, seeking to dissolve all structures, systems or myths produced to contain this crisis (RPL, SP; SNS, IR); a *sublimatory, transubstantiating modernism* that takes pleasure in the infralinguistic music of the body, elaborates suffering into a style and sustains our intimate space (RPL, SP, PH, TL, NMS, SNS, IR, HF, PST, TAS, C, SH); an *abject modernism*, symptom of the apocalyptic horrors that have marked the twentieth century and a tentative response to these horrors in its attempt to violently expel what disgusts or horrifies, while remaining in quest of 'a ridiculous little infinite'[12] that might alleviate the pain and re-channel the death drive (PH, HF); a *melancholic modernism*, experienced as aesthetically awkward, non-cathartic in its clinical treatment of trauma and powerless in its mute confrontation with an affect that resists logic or naming (BS); and finally, a modernism that, irrespective of its face, remains for Kristeva the indisputable index of a *(self-)critical culture* that needs to be reclaimed and transposed on to our contemporary historical, geographical, political, aesthetic and moral coordinates.[13] As some of the contributors in this volume suggest, such reclamation will inevitably demand a move beyond Kristeva's acknowledged Eurocentrism[14] and her (less explicitly acknowledged) modern orientalist patterns of thought.[15] Significantly, *Understanding Kristeva, Understanding Modernism* will amply demonstrate that the theoretical resources for this move can be found in Kristeva's own work.

Following the template set for the series, the volume is structured in three parts. The first part, 'Conceptualizing Kristeva', includes seven essays, all aiming to offer original readings of key individual texts or central concerns in Kristeva's oeuvre, approached as a negotiation with the aesthetic, cultural, religious and political traditions of modernity. The first three chapters focus on the early period of her development as a theorist. They attempt to appreciate anew, from the perspective of the present, some very important but controversial aspects of her thinking, namely, her long affiliation with *Tel Quel* and its aesthetic-cum-political agenda; her 1960s–1970s reliance on mathematical abstraction and, in particular, Georg Cantor's concept of infinity; and her persistent invocation of a notion of the 'feminine' which (initially at least) remained rather vague.

Drawing on her seminal book *The Cultural Politics of Tel Quel* (1996), Danielle Marx-Scouras seeks to understand the complexity of the philosopher's political stance in the 1960s and 1970s as both an immigrant (as well as a dissident) from a communist European country and a leading member of a French avant-garde journal which pursued its own cultural/ aesthetic ends through cultivating an ambiguous fort/da relationship with the French Communist party. Marx-Scouras' intervention in this chapter is most pertinent and a much-needed corrective to the scandal-mongering media accounts of Kristeva's alleged secret collaboration with the communist regime in her native Bulgaria.

John Lechte and Miglena Nikolchina, in their turn, traverse similar territory (i.e. Kristeva's early formalization of avant-garde writing and the semiotic through the conceptual lens of set theory), in order to address very different theoretical questions. On the one hand, Lechte traces the fate of mathematical concepts such as 'number' and 'infinity' in Kristeva's post-1973 work in order to point to Kristeva's gradual break away from her early formalist period and her increasing concern with a psychoanalytic understanding of materiality and the body. Miglena Nikolchina, on the other hand, focuses on the relationship between the mathematical concept of *'le nombrant'* in her pre-1973 work, the *chora* in *Revolution in Poetic Language* and 'the feminine' in her later, psychoanalytically indebted writings, wishing to demonstrate the development in Kristeva's thinking of an 'indifferent feminine' (neither sex- nor gender-based) and its constitutive role in her theorization of modernist innovation.

The next two chapters turn to Kristeva as a novelist, one who employs familiar modernist techniques and engages (more or *less* critically) with some of the foundational problems of modernity. As Carol Mastrangelo Bové and Martha J. Reineke argue in their analyses of Kristeva's most recent novels (i.e. *The Enchanted Clock* and *Teresa, My Love* respectively), these problems include: (a) the domination in the West of a liberal, capitalist, patriarchal model of democracy, a pragmatic individualist ethics and a market-based idea of freedom; (b) the confrontation between knowledge and faith, secularism and religious fundamentalism; (c) the nihilistic crisis that followed both the rise of the economic as a prime cause and post-Enlightenment scepticism; and (d) finally, the colonial progressivist paradigm of history that has favoured the West (over 'the rest') and promoted the increasing mechanization of the world. While Reineke traces the tension in Kristeva's account of Saint Teresa between the dialectical structure she adopts, based on entrenched modernist assumptions about 'true' faith, and her distinct ethics inspired by the figure of the stranger, Bové foregrounds instead her critique of American pragmatism.

The last two chapters of Part One continue to invoke a number of the problems above as a crucial theoretical context within which to re-evaluate Kristeva's attitude to some of the political impasses that are part of our contemporary global landscape. Examining her differential treatment of the aesthetic strategy of veiling as opposed to women's veiling as a cultural and religious practice, Tina Chanter contends that Kristeva leaves unthought 'the foundational fantasies that govern Eurocentric provincialism' and, despite her critique of secularism, ends up reproducing some of its myths which otherize non-Western, non-Christian cultures. In her own chapter Robin Truth Goodman has chosen to focus on Kristeva's productive intellectual encounter with Hannah Arendt, one of the seminal thinkers of the concept of the political and its crises throughout the twentieth century. Goodman sets out to elucidate the important divergences in the thought of these two philosophers, more particularly, in their understanding of singularity and plurality but also in their theorization of the modern experience of precarity. Her aim is to show the usefulness of reading their perspectives side by side in light of the split between politics and the subject that the spread of neoliberalism has brought about.

Part Two, 'Kristeva and aesthetics', consists of six chapters which either engage with Kristeva's influential readings of key modern(ist) figures (i.e. Woolf, Céline, Joyce and Arendt) or draw on her analyses of poetic language, melancholia, love, abjection and motherhood, in their attempt to offer new interpretations of both major and 'minor' modernists in literature, the visual arts and dance. The first three chapters converge in their concern with the continuing relevance of Kristeva's theory of psychic, social and political abjection, including its diverse and haunting manifestations in literature and art. Constantinou's chapter opens Part Two and brings together a number of the threads pursued in Part One, specifically, Kristeva's privileging of Western European cultural and religious traditions, her uneasy encounter with Arendt as well as her ambivalent attitude to some of the seductions and entrapments of modernity. He re-weaves these threads in a critical project that reconstructs (piece-by-piece, voice-over-voice, text transposed to text) the complex puzzle of Kristeva's tale of the twentieth century. Reading Arendt, Joyce and Céline against Kristeva's own writings on these authors, Constantinou elaborates a conceptual pattern that aims at exposing the audacity of Kristeva's venture into the modern territory of the abject. At the same time, he throws into relief the proliferating obstacles she encounters on her way, given her difficulty with appreciating the close connection between the domination in modernity of a bourgeois metaphysics of motion, the imperial process that develops hand-in-hand with the systematic exploitation of the earth and the modern experience of displacement that produces political abjection. As he argues, if Kristeva's frame of abjection is to preserve its theoretical force, it needs to be remobilized in the context of the contemporary critique of imperialism and the Anthropocene.

In their own employment of the frame of abjection, Nicholas Chare and Rina Arya make a strong case for the sublimating power of art and literature, their ability to express fears and anxieties that persist alongside (indeed, despite) the modern compulsion for order, classification, boundary-drawing, homogenization and conformity. Interestingly, Chare suggests that gothic fiction, a genre disparaged by modernists because it was connected with mass entertainment, is paradigmatic in this respect. He chooses to focus on a ghost story by M. R. James, a writer who was explicitly critical of modernist experimental techniques and remained at a distance from his avant-garde contemporaries. Examining James' style, themes and motifs (especially his use of drapery) against the abject landscape that Céline's writings painfully confront us with, Chare concludes that, unlike Céline, the gothic writer succeeds in shielding his readers' eyes from Medusa's gaze, keeping the powers of horror in check.

By contrast, the three visual artists Arya discusses render viewing a wounding experience. Arya's aim is to demonstrate the impact of what Kristeva has theorized as 'abjection' on Modernist art. To this end, she turns to the reconfiguration of human identity and the body in the works of Hans Bellmer, Francis Bacon and Maria Lassnig. What all these artists share, she argues, is a concern with the abject(ed) fragment, the body-part rather than the fully integrated organism, the sensation of embodiment rather than its sense, the unruly flesh overflowing the body's boundaries rather than the unified body-image or its exterior form.

The remaining three chapters of Part Two take on the task of examining Kristeva's theory of twentieth-century literature and aesthetics (a theory that is paradoxically privileging male modernists while grounded in a concept of the 'feminine') from the perspective of women's writing and artistic production. Intrigued by Kristeva's brief (and occasionally dismissive) references to Virginia Woolf, Christina Kkona sets out to reread Woolf's *Orlando* in ways that enable her to engage critically with Kristeva's problematic treatment of female authors and homosexuality, while insisting on the political potential of her post-1990s rethinking of femininity in terms of disillusionment, strangeness, exile and irony. The female experiences of displacement and liminality continue to be important in Rossitsa Terzieva-Artemis' interpretation of Jean Rhys' interwar Parisian novels. Drawing on Walter Benjamin's reflections on melancholic modernity and Kristeva's clinical and literary analyses of melancholia, Terzieva-Artemis pursues the development in Rhys' writings of a melancholic modernist sensibility that exposes the writer's as well as her characters' infatuation with discourses of love and death, rather than with the bankrupt ideals of control and reason. As Terzieva-Artemis shows, despite the prevalence of mortality and irrational forces in Rhys' interwar novels, a strong conviction in the characters' psychic resilience and in the possibility of a trajectory of becoming *within* melancholia remains.

Finally, Robert R. Shane ventures in the fascinating territory of modern dance, compellingly arguing in favour of its revolutionary potential as a poetic *writing in space* through movement. With close reference to Kristeva's theory of subject-formation and her revision of Jacques Lacan's mirror stage, Shane points to the temporal paradoxes of the self-reflexive act of mirroring employed by Martha Graham in *Hérodiade*. Positing herself at the modern sites of collective and individual trauma, Graham feminizes the space of traditional dance, reinscribing in it the corporeality of the female dancer, the rhythms of maternal pain and sexuality, as well as the timelessness of the unconscious that complicates the subject's endurance in time and her desire to transcend linear temporality.

Part Three of *Understanding Kristeva, Understanding Modernism* takes the form of a Glossary. Written by experts in their respective fields, each of the entries traces the evolution of central concepts or terms in Kristeva's oeuvre across the different stages of her theoretical development. Despite their comparative brevity, all chapters in this part offer substantial treatments of the relevant texts, contexts and intertexts that have marked the signifying history of each of the chosen concepts. More importantly (inevitably perhaps) they leave the reader at an aporetic crossroads or in suspense, for no one can foretell the afterlives of concepts and ideas which, notwithstanding existing uses and appropriations, remain productive of innovative thought. As Kristeva has taught us, every return is a form of revolt, a commitment to reflect on past meanings again, anew, from the perspective of emerging needs and challenges. Isn't this why, as Leslie Hill insightfully suggests, one of Kristeva's key contributions as a theorist of modernism is that she has enabled us to approach it *no longer* as an exceptional period or form of writing but as 'a dynamic process' inherent potentially in all forms of literary and aesthetic production (Hill 1990: 145)? If we agree with Hill, then the driving force that seems to carry this volume of the *Understanding Philosophy, Understanding Modernism* series needs to be traced beyond the desire to appreciate the value and remnants of the tradition of modernism. What is at stake, indeed, is to identify the contemporary edges of this (still) bleeding legacy and (with the help of one of its most vibrant theorists) to continue to generate questions, discourses, practices or thoughts inspired by it.

Notes

1 See her *Intimate Revolt* (2002 [1997]).
2 See, for example, Moi's introduction in *The Kristeva Reader* (KR 1–22), Lechte (1990), Sjöholm (2005), Chen (2008) and Nikolchina (2020).
3 See, for example, Michel Beaujour's critique of Kristeva's *Révolution du langage poétique* (2003) and Alison Tate's 'A Semblance of Sense: Kristeva's and Gertrude Stein's Analysis of Language' (1995).
4 In 'The Semiotic Revolution' I have emphasized the significance of Kristeva's mobilization of a materialist concept of 'practice' in her theorization of the avant-garde text and the *sujet-en-procès*. See Lechte and Margaroni (2004).
5 See Kristeva's *Sense and Non-Sense of Revolt*, where she explicitly argues that *Tel Quel* takes up and renews the legacy of the European avant-gardes from Rimbaud, Lautréamont and Mallarmé to the Surrealists.

6   See Cavanagh (1993).
7   Cavanagh strategically avoids to give the full quote from 'Psychoanalysis and the Polis' where Kristeva offers the following qualification: 'Now, from the position of the post-Freudian, post-phenomenological analyst… it is clear that there is no World (or that the World is not all there is)' (KR 313).
8   In *Revolution in Poetic Language* Kristeva defines 'transposition' as 'the passage from one signifying system to another' that 'demands a new articulation of the thetic' (60).
9   I discuss the 'black laughter' Kristeva hears in modernist literature in 'Artaud's Madness and the Literary Obscene: Humanism and its Double in Julia Kristeva' (2020).
10 See Nikolchina's chapter in this volume. Hill emphasizes Kristeva's turn away from a transgressive model of avant-gardism but he associates this turn to Kristeva's exposure post-1977 to alternative models flourishing in the United States (1990: 151). Peter Buse (2005) also foregrounds Kristeva's encounter with more 'primitive' experimentations in American art.
11 For an extensive account of Kristeva's concern with the experiences of exile and estrangement, see Smith (1996).
12 Céline quoted by Kristeva in PH 134.
13 In her 'Intellectual Autobiography' Kristeva draws a distinction between 'culture', which she defines as 'a memory reassessed and reordered by means of singular discourses and behaviours, through interactive histories and life stories', and 'civilization'. As she tells Samuel Dock, 'By *civilization* I mean a social organization dominated by the administration of labor and procreation, based on specific rules corresponding to regulatory priorities' (2020: 118; emphasis in the original).
14 Even in her recent conversation with Dock, Kristeva insists that 'this *culture* has a better chance of deepening in Europe than in the United States' (2020: 119; emphasis in the original). She does qualify this statement by adding a few pages later: 'I don't idealize Europe by any means, and while I'm betting on the Europe of the Renaissance and the Enlightenment, I don't discount the Europe of the crusades, the pogroms, and radical evil, and frequently insist on it' (2020: 123).
15 See in particular the chapters by Reineke, Chanter, Constantinou, Postl and Jaspers.

References

Beaujour, M. (2003 [1975]), 'A Propos of a Separation in Julia Kristeva's *La Révolution du Langage Poétique*', trans. J. Lechte, in J. Lechte and M. Zournazi (eds), *The Kristeva Critical Reader*, 15–35, Edinburgh: Edinburgh University Press.
Buse, P. (2005), '*Tel Quel* in Manhattan: America and the French avant-garde 1960–1982', *Nottingham French Studies*, 44 (3): 69–82.

Cavanagh, C. (1993), 'Pseudo-Revolution in Poetic Language: Julia Kristeva and the Russian Avant-Garde', *Slavic Review*, 52 (2): 283–97.
Chen, Szu-chin Hestia (2008), *French Feminist Theory Exemplified through the Novels of Julia Kristeva: The Bridge from Psychoanalytic Theory to Literary Production*, Lewiston, NY: Edwin Mellen Press.
Hill, L. (1990), 'Julia Kristeva: Theorizing the Avant-Garde?', in J. Fletcher and A. Benjamin (eds), *Abjection, Melancholia, and Love: The Work of Julia Kristeva*, 137–56, London: Routledge.
Jardine, A. (2020), *At the Risk of Thinking: An Intellectual Biography of Julia Kristeva*, ed. M. Ruti, London: Bloomsbury.
Kristeva, J. (2020), 'Intellectual Autobiography of Julia Kristeva: *Je Me Voyage*, a Journey across Borders and through Identities', in S. G. Beardsworth (ed.), *The Philosophy of Julia Kristeva*, 3–152, The Library of Living Philosophers, 36, Chicago: Open Court.
Lechte, J. (1990), *Julia Kristeva*, New York: Routledge.
Margaroni, M. (2004), 'The Semiotic Revolution', in J. Lechte and M. Margaroni (eds), *Julia Kristeva: Live Theory*, 6–33, London: Continuum.
Margaroni, M. (2013), 'The Vital Legacy of the Novel and Julia Kristeva's Fictional Revolt', in B. Trigo (ed.), *Kristeva's Fiction*, 155–73, New York: State University of New York Press.
Margaroni, M. (2020), 'Artaud's Madness and the Literary Obscene: Humanism and Its Double in Julia Kristeva', in S. G. Beardsworth (ed.), *The Philosophy of Julia Kristeva*, 249–64, The Library of Living Philosophers, 36, Chicago: Open Court.
Marx-Scouras, D. (1996), *The Cultural Politics of* Tel Quel: *Literature and the Left in the Wake of Engagement*, University Park, PA: Pennsylvania State University Press.
Nikolchina, M. (2020), '*Signifiance* and Transubstantiation: The Returns of the Avant-Garde in Kristeva's Philosophy of Literature', in S. G. Beardsworth (ed.), *The Philosophy of Julia Kristeva*, 265–81, The Library of Living Philosophers, 36, Chicago: Open Court.
Sjöholm, C. (2005), *Kristeva and the Political*, New York: Routledge.
Smith, A. (1996), *Julia Kristeva: Readings of Exile and Estrangement*, New York: St. Martin's Press.
Tate, A. (1995), 'A Semblance of Sense: Kristeva's and Gertrude Stein's Analysis of Language', *Language and Communication*, 15 (4): 329–42.

PART ONE

Conceptualizing Kristeva

1

Kristeva telle quelle: A seductive encounter

Danielle Marx-Scouras

Tel Quel was one of the most influential literary journals and controversial intellectual currents in twentieth-century France. For two decades (1960–82), it published the very best in French intellectual thought and writing, including Roland Barthes, Georges Bataille, Jacques Derrida, Jean-Pierre Faye, Michel Foucault, Gérard Genette, Julia Kristeva, Marcelin Pleynet, Philippe Sollers and Tzvetan Todorov. Nonetheless, few women were closely associated with the journal. Only two made it to the editorial board: Jacqueline Risset (1967–82) and Julia Kristeva (1970–82).[1]

The editorial board was plagued by acrimonious polemics, departures and expulsions, with only Philippe Sollers remaining from the first to the last issue, and onward to *L'Infini*. In a 1988 interview with *France-Culture*, Kristeva stated:

> People have no idea how virulent its [Tel Quel group] criticism, rejections, diatribes, and invectives were. It was all a bit surreal, and I realize that we were contemptuous of those who were not members of the group. Yet those of us who experienced these inner struggles felt very overwhelmed by it all. People do not realize this, and we (I should say 'I') kept a stiff upper lip. I felt quite vulnerable during my years with 'Tel Quel' because I found myself caught between all those angry men. I had a hard time of it.
>
> (I 7)

Nonetheless, the two women fared better and longer on the editorial board than the majority of the men, most of whom left in quite an uproar.

Unquestionably, one of the reasons Kristeva fared so well and so long with *Tel Quel* is due to her association with Sollers, whom she quietly married in August 1967. They would remain lifelong amorous as well as intellectual partners. In her exhaustive biography on Roland Barthes, Tiphaine Samoyault writes, 'Barthes was fascinated by the eroticism that imbued this couple, by the overlap of sexuality and theoretical productivity in them (this was common at that time)' (2017: 353). Sollers, himself, states, 'These years prior to the explosion of May are amazing. I'm still leading a disorganized life, but another feminine encounter takes place – a fundamental encounter and love at first sight. It's Julia (Kristeva) who arrived from Bulgaria in 1966, with a graduate fellowship. She's twenty-five, remarkably beautiful. She comes to interview me; we haven't left each other since' (2007: 101, my translation). He also adds, 'She is the most intelligent woman I have met' (102). Sollers is referring to their first meeting at his office at the Éditions du Seuil in May 1966. What is also striking about these remarks is that he has placed them in the '*Tel Quel*' chapter of his book. Simply put, the Kristeva-Sollers relationship is quasi synonymous with *Tel Quel*.

Similarly, Kristeva repeatedly references this vital connection in her writings and interviews, beginning with her autobiographical piece, 'Mémoire' ('My Memory's Hyperbole'). Strategically positioned in the very first issue of *L'Infini* (the continuation of *Tel Quel* at Gallimard) in winter 1983, it recounts the *Tel Quel* trajectory from her perspective. Decades later, Kristeva acknowledges her profound debt to Sollers, for 'her life-story, since her arrival in France, would never have existed and become what it is, had she not been welcomed and accompanied by Philippe' (JMV 111–12). In these same interviews, she also recognizes that 'her intellectual adventure cannot be reduced to her sole readings and research', but that it 'encompasses emotional ties with personalities who animated intellectual life for half a century. And even the political outbursts that shake up our contemporaries' (96). 'Mémoire' will thus be 'an autobiography in the first-person plural, a "we" of complicity, friendship, love. This "we" is the setting commonly recommended by the social contract for illusions, idealizations, errors, constructions' (PK 3–4).

The first subtitle of 'Mémoire' is, not surprisingly, 'l'expérience telle quelle', with its double sense of 'as is' and, of course, its direct connection to the journal. The account begins with Kristeva's initial arrival in France in December 1965, 'in a bleak and rainy Paris' saved only by midnight mass at Notre Dame (5). With only five dollars to her name, and a contact who stands her up at the Bourget airport, Kristeva, nonetheless, will benefit from generous encounters from the onset. Her Franco-Bulgarian scholarship, which facilitated meetings with writers and academics, immediately plunged her into an intellectual universe which, in favouring critical Marxism, sought out 'socialism with a human face' and yet missed it entirely (6). She avows that she had been trained as a true French intellectual despite a Marxist-Leninist formation in Bulgaria: 'I even had the impression, when I wasn't viewed as a more or less monstrous anomaly, that people saw in me, aside from my Stalinism, a perfect product of the French system projected into the future' (6). This statement is fundamental for understanding Kristeva's positioning in French (or at least Parisian) intellectual thought and cultural practice in 1966, and even in subsequent years. Kristeva brings this apparently antagonistic formation to bear on a watershed moment. What she brings is as crucial as what she encounters.

Sollers claimed that there was a 'revival of memory' in 1964–6 (1974: 73). These years mark the end of 'the naïve and instrumentalist conception of language', which coincides with a rebirth of the avant-garde: 'It is only with delay, and after so many censors and obliterations, that our era takes note of Russian futurism and Formalism, surrealism, the great endeavours of narrative, linguistics, and even of psychoanalysis' (1974: 73). This revival went hand in hand with an explosion in French intellectual thought that took place at the time of Kristeva's arrival in Paris. Given her cultural baggage, she could not have arrived at a more opportune moment. Between 1965 and 1966, the following key works appeared: Louis Althusser's *Reading Capital* and *For Marx*, Roland Barthes' *Criticism and Truth* (*Critical Essays* came out in 1964), Émile Benveniste's *Problems of General Linguistics*, Jacques Derrida's 'Of Grammatology' in the journal *Critique* (the book appeared in 1967), Foucault's *The Order of Things*, and Jacques Lacan's *Écrits*.

Underlying this unique, intellectual explosion was an acute preoccupation with the workings of language, which gave *Tel Quel* its theoretical basis for re-actualizing the avant-garde venture.[2] A new conception of writing (*écriture*) began to permeate literature, linguistics, philosophy and psychoanalysis, and the works listed above provided *Tel Quel* with a theoretical orientation that mirrored its own literary preoccupations. *Tel Quel* was now ready to resume the avant-garde wager abandoned by surrealism. More importantly – for what interests us here – *Tel Quel* would not be the sole beneficiary of this avant-garde venture that it spearheaded. It would meet up with the French Communist Party as it began to undergo cultural and intellectual de-Stalinization as a result of the French Communist Party Central Committee meeting at Argenteuil in March 1966.

Kristeva came to Paris at a much more propitious moment than her compatriot Tzvetan Todorov, who upon his arrival in 1963 found no literary theory or poetics being offered at the Sorbonne (Dosse 1997: 194). He subsequently enrolled in Barthes' seminar at the École Pratique des Hautes Études. Bilingual in Bulgarian and Russian, he began translating and publishing on the Russian formalists. His translations and introductions to Victor Shklovsky's 'Art as technique' (1917) and Roman Jakobson's 'On artistic realism' (1921), respectively, appeared in *Tel Quel* issues 21 (spring 1965) and 24 (spring 1966). Several Telquelians (including Faye and Genette) claimed to have encouraged Todorov and *Tel Quel* to publish the edited volume *Théorie de la littérature*, containing his translations of the Russian formalists, in the *Tel Quel* collection at Seuil in 1965. As Kristeva's compatriot, Todorov reached out to her early on, encouraging her to do her dissertation under Lucien Goldmann, even though she would also join Barthes' seminar shortly after, where she would make her mark, by presenting her work on the post-formalist Mikhail Bakhtin, whose work was not yet diffused in France. Her initial work on Bakhtin, 'Word, Dialogue, Novel' was published in *Critique* in April 1967 and subsequently in her collected essays, *Séméiotiké, Recherches pour un sémanalyse* in the *Tel Quel* collection in 1969. Through Bakhtin's work on dialogism and the carnivalesque, Kristeva discovers that 'writing' (*écriture*) can challenge structural analysis and semiotics as a 'science'. A writer as well as a 'scholar' (*savant*),

> Bakhtin was one of the first to replace the static hewing out of texts with a model where literary structure does not simply *exist* but is generated in relation to *another* structure. What allows a dynamic relation to structuralism is his conception of the 'literary' word as an *intersection of textual surfaces* rather than a point (a fixed meaning), as a dialogue among several writings: that of the writer, the addressee (or the character), and the contemporary or earlier cultural context.
>
> (DL 64–5)

Kristeva impressed not only Barthes with her presentation on Bakhtin but also René Girard, who asked her to join his department at Johns Hopkins University. Kristeva declined, citing US imperialism in Viet Nam as a reason for her refusal. Goldmann had nonetheless encouraged her: 'Listen. Capitalism? You have to take it from the inside!' (Jardine 2020: 85). Years later, Kristeva stated, 'That was during the Vietnam War, and because I was even more political then than I am now, I had problems with the idea of going to America' (I 5).

Kristeva's first piece to appear in *Tel Quel* (no. 29, spring 1967) was 'For a semiology of paragrams', where she acknowledges the importance of both the Russian formalists and Saussure's 'Anagrammes' for a notion of the text bound up with language as productivity that would distinguish *Tel Quel* in the late 1960s. In emphasizing the nonlinear functioning of the poetic signifier and thus a textual logic different from the one of the sign, the formalists, along with Saussure, were the first to open up linguistics to a semiotics of literary texts. In so doing, they challenged the very bases of structural linguistics. In 'For a semiology of paragrams' Kristeva notes that the text is precisely that which cannot be considered by a certain conceptual system whose limits it marks (S 24). The essay brings together metamathematics and mathematical logic and the structures of modern poetic language for a semiology that is not only *grammatic* (scientific, monologic) but also *paragrammatic* (contestatory, dialogic) (TSP 47). It demonstrates how Kristeva was already transitioning from semiology to (critical) semiotics and how *Tel Quel* would become 'the privileged link where the structuralist advance turned into an analysis of subjectivity' (PK 10). What Kristeva calls literary semiology in her inaugural text for *Tel Quel* bypasses the inherent limitations of structuralism, 'its "staticism" and its "non-historicism", by setting itself the task that will justify it: the discovery of a formalism that corresponds isomorphically to literary productivity's thinking itself' (TSP 25). *Tel Quel* also added a new subtitle, 'Science/Literature', to this issue. It would remain in place until autumn 1970 (issue 42) when it became 'Literature/Philosophy/Science/Politics'.

It can never be emphasized enough that *Tel Quel* was a journal founded by writers and not academic critics. From the onset, they opposed Sartrean engagement and its disdain for literature, and especially poetic language. The opening Declaration – which many considered reactionary for its times – demanded that literature, 'forever despised and yet triumphant', be once again taken seriously and freed from the ideological determinations of the post-war and Cold War years: 'Ideologues have ruled long enough over expression... it's about time a parting of the ways took place; let us be permitted to focus upon expression itself, its inevitability and its particular laws.'[3] Reactionary or not, *Tel Quel*'s initial premise did not deter French Communist Party journals from taking an immediate interest in their endeavour. In February 1960 – even before the first issue of *Tel Quel* appeared – Hubert Juin published an interview entitled 'Pourquoi une nouvelle revue?' [Why a new journal?] in Louis Aragon's *Les Lettres Françaises*. There were no overt political remarks on the part of the young Telquelians. Jean-René Huguenin stated that they were not simply returning to poetry – a genre that had been neglected in the post-war years in favour of a 'politics of prose' (Hollier 1986) – but, more importantly, transcending the traditional generic distinctions of prose and poetry and seeking the poetic dimension in the novel and essay (Juin 1960: 4). This new manner of examining the poetic, outside of generic distinctions, became one of the distinctive and lasting trademarks of *Tel Quel*. It subsequently took on linguistic, philosophical and political dimensions. The transgeneric and transdisciplinary ambition of *Tel Quel* was only fitting for a group that had chosen the collective and hybrid review form as its vehicle for cultural renewal. It chose to work from a site beyond the traditional distinctions of narrative, poetry and criticism, called 'écriture', which integrated other topologies such as the 'text' and 'signifying practice', at the heart of Kristeva's work. These notions revealed a new relationship between literary practice and semiotic theory that would reciprocally impact both: 'What we call *écriture textuelle* is the work site between a scriptural practice and its theory' (Sollers 1968: 70, my translation). Opposed to the separation of the creative and critical functions of writing, *Tel Quel* demanded that writers 'take a critical, virtually a scientific attitude towards themselves, that they break permanently with the individualism of the would-be creator of forms' (Sollers 1983: 191).

Although *Tel Quel*'s early years were characterized by a lack of political positions, from its onset, it nonetheless rejected the 'ideology of the text as reflection' inherent in the novel and central to debates on literary realism, as well as an aestheticizing ideology attributed to poetry by a belletrist tradition bound up with Western metaphysics. Kristeva contends that the logic of paragrams is a 'means of crushing that vulgar psychologism and sociologism which sees poetic language as mere expression or reflection and effaces hereby its particularities' (TSP 47). Clearly, the impact of both Jakobson and Bakhtin is evident here, for Kristeva; however, Barthes' critique of literary realism was also essential for *Tel Quel* in general.

Kristeva certainly did not come to *Tel Quel* as a writer, at least not in 1966. However, her pioneering work related to the act of writing in Bakhtin clearly reveals her strategic relevance for the *Tel Quel* enterprise. Her position with respect to *Tel Quel* must also be viewed in light of the Barthes-Picard polemic that took place the year she arrived in France. In *Criticism and Truth* published in the *Tel Quel* Collection in 1966, Barthes affirmed that the 'journey across writing' was leaving its mark on the twentieth century as it challenged intellectual discourse as a whole.[4] If the writer was still a viable player on the intellectual scene, it was no longer because he was defined by his role or value 'but only by a certain *awareness of discourse*. A writer is someone for whom language constitutes a problem, who is aware of the depth of language, not its instrumentality or its beauty' (1987: 64). In 1977, Foucault claimed that, as the writer disappeared as a figurehead, the university and the academic emerged (1980: 127). If this is true, it is nonetheless important to recognize that the upheaval of the university symbolized by May 1968 was also the result of explosions that had taken place in institutional sites directly opposed to the university, such as the École Pratique des Hautes Études and *Tel Quel*.

Kristeva's theoretical work complemented but also broadened the one of Todorov, who, along with Genette, took his distance from *Tel Quel* around 1967–8 as it embarked on its politico-theoretical course. In her second contribution to *Tel Quel*, 'Distance and anti-representation' (issue 32, winter 1968), she introduced the contemporary work of a group of semioticians – Juri Lotman, Boris Uspensky, Vyacheslav Ivanov, Isaak Revzin and others associated with the University of Tartu. She also presented their work in 'Semiology Today in the Soviet Union' in issue 35 of *Tel Quel* (autumn 1968). An essay by Todorov on 'Formalists and Futurists' figures in a separate section of this issue. His *Théorie de la littérature* included texts first published in Russian between 1917 and 1928. Todorov's project was very important considering that the futurists and formalists were subsequently censored by Stalinism and Zhdanovism. Jakobson, who was very interested in Bakhtin's work, convinced Kristeva that it was their duty to revive both the past and a more recent memory of their old Europe (JMV 96). Her special number for *Tel Quel* thus updates Todorov's work on the earlier period of Russian formalism, since the majority of these essays were presented at a conference in Tartu in May 1968.

Kristeva begins her introduction to this special issue by citing the work of Sebastian Saumjan and P. A. Soboleva, which is critical of Chomsky's generative linguistics. Referring to the polyglotism of all the authors featured here, she emphasizes how their work departs from an ethnocentric perspective bound up with structuralism in France. Aside from Vyacheslav Ivanov's structural analysis of a poem by the Futurist Velimir Khlebnikov, this issue focuses for the most part on the role of the number (rather than the sign) in cultural history, the topic of the Tartu conference, and includes essays by Juri Lotman, Vladimir Toporov, Ivanov and others. Lotman and his colleagues formulated a semiotics of culture: 'a discipline that examines the interaction of differently structured semiotic systems, internal unevenness in a semiotic space, and the necessity of cultural and semiotic polyglotism' (Lotman 1988: 52–3). Even though Kristeva acknowledges the highly formalized linguistic work of Saumjan and Soboleva, she believes that semiology in the Soviet Union is creating a breach in the homogeneous discourse of the human sciences, which are usually subordinate to positivist scientism. Recognizant of the heritage of the futurists and formalists, the work of these contemporary semioticians further contributes to the subversion of Western discourse that Russia (and Europe) experienced on the eve and in the aftermath of the October Revolution (1968a: 3, 7–8).

Despite the pioneering perspective Kristeva brings to French semiotics here, this issue of *Tel Quel* does not exist in isolation from a larger context, one heavy with political considerations. While many of the semioticians cited in this work faced problems with Soviet authorities due to their work or identity, this special number does come out in autumn 1968, with no mention whatsoever of the Prague Spring.[5] Faye, who had already left *Tel Quel*, objected to the mention of the Soviet Union in the title of this issue (the Tartu-Moscow school was a joint venture between academics from both cities but was linked to Estonia, after all). He also criticized *Tel Quel*'s silencing of Prague and even stated that several Telquelians had supported the Soviet invasion of August 1968 (Faye 1979). There were Communist militants, like Pierre Daix, with whom Kristeva had actually corresponded from Bulgaria and whom she subsequently met in Paris (Jardine 2020: 55, 80), who courageously opposed the Soviet invasion in *Les Lettres Françaises*. It is possible that Kristeva, an émigré herself from a Soviet satellite country, was exercising caution here. However, what is certain is that during May 68, *Tel Quel* would side with the Confédération Générale du Travail and the PCF against the students, with exceedingly hardline positions in issue 34 (summer 1968), the issue preceding the one on contemporary Soviet semiotics. *Tel Quel*'s position during May 68 inevitably elucidates their silence during the Prague Spring.

In order to understand this critical phase of *Tel Quel* and also why Kristeva took this route, whereas her compatriot Todorov opted for the university, we must return to Kristeva's 'Mémoire' and, more specifically, to the second section entitled 'What's the Use of Politics in Times of Distress'. She writes:

> *Clarté*, the journal of Communist students, had published, at the end of 1965, I think, a large picture of Sollers along with a text in which he explained, in essence, that only the socialist Revolution could provide a social setting propitious to avant-garde writing. This was, before the mediation of Genette, my first encounter with *Tel Quel*. And the first seduction.
>
> (PK 13)

Seduction is an interesting word choice here, considering that the verb means to drag aside or lead astray. Therefore, how could an intellectual who had just turned her back on a socialist regime possibly be captivated by *Tel Quel* precisely at that very moment when *Tel Quel* was lured by revolutionary politics? Apparently, Kristeva and fellow Telquelians were led to believe that 'in France, it would be different' (PK 13). Hadn't Althusser 'taken the toughest ([for Kristeva] the most "Stalinist") points of Marxism in order to instil new hope in the French Communist Party and all of French society, the harbinger of a worldwide Marxist spring?' (PK 13–14). However, Kristeva remained 'less sensitive to the arguments of the director of studies of the rue d'Ulm than to the revolutionary aestheticism of *Tel Quel*, which seemed, after all, to bode well for the success of the futurist utopia' (PK 14). Could she make a difference, as an intellectual refugee from Eastern Europe, in contributing to a dissident Marxism in France: How would her unique background contribute to this curious wager of revolutionizing society by revolutionizing language? Were the stakes that low or did Kristeva glimpse a new manner in which to embrace her intellectual present without entirely forsaking her Marxist upbringing? It is noteworthy that there are no comments pertaining to her Bulgarian, Marxist background during this period.

Kristeva's optimism regarding a 'Marxist spring' reinforced that of *Tel Quel*. As I have already mentioned, a certain de-Stalinization of the PCF took place after the Central Committee meeting at Argenteuil of 11–13 March 1966. After decades of intense conflict with their intellectuals, the party chose to devote an extra day to ideological and cultural concerns. Communist writers and artists were considered important by the Central Committee during the 1950s only insofar as they adhered to the party line and subordinated their artistic expression to party ends – the class struggle at whose head was the party. At Argenteuil, the Central Committee officially proclaimed that it would no longer intervene in scientific and artistic matters. Many militants interpreted this gesture as a desertion. The late Jean-Louis Houdebine, who played a key role in bringing *Tel Quel* and Communists affiliated with *La Nouvelle Critique* together, claimed that the political apparatus of the PCF was not the least bit interested in the intellectual discussions of the 1960s: Central Committee politicians certainly could not fathom what an avant-garde current like *Tel Quel* could contribute to Communism. However, if having Telquelians as fellow travellers meant influencing French youth and getting their vote, then the party favoured encounters with them (Houdebine 1987). In the March 1967 legislative elections, the PCF obtained 22.4 per cent of the vote; the Gaullists barely won with a 37.7 majority through a coalition (Comité d'Action pour la Vième Republique). The party was still a viable political force. *Tel Quel*'s journey on 'the Communist Party vessel' thus made sense to Kristeva in that the PCF 'was, and still remains to a large extent [in 1983], the only French party to have a cultural politics' (PK 14). She also notes that it is the only party 'to have drawn a lesson from having closely witnessed the great adventures of twentieth century thought and art' (PK 14). This latter remark is important.

Tel Quel's liaison with the Communist Left did not begin in 1966–7. Even before Juin's interview with the young Telquelians in 1960, Aragon had already launched Sollers in 1958. In a very lengthy review of *Une curieuse solitude* published in *Les Lettres Françaises*, Aragon ends up not only praising this apolitical novel but also going back in time to his beloved and much criticized *Aurélien* (1944): 'It's that *Aurélien* is bourgeois literature, and I'm committing the crime of liking bourgeois literature. And so what?' (1959: 37–8, my translation). As the writer who relinquished the surrealist wager and became a PCF leader, Aragon is clearly confessing his profound disillusionment with Stalinism and socialist realism here. Kristeva also alludes to Aragon's launching of the young Sollers, but adds:

> But starting in 1966, the entire machine of the PCF awakened to the experiments of the avant-garde. Let's not forget that in France, institutional recognition of Russian formalism, futurism, and, by analogy, contemporary writing, with literary theory as one of its facets, first came with the publications of the PCF, *Les Lettres Françaises* and the *Nouvelle Critique*, and the colloquia it organized (Cluny I and Cluny II).
>
> (PK 14)

Kristeva referred to the first Cluny encounter as an 'event'. Although this was merely an intellectual gathering on 'Linguistics and Literature', it would have significant repercussions for *Tel Quel* in propelling the journal on its political (Marxist) course, as well as rerouting certain PCF intellectuals towards *Tel Quel*.

Kristeva has elaborated in considerable detail on her relationship to the PCF, as well as on the reverse – the PCF's interest in *Tel Quel* from 1958 to 1960 onwards. Yet, when queried by *The New Yorker* in 2018, regarding whether *Tel Quel* had been affiliated with the PCF, she simply replied no. This query was obviously in conjunction with Kristeva's alleged activity as a Cold War spy. I was subsequently contacted by the journal to confirm or deny her response. Affiliated usually implies being a card carrier of the party, which of course they were not.[6] Nonetheless, they had a complex relationship with the PCF that I tried to impart to the fact checker at *The New Yorker*. In the end, *The New Yorker* simply wrote: 'She also disputed the notion that her husband and the magazine he edited had ties to the French Communist Party, though this is a matter of scholarly consensus. (Danielle Marx-Scouras, the author of *The Cultural Politics of Tel Quel*, said that the magazine supported the Party from the mid-1960s until 1971.)' I suspect the author of the article sought further ammunition to confirm that she was indeed a spy because Tel Quel had been 'affiliated' with the PCF.

With respect to the question of affiliation, I wish to reverse the question and perhaps shed more light on this relationship, which indeed represents a curious moment in Parisian intellectual history. There are two ways of looking at fellow travellers here: the traditional way – intellectuals following Communist parties; and the reverse – PCF intellectuals abandoning the party for *Tel Quel*. Many intellectuals have historically abandoned their respective Communist parties, but what matters here is the hegemonic position *Tel Quel* would acquire as a result. We have a number of PCF intellectuals and cultural organs (*Les Lettres Françaises, Clarté, France Nouvelle, Promesse, La Nouvelle Critique*) closely following the singular trajectory of a supposedly 'reactionary', in any case, initially apolitical review, over the years, as well as several militants (Pierre Guyotat, Jacques Henric, Jean-Louis Houdebine, Guy Scarpetta) who leave the party – even after the supposed de-Stalinization that took place in 1966 – because of *Tel Quel*. In 'Le refus d'hériter' [The refusal to inherit] published in *Le Nouvel Observateur* of 30 April 1968, Barthes provocatively asked why there was 'A Communist in *Tel Quel*'. Why not?, he replied, if this meant 'unwriting the traditional distaste for formalism among Communist intellectuals' (1987: 70). In *Les Lettres Françaises* of 7–13 July 1966, Daix wrote, 'The big event for us French of 1966, is the discovery of the Formalists of the '20s' (1966: 12). This discovery happened to coincide with a new intellectual climate characterized by the cultural de-Stalinization that took place at Argenteuil that very same year. Communist intellectuals could now discard socialist realism. Raymond Jean, one of the most enthusiastic participants at Cluny I, claimed that when he came to literature in the late 1950s, an entire generation already distrusted the subservience of literature to engaged thought. Socialist realism was at the origin of the worst deceptions in both Eastern Europe and France (1980: 12). Both groups actually had a common foe in that *Tel Quel* opposed Sartrean engagement from the onset. Communist writers and academics were now more willing to consider the specificity of the literary text and shift their attention to formal concerns. They also considered the human sciences essential for the renewal of Marxist thought. Louis Althusser would be chief among them.

From 1965 to 1968, the various Communist journals published numerous texts and interviews by the Telquelians, including Kristeva's 'Semiotics: A Critical Science and/or a Critique of Science'. The *Lettres Françaises* publication (20 April 1967) on 'Literature and Linguistics: Is collaboration between literati and linguists possible?' featuring a discussion, led by Henri Mitterand with academics such as Jean-Claude Chevalier, Jean Dubois, Todorov and Daix, foreshadowed the first Cluny encounter (Mitterand 1967). The 16–17 April 1968 colloquium, 'Linguistics and Literature', organized by *La Nouvelle Critique* brought together eighty participants – academics and writers – associated with the linguistic section of the Centre for Marxist Studies and Research, *Tel Quel* and the Vaugirard Group for Interdisciplinary Studies and Research (the latter was comprised of a group of university faculty led by PCF militant Jean Peytard). Four Telquelians (Kristeva, Sollers, Pleynet and Jean Louis Baudry) joined such academics and Communist intellectuals as Henri Meschonnic, Annie Ubersfeld, Michel Arrivé, Philippe Bonnefis, Jean, Mitterand, Peytard and Houdebine. Kristeva, twenty-six at the time, was only one of two women presenters, along with Ubersfeld, a well-known theatre scholar and French Jew who had been a resistant during the war and a member of the PCF. Nonetheless, Kristeva would be cited in the Introduction to the Proceedings for referring to the encounter as an 'event'. As an official encounter between the avant-garde and the political Left, Kristeva noted that the conference played 'a historical role, and one that was not limited to the development of literary theory'.[7] Jean proclaimed it a 'great ideological moment that benefited all'. Thanks to Cluny, 'the Party was less stiff and dogmatic, the avant-garde more responsible and militant' (1980: 13). Sollers claimed that the PCF had come to them for non-Marxist reasons, whereas they had approached the PCF for Marxist ones (Sollers 1979). Even if we question *Tel Quel*'s motives, it is true that the party wished to recover the intellectual hegemony it had lost as a result of Stalinism. It sought to unite all 'specialists working for the progress of knowledge – Communists and non-Communists'.[8] Outnumbered twenty to one by party intellectuals and academics, the Telquelians nonetheless stood their ground. Jeannine Verdès-Leroux claims that certain Communist intellectuals present felt theoretically incompetent with respect to questions of ideology, literature and art. As a result, the Telquelians gained the upper hand and Kristeva was even viewed as a diva (1987: 124–5). Kristeva's presentation 'The Problems of the Structuration of the Text' had considerably fewer Marxist references compared to the presentations of Baudry and Pleynet. She drew from her dissertation on

The Text of the Novel, which she would publish in 1970, focusing on such concepts as the text as signifying practice, the production of meaning, geno/phenotext, intertextuality and the text as ideologeme.

Cluny not only allowed for a dialogue between the avant-garde and the party but more importantly – for *Tel Quel* – questioned whether linguistics was the best vantage point from which to discuss literature. This also proved fruitful for PCF participants in that *Tel Quel's* notion of literary practice, which was incorporating more and more Marxist notions, undermined structural linguistics, which had been accused of supplanting dialectical materialism years earlier. In 'Semiotics: A Critical Science and/or a Critique of Science', Kristeva argued that the concept of production could become the crucial connection among Marx, Freud and semiotics. She contends that 'Marx's critical reflections on the system of exchange resemble the contemporary critique of the sign and the circulation of meaning' (KR 83) and that Marxist thought is crucial for the development of semiotic theory because it is 'the first to pose the problematics of productive work as a major element in the definition of a semiotic system' (KR 81). Baudry would even argue at Cluny that it wasn't 'by chance that linguistics developed in the West, whereas semiotics as a science of trans linguistic practices, developed in the Soviet Union or in zones marked by Marxism'.[9] Peytard also noted that *Tel Quel's* critique of structural linguistics was inscribed in the prolongation of Russian formalism and post-formalism. He added that it was 'heartening to note that the questioning of linguistics came from the best of our contemporary literature'.[10] Whatever we may think of the above comments, it is clear that *Tel Quel* was not about to relinquish the hegemonic position it had acquired at Cluny, nor abandon the Party that readily. Kristeva would later argue that 'the PCF was the best mouthpiece for experimental literary or theoretical work' (PK 16). She also added 'the idea was to use the Communist Party, not be used by it' (PK 16).

Thus, in May 1968, *Tel Quel* was not as Kristeva later claimed with 'a foot on the barricades' (PK 16), but instead embarked on the Communist 'galley'. Despite divergences among Telquelians (with several already favouring Maoism), the summer 1968 issue of *Tel Quel* (no 34) opened with an aggressive seven-point manifesto entitled 'The revolution here and now', signed not only by Kristeva and other Telquelians but also by Pierre Boulez, Hubert Damisch, Denis Hollier and others. It concluded with the following:

> Any ideological undertaking which does not today present itself in an advanced theoretical form and settles instead for bringing together under eclectic or sentimental headings individual and under-politicized activities, seems to us counter-revolutionary, inasmuch as it fails to recognize the process of the class struggle, which has objectively to be carried on and reactivated.[11]

In conjunction with the programme noted above, *Tel Quel* founded a 'Theoretical Studies Group', which met weekly from October 1968 to June 1969. Kristeva also participated in these discussions pertaining to textual production and ideological confrontation. The only Communist present was Houdebine. An explanatory remark in *Tel Quel* (issue 38) indicated that the group had been established in opposition to 'the reactionary politics of teaching in France'.[12]

The other 'May 1968' manifesto, which appeared at the end of this same issue, unsigned, severely criticized the student movement. More political than the first manifesto, which focused on the central place of theory in revolutionary struggle, this text underscored the essential and impassable role of the working-class party and criticized the petit bourgeois contestation of the students that had been substituted for the class struggle.

Tel Quel clearly wished to stay in the good graces of the PCF, but the second Cluny encounter with *La Nouvelle Critique* of 2–4 April 1970 on 'Literature and Ideologies' would prove otherwise. *Tel Quel* would not be the privileged minority here as was the case in 1968; instead it would be competing with other avant-garde currents represented by the journals *Action Poétique* and *Change*. The latter was founded by Faye in 1968, a year after leaving *Tel Quel* in a fury. Elisabeth Roudinesco writes, '[t]he struggle between the two journals was violent and pivoted on the imaginary conquest of the proletarian fortress' (1990: 536). After being played out in the respective journals and in the French and foreign press, it reached a climax at Cluny II, where *Change* was joined by *Action Poétique*, directed by Henri Deluy (1990: 536).

Faye claimed to have joined *Tel Quel* because of a common love for Mallarmé and the Russian formalists. He and Kristeva differed on many points. He did not think that highly of her linguistic expertise and certainly did not share her negative appraisal of Chomsky's work. He was also disturbed by the analogies between linguistics and Marxism made by Kristeva, Sollers and others, as a result of the Althusserian notion of theoretical practice that they exploited (1979). At Cluny, his colleague Mitsou Ronat of *Action Poétique* attacked the linguistic and philosophical work of Kristeva. Sollers was in an uproar and demanded that she be censored, or he would 'withdraw his troops'. In an attempt to appease all sides so that the conference could continue, it was agreed that a modified version of Ronat's presentation appear in the Introduction to the Proceedings, apparently also without the polemical discussion that had ensued.[13] Both Faye and Roudinesco claimed that *Tel Quel* subsequently broke with *La Nouvelle Critique* because they had not taken a stronger position against Ronat (Faye 1979; Roudinesco 1990: 540).

Did *Tel Quel* lose its hegemonic position with the PCF in 1970 at Cluny II? Not entirely and not exactly with respect to the question of literature, which Kristeva also elaborated in her presentation on 'The Ideology of

Discourse on Literature'. *Tel Quel* would justify its turn to the Chinese Cultural Revolution via a critique of PCF revisionism in its 'Positions of the June 71 Movement' proclamations. Its trajectory until 1982 would be an intricate one as it turned from the Chinese Cultural Revolution to the United States, and finally dissidence, to name but a few of its major stops.

Tel Quel's final destination was, in many respects, Kristeva's departure point in 1965. In 'Mémoire', she concedes that despite her initial 'seduction', Sollers' wager

> seemed to me completely unrealistic from the standpoint of the socialism I had experienced. I knew to what extent a regime born of a Marxist social mutation rejected not merely all aesthetic formalism deemed individualistic or antisocial, but also all individual stylistic experience that could question or explore the common code and its stereotypes in which ideology must seek shelter in order to dominate.
>
> (PK 13)

When I asked Kristeva, at the time of their dissident turn, who read *Tel Quel* and whether the elitist nature of the journal was not incompatible with the intellectual stance they had adopted in the late 1960s, she immediately responded, 'But who reads Mallarmé?' According to Kristeva, *Tel Quel* 'does not address people as individuals determined by their places in production. It addresses people as determined by their dreams, their sleep, their sex; in that instance, their social status is not essential', For Kristeva, 'There is no mass culture. Mass culture is a fantasy for a homogenous society that has never existed' (Kristeva, personal interview, 1978a). What disturbs Kristeva about the democratization of culture is that it implies a homogenization that always begins from the base. It always eliminates what exceeds: a Dostoevsky or a Kandinsky.

These remarks coincide with her concepts of politics as the common measure and the subject on trial/in process. The eccentric subject historically relegated to art and literature – if not to madness – became her basis for considering social change in a manner that coincided with dissidence in the late 1970s. This is exemplified in 'A New Type of Intellectual: The Dissident' in *Tel Quel* 74 (winter 1977), where she is viewing dissidence from multiple identity formations (intellectuals, psychoanalysts, writers, women, exiles). In the end, Kristeva remains closer, as a former citizen of a Soviet satellite country, to three French Communist militants who abandoned the PCF for *Tel Quel* in 1971–2. The respective essays of Jacques Henric, Guy Scarpetta and Houdebine in *Tel Quel* and *Art Press* converge with the work of Kristeva. The statement that best describes their common trajectory is perhaps the one of Henric, who affirmed, in 1986, that contrary to the avant-garde writers who had preceded them, they had caught themselves in time: 'Whatever may have been our mild or not so mild ideological deliriums, we never sacrificed our literary and artistic convictions to the political slaughterhouse. Literature is what saved us' (Henric 1986). Henric is implying that literature saved *Tel Quel* not only from engagement – 'We never gave in there. We were engaged but we never made engaged literature' – but from politics itself (Henric 1986). Jean-Paul Sartre, on the other hand, went to Prague in 1963, where he extolled socialist realism to an audience of Czech students and intellectuals, who had already rehabilitated Kafka and were paving the way for the reforms of 1968: 'Your Sartre dropped his pants in front of the authorities', lamented Ilios Yannakakis' students (Yannakakis 1980: 39). Was Sollers entirely wrong in 1967 when he claimed that Sartre did not really understand Marxism, given his literary views? (1967: 85).

Scarpetta would second Henric's assertion that their literary and artistic choices never faltered: 'Let those who talk about our "changing colours" reflect on this little detail, not the least trivial' (1987). Before we dismiss these comments as purely idealistic ruminations having no real social bearing, we must recognize that they are not coming from ivory tower academics but from former militants who joined ranks early in their youth. If artists and writers are indeed privileged, then why, asks Albert Camus, have they traditionally been the first victims of modern tyrannies, be they left- or right-wing? (2008: 263). If art and literature are superfluous, elitist endeavours, then why do all totalitarian regimes take artists and writers so seriously and punish them accordingly? At the 1977 Biennale of Dissent, Joseph Brodsky remarked that he didn't want to be viewed as a dissident writer, but simply as a writer (in Pasti 1977: 15). In fact, during his 1963 trial, he was charged as a writer, a 'parasite of the nation' by Soviet authorities. Andrei Sinyavsky, who along with Yuli Daniel, was the victim of the first Soviet show trial in 1966 openly directed at literary works, stated the following at the Biennale: 'Dissidence is finally but the synonym of art' (Sinyavsky 1978: 57). 'Art is indeed the equivalent of a crime… It has a value! It is a reality' (Sinyavsky 1978: 58). And several months before his assassination (2 November 1975), Pier Paolo Pasolini was asked how he wished to be defined. He responded, 'WRITER' (Macciocchi 1978: 27). Finally, Gyorky Konrad, the only Eastern European-based writer (not already in exile) authorized to attend the Biennale, stated, 'The word "dissident" is nothing other than an improper adjective next to the substantive literature' (Konrad 1978: 68). These pronouncements lend credence to Kristeva's and *Tel Quel*'s equating of the aesthetic and ethical prospects of literature with dissidence. They propose an ethics deriving from the literary experience itself, founded on the premise that questions of political oppression and ideological totalitarianism are initially implanted 'in the relation that each subject holds with their language and culture, and with what goes beyond them' (Scarpetta 1981: 290). It needs to be noted that at this time, *Tel Quel* is also moving beyond East-West divisions, as well as Left-Right binaries, through their affiliation with CIEL (Committee of Intellectuals for a Europe of Liberties).

Issue 76 of *Tel Quel* (summer 1978) is dedicated to the 1977 Venice Biennale on Dissent. Along with texts by Konrad, Brodsky, Sinyavsky and Yannakakis, there is also an essay by Maria-Antonietta Macciocchi, who envisages Pier Paolo Pasolini's assassination in light of the Italian historic compromise and the crisis of Eurocommunism. Kristeva's 'Dissident Literature as the Refutation of Left Discourse' introduces this issue. The original Biennale talk is reviewed by Daniela Pasti in *La Repubblica* (4–5 December 1977: 15). It is a seductive journalistic piece that features Brodsky and Kristeva (with their two photos) under a title taken from her Biennale presentation: 'To recover the memory of the discourse of the Left'. This is probably one of those rare moments when Kristeva is indirectly featured as an East European émigré (even if references are to her *Tel Quel* connection), although her exile was certainly not involuntary like Brodsky's.

Sinyavsky notes that 'the artistic situation of an era is not defined solely by what is created at that time, but also by what, arising from the past, enters our perception with a particular intensity, abolishing the distance of time and space' (57). Does *Tel Quel* succeed in masking the distance of time and space by emphasizing the literary and artistic dimension of dissidence in 1977–8? It is not for literary reasons that the dissident writers featured in this issue were completely ignored by the journal during the 1960s. *Tel Quel*'s interest in Russian formalism and post-formalism in the 1960s does not exclude the fact that these writers were sent to forced-labour camps or psychiatric prisons. In his 1931 essay, 'On a Generation That Squandered its Poets', Jakobson writes, 'There are countries where Marxist theory is answered by Leninist practice, and where the madness of the brave, the martyr's stake, and the poet's Golgotha are not just figurative expressions' (1987: 298). The writers featured belatedly in the 1978 issue *of Tel Quel* paid a tremendous price for freedom of expression, while *Tel Quel* kept silent. How tragic that it takes the crisis of Marxism-Communism in France in the late 1970s to take note of a resistance that was already present decades earlier. There is still much to be said about the lost opportunities for French intellectuals from 1956 to 1974 that the late Tony Judt so grievously reiterates in *Past Imperfect*:

> Starting from a shared premise – that November 1956 marked the end of an era in which communism had dominated the radical imagination – they moved not closer to their eastern European audience but further away, to the point of losing all contact with a large part of their international constituency. In 1956, French intellectuals thus parted company from much of the rest of the European intellectual community at just the moment when they could still have reasserted their leadership, in East and West alike.
>
> (1992: 281–2)

The Italian backdrop of the Biennale presented yet another lost opportunity for Kristeva and *Tel Quel*. The focus on the Soviet Union and Eastern Europe at the Biennale eclipsed the crisis of Eurocommunism taking place in Bologna and Rome. The Italian Communist Party revealed its true Stalinist colours in supporting Soviet opposition to the Biennale, while, at the same time, violently opposing demonstrations in the municipalities it actually controlled. In going from opposition to power through the notorious 'historic compromise', the PCI was also held responsible for political repression. During the March 1977 student uprisings in the Communist-run cities of Bologna and Rome, it supported police intervention and brutality, and positioned the working class against the youth movement. These events led to the 'French Appeal Against Repression in Italy', signed by Gilles Deleuze, Félix Guattari, Foucault, Sartre, Barthes, Sollers, Macciocchi, Denis Roche and others, and to the Bologna mass rally of 23–25 September 1977. That very same month, the Common Program was dissolved in France.[14] Telquelians were not in 'red' Bologna, whose police intervention sanctioned by the Communists was called the 'Little Prague'. But then they weren't with Prague in 1968 either, nor with the students in Paris for that matter.

Kristeva's presence at the Biennale commemorating the sixtieth anniversary of the October Revolution was certainly opportune. After all, Jakobson had insisted that they keep the memory of their old Europe alive lest the future no longer belong to them either. She positions herself on two fronts at the Biennale by allowing the 'anachronistic' project of the Eastern European dissidents to dispel any lingering, progressive illusions with respect to Marxism/Communism in Western Europe. This also allows her – both as the Bulgarian émigré and the French intellectual – to finally come to terms with the spectres of Marxism and Communism that haunted her since her arrival in Paris in 1965.

However, dissidence could not be contained within the Biennale walls of Venice, nor limited to the Soviet Union and Eastern Europe for that matter. Kristeva had as many 'tools' – if not more – available to dismantle the discourse of the Left from what had taken place between March and September 1977 in Italy as she had from the Eastern European and Soviet past. Had she also turned her gaze sideways from the 'white' Veneto and the 'anachronistic' resistance of Eastern Europe to the 'red' cities of Bologna and Rome, she would have witnessed a contemporaneous mass movement challenging the discourse of the Left in its very praxis. The only mention of these momentous events in *Tel Quel* were a few remarks by Bernard-Henri Lévy (issue 77, autumn 1978), whereby he lauds this New Left Movement as one 'thinking elsewhere' rather than simply 'against' the PCI (32).

Kristeva had little faith in the masses – she left them the *maisons de la culture* so that intellectuals could go on with their research.[15] Yet what was taking place between March and September 1977 by those whom Enrico Berlinguer called the *untorelli* (plague carriers) – better known as Indiani

Metropolitani, Autonomia and Radio Alice, to cite but a few 'keywords' – was definitely a concrete manifestation of the subject in process/on trial and of resistance to political consensus: 'Revolutionary politics, when it isn't repetition, should be the time when politics (the common measure, thus language) ruptures' (PL 13).

Gianni Scalia aptly noted, 'It isn't freedom of speech that is lacking, but rather the freedom to be heard' (1960: 639, my translation). The dissidents could finally be heard within the official premises of the Biennale, but the diverse voices emanating from the occupied streets of Bologna and Rome, the bodies being arrested, brutalized or killed (students Giorgiana Masi and Francesco Lorusso) depended on the pirate Radio Alice (whose collective would also be arrested). Was Radio Alice all that different from the Samizdat of Eastern Europe? Bakhtin would certainly have been pleased to witness the carnivalesque ambiance made possible by thousands of individuals at the September rally in Bologna, where a new, heterogeneous subject, ex-centric with respect to the powers that be and their institutions, was turning a rally against repression into a cultural *fête* marked by spontaneous conversation, music, dance, theatre, art, laughter – and certainly a new relation to language and power.

Notes

1. Risset was an Italianist and Dante scholar. She published ten articles in *Tel Quel*, beginning with her text on Ponge in no. 22 (summer 1965). Kristeva published twenty articles in all. Although there were not many texts by women in the early years of the journal, issue 2 did have a text by Janine Aeply and subsequent issues included an interview with Natalie Sarraute (9), a text by Marthe Robert on Kafka (18), by Lucette Finas on Sarraute (20) and Hélène Berger (Cixoux) on Joyce (22). Other women contributors included Paule Thévenin, Luce Irigaray, Maria-Antonietta Macciocchi, Susan Sontag, Shoshana Felman, Dominique Desanti, Meredith Monks, Françoise Giroud, Viviane Forester, Dominique Rolin, Sophie Podolski and Christine Glucksmann.
2. For a full analysis of the journal's role in renewing the French intellectual scene between the 1960s and late 1970s, see Marx-Scouras (1996).
3. 'Déclaration', trans. Bettina Knapp, 3.
4. Barthes is quoting Sollers here. Barthes (1987: 65).
5. *Tel Quel* subsequently apologized for its silence in issue 47 (autumn 1971). See 'Positions du Mouvement de Juin 71', 136.
6. Kenarov (2018).
7. Kristeva, response in 'Linguistique et littérature' (Colloque de Cluny I, 16–17 April 1968), 170.

8   Introduction to 'Linguistique et littérature', *La Nouvelle Critique*, 6.
9   Baudry (1968: 54).
10 Peytard (1968: 14).
11 'La Révolution ici maintenant', trans. Keith Reader, 4.
12 Groupe d'Etudes Théoriques de Tel Quel année 1968–1969, 103.
13 Faye (1979); Forest (1995: 350–4); Matonti (2005: 195).
14 In March 1972, the Communist and socialist parties, along with the Movement of Radicals of the Left signed a 'Common Programme for a Government of Left Union'. The Left did very well in the municipal elections of March 1977, obtaining 51.5 per cent of the vote. However, disagreement between the two major parties (essentially a powerplay with the Socialists gaining the upper hand) led to the rupture of the Common Program in September 1977 and their loss in the legislative elections of March 1978.
15 She stated, 'The masses have the "maisons de la culture", where one can see a play by Beaumarchais or Molière, which is not bad in itself, but as far as intellectuals are concerned, it is essential that we continue our work in language.' Personal interview, Paris, 15 February 1978a.

References

Aragon, L. (1959), *J'abats mon jeu*, Paris: Réunis.
Barthes, R. (1972), *Critical Essays*, trans. R. Howard, Evanston, IL: Northwestern University Press.
Barthes, R. (1986), *The Rustle of Language*, trans. R. Howard, New York: Hill and Wang.
Barthes, R. (1987), *Criticism and Truth*, trans. P. Thody, Minneapolis, MN: University of Minnesota Press.
Baudry, J. L. (1968), 'Linguistique et production textuelle', *La Nouvelle Critique*, special issue: 48–54.
Brochier, J.-J. (1972), 'Tel quel, du nouveau roman à la revolution culturelle', *Magazine Littéraire*, 65 (June): 9–10.
Camus, A. (2008), *Oeuvres complètes*, vol. 4, Paris: Gallimard.
Daix, P. (1966), 'Et si nous étions passés à côté de la littérature soviétique?', *Les Lettres Françaises*, 7–13 (July): 11–12.
Dosse, F. (1997), *History of Structuralism: The Rising Sign, 1945–1966*, vol. 1, trans. D. Glassman, Minneapolis, MN: University of Minnesota Press.
Faye, J. P. (1979), personal interviews, Paris, 23 and 30 May.
Forest, P. (1995), *Histoire de Tel Quel*, Paris: Éditions du Seuil.
Foucault, M. (1980), *Power/Knowledge: Selected Interviews and Other Writings (1972–77)*, ed. C. Gordon, New York: Pantheon.
Henric, J. (1986), 'Quand une avant-garde (littéraire) rencontre une avant-garde (politique) ...', unpublished paper.
Hollier, D. (1986), *The Politics of Prose*, trans. J. Mehlman, Minneapolis, MN: University of Minnesota Press.

Houdebine, J. L. (1987), personal interview, Paris, 23 June.
Jakobson, R. (1987), *Language in Literature*, ed. K. Pomorska and S. Rudy, Cambridge, MA: Harvard University Press.
Jardine, A. (2020), *At the Risk of Thinking: An Intellectual Biography of Julia Kristeva*, London: Bloomsbury Academic.
Jean, R. (1980), 'Trajet politique et romanesque', *Magazine Littéraire*, 166 (November): 12–14.
Judt, T. (1992), *Past Imperfect: French Intellectuals, 1945–1956*, Berkeley, CA: University of California Press.
Juin, H. (1960), 'Pourquoi une nouvelle revue?', *Les Lettres Françaises*, 18 (February): 4.
Kenarov, D. (2018), 'Was the Philosopher Julia Kristeva a Cold War Collaborator?', *The New Yorker*, 5 September. www.https://newyorker.com/news/dispatch/was-the-philosopher-julia-kristeva-a-cold-war-collaborator (accessed 12 September 2020).
Konrad, G. (1978), 'L'autre littérature: crise de l'hégémonie et contradictions dans les cultures de l'Europe de l'Est', *Tel Quel*, 76 (summer): 61–70.
Kristeva, J. (1968a), 'Distance et anti-représentation', *Tel Quel*, 32 (autumn): 49–53.
Kristeva, J. (1968b), 'Présentation' to 'La sémiologie aujourd'hui en U.R.S.S.', *Tel Quel*, 35 (autumn): 3–8.
Kristeva, J. (1977), 'Un nouveau type d'intellectuel: le dissident', *Tel Quel*, 74 (winter): 3–8. Reprinted in KR.
Kristeva, J. (1978a), personal interview, Paris, 15 February.
Kristeva, J. (1978b), 'La réfutation du discours de gauche', *Tel Quel*, 76 (summer): 40–44.
La Nouvelle Critique (1968), 'Linguistique et littérature', *La Nouvelle Critique*, special issue (Colloque de Cluny, 16–17 April).
Lévy, B. H. (1978), 'La prévue du pudding' (interview with Ludovic Bessozzi), *Tel Quel*, 77 (autumn): 25–35.
Lotman, Y. (1988), 'The Semiotics of Culture and the Concept of a Text', *Soviet Psychology*, 26 (3): 52–8.
Macciocchi, M. (1978), 'Pasolini: assassinat d'un dissident', *Tel Quel*, 76 (summer): 27–39.
Marx-Scouras, D. (1996), *The Cultural Politics of 'Tel Quel': Literature and the Left in the Wake of Engagement*, University Park, PA: Penn State University Press.
Matonti, F. (2005), *Intellectuels Communistes: Essai sur l'obéissance politique ('La Nouvelle Critique', 1967–1980)*, Paris: La Découverte.
Mitterand, H. et al. (1967), 'La collaboration entre littéraires et linguistes est-elle possible?' *Les Lettres Françaises*, 20 April: 3–7.
Pasti, D. (1977), 'Per ritrovare la memoria del discorso di sinistra', *La Repubblica*, 4–5 (December): 15.
Peytard, J. (1968), 'Rapports et interférences', *La Nouvelle Critique*, special issue: 29–34.
Ristat, J. (1975), *Qui sont les contemporains?*, Paris: Gallimard.
Roudinesco, E. (1990), *Jacques Lacan and Co. (A History of Psychoanalysis in France, 1925–1985)*, trans. J. Mehlman, Chicago: University of Chicago Press.

Samoyault, T. (2017), *Barthes: A Biography*, trans. A. Brown, Cambridge: Polity.
Scalia, G. (1960), 'L'esempio del Politecnico', *Letterature moderne*, 10 (5): 638–44.
Scarpetta, G. (1981), *Éloge du Cosmopolitisme*, Paris: Grasset.
Scarpetta, G. (1987), personal interview, Paris, 23 June.
Sinyavsky, A. (1978), 'L'art est supérieur à la réalité', *Tel Quel*, 76 (summer): 56–60. All translations from this issue are the author's.
Sollers, P. (1967), 'Un fantasme de Sartre', *Tel Quel*, 28 (winter): 84–6.
Sollers, P. (1968), 'Écriture et révolution' (interview with Jacques Henric), *Théorie d'Ensemble*, 67–79, Paris: Seuil.
Sollers, P. (1974), 'Littérature: Le retour des précieux', *Le Nouvel Observateur*, 2–8 December: 73.
Sollers, P. (1979), personal interview, Paris, 5 July.
Sollers, P. (1983), *Writing and the Experience of Limits*, trans. P. Barnard and D. Hayman, New York: Columbia University Press.
Sollers, P. (2007), *Un Vrai Roman, Mémoires*, Paris: Plon.
Tel Quel (1960), 'Déclaration', *Tel Quel*, 1 (spring): 3–4.
Tel Quel (1968), 'La révolution ici maintenant', *Tel Quel*, 34 (summer): 3–4.
Tel Quel (1969), 'Groupe d'études théoriques de *Tel Quel* année 1968–1969', *Tel Quel*, 38 (summer): 103.
Tel Quel (1971), 'Positions du mouvement de juin 71', *Tel Quel*, 47 (autumn): 135–41.
Todorov, T., ed. and trans. (1965), *Théorie de la littérature*, Paris: Seuil.
Verdès-Leroux, J. (1987), *Le Réveil des Somnambules: le Parti communiste, les intellectuels et La culture, 1956–1985*, Paris: Fayard.
Yannakakis, I. (1980), 'Concilier Sartre et la dissidence', *Libération*, special issue on Sartre: 39.

2

Julia Kristeva: *Chora*, infinity, modernism

John Lechte

If modernism is not completely captured in the notion of formalism, the latter has certainly been held to be one of its fundamental elements.[1] As a result, an important question posed in this study is: how does Julia Kristeva's notion of number, set theory and infinity that is so visible in her early work play itself out in relation to the *chora* and *le sémiotique* (the semiotic) after 1973? If, as she claims explicitly (clearly echoing Cantor), 'language is, practically, the only *real infinity*' (S 200), and poetic language is an incarnation of infinity in Cantor's sense (200), we want to know whether the *chora*, base of the semiotic, might also be understood in these terms. Does Kristeva's conception of number change in the post-1973 texts? In relation to the latter, one should note – as Quentin Meillassoux (2011) has done – references to number in Mallarmé's '*Un coup de dés*' – a key text in both Kristeva's pre-1973 texts and in the development of '*le sémiotique*' in *La Révolution du langage poétique* (RLP). More broadly, though, could there ever be an *incarnation* of infinity if the mathematics of it are taken seriously?

In 'Le mot, le dialogue et le roman' (S 143n73; DL 64–91) there is a reference to Cantor and set theory and the 'logic of the "*transfinite*"' and of a countable infinity as a way of illuminating the notion of dialogism (S 153; DL 72). But then this is offset by a footnote saying that such references in relation to poetic language are only 'metaphorical' and 'analogical' (S 153 n.10; DL 72 n.15).

Later, in 'Pour une sémiologie des paragrammes' ('Towards a Semiology of Paragrams') (S 174–207), a section is entitled, 'Le Langage poétique comme infinité' ('Poetic Language as Infinity') (S 176–80). There, it is said that only in poetic language is the 'totality (we prefer *to this term* that of "infinity") of the code practically realised' (S 178; emphasis added). This leads one to think that poetic language may well be the *incarnation* of infinity, a highly problematic notion, as we as shall see. It is more likely, though, that the infinity invoked is a potential infinity (recalling Aristotle) rather than the infinity Cantor brought into being. Then again, Kristeva's text is ambivalent. For it is said that 'the rules that govern the paragrammatic network can be spelt out *by set theory*, by the operations and theorems that flow from or relate to them' (S 183; emphasis added). Moreover, as I noted above, language is said to be a *'real infinity'*. Consequently, the issue arising later in this chapter in relation to the semiotic is the extent to which Cantor's notion of an infinite set can be brought to bear on language and literature in general and on the semiotic *chora* in particular.

Even though it might be possible to draw a vague parallel between the geno- and pheno-text of Kristeva's early work (1966–73) – the work of *'sémanalyse'* – and the semiotic and the symbolic made famous by *La Révolution du langage poétique*, it would seem (and this is what needs to be confirmed) that the semiotic is discontinuous with what went before. Specifically, to all appearances, a difference arises between a formalist and structuralist – indeed, mathematical – approach to textuality adopted in the major texts of the 1960s and early 1970s, and the more 'concrete' approach implied by the notion of the semiotic in Kristeva's post-1973 writing. This is not to deny that the effort to conceptualize the semiotic, the *chora* and the Freudian drives also brings with it a degree of formalization. but the latter is at the antipodes of the formalism of texts like: 'Pour une sémiologie des paragrammes', 'La productivité dite texte' ('A Productivity called text') (S 208–45), 'Poésie et négativité' ('Poetry and Negativity') (S 246–77) and 'L'engendrement de la formule' ('Engendering the Formula') (S 278–371).

An important inspiration and stimulus to the formalist approach of sémanalyse were Philippe Sollers' hyper-modernist novels such as *Drame* (1965), *Nombres* (1966), *Lois* (1972) and – to a lesser extent – *H* (1973), novels in which number and numbers figure prominently, either explicitly (*Nombres*) or implicitly (*Drame*), and where the focus is as much on the act of writing as on its content, with little effort being made to respect existing narrative or grammatical conventions.

Significantly, in her early works, set theory is invoked by Kristeva, along with a number of mathematical procedures, such as the axiom of undecidability, the law of commutativity, lattice theory and the axiom of choice. With infinite sets, the part becomes equivalent to the whole. As is frequently pointed out, Cantor's concept of infinity is to be distinguished from a 'potential infinity' (counting approaching infinity but never reaching it). As Jean-Louis Houdebine (Kristeva's one-time colleague at the Université de Paris-VII) explains,

> at no time could the infinite be defined in terms of the accumulation of finite units, however large one might envisage them to be. Cantor shows on the contrary that to accede to an infinite dimension, it is necessary beforehand to carry out an operation of an entirely different order, definable in terms of a *break* (*coupure*); a break which is, at the same time, a *nomination*.
> (Houdebine 1983: 99, my translation)

According to Houdebine, Kristeva is one of the few to have worked with literature in terms of an 'infinitist problematic' (1983: 89). The closest that one could come to this is if literature were the incarnation of the violation of the principle of the whole being greater than the part.[2] But this would also mean that literature is the *incarnation* of an infinite set, or, to put it another way, that there is a continuity between mathematics and a real object. The latter would, for a contemporary mathematics of the infinite, be considered highly problematic. As the philosopher of mathematics Penelope Maddy has pointed out in relation to the object of mathematics, 'It isn't clear that the world contains any literally infinite structures... If the full theory of numbers has a subject matter, it isn't to be found in the physical world' (2007: 362).

Despite this, and before going into more detail about set theory, it still seems legitimate to ask whether Kristeva's notion of *chora* has a mathematical aspect. On the face of it, the answer seems to be 'no'; for mathematics in general – and set theory in particular – would be part of the symbolic, the very opposite of the semiotic. On this basis, in coining the term *le sémiotique* (as opposed to the conventional, '*la sémiotique*) to refer to the drives and their stases, Kristeva at the same time appears to separate her early work dominated by a formalist impulse from her post-1973 work dominated by the semiotic. In other words, when Kristeva says in 1966 that 'The application of mathematics (more especially set theory), dominated by the idea of the infinite, to this potential infinity of the language of the writer, will help to bring back to the consciousness of every user of the code the concept of the infinity of poetic language' (S 200, my translation), this does not refer to the semiotic. To be sure about this, though, we need to consider once again what we are dealing with when approaching the *chora* as the basis of the Kristevan semiotic.

Chora reconsidered

In this regard, two general observations can be made. The first relates to the philosophical context in which *chora*, in Kristeva's appropriation of it, appears. As is known, this is, in the first instance, in relation to Plato's *Timaeus*, which is embedded in Greek thought of around 350 BC. Basically, the *chora*, in one of its incarnations, is a receptacle, or container, that, according to what Plato says at one point, does not in any way mix with what is contained in it. Thus, Timaeus says, 'that which is to receive all forms should have no form' (50e) (Plato 1980: 1177). The mother, it is then claimed, is analogous to that which has no form (51a) (1178). In set theory, it is said the elements of a set are distinct from the set itself. The empty set, for example, is the set which has no elements, but which can be a sub-set of itself. It thus includes itself. But, as we shall see, the zero set {Ø} is a subset of every set, in which case the *chora* could be a sub-set of all the elements contained in it, even if it does not appear as such. In short, as a zero set includes itself, Plato's *chora* is perhaps analogous to a set even after it receives the elements germane to it. Later, we ask whether it is plausible to apply set theory to the *chora* in this way.

But what does Kristeva make of this? The *chora* is initially defined 'as "energy" charges, as well as "psychical" marks' (RPL 25), and thus as 'outside' (so it would seem) the symbolic. Hardly any mathematical indications here, unless stochastics and equations for turbulence are evoked by implication. In any case, in *Revolution in Poetic Language*, mathematics is referred to as a metalanguage (RPL 62). However, the semiotic is made present through musicality, which reminds us of the importance of music for Pythagoras. But Pythagoras stands for mathematics as harmony and pattern *in* the world, while mathematicians today would be sceptical of the continuity between number and the world. The semiotic evokes the origin as chaotic. How ironical it is, then, that the *Timaeus* is often described as the work where Plato's Pythagoreanism is most evident (cf. Tubbs 2009: 28).

Even so, perhaps a mathematical aspect enters the scene when it is a matter of number. We shall keep an eye out for this when discussing Kristeva's commentary on Mallarmé's *Un coup de dés* (1945) as compared to Meillassoux's approach in *Le Nombre et la sirène*.

The other aspect of context I want to mention regarding the semiotic and mathematics is the ancient Greek privileging of space and geometry. Once again, Pythagoras features here. But rather than discussing Pythagorean thinking on space, let us note the timely reminder given by Keimpe Algra: 'Since in antiquity neither empirical experiment nor mathematics played any role of importance in philosophies of space, the ways in which spatial terms were commonly applied constituted, so to speak, the raw material of the philosophical debate' (1995: 31). Significantly, Plato initially calls the *chora* 'invisible' and 'formless' and says that it 'partakes of the intelligible and is most incomprehensible' (51b) (1980: 1178). It is an entity that is certainly not known through the senses and hardly even through the intellect. It is thus only knowable via a kind of 'bastard reasoning'. By contrast to this, Kristeva, while certainly acknowledging 'bastard reasoning', nevertheless makes the *chora* a sensible entity, playing up Plato's analogy between the mother/receptacle and the *chora*. For Plato, too, if the *chora* is space (and *chora* can be translated as space in Greek), space in its turn is eternal, that is, timeless. Plato elaborates by saying that space 'provides a home for all created things, and is apprehended, when all sense is absent, by a kind of spurious [bastard] reason, and is hardly real' (52b) (1178–9). The 'spurious' or bastard reasoning gives rise to dream and image as the mode of apprehension of the *chora* (52c) (1179).

Alexander Hope, in a scholarly article on the *chora* and metaphor, says, 'The temptation to simplify *khôra* by reducing it anachronistically to modern conceptions of space is obvious; however, this is clearly not the case as this would be to translate Plato's ontology into an epistemology that excludes the division between the eternal eidos and the visible world' (2015: 615). Certainly, while modern conceptions of space should, clearly, not be projected on to the *chora*, the fact that, on one possible reading, it has an eternal, or 'ever-lasting', status brings it within the bounds of how Greek thought conceived space, even if the latter was not presented in an abstract fashion, but rather as 'land/region/ground' (Algra 1995: 33).[3] John Sallis proposes that it may be 'intrinsically untranslatable' and goes so far as to add that 'It is such as to disrupt the very operation of translation' (1999: 115). But then Sallis realizes that things cannot be left there as the very effort to study the *chora* at all would be compromised. Consequently, the philosopher concedes that it may be possible to translate *chora* in relation both to the Greek language as a whole and to other parts of the *Timaeus*, where it might mean 'place', 'land' or 'country' (1999: 116).

Whatever difficulties there are in translating *chora*, the history of scholarship shows that the overriding issue of interpretation has centred on a receptacle that does not appear at all because it is formless, or on one that only appears through the forms it receives. As Sallis succinctly explains, *chora* 'comes to have, to receive, forms, and yet it does not have them itself'; it appears 'by way of those things that enter it' (1999: 109). Confusingly, in light of the latter remark, Sallis adds that the *chora* is 'formless' (110), 'has no determination whatsoever' (110–11). We see, indeed, that Sallis' own discourse is torn between the *chora* never appearing as such and its appearing as movement, as the following passage confirms:

> It is not without paradox that one can speak of the χώρα [*chora*] as itself in movement, as something – though not of course, some thing – that moves. For the χώρα is not only utterly amorphous but also invisible, even insistently invisible, whereas the things that can be said, without further

ado, to move are visible things, things that occupy some place and move to another, or at least that alter their position or state within a place. But how can the χώρα be in a place in which or from which to move?

(1999: 127)

In the latter part of his study where he responds to Aristotle's criticism that after introducing the *chora* Plato makes no further use of it in the rest of the *Timaeus*, Sallis defends Plato by again evoking the indeterminacy of the χώρα: 'It does not itself become present but only appears as something else, not as itself. It cannot be presented even in the sense of being the theme of a discourse that would determine it, for it withdraws from all determination and allows only a bastard discourse' (1999: 132). As a result, Sallis seems, finally, to line up with those who comprehend the χώρα as other than matter or anything that appears.

In this regard, Derrida's thinking the *chora* as *khôra*, without the definite article, is, seemingly, to make an a priori gesture in favour of indeterminacy and thus the difficulty, if not the impossibility, of thinking the *chora* as such. Without the definite article *chora* becomes a name not a thing. In line with the first part of the *Timaeus*, Derrida confirms that *chora* receives 'all determinations but possesses none of its own' (1993: 37, my translation). Nowhere does Derrida directly address the difference between *chora* as that which does not appear and its appearing in what it receives. Instead, he prefers to think the intricacies of the *Timaeus* text as itself a receptacle, receptacle of myths, stories (*récits*),[4] memories, images and dreams, and even of a certain 'Platonism'.[5] *Khôra* itself cannot, of course, 'become the subject of any *narrative* (*récit*)' (1993: 76, my translation).

To all appearances, then, modern interpreters of the *Timaeus* have always been divided, some giving precedence to the *chora* as invisible, formless and indeterminate,[6] and others saying it is matter, and that along with its contents, the *chora* also moves or 'shakes'.[7] For Cornford in the 1930s, '[t]here is no justification for calling the Receptacle "matter" – a term not used by Plato' (1937: 181). Some scholars have thus played down the importance of *chora* as matter or as being effectively equivalent to, or only appearing through, what it receives, while others have placed emphasis on the *chora* as space writ large and thus as invisible, amorphous, without 'qualities of its own' (Cornford) and barely thinkable (hence the need to resort to a 'bastard' reasoning).[8]

Sallis points out that, at least since Aristotle, distortions have crept into interpretations of the *Timaeus*, one of them being the characterization of the *chora* as matter, such as is found in Plotinus (*c*. AD 204/5–270), Plutarch (*c*. AD 46–*c*. 120) and in a forged text, *On the Nature of the World and the Soul* purportedly by a 'Timaeus of Locri'.[9] Sallis is critical of the definition of the *chora* as matter, a definition given by those influenced by this tradition (such as Irigaray, who refers exclusively to ὕλη (hyle), 1985: 173) (see Sallis 1999: 151 and n. 9).[10]

Hope, in the work already cited, seems to want to have it both ways. Thus, after acknowledging that 'Khôra affords a place for all things to come into being, but is itself unaffected by the creation and destruction that it gives place to' (2015: 615), he adds that 'Khôra certainly cannot be said to be eternal in the sense of eternally unchanging, since it takes on the shapes of the forms that enter it' (2015: 617) – that is, it seems to become what enters it. So, one might wonder how the later gloss could be valid when, as we have seen, *chora* is such that it does not mix with what it contains.[11]

What, then, are we to make of the link Kristeva draws between the Platonic *chora* and mobility (RPL 25)? For – at least in my reading – while the contents of the *chora* might be mobile, for Plato, the *chora* itself is not. Again, when the *chora* is described as a 'nonexpressive totality formed by the drives and their *stases* in a motility that is as full of movement as it is regulated' (RPL 25), it seems that we are already in psychoanalytic territory. As such, rather than being the basis of an interpretation of the *Timaeus*, *chora* operates as a device for shifting attention away from both phenomenological and Cartesian explanations of the subject and from a conventional linguistic approach to poetic language. Indeed, instead of using *chora* to explain the working of the drives and the 'so-called *primary processes*' (RPL 25), psychoanalysis is used to illuminate the *chora*. This is the conclusion that must be drawn in the wake of the majority of scholarly interpretations of the *chora*, which emphasize its enigmatic status, interpretations that, consequently, in no way resemble Kristeva's ultimately psychoanalytical characterization of the *chora* as harbinger of the drives. Kristeva nonetheless recalls that the 'receptacle' – also called 'space' – is ambiguous, amorphous, unnameable, prior to number and forms and, once named, becomes ontologized.[12] The question is: 'Why then borrow an ontologized term in order to designate an articulation that antecedes positing?' (RPL 239, n.13). Basically, the answer given is that the *chora* brings to the fore an 'insurmountable problem for discourse', namely, the problem of the pre-symbolic, and that (our author insists) the '*motility*' made explicit is 'the precondition for symbolicity' (RPL 239–40, n.13; emphasis added).

Debate centres, then, on whether the Platonic *chora* itself moves and to this extent is present, or whether it is only the items inside the *chora* which move. In his well-researched chapter devoted to the *Timaeus*, Algra sums up this debate: 'Most interpreters have been of the opinion that the two different descriptions [*chora* as receptacle that does not appear and as matter that does appear] were incompatible and that consequently only one of them conveyed Plato's *real* thoughts' (1995: 77). In Algra's view, 'from antiquity onwards the problem of the identification of the *hupodochê* [receptacle], the third factor introduced in the course of Plato's famous cosmological account, has kept scholars busy trying to fit the relevant passages into a coherent framework' (1995: 72). Although, Algra says, 'most interpreters' have tried to reconcile one or other interpretation of the *chora* with what Plato might have intended, his judgement is that 'Plato's presentation of the receptacle is in the end fundamentally incoherent' (1995: 78). But, in any case, says Algra, just to call the receptacle *chora* goes against it being matter, which implies that it does not have a material character.

The Kristevan *chora* as Freudian maternal thing

Clearly, Kristeva bypasses the scholarly debate on the nature of the *chora*, perhaps the better to appropriate it for her own purposes. So, not only is the *chora* essentially mobile (evoking the operation of the winnowing instrument in the *Timaeus*, 53a) but – as she says in her now well-known thesis – it becomes the incarnation of the drives and their energy flows: 'their ephemeral stases' (RPL 25). In short, the *chora* is not the formless receptacle that does not appear as such, the better to allow the manifestation of what it receives. This approach hardly allows the *chora* to be grasped by set theory, as the latter would depend, as I see it, on it being an empty set, one that contains no elements.

The Kristevan *chora* is, then, a mass of energy charges in motion in its own right, whereas, even as the instrument that also moves along with what it receives, the Platonic *chora* (χώρα – translatable as a variant of space, if not as space as such) lays claim to being *universal* and all-encompassing (this is why it can only be accessed, if at all, via a 'bastard' reasoning) – the recipient of everything. This contrasts with the *chora* as a very *particular* entity, despite it being designated by Kristeva as a 'nonexpressive *totality*' (RPL 25, emphasis added). That the *chora* is not a totality in Plato's sense is confirmed by Kristeva equating it with the term 'semiotic', understood as the now familiar Greek 'σημεῖον' (semeion) defined as 'distinctive mark, trace, index, precursory sign, proof, engraved or written sign, imprint' (RPL 25). Such an etymology allows the theorist to connect it to the 'modality' of the Freudian drives, as it also indicates that the *chora*, in Kristeva's hands, is *perceptible*, whereas in the *Timaeus* the *chora*'s perceptibility is its most doubtful aspect. But also, as if the Platonic context were only a pretext, the *chora* is quickly equated with the Freudian '*primary processes*' and thus with the drives as 'discrete quantities of energy' that 'move through the body of the subject' (RPL 25). The 'body of the subject' – how much more particular can one get than this?

While Kristeva, along with others, says that, in Plato's terms, the *chora* is a mother (RPL 240, n.14 and RLP 25, n.17), translations of the relevant passage are rendered as being *like* a mother (50d 1980: 1178, Jowett trans.), or is that which we may *compare* to a mother (Cornford 1937, trans. 185). The *chora* is only maternal by way of illustrating how the receptacle must, to be what it is, remain distinct from its contents. It could thus be argued that it does not have to have a feminine bearing. Least of all is it *essentially* feminine or female. Moreover, to bring corporeality into relation with the *chora*, which, for many readers, is what the designation of the mother-female implies, is quite out of keeping with the receptacle as that which does not appear as such – which is not present, as it were.

Chora as a set in relation to the axioms of set theory

Despite the implausibility of set theory being applicable to Kristeva's project, let us turn, nevertheless, to a simplified version of it the better to see how the *chora* measures up. It should, to begin, be noted that it only makes sense to contemplate posing the *chora* as a set and speculating about this because it is an entirely imaginary, not a real, entity. Thus, in set-theoretic terms, we can say, axiomatically: suppose that the *chora* exists.[13]

Now, by way of illustration, let us focus on the 'axiom of extension' as it is understood in set theory the better to see if it explains anything about the *chora*. Two sets are equal if and only if they have the same elements, a set being defined as a collection of objects.

Symbolically: $A \subset B$ (= inclusion, which is reflexive: A includes A is transitive: that is, a set can include a set which includes a set... cf., organization of organizations). $A \, \varepsilon \, B$ (= belonging). $A = B$ (= equality, which is symmetric $B = A$). Inclusion is 'antisymmetric' (if $A = B$ and $B = C$, then $A = C$). While inclusion is always reflexive, it is not clear that the same is true for belonging, given that belonging relates to elements, while inclusion relates to sets (see Halmos 1960: 1–3).

Intuitively, we say that mathematics depends on axioms and definitions, not on how things are. Interestingly, this is how the *chora*-receptacle can be approached; for its empirical reality is its least important aspect given that it is an object of pure speculation and supposition, if not of myth. Treating it as something entirely abstract would not be a betrayal of it. If we define it as appearing when it shakes along with its elements, it is still possible to say that the receptacle as a set includes itself: $R \subset R$. To the extent that the Platonic *chora* does not appear, and that it is empty (prior to receiving any elements), it can nonetheless be defined in set theory terms as including itself. But also, if we define *chora* as set {C}, the elements it receives would belong to C. If it received a set of all D, the latter would be included in C. If D is included in the *chora*, then D is a 'proper' sub-set of C (is included in C). With the *chora* as receptacle, it is not clear that it is included in what it receives – that is, it may be a matter of belonging, namely, C ε D, which entails that the reverse is not true. For belonging is not transitive (Halmos 1960: 3).

To take a slightly different tac: suppose that the *chora* is an infinite set C because every element that exists – including all the counting numbers and that, through creation, will exist (whether sensible or intelligible) – is a member of C. To consolidate this point in light of what Tubbs shows, we define the elements just mentioned as a completed infinity. As such, the set violates the principle that the whole is greater than the part, which is true for finite collections, or sets (see Tubbs 2009: 247).

All this, however, is speculative, not least because, from a set-theoretic perspective, it appears – as was proposed earlier – that the *chora* might be the empty set {Ø}. As such it is a sub-set of every set. Thus, if the elements were defined as sets (but not everything is a set), which would entail that there is a unity manifest in them, the *chora* would be present in every element. No doubt this is where a mathematical approach ceases to be applicable or illuminating as far as the *chora* is concerned, if only because, for Plato, it is the diversity, not the unity of elements which is at issue. This speculative approach[14] has served to indicate a route that Kristeva could have taken in relation to the *chora* following her theoretical work of 'sémanalyse' of the late 1960s and early 1970s. The focus in the early part of *La Révolution du langage poétique* on the *chora* as content (as opposed to the *chora* as formless and not appearing) confirms that Kristeva is indeed taking a materialist approach to the receptacle. To take a materialist approach is to return to the principle that the whole is greater than the part – not that this principle figures explicitly in the theory of the Kristevan semiotic. Furthermore, the semiotic is materialist in the sense that, as opposed to formalization, it encapsulates the enactment, or performance, of language, or, more broadly, of the semiotic–symbolic dyad.

But with regard to the infinite and to mathematical objects in general, the near consensus now is that, unlike the approach of a Newton or a Leibniz in the eighteenth century, for whom the order of the universe and mathematics were one (see Maddy 2011: 14), the mathematical object is discontinuous with the material world. In other words, we truly are in the era of what Cantor called 'free mathematics', rather than 'pure mathematics' (cited in Dauben 1990: 132). And David Hilbert, after Cantor, reiterates that 'the infinite is nowhere to be found in reality. It neither exists in nature nor provides a legitimate basis for rational thought' (1998: 201). If what Cantor and Hilbert say is true, there is little chance of a cross-over between the infinite and the semiotic, as articulated by Kristeva. Thus, the formalist approach of Kristeva's early work cannot be carried over to the theory of the semiotic in poetic language in 1974.

The semiotic, Mallarmé's poetics and Meillassoux's claim

The semiotic, to turn now to it, includes the child's prelinguistic, or translinguistic 'phonatory' explorations of sounds that are even prior to holophrastic utterances as well as its rhythmic and repetitive body movements and the making of marks – what are termed 'concrete operations' that are the result of the energy charges of the drives. Such processes manifest in childhood are also deemed to be at the origin of the modernist avant-garde's creative process. Included here are sound patterns and the disposition of the text on the page, the *timbre* (*Klangfarbenmelodie*) of early twentieth-century music, the abstract (not to say formalist) colour, line and point arrangements of modernist painting,[15] and the exposure of infrastructure in modernist architecture.[16] What are the implications?

Perhaps in order to make the semiotic explicit in avant-garde art, the notion of infinity appears in *La Révolution du langage poétique* in the analysis of Mallarmé's poetics, where reference is also made to the *chora*. Part of this analysis appeared in English in 1974, and most notably the following:

> Thus, the signifying differentials condense phonetic values and phonological values and, through this very process, connect the *semiotic chora* to language as a symbolic system. It is also in this way that the signifying differentials open the given pheno-text to the code of the language as infinity: to the infinite possibilities, be they transgrammatical or agrammatical, of impulsionally invested morpho-syntactic transformations.
>
> (Kristeva 1974: 34)

Here, 'infinite' evokes the potential, not completed, infinity, as is confirmed by the phrase, 'infinite possibilities'. It does, however, take second place to the notion of drives and their articulation as the basis of the *chora* – a basis that gives way to the symbolic, or what could be called language as defined linguistically. Indeed, without going through the phase of the *chora*, entry into the symbolic is foreclosed. Mallarmé's poeticizing discloses the semiotic as *timbre* (Kristeva 1974: 35). The blanks in writing are, in Mallarmé's poetry, the equivalent of the child's exploration of sounds as different phonemes, the range of which would exceed what is necessary for the acquisition of the national language. The *timbre* of language emerges with a 'rhythmic structure of sound' (1974: 37) and is present in communicative language but is not reducible to it.

This *timbre rythmé* ('rhythmical timbre') is a key aspect of what we can call Kristeva's materialist view of language understood as the coincidence of the semiotic and the symbolic – of drives and passion and of communication and reason. If the semiotic is drive- based it becomes analysable by way of the Freudian theory of the primary processes (particularly as revealed in the interpretation of dreams) and most notably through the concepts of condensation and displacement, which Jakobson (and after him, Lacan) dubbed metaphor (similarity) and metonymy (contiguity), respectively. Kristeva invokes these terms in her analysis of Mallarmé's poetic strategy, revealing that through transposition, in the case of displacement, and through the suppression of elements of syntax (as found in Mallarmé's *Un coup de dés*), both become vehicles for the appearance of the drives in the symbolic (RLP 232–3). In other words, in certain key examples of modern, poetic language the semiotic comes to take precedence over the symbolic, which includes the conventions of grammar, syntax and semantics of communicative language.

As the reference to Jakobson implies, some of the terminology employed by Kristeva is a modification of that found in conventional linguistics. The aspect of poetic language that really brings the semiotic to the fore is rhythm and, in particular (as has already been mentioned), the '*timbre rythmé*' of *Klangfarbenmelodie*. Mallarmé and Joyce – as exponents of poetic language – exploit the 'rhythmic and drive possibilities of the semiotic' (RLP 262, my translation).[17] The rhythm and musicality of poetic language, then, constitutes, Kristeva tells us, the '*jouissance* for the speaking subject' (RLP 263). Consequently, of this we are reminded that of equal importance with plumbing the depths of the substance of poetic language is the latter's role in the constitution of the 'psychic reality' of the subject – the *sujet en procès*. If in her work of the 1960s, it was the literary text as such that assumed pride of place, in *La Révolution du langage poétique* and work subsequent to it, the formation of the subject and its semiotic and symbolic dispositions are at issue. At the same time, with the speaking subject in process/on trial moving to centre stage, the mathematical sub-structure that characterized Kristeva's initial foray into textual theory falls into the background, if it does not entirely disappear.

In its contemporary rendering, Mallarmé's hyper-modernist poem *Un coup de dés jamais n'abolira le hasard* (*A Dice Throw Will Never Abolish Chance*) is printed[18] after the first single page on double pages in different typefaces. According to the author's intentions, 'on évite le récit' ('one avoids narrative')[19] – that is, one avoids attempting to piece together a coherent story or theme in the poem (see Mallarmé 1945: 455). However, mentioned in the poem is 'l'unique nombre' (1945: 462) ('the unique number') along with a reference to infinity and to 'LE NOMBRE' ('THE NUMBER') (1945: 473). While Quentin Meillassoux sets out on a quest to reveal the actual number that he thinks is implied here (the number 707, which is also, according to a certain count, the number of words in *Un coup de dés*),[20] Kristeva avoids any reference to number or to what might be called the semantic aspect of the poem. Indeed, Meillassoux fails to 'évite le récit', which might be legitimate, if the Preface containing the injunction is not part of the poem.

For Kristeva, poetic rhythm breaks up the linear syntax (RLP 270). Moreover, as far as *Un coup de dés* is concerned:

> [E]ven with the hypothesis of a possible reconstitution, the graphic disposition of the text has precisely the effect of blurring, of breaking the syntactic linkages and consequently of rendering phrases semantically and syntactically polyvalent.
>
> (RLP 271)

As opposed to Meillassoux, Kristeva reads the Mallarméan text *as a text* – that is, as it is distributed on the page in black and white – and not as a concealed 'denotative message' (RLP 271), the message of language as communication. The sound pattern of *Un coup de dés* alone begins, in Kristeva's terms, to pluralize associations and therefore meaning. As an example, we read that 'soit /swa/, by displacement and condensation, connotes the sememes,[21] "soie" [silk], "lisse" [smooth], "clarté" [clarity]', etc. which is opposed to 'abîme' [abyme] but tallys with 'blanchi' [whitens]' (RLP 383). Pluralization (of both sounds and associated meaning) is the key, and this is equivalent of the semiotic at work in the interior, as it were, of the symbolic system.

Given that *Un coup de dés* clearly breaks with the conventions of communicative language, it seems reasonable to treat the text as it is articulated on the double pages upon which it is set. Rhythm (as has been noted), the blanks of the text, a topographic strategy that breaks with conventional linearity leading to ambiguity, the absence of punctuation that heightens ambiguity, a variety of different fonts leading to a pluralization of possible readings – all this and probably more reinforces the semiotic tenor of *Un coup de dés*.

Meillassoux's reading strategy (like that of numerous critics)[22] is the opposite of this and geared to discover the coded message that it is claimed Mallarmé concealed in the poem, especially as regards number. In the end, Meillassoux presents a case for the symbolic significance of number in Mallarmé's hands. Such a view of number, however, implies that specific instances of it are inscribed in the real world, that number and reality are imbricated in one another. From what has been said earlier in this chapter such a view of number is pre-Cantorian. Or, if Cantor can for a moment be considered the Einstein of mathematics, the view of number as embedded in reality is Newtonian. For, indeed, as has also been remarked, Newton's view was that the universe itself is mathematical.

For her part, Kristeva returns to the theme of the infinite when discussing the nineteenth-century notion of the State (issue of the illusion of the state as 'the set of all sets'; RLP 379–83) as well underpinning the Name-of-the-Father as a 'second order' representation: 'a representation of the murder which is already the representation of an infinite denied and diffused, stuffed into a signifying set' (RLP 553). The infinite is deemed to be threatening to a 'productivist society' such as late nineteenth-century France. Thus, it must be exiled (RLP 554). This suggests that it is less Cantor's infinite with which we are dealing and more an infinite implicated in the violent sacrifice supposedly at the foundation of society.[23]

Reference to the infinite appears again with regard to Mallarmé's artistic strategy: '"Music in letters" ("La musique dans les lettres")[24] replaces the unary aspiration by making *unity*, not a *centre* to safeguard, but a *limit* to the infinite process of renewal' (RLP 567). Such a strategy, clearly, is linked to the play of the semiotic, as Kristeva acknowledges (RLP 567). The semiotic and the infinite would thus seem to be linked – but in a common-sense way, rather than in a mathematical sense. Certainly, as has been said, the semiotic pluralizes language in its social context as well as meaning and possibilities, perhaps to the point of infinity (RLP 603); but this would be a potential (Aristotelian) infinity. Even more explicitly, Kristeva, in the conclusion of *La Révolution du langage poétique*, writes: 'La jouissance is an *infinitization* of meaning: a possibility of opening to infinity the *process* of signification by way of the irruption of the drive in the *position* of meaning itself which, in this regard, acts as a limit and turning point' (RLP 613).

The 'infinity' – or infinitization – in question, then, is practical before being mathematical, a practice of poetic language (its process [musicalization] as much as its result [the polyphonic novel]) rather than the basis for a critical metalanguage marked by a strict formalism. Specifically, Kristeva points to the 'pluralization' of meaning that one finds in Joyce as the successor to Mallarmé and Lautréamont. It is a pluralization that is also the result of the drives becoming socially visible in art instead of remaining repressed.

If the *chora* as the drives and their stases[25] is prior to the formation of the symbolic – that is, prior to number, prior to metalanguage and formalization – the question becomes: how is it possible even to refer to it, let alone conceptualize it? For to do so, obviously, is to invoke the symbolic that the semiotic would 'pulverize'. At one point, Kristeva gives a tentative response to the question raised: 'the semiotic that "precedes" symbolization is only a *theoretical supposition* justified by the need for description. It exists in practice only within the symbolic' (RPL 68). This echoes Freud's reference to the primary process that, because it is only accessible via the secondary process (the symbolic), it 'is to that extent a theoretical fiction' (Freud 1976: 763). The Kristevan notion that the semiotic exists 'only within the symbolic' – that it is within the symbolic as the *receptacle* of the semiotic, which is its opposite, is open to paradox. For, to begin, it implies that the very constitution of the symbolic includes the semiotic so that the definition of the symbolic must include the semiotic. But, in addition, the issue of the *chora* as outlined in the *Timaeus* seems to reappear, as the symbolic becomes the receptacle that would remain distinct from what it 'contains'. In other words, aspects of the Platonic discourse on the *chora* that Kristeva ignores seem to re-emerge, willy-nilly, in Kristeva's own text without this being acknowledged. Perhaps, to avoid the paradox, mathematical formalization typical of axiomatization could have been activated. And this, of course, would return us to the formalization strategies of the Kristevan texts of the 1960s and 1970s. Have we then now gone full circle in the effort to expose Kristeva's modernism?

Notes

1 As T. J. Clark writes, 'I shall start with the obvious, the indisputable. Modernism, so everyone roughly agrees, was a kind of formalism. Modernists put a peculiar stress on the physical, technical facts of the medium they were working in' (2002: 162).

2 Mathematician Robert Tubbs thus states in relation to sets: 'A set is infinite if it can be put into a one to one correspondence with part of itself' (2009: 247).

3 According to Liddell and Scott's *Greek-English Lexicon* there is no difference in meaning between *chora* [χώρα] and *choros* [χῶρος]. However, only *chora* [χώρα] appears in classical Attic Greek – that is, in Plato's Greek – and means 'the space or room in which a thing is'. The second meaning given is 'land'.

4 Cf. 'Each story (*récit*) is the *receptacle* of another' (Derrida 1993: 75, my translation).

5 Cf. 'Socrates is not *Khôra* but it would very much resemble him if it was some one or some thing' (Derrida 1993: 63, my translation).

6 Outside of modernity, perhaps, it is impossible, according to Derrida, to characterise interpretative tendencies, since Antiquity, in the 'immense literature' devoted to the *Timaeus* (1993: 26). Derrida, considers that a key problem of *chora* interpretation has been that so many interpretations end up giving it form (see Derrida 1993: 26).

7 This is especially true for those who lay emphasis on Plato's simile, which says that the *chora* is 'moving like a winnowing machine' (53a; Plato 1980: 1179) in the threshing of corn, the corn presumably being like the contents of the *chora* as receiving vessel.

8 As I. M. Crombie explains: 'Why is the reasoning "bastard"? Not, I think, because the inference is illegitimate, but because the mind cannot "grasp" or understand the entity which it has to postulate. We can neither understand what "space" is nor dispense with it' (1963: 217, n.1).

9 As to the latter, Sallis argues that it is undoubtedly a forgery (1999: 148).

10 Derrida points to 'the problem posed by the Aristotelian interpretation of *khôra* as matter' (1993: 97).

11 Aristotle was probably the first to query Plato on this point. In *On Generation and Corruption*, Aristotle states that Plato 'has not stated clearly whether his "Omnirecipient" exists in separation from the "elements"' (Aristotle 1941: 508).

12 This is so despite notes in RPL that give the impression of a close reading of the *Timaeus*. For example, note 12 of the section 'The Semiotic and the Symbolic' says, in part, that, 'Plato emphasizes that the receptacle (ὑποδοχεῖον), which is also called space (χώρα) vis-à-vis reason, is necessary – but not divine since it is unstable, uncertain, ever changing and becoming: it is even unnameable, improbable, bastard' (RPL 239). But the quotation immediately given to confirm the 'ever changing' nature of the *chora* does not do this: 'Space which is ever lasting, not admitting destruction, providing a situation for all things that come into being, but itself apprehended without the senses by a sort of bastard reasoning and hardly the object of belief. This, indeed, is that which we look upon as in a dream and say that anything that is must needs be in some place and occupy some room' (52a-b, Cornford trans.) (239).

Note 13 offers a nuanced account of the *chora*, saying that the receptacle is ambiguous, 'mobile', 'separable and divisible', a 'separability and divisibility' that is prior to 'numbers and forms' and because of this, 'the space or receptacle is called *amorphous*' (239). 'Once it is named it immediately becomes a container that takes the place of infinitely repeatable separability. This amounts to saying that this repeated separability is "ontologized" the moment a *name* or a *word* replaces it, making it intelligible' (239). The note goes on to discuss the relation between *chora* and motility with some subtlety. However, in the main text this nuanced approach and this subtlety of interpretation seem to fall away in the interests of a psychoanalytical approach that endeavours to appropriate the *chora* to construct a theory of the subject (in process/on trial).

13 The relevance of subjecting a notion of *chora* as a kind of totality to aspects of set theory and the notion of infinity is that it brings out what *chora* would have to be for it to be illuminated by set theory. By implication, at least, the *chora* as Kristeva presents it does not lend itself to such an illumination, largely because the theorist has by 1974 moved away from the literary theoretical concerns of the work of the 1960s, where a mathematical approach was much more the order of the day. Nevertheless, it should be noted that references to infinity (key element in set theory) still abound in RLP and elsewhere, as we shall see.

14 An approach that is speculative also in that, without including all the counting numbers, the membership of the set C {C} would be finite rather than infinite. Without the counting numbers existence would have to be taken to be, like the counting numbers, infinitely extendable by addition, which is debatable. But also, according to Halmos, 'nothing contains everything' (1960: 6), or 'there is no universe' (7), even if such were the case for Plato. In addition, though, if the *chora* contains everything, it evokes the idea of the absolute set, or the set of all sets, which does not exist. As I have indicated, it is only because the *chora* is in fact an imaginary entity that it makes any sense at all to speculate about it in set theoretical terms. Since Hilbert's work on axiomatization, the 'set of all sets' is no longer an issue, as it was for Russell.

15 As an example of the semiotic in painting, see Kristeva's essay on Jackson Pollock (1989).

16 Although Kristeva has not (to my knowledge) ever discussed the nature of modernist architecture from the point of view of the semiotic, it could be that the latter is found in the exposure of a building's infrastructure, for which the *Centre Georges Pompidou* could be taken as exemplary (cf., the exposure there of the frame, of the escalators 'glued' to the exterior, of exposed interior and exterior water pipes, of the exposed pipes for heating and cooling, of exposed lighting fittings and cables, of exposed air extractors as features, etc.). In short, what is normally concealed (the building process) is not just exposed but featured. Nevertheless, despite this exposure the *Centre* is still consciously experienced as a completed and meaningful building – that is, at the level of the symbolic.

17 All translations from RLP are my own.

18 As Quentin Meillassoux notes, there are two versions of the poem, the first appearing in *Cosmopolis* magazine in May 1897, but not exactly in accordance with Mallarmé's specifications, and a second version called the Vollard edition, eventually published in book form in 1914 by the *Nouvelle Revue Française*.

19 All translations from Mallarmé's *Un coup de dés* are my own.

20 Meillassoux affirms: 'a) that Mallarmé's poem is coded; b) that the deciphering of this code is a condition for the correct understanding of the *Coup de dés*, since it illuminates one of its essential components, namely, the nature of Number' (2011: 9; all translations from Meillassoux's French text are my own). In terms of what has been outlined concerning Cantor's infinite in the history of mathematics, Meillassoux's claim would seem to be somewhat inflated. The question is: could there ever be a truly unique number, and if there were such a thing, could it really be a number, mathematically speaking? The answer implied from what has been said above is: 'no'.

21 'Sememe': a unit of meaning that is indivisible.

22 Critics who sometimes do not respect Mallarmé's presentation of the poem. See, for example, Badiou (2016).

23 Cf. 'Sacrifice sets up the symbol and the symbolic order at the same time, and this "first" symbol, the victim of a murder, merely represents the structural violence of language's irruption as the murder of soma, the transformation of the body, the captation of drives' (RPL 75). For its part, 'the sacred does not… celebrate pure violence; it celebrates instead the *positing* of violence, the "*boundary to the infinite*"' (RPL 79, emphasis added). Whether this infinite is potential or completed will be discussed below in relation to *jouissance*.

24 Mallarmé gave a lecture at Oxford and Cambridge in March 1894 called, 'La Musique et les lettres' ('Music and Letters'). See Mallarmé (1945: 633–57).

25 Of course, implied here is the whole of the Freudian primary processes in the formation of the subject, which has to a large extent been left in abeyance throughout this chapter.

References

Algra, K. (1995), *Concepts of Space in Greek Thought*, Philosophia Antiqua, 65, Leiden: Brill.
Aristotle (1941), *De Generatione et corruptione (On Generation and Corruption)*, trans. H. H. Joachim, in R. McKeon (ed.), *The Basic Works of Aristotle*, 467–531, New York: Random House.
Badiou, A. (2016), 'Is It Exact that All Thought Emits a Throw of Dice?', trans. Robert Boncardo and Christian R. Gelder, *Journal of the Circle for Lacanian Ideology Critique*, 9: 16–30.
Clark, T. J. (2002), 'Modernism, Postmodernism, and Steam', *October*, 100 (spring): 154–74.
Cornford, F. M. (1937), *Plato's Cosmology. The Timaeus of Plato with a Running Commentary*, London: Routledge and Kegan Paul.
Crombie, I. M. (1963), *An Examination of Plato's Doctrines, Vol II: Plato on Knowledge and Reality*, London: Routledge and Kegan Paul.
Dauben, J. W. (1990), *George Cantor: His Mathematics and the Philosophy of the Infinite*, Princeton, NJ: Princeton University Press.
Derrida, J. (1993), *Khōra*, Paris: Galilée.
Freud, S. (1976), *The Interpretation of Dreams*, trans. J. Strachey, The Pelican Freud Library, vol. 4, London: Penguin.
Halmos, P. R. (1960), *Naïve Set Theory*, Princeton, NJ: D. Van Nostrand.
Hilbert, D. (1998), 'On the Infinite', in P. Benacerraf and H. Putnam (eds), *Philosophy of Mathematics: Selected Readings*, 183–206, Cambridge: Cambridge University Press.
Hope, A. (2015), 'Khōra – plus de métaphore', *Textual Practice*, 29 (4): 611–30.
Houdebine, J.-L. (1983), 'L'expérience de Cantor', *L'Infini*, 4: 87–110.
Irigaray, L. (1985), *Speculum of the Other Woman*, trans. G. C. Gill, Ithaca, NY: Cornell University Press.
Kristeva, J. (1974), 'Phonetics, Phonology and Impulsional Bases', *diacritics*, 4 (3): 33–7.
Kristeva, J. (1989), 'Jackson Pollock's Milky Way, 1912–1956', *Journal of Philosophy and the Visual Arts*, 1: 34–9.
Maddy, P. (2007). *Second Philosophy: A Naturalistic Method*, Oxford: Oxford University Press.
Maddy, P. (2011), *Defending the Axioms: On the Philosophical Foundation of Set Theory*, Oxford: Oxford University Press.
Mallarmé, S. (1945), *Oeuvres complètes*, 'Bibliothèque de la Pléiade', Paris: Gallimard.
Meillassoux, Q. (2011), *Le Nombre et la sirène. Un déchiffrage du Coup de dés de Mallarmé*, Paris: Fayard.
Plato (1980), *Timaeus*, in *Plato: The Collected Dialogues*, ed. E. Hamilton and H. Cairns, trans. B. Jowett, Bollingen Series LXXI, Princeton, NJ: Princeton University Press.
Sallis, J. (1999), *Chorology: On Beginning in Plato's Timaeus*, Bloomington, IN: Indiana University Press.
Sollers, P. (1965), *Drame*, Paris: Seuil.

Sollers, P. (1966), *Nombres*, Paris: Seuil.
Sollers, P. (1972), *Lois*, Paris: Seuil.
Sollers, P. (1973), *H*, Paris: Seuil.
Tubbs, R. (2009), *What Is Number? Mathematical Concepts and Their Origins*, Baltimore, MD: Johns Hopkins University Press.

3

Indifferent feminine: Kristeva and the avant-garde

Miglena Nikolchina

Julia Kristeva's concept of the feminine[1] is elaborated as a crucial aspect of creativity and of the capacity for transformation and renewal; as such, it is not reducible to the problematic of sexual difference and gender identity – not reducible, perhaps, to the problematic of difference and identity at all. As an agent of change, it is revealed to be constitutive for the innovative thrust of modernism and the avant-garde, which have always been at the centre of Kristeva's work. However, although present from very early on in her writing, the conceptualization of the feminine is probably the one that took the longest to unfold and is, in fact, still evolving.

This evolution runs parallel to certain major methodological shifts in Kristeva's work. The shifts from linguistics to psychoanalysis and from revolution to revolt have been explicitly articulated by her and have become the habitual grid for the study of her work.[2] They have been accompanied by a shift from a modernist aesthetics of 'pulverization' to one of 'transubstantiation': a shift which involves a greater emphasis on the novel and fiction rather than poetry. If in the early writing the 'work of the text' is compared to a sacrificial pillar where the body and all incarnation is put to death (S 285), from *Tales of Love* on Kristeva's focus increasingly will be on transfigurative embodiment and will look for venues in Proust's sensuous monsters, feeding on time, and in Colette's writing as 'powerful arabesque of flesh, a cipher of tangled members', 'chiselled by the temporality of beginning, of rebirth, of astonishment' (C 3, 402). Yet there is a continuity in these shifts, and looking at them from both ends, as I will try to do here, might grant a clearer vision of the systematicity with which Kristeva approaches a difficult problem.

And notoriously difficult it is. As radical as it is ungraspable, the feminine implicated in modernist writing has been discussed by Kristeva as a theoretical impasse and a challenge to thought, as a confrontation with the impossible, and, ultimately, as the capacity for infinite rebirth resulting from the tireless and interminable conquest of the two phases of the (girl's) unfinished Oedipus. Repeatedly, Kristeva would refuse to assuage the complexity of the problem in the face of various ideological pressures. She would persistently decline to substitute political wishful thinking for the lack of the conceptual answers which she would need decades to elaborate. Art, one should not forget, is, according to Kristeva, a material force in individual and social transformation. The question is what makes the feminine a decisive aspect of this force.

Preliminaries: A stagehand

Broken syntax, fragmented narrative, illogicality, foregrounding the materiality of sound and the printed letter ... on top of everything, as Kristeva will say apropos of Philip Sollers' *Numbers* – a novel dedicated to her – an anonymous, mortal, scandalous, non-romantic, dry, beastly, sordid rendering of amatory experience with a 'she' in whom, Kristeva notes, Dante's Beatrice joins Bataille's *My mother* (S 295). In the social and intellectual turmoil of the 1960s, Paris immediately enhanced the thrust for coming to terms with modernism which was part of Kristeva's pre-Parisian motivation.[3] Later on, Kristeva will claim that her shift from linguistics to psychoanalysis was prompted by the desire to understand better what avant-garde poets were doing (I 19–20). What in this case is referred to, rather generally, as linguistics names, in fact, *again* a project born of the desire to understand the avant-garde: Russian formalism and, more specifically, Jakobson, who coined the term structuralism, relied on phonetics and the science of language in an effort to construct analytic tools adequate to modernist artistic practice. Jakobson's work is initially connected to the Russian and the Czech avant-garde.[4] When he enters the French scene, it is once again via a modernist poet, in fact, the father of modernist poets: Jakobson's and Levi-Strauss' joint article, which acted as a sort of manifesto of French structuralism, is an analysis of Baudelaire's sonnet *Les Chats* (Jakobson 1987).

Many of Kristeva's early texts follow the structuralist interest in modernist poetry as well as the structuralist sensitivity to the work of sheer sound. Her insistence in these explorations, which will ultimately take her on a different path, is on problematizing the methodological standing of the Saussurean sign. In fact, her very first publication in *Tel Quel*, a year after her arrival in

Paris, purports to demonstrate how Saussure's own work cannot be reduced to the concept of the sign attributed to him.[5] The critique of the 'matrix of the sign' (S 20) underlies her reading of Bakhtin, whom she introduced to the West. It should be noted that in Bulgaria, before she left for France, Kristeva was closely connected to anti-structuralist Bakhtin-oriented circles, Bulgaria being probably the first country outside of the Soviet Union where Bakhtin became popular.[6] In Soviet Russia, it has been claimed, Bakhtin was taken out of the freezer in order to be opposed to the rising star of semiotician Jurij Lotman. The idea apparently was to tolerate Lotman for export to the West (his publications were extremely difficult to get hold of in Eastern Europe) and levy 'Marxian' Bakhtin for East European usage: that things have taken a rather different turn, not without Kristeva's mediation, is one of those beautiful ironies of failed ideological control. Kristeva knew Lotman and has referred to him both in her early and her later writing. His work on 'sign systems' played a major role for the establishment in 1969 of the International Association for Semiotic Studies, with Émile Benveniste as the first president and Kristeva as the first general secretary (Jardine 2020: 386, n.102). Rather than extend the 1930s controversy between protostructuralist Russian formalists and Bakhtin's Marxian circle[7] – that is, rather than play the anti-Bakhtinian part expected of him – Lotman elaborated the 'dual codes' of their theoretical confluence; so did Kristeva in her early work (Spassova 2018). Recent research has recovered the name of Emilia Litauer, an interwar Russian emigrant in Paris, who attempted an early theoretical reconciliation of the two factions (Tihanov 2019: 59 and *passim*). Kristeva could hardly have heard of Litauer, who had a couple of publications in obscure emigrant venues and then had the imprudence to return to the Soviet Union and become one of Stalin's innumerable victims. Yet Litauer's emphasis on the production of the literary text – on productivity rather than product – is indicative of the 'intertextual' (to put it in Kristeva's terms) potentials of the debate.

For Kristeva, the understanding of the avant-garde and modernism would be impossible without considering productivity, and, consequently, without dismantling the static and closed character of the Saussurean sign. In her early essays, this involves turning to the phonic and visual materiality pestering the sign; to translinguistic ingredients, be they gestural or paragrammatic; to an unsettling verticality co-present with the linear unfurling of signification; to a figurability as opposed to the stable figure; to the infinity of a 'genotext' 'insisting' in the articulation of the 'phenotext'; the mystery of 'engendering the formula'. Kristeva summons a plethora of schools, perspectives and sciences in order to capture this seething which she calls *signifiance*, a major term which has kept its centrality in her thought.[8] Translinguistic in its operations, the work of *signifiance* is eventually flattened in a signifying chain which is communicative, grammatically structured and squeezed on the 'line of the speaking subject' (S 11). Yet it is not reducible to this chain and this line; it traverses and exceeds them. Avant-garde practices find a way to speak about and represent the revolutionary productivity of *signifiance* on condition they find an equivalent on the stage of social reality. Like mathematics, *signifiance* engenders formulas which may or may not apply to (social) reality as they have their own logic without exteriority. The accumulation of heterogeneous perspectives characteristic of *Semeiotike* will continue in *The Revolution in Poetic Language*. Linguistics – as the model of all semiotics (S 20) – is still the major reference point. Yet already in *Semeiotike* there is the assertion that the production and the transformation of meaning is the 'place in semiotic theoretization where the science of psychoanalysis intervenes in order to provide conceptualization capable of grasping the figurability in language across the figured' (S 27).

Out of this crossing of linguistics and psychoanalysis two of Kristeva's major concepts will emerge – the semiotic as opposed to the symbolic. They are conceived as two dimensions of *signifiance*, the translinguistic process producing meaning and the subject. One is never without the other, although to a different degree depending on the type of discourse: the symbolic is the realm of syntax, logic and the law; the semiotic 'accounts for this archaic pressure, which is pre-symbolic and anterior to the constitution of signs and syntax in speech and which bears the trace of the intense relation of the child to its mother' (SUF Kindle 1406). The semiotic manifests itself as rhythm, echolalia, gesture, coloratura, abstract pattern, music, dance … in short, as ordering irreducible to meaning. Its job is to shake, traverse, shatter and in all possible ways annoy the smooth work of the symbolic, which, being logically and chronologically posterior to it, and in fact supported by it, can never quite get rid of it. The semiotic thus unfurls abstract sensorial articulations preceding signification: it encompasses 'functions and energy discharges that connect and orient the body to the mother' (RPL 27).

Thus, although the conceptualization of the semiotic explicitly provides a continuation of the preoccupation of structural linguistics with sound and with the two axes of metaphor and metonymy, this is 'not all' (RPL 41). One obvious inspiration for Kristeva's term is Émile Benveniste, whom she calls her teacher and whom she describes as the rare case of a linguist interested in psychoanalysis (JMV 98). His distinction between semiotic and semantic as precursor to Kristeva's distinction between semiotic and symbolic has been discussed, although infrequently (Mechelen 2017). Benveniste is mentioned by Jakobson and Levi-Strauss as having read their joint text on Baudelaire's *Chats* in manuscript (Jakobson 1987: 520, n.6); what has become known only later, however, is that Benveniste was probably contemplating an answer. His notes towards this unrealized project include the claim that 'Baudelaire is a poet who does not speak; for whom language disappears in something else' (Laplantine 2011: 48). Towards the end of his career Benveniste seems to have been making these notes on Baudelaire while planning a 'general theory of poetic language' with 'evoker' (évocant) and 'evoked' (évoqué) replacing the signifier/signified pair of Saussure's general linguistics (Laplantine 2011).

What is this 'something else' in which language, in a poem, disappears? It would be futile, of course, to compare what Kristeva did to an unrealized project; nevertheless, her conceptualization of the semiotic provides an answer to Benveniste's question. As pointed out, Kristeva ties this interface to the early skin-to-skin relationship between the infant and its mother. In an interview first published in 1975, in the wake of *The Revolution in Poetic Language*, Kristeva sums up the consequences of her theory of the semiotic so far as women are concerned.[9] The semiotic is connected to what Kristeva terms the maternal function and the woman-effect, both of which can be analysed only on the level of the symbolic where 'feminine identity' appears as 'one way of living oneself (*se vivre*) in the face of social cohesion and the power of language' (SUF Kindle 1188). This way of living amounts to not possessing but being the silent backing of power: power's behind-the-scenes stagehand (*une coulisse ouvrière*). Kristeva thus stresses 'the social aspect of the "woman-effect" in so far as it is neither power, nor the system of language, but their mute support which works and exceeds them' (SUF Kindle 1190). What needs re-evaluation, according to Kristeva, is the role of the maternal function not just as explosive repression but as a prop (*étayage*) of certain practices perceived as marginal (including artistic ones) and, ultimately, of 'all innovation' (SUF Kindle 1270).

Femininity (the 'woman-effect') as a mode of living oneself with respect to power (meaning, social structure, the symbolic) is thus quite distinct from the 'maternal function' as behind-the-scenes stagehand and mute excess yet at this point, the point when the interview was taken, the distinctness is theoretically still rather hazy. It will take years for Kristeva to disentangle this bundle through an elaboration of the two-faced (and one might say, two-phased) Oedipus of the girl. Femininity will appear with respect to the second phase, Oedipus two, in an 'as if', a 'whatever', an oscillation between illusion and disillusionment. Its inherent incompletion will be indicated in Kristeva's latest reflections as the engine for the proliferation of genders we witness today (Kristeva 2019a). The maternal function, on the other hand, approached as *chora* and semiotic, will be elaborated with respect to the first Oedipus and will entail the addition of the concept of the imaginary father (TL 26–48 and *passim*) and, later on, a reassessment of Freud's theory of language, with the feminine defined as 'psychic depth' (C 419) and as 'a factor of the transformability of psychic life' (Kristeva 2019a). Psychic depth is one of Kristeva's major concerns vis-à-vis her unease with contemporary 'robotization'.[10] Yet her own writing on Proust, Colette and elsewhere, including some of her novels, reveals psychic depth as ultimately a-psychic, as an interface of the imaginary and the inhuman. For all the impossibility to neutralize it, the feminine would hence seem to mark precisely the sexually indifferent:[11] a matter of fact which might make us want to return to Kristeva's earliest concepts, the ones preceding the psychoanalytic turn.

An aside: Privileging male artists

The feminine with its hazardous power for innovation is more accessible for male artists. This claim caused a lot of heated discussions. Even today, after Kristeva's trilogy on Hannah Arendt, Melany Klein and Colette, after *Teresa, My Love*, after her novelistic turn to historical figures like the medieval Byzantine princess and intellectual, probably the first woman historian Anna Comnena, or the French Enlightenment scientist marquise Émilie Du Châtelet, Kristeva, never apologetic, keeps maintaining that the life of the spirit is more difficult for a woman and that 'taming the feminine', which is as 'rare, craved, desirable, and impossible as the quadrature of the circle', has only been achieved by a few saints and geniuses, quoting Joyce as her example once again (SUF Kindle 115).

An interview from 1989 entitled 'What Avant-garde Today?' (SUF) pretty much summarizes the debate. The interviewer Françoise van Rossum-Guyon voices the common perplexity that Kristeva has, on the one hand, forged the concept of the semiotic and has attributed a crucial role to the feminine-maternal continent in the genesis of artistic creativity; while, on the other hand, she has neglected women artists and has frequently expressed her scepticism regarding productions which are intended as specifically feminine. Kristeva's answer follows two lines of argumentation. One concerns the negative consequences of the very articulation of the problem. Focusing on the achievements of women qua women on the basis of ideological considerations risks turning into a new dogma and thus levelling the uniqueness of individual women's work. It may lead to disregarding quality while at the same time deepening segregation – 'to everyone their toy'. Feminism thus partakes of the familiar tensions between movements and the thinkers whom they choose as representing their ideas but who are frequently condemned as elitist and not properly following the party line. Kristeva makes no exception to this type of tension and has been at times perceived as both too difficult and too wayward. There is, besides, the paradox of identitarian politics of any kind: as Kristeva points out, 'the more we stigmatize "exclusion," the more we barricade ourselves behind personal and community cults' (SUF Kindle 129).

The second line of Kristeva's argumentation is a direct consequence of her conceptualization of the semiotic. Approaching the semiotic is a perilous undertaking; it entails a battle with the archaic mother. For a man, erotization of the battle and thus averting its deadly aspects would be easier; for a woman, it would be a far more violent and demanding affair. This difficulty appears both on the side of women's creativity per se and on the side of its recognition which would amount, once again, to a stifling encounter with maternal power. In any case, the difficulties lead to cultural matricide, a universal reluctance in acknowledging women's contributions to the life of the spirit.[12] Not without self-irony, Kristeva illustrates this point with her belated acknowledgement of her indebtedness, in theorizing the maternal, to her female analyst (Kristeva 2016: 83–5).

Mère-version of the Muse

Up and against the more general and abstract frameworks which she employs, Kristeva never fails to emphasize the historically specific manner in which the feminine manifests itself in artistic practice. Going back to the confluence of Dante's Beatrice and Bataille's obscene 'mother', which characterizes French modernism, she insists on dissociating the avant-garde erotic from psychoanalytic influences and relates it, rather, to 'the obsession with the feminine that has haunted the decomposition of Catholicism and its esoteric aspects since the nineteenth century' (SNS 122). The point is that psychoanalysis investigates something which is not its own product, which is there in shifting forms and 'tales of love' and which acquires a more drastic visibility in the three consecutive waves of French avant-garde literature. These three waves include the 'precursors' whom Kristeva studies via Lautréamont and Mallarmé in the *Revolution in Poetic Language*, the first half of the twentieth century studied by her through a plethora of pivotal writers (Céline and Aragon, among others) and the era of *Tel Quel* with Philippe Sollers.

In the context of these stages of the French avant-garde but also outside of it, working with other periods and cultural settings, Kristeva's exploration of the feminine increasingly elaborates an important bifurcation. I say this, increasingly, because *signifiance* as a process in which the feminine is crucially implicated has been described by Kristeva from very early on as a double-edged practice of structuring *and* de-structuring (RPL 17). Maintaining at all times the inherent ambiguity, the subsequent theoretical developments move, on the one hand, towards concepts which capture the menace, the danger, the violence, the pulverization of the subject and the risk of dissolution vis-à-vis the terrifying insistence of creation. This slant is summarized through the concept of abjection in *Powers of Horror* and Kristeva keeps returning to its literary and artistic manifestations, maintaining her emphasis on the annihilating and all but unresolvable confrontation, for a woman, with the abject. Neither subject nor object, a precarious and most archaic separation between a subject-to-be and an undifferentiated everything else conflated with the maternal body, the abject is 'something rejected from which one does not part, from which one does not protect oneself as from an object. Imaginary uncanniness and real threat, it beckons to us and ends up engulfing us' (PH 4). Kristeva's analysis of *Irene's Cunt* by Louis Aragon provides one of her drastic illustrations of the abjected Muse, staggering in its savagery and obscene beauty. *Irene's Cunt* was part of a larger text, *Défense de l'infini*, whose manuscript Aragon burnt; later he sold the surviving pages to a collector and they underwent a number of anonymous editions (SNS 132). Like Proust displaying his family's furniture and his mother's photos in a brothel (Kristeva 1996: 174, 183, 240), the very history of the manuscript exemplifies the brutality accompanying the troubled experience of 'an X ray of the pulverized identity, laid bare and laid to rest in Irene's jouissance' (SNS 135).

The other direction appears as incorporation and, at the far end, as transubstantiation. The last term emerges in Kristeva's study of Proust's search 'of an "embodied" imaginary, a space where words, along with their unconscious and obscure emergences, knit the unbroken flesh of the world' (TAS 169). As Kristeva notes, 'the sensory subtext of metaphor will see that metaphor realizes Proust's vision of transubstantiation' (SNS 212). It should be noted that from her earliest elaboration of the semiotic, Kristeva's notion of *signifiance* implicates the making of a body in the making of the subject. An observation of Diderot's daughter, which Kristeva quotes in *Teresa, My Love*, pretty much sums up her own position: 'you make soul by making flesh' (TML 588). Incorporation is hence the process through which *signifiance* grants a body *and* a soul to the speaking being and to which literature provides a privileged exemplification. With transubstantiation, however, the writer (and the reader) is metamorphosed into the writing, but the writing is then metamorphosed into Proust's 'flesh of the world' (TAS 169). Kristeva introduces the concept of the imaginary father as the instance allowing these transitions (TL 26–48). The pre-Oedipal imaginary father – with Freud, father of individual pre-history and of *Einfühlung*, primary identification – is a hybrid maternal/paternal figure, a coagulation of the father with maternal desire, an incestuous perversion sublimated into *père-version*, a leap of the subject-to-be into a metaphoric fusion with a father-capable-of-loving-like-a-mother. Although the imaginary father is not mentioned in Kristeva's book on Proust, the exploration of Proust's use of metaphor as translation into flesh is based both on Proust's own theory of metaphor and on a re-examination of Freud's theory of language which involves primary identification. This crucial re-examination marks a new stage in the integration of the 'linguistic' and 'psychoanalytic' Kristeva. She elaborates it further in *The Sense and Nonsense of Revolt*, where the imaginary father is described as 'the keystone of our loves and imagination' (SNS 53). Implicitly or explicitly, Kristeva attributes her own inspiration to the radiance of this paternal support (Jardine 2020: 29), which, however, is ambiguous not only sexually but also with a view of its precarious and fragile be it luminous spirituality.

It is only with Kristeva's book on Colette, however, and especially with the analysis of Colette's dealing with the death of her mother that female artistic inspiration becomes localized in 'sharing with the mother a mutual osmosis in the alphabet of the world' (C 381). Kristeva describes it as *mère-version*: a perverse, yet 'pure' turning to the mother as one possible response to the girl's two-faced Oedipus. It is an osmosis between play and chaos, between a 'metamorphic body diffused in the world's flesh' and the 'monstrosity of its "misshapen, expanding, whirling" underside' (C 225). Through *mère-version* the 'cavernous and hypersensitive receptivity' of the girl becomes metabolized into what, with Colette, will appear as an interpenetration of language and the world, so that 'there is no longer ego or self but rather, plants, beasts, monsters, and marvels' (C 12). Furthermore, 'the two-faced Oedipus, interminable, always beginning again, [could be] the source of this insistence on the rhythm of renewal, against the linear time of faced completion' (C 424). As Colette puts it, 'Turning over a new leaf, rebuilding, being reborn, has never been beyond my strength' (C 424).

Kristeva (2019a) returns to this dynamic in her recent 'Prelude to an Ethics of the Feminine'. In it, the transformative aspect of the feminine, including contemporary proliferations of gender identities, is attached to the interminable Oedipus of the girl. This amounts to re-orienting the thinking of sexual difference(s) no longer with respect to the symbolic, language, the realm of the sign but with respect to the feminine as manifesting and disclosing the 'original disjunction' which constitutes the human subject (Kristeva 2019a). With this re-orientation sexual difference and heterosexuality face the prospect of infinite metamorphoses, on the one hand, and, on the other, to put it in Colette's terms, a 'nauseous chaos without beginning or end [of which] certain arabesques can be read like characters of an alphabet' (C 2). The feminine, hence, not only manifests sexual difference but also haunts this difference as its suspension.

Keeping one's head

This conceptualization of the feminine whose psychoanalytic elaboration took decades of Kristeva's thought might acquire an additional dimension if we revisit a split rarely traversed: a split in Kristeva's reception, in fact. Her early work is claimed in semiotic studies where it is still considered to be Kristeva's most important achievement; the predominant part of Kristevan studies today, however, is concerned with her later work, focusing on it in a psychoanalytic perspective, or elaborating its political implications.[13] This split entails the risk of overlooking the consistency of Kristeva's thought. I will hence turn to one of Kristeva's most influential early essays, 'Engendering the Formula' (S 217–310), which first appeared in 1969. It is a continuation of Kristeva's preoccupations with the infinity of poetic language qua critique of Saussure's concept of the sign (TSP). 'Engendering the Formula' is a theoretical response to Philippe Sollers' novel *Numbers* (Sollers 1968b). Derrida's essay 'Dissemination', published a couple of months before Kristeva's, addresses and disseminates, so to say, the same novel. Kristeva refers to Derrida's text (S 231, n.18). The more intriguing reference, however, is to Alain Badiou's 'La subversion infinitésimale' ['Infinitesimal Subversion'] (S 234). Badiou's text (1968), it has been claimed, 'anticipates, perhaps more than any other of Badiou's early texts, many of the distinctive concerns of his later philosophy' ('Synopsis'). In 'Engendering the Formula' Kristeva sees it as the first of a necessary future line of epistemological disentanglements of the mathematical notions of number (S 234). Many years later, Badiou's title will pop up in her novel *Teresa, My Love*, in a postscript entitled 'Letter to Denis Diderot on the Infinitesimal Subversion of a Nun' (567–96). I will return to this.

Some sort of agreement, however general, is needed here: an agreement as to the propensity of ideas to travel from one discourse to another and from one discipline to another – a propensity we might call transmodality.[14] It is a regular occurrence that no one can really prohibit from forcing, entangling or, indeed, charming its way into the world: examples may include ontology in computer science or naïve set theory in mathematics (the rest of set theory, I assume, is sentimental). In addition to this there is the phenomenon of autotextuality: 'a text remembers a previous one [by the same author], using it as the matrix of its own development, while returning to it as its reading and interpretation' (Kolarov 2009: 228). And finally, at the crossroads of the transmodal and the autotextual, why not proffer conceptual metempsychosis, emphasizing the fact that the mobile concept might, or might not, be aware of its past life? I say this by way of exonerating my claim that what took its latest shape in Kristeva's conceptualization of *the feminine* initially surfaced into her writing as le *nombrant* before it metamorphosed into *chora*. From mathematics to philosophy (the *chora* is a Platonic term) to psychoanalysis: something was lost and something was acquired in the process, yet the very trajectory of the concepts is illuminating.

Sollers' novel *Numbers* is dedicated to Юлия, which happens to be the name Julia spelled in Cyrillic. This spelling is one among other transplantations from alien alphabets and systems of writing, interspersed in the novel as impenetrable pictograms. Written shortly after Kristeva and Sollers' marriage, the novel might be seen as a sort of love letter. And indeed, this is a novel as much about numbers as it is about *elle* (she, her). While the word *femme* (woman) never (if I am correct) appears in *Numbers*, *elle* is introduced as a query whether she were not: 'More inaccessible now that she was entirely here, just here, like a corpse with a severed head ... However, I knew that if I reached out to her, I could not verify whether she had not become, during my sleep, her own sleep, bloody and deaf' (Sollers 1968b: 12).

The severed head probably did not go unnoticed by the young bride, yet it will take some thirty years before Kristeva focuses on the severed head as a theorist, novelist and, at some point, even curator (see SNS; PO; SH). In Sollers' novel the turning to 'numbers' evokes, among other things, the number symbolism of Dante, who weaved figures into his poetic language and transposed his idealized beloved Beatrice into threes, nines and their products. Written before *Numbers* but included in a collection which appeared in the same year, Sollers had an essay on Dante quoting him say that 'Beatrice *is* a nine' (Sollers 1968a: 57). Kristeva evokes this essay in 'Engendering the formula' in order to remind us that, for a good part of Dante's writing, Beatrice is *dead*. To the Medieval tradition, the French avant-garde will add its 'erotic excitation with [the] decapitated feminine' (SNS 122), which Kristeva addresses in *The Sense and Non-Sense of Revolt*. Sollers' *elle* in *Numbers* is a continuation of this tradition of 'unhinged' femininity which includes Villiers de L'Isle-Adam's fantasy of making love with a headless woman, fin-de-siècle fascination with Salomé, André Breton's *Nadja* with its 'diabolical, mechanical, and sadistic vision of a feminine at once powerful and dethroned', and 'other chimeras, constructing the image of an intractable and entrancing femininity that re-emerges in Aragon's *Irene's Cunt*' (SNS 122).

'Engendering the Formula' thus marks the beginning of Kristeva's project to understand theoretically what avant-garde artists in general but also what this particular avant-garde writer was doing: it was a question, after all, of keeping her head. My point here is to emphasize Kristeva's lucidity as to her own inscription as Юлия, l'étrangère,[15] in the avant-garde phantasmatic of femininity – and in the phantasmatic of femininity *tout court*. Too close yet too distant, a stranger and a headless corpse, and yet, perhaps, an undead dreamer of unfathomable bloody dreams, Kristeva's sustained response to the risk of being trapped in this chimera was to keep her head: answering the avant-garde erotic with a passion for thinking. 'Engendering the Formula' is thus the first instance – in a long series to come – of Kristeva's coupling of a female theorist with an avant-garde artist who, like Aragon, 'identifies with a feminine hypostasis, he absorbs it, he is she: he ... writes the impossible of femininity, assimilates it, sucks its blood' (SNS 145). But there is a cool-headed witness to tell.

Cutting a long story short, with Beatrice as a number and Юлия as the Beatrice of *Numbers* (the Number of Numbers?) we might be opening a new perspective on a concept which appears in 'Engendering the Formula' but is then quickly abandoned: not without a trace, I believe. *Le nombrant*.

Nombrant, prefiguring the *chora*

Kristeva introduces the 'semiotic' and the *chora* in *The Revolution in Poetic Language* as closely connected terms without really explaining why we need them both. Persisting in her later work, and ubiquitously accepted by commentators, the semiotic has gradually been trimmed as the shorthand for rhythm, alliteration, gesture, colour and all manner of abstract sensorial orderings which transmit sense but no meaning. Music and dance would come closest to pure semiosis but not, of course, in cases when they function as language as, for example, certain genres of dance do in India. Kristeva connects the charms but also the corrosive (with respect to meaning) aspects of semiosis to the pre-linguistic exchanges (echolalia, rhythmic motion, laughter) between the infant and the 'maternal container': it all begins in this archaic holding, in the barely distinguishable skin-to-skin autoerotic dyad. Hence the *chora*. The semiotic was thus retained to designate the material, observable, tangible aspect of this pre-linguistic ordering as it appears in symbolic structures, more or less rebelliously as the case may be. As such, the semiotic, somewhat trivialized, belongs to the area of literary or other media studies and is a phenomenon of aesthetics and rhetoric. The *chora*, on the other hand, seems to be there to remind us of the logical and chronological positioning of the semiotic in a time before time, the 'hors temps' of maternal embrace. The *chora*, therefore, would be the term which allows the connection to be made between the semiotic and the feminine. And while psychoanalysis is the tool which allows Kristeva to articulate this concept in its relevance for both the becoming of the speaking being and avant-garde artistic practices, its philosophical provenance persists in the psychoanalytic optics.

The term is taken out of Plato's *Timaeus* as one of those concepts apprehended through difficult reasoning: lost as soon as they are posited but non-existent without this positing. Supporting her definition of the *chora* with quotations from Plato's dialogue, Kristeva describes it as a dynamic space beyond representation, unstable, uncertain, seething and, although named, unnameable. The transplantation of the term into the psychoanalytic narrative of the speaking being's formation is supposed to strip it of Plato's ontological implications. Yet there is a residue which seems to resist this narrativization. What does this term add to the understanding of the semiotic? How is it distinguishable from it? Is it not a redundant redoubling of the same? The *chora* is sometimes described as semiotic, sometimes as semiotizable. Unnameable it is but made tangible by semiosis. The question is, is there a *chora* outside of semiotization, a not-yet-semiotized chora? On the one hand, there is not because we would not know about such a thing; on the other hand, there is because this is the crux of the paradox with this concept. If this undecidable existence of the *chora* were not needed, Kristeva could have stayed with the semiotic as the persistence of echolalia in the language of adulthood.

As already pointed out, the task to understand what avant-garde artists are doing involves, with Kristeva, a critique of the Saussurean conception of the sign. What is it, this thing which is not a sign and operates in avant-garde writing; are there units of *signifiance* as a trans-linguistic process which unfurl its revolutionary action in and across meaning and representation? In 'Engendering the Formula' this *other* articulation of the materiality of the text, an articulation which is not under the auspices of the sign, is called *numbers*, the numbers of Sollers' title, of course. The number, Kristeva says, is the 'graphic or phonic unity' of the 'smallest signifying set' which can be isolated in the text; it is 'the first movement of organization, i.e. of demarcation and ordination. A movement that differs from the simple "signify" and, we will say, covers a larger space where "to signify" can be understood and put in its place' (S 233). Like numbers in mathematics, these textual numbers can mean – count or give account of – one thing or another, or, indeed, an indefinite host of things.

Kristeva will abandon numbers in favour of the semiotic for, I presume, a couple of major reasons: the material and sensorial aspect of those minimal units of ordering is too important to her; as well as what will emerge as their indebtedness to the maternal body in terms of this ordering. I would venture to call this apparatus which she will keep elaborating in all her subsequent work a *filter of humanization*. Notably, the semiotic concerns mostly those aspects of art which seem closest to translatability into frequencies (sound), wave lengths (colour), muscular contractions (gesture) and so on. This is what they are, a border between the inhuman and the human, the precarious insistence of the biological and the inanimate in the human. They are the sustained presence of a miraculous occurrence, the extraction of the human being – before it can address another or, indeed, express itself – from the cosmic fabric ('the corporeal-ecological continuum' PL 440) by filling the void[16] with its own rhythm while 'learning to differentiate the body, to cut it up, to break it up into systems and levels' (PL 442). Melody comes later, together with syntax (how much later may depend on the linguistic environment); rhythm is the primordial ordering in which a future subject comes into being (PL 449–51). Rhythm is the primary structuration – the coalescence of 'intensities, frequencies and time' – yet it is as much sound as it is bodily motion and muscular contraction: to quote once again Diderot's daughter as quoted by Kristeva, 'you make soul by making flesh' (TML 588).

Like numbers in 'Engendering the Formula', the semiotic is devoid of exteriority; it produces differentiation without enunciating or addressing anything. The resurgence of the semiotic in the practice of modernist artists is hence something that is not exactly an aspect of their psychological insight: it is, on the contrary, something which leads beyond subjectivity, beyond psychology, beyond biology, into vibrations, pulsations, currents and quanta of energies. Looking at the semiotic via 'Engendering the Formula' makes this inhuman aspect more visible insofar as 'while showing itself in the language, [*signifiance* as manifest in avant-garde writing] does not enunciate anything about anything, but is produced in its own track where words are notations of applied sets (*ensembles appliqués*). Without externality, then, but in the ever-renewed germination of its differences, the domain thus described is equal to the inhuman of the formal sciences – mathematics' (S 263). In fact, I am tempted to say, mathematics should be the purest form of the semiotic. If Kristeva abandons her mathematical analogies and elevates music to this supreme purity, it is, I presume, because this art, notoriously attracted to mathematics, is a sensory phenomenon while mathematics, for all its beauty, not that obviously so. And, *stricto sensu*, they both mean nothing.

In 'Engendering the Formula', on the other hand, numbers as the smallest graphic or phonic unities in the text are nothing if not sensorial. What 'germinates' them in the engendering which interests Kristeva is called by her *nombrant*. I will leave the term in French in view of Kristeva's unique take on it. Sollers does not use *nombrant* in *Numbers*, nor does Derrida in 'Dissemination'. Nor, for that matter, Badiou in his 'Infinitesimal Subversion' although this essay (rather than Leibniz, who is Kristeva's major reference here – see S 237) is closer to the spirit of Kristeva's 'infinity points': they both, after all, unlike Leibniz, are on the lookout for subversion. In Jules Vuillemin's *Philosophy of Algebra*, which is quoted by Kristeva, *nombrant* does not seem to be an important term: Vuillemin simply points out that *nombres nombrants* are ordinal numbers; they show the position of something (first, second, etc.), while cardinal numbers, *nombres nombré*, tell us the number of things (Vuillemin 1993: Kindle 4163).[17] In fact, this somewhat antiquated pair tends nowadays to pop up mostly in discussions of Plato, Aristotle and Plotinus.[18] Aristotle, who appears in Kristeva's epigraph to the section on the *nombrant* (S 229), as well as Pythagoras and Neo-Platonism (S 233), might have played a role but certainly not in an obvious way. In any case, it is clear that the *nombrant* qua ordinal number is summoned to order Sollers' *Numbers*, those infinitesimal units of avant-garde subversion, and, in the line of reasoning I am pursuing, it is not surprising that the semiotic *chora* will be announced in *The Revolution of Poetic Language* as *ordering* the drives (RPL 25).

Whatever the case, the *nombrant* is defined by Kristeva as signifying infinity composed of everything that has been or will ever be conceived in any language past, present or future (S 232–6 and *passim*). It knows no lack. It is 'white' (like white light or white noise?). It is spatial and timeless. It infuses with infinity the number qua graphic and phonic unit and restores to it its function as 'infinity-point'. It will eventually be flattened into the plane of Saussure's two-dimensional sign as signifier/signified and into the line of enunciation: even avant-garde writing cannot evade this fate. Formulas will be engendered. Avant-garde writing, however, as exemplified by Sollers' *Numbers*, is the practice that, by sabotaging the sign, which nevertheless it includes in its deployment, bears witness to the *nombrant*'s infinity as infinite engendering. As has been justly noted and Kristeva makes sufficiently clear, this model of textual germination evokes Leibniz's theory of compossibles, according to which the entity that comes into being 'must by necessity bear marks of the virtual entities which have not been realized in its place, but which could have been' (Johnson 1988: 81).

There is still the mystery of what exactly gets engendered in the formula or, to exemplify it in terms of Sollers' *Numbers*, how out of the white *nombrant* does the bloody headless *elle* get conjured. The thorough overhaul of the conceptualization of engendering in the *Revolution in Poetic Language* might be seen as provoked by this query. With it, the *nombrant* and the infinity points of its numbers seem to have completely disappeared, opening the way for the *chora* with its semiotic and for Kristeva's further search for the 'Higgs boson' of the feminine (Kristeva 2019a). Yet has the *nombrant* disappeared, really? Or perhaps it is still there, holding the key to understanding why the semiotic needs to be coupled with the *chora*: semiotizable but perhaps, at some level, not yet semiotized, infinite, timeless, 'white'? The re-emergence of the conceptual package of 'Engendering the Formula' decades later in 'Letter to Denis Diderot on the Infinitesimal Subversion of a Nun' is quite telling. Echoing in its title the title of Badiou's youthful essay, this letter is an invocation to imagine the subject 'as the infinitesimal, giving back to the number its infinity-point' (TML 589). 'Teresa's extraordinary innovation – says Kristeva adding a strikingly modern sixteenth-century saint to her trilogy of female geniuses – consists in this incorporation of the infinite, which, working backward, against the grain, returns the body to the infinite web of bonds' (588). Beyond Colette's transubstantiation as 'plants, beasts, monsters, and marvels', the mystic nun seems to have found a way for (dis)incorporation directly in the *nombrant*. Kristeva defines both feats of the feminine as 'fiction' but what exactly she means by that will have to be the topic of another study.

Notes

1 As the principle of tireless incompletion, the feminine is not to be confused with 'reactive femininity and its parades of embellishment or narcissistic reparation, with which the woman's later phallicism reacts to the castration complex' (Kristeva 2019a).

2 Beardsworth's assertion that 'a genuine and deep-rooted departure from the revolutionary standpoint takes place in the later writings' (Beardsworth 2004: 26) is shared by many Kristevan scholars although it may be conceptualized and assessed differently. While some see it as continuation of her search for an embodied subject (Lechte and Margaroni 2005), others tend to criticize it as a conservative turn and a betrayal of the avant-garde. As William Watkin

puts it, 'Kristeva, having touched on the truth of the radical loss of significance as an ontological revolution in her early work, then systematically withdraws from it through a redefinition of terms and a re-consideration of the role of heterogeneous materiality' (Watkin 2003: 92).

3 I deal with this in greater detail in Nikolchina (2017).
4 He was part of the Russian avant-garde also as an artist. See Cutler 2008: an amazing sound and text collection which includes original recordings and reconstructions of Jakobson's own 'trans-rational' (*zaum*) experimentations.
5 The essay 'Pour une sémiologie des paragrammes' appeared initially in 1967 in *Tel Quel* and was reprinted in S 113–46. For the English translation, see Ffrench and Lack (1998).
6 On the early reception of Bakhtin in Bulgaria, see Stoyanov (2019).
7 On the disputes between Russian formalism and Marxism, see Tihanov (2019: 36–8) and *passim*.
8 I deal in greater detail with *signifiance* in Nikolchina (2020).
9 'Une(s) femme(s)' (SUF).
10 As in 'mechanized, roboticized, lobotomized, a sorry and embarrassing version of the human' (SNS 87).
11 As has been rightly noted, 'It is true that Kristeva's embodied subject, remains curiously (even disturbingly) unsexed' (Lechte and Margaroni 2005: 23). My claim here will be that the sexual indifference of the feminine is not only psychoanalytically but also ontologically viable. With all the persistence of Leibniz's differential in Kristeva's thinking, her work involves levels of the suspension of difference, which need a more careful analysis. An example I cannot tackle here would be the opaque foreigner that everyone is to oneself proposed as the ground for a new universalism (SO). The need to rethink the post-Kantian philosophy in terms of indifference has been powerfully articulated by William Watkin, whose readings of Agamben and Badiou inspired my approach here (Watkin 2014, 2017).
12 I discuss the retroactive disappearance of women's cultural contribution in Nikolchina (2004).
13 In the Anglophone context this is partly due to – or reflected by? – the 'curiously partial' translation of her work. See Ffrench and Lack (1998: 247, n.1).
14 'The transmodal idea is the bare descriptive ingredient of a scientific idea, which, in its "purified" logical form, is reproduced in heterogeneous contexts; it transgresses the boundaries of scientific theories' (Kolarov 2009: 221).
15 In a recent interview, Kristeva reiterates, 'I am and will remain a foreigner' (Kristeva 2019b).
16 'La voix prendra la relève du vide' (the voice will replace the void) (PL 442). Based on the observation of infants, Kristeva's claim is that all emissions of sound at this early stage are in response to something missing or some disturbance in corporeal equilibrium: they aim to fill the gap and restore the balance.

17 Kristeva refers to Vuillemin's book in S 235, note 24; 236, n.26.
18 See, for a recent example, Collette-Dučić (2007). Or, an older one, Amado (1953).

References

Amado, É. (1953), 'A propos des nombres nombrés et des nombres nombrants chez Plotin', *Revue Philosophique de la France et de l'Étranger*, 143: 423–5.
Badiou, A. (1968), 'La subversion infinitésimale', *Cahiers pour l'Analyse*, 9 (8): 118–37.
Beardsworth, S. (2004), *Julia Kristeva: Psychoanalysis and Modernity*, Albany, NY: State University of New York Press.
Collette-Dučić, B. (2007), *Plotin et l'ordonnancement de l'être*, Paris: Librairie Philosophique J. Vrin.
Cutler, C., ed. (2008), *Baku: Symphony of Sirens. (Sound Experiments in the Russian Avant Garde)*, London: ReR Megacorp.
Ffrench, P. and R. F. Lack, eds (1998), *The Tel Quel Reader*, London: Routledge.
Jakobson, R. and C. Lévi-Strauss (1987), 'Baudelaire's "Les Chats"', in R. Jakobson, *Language in Literature*, 180–97, Cambridge, MA: Harvard University Press.
Jardine, A. (2020), *At the Risk of Thinking*, New York: Bloomsbury.
Johnson, C. M. (1988), 'Intertextuality and the Psychical Model', *Paragraph*, 11 (1): 71–89.
Kolarov, R. (2009), *Povtorenie i sutvorenie: Poetika na avtotekstualnosta* (Repetition and Creation: Poetics of Autotextuality), Sofia: Prosveta.
Kristeva, J. (1996), *Time and Sense: Proust and the Experience of Literature*, trans. Ross Guberman. New York: Columbia University Press.
Kristeva, J. (2016), *Je me voyage. Mémoires. Entretiens avec Samuel Dock*. Paris: Fayard.
Kristeva, J. (2019a), 'Prelude to an Ethics of the Feminine', http://www.kristeva.fr/prelude-to-an-ethics-of-the-feminine.html (accessed 2 November 2021).
Kristeva, J. (2019b), 'Je suis et resterai une "étrangère"', *Philosophie*, 135, http://www.kristeva.fr/philosophie_magazine_135.html (accessed 2 November 2021).
Laplantine, C. (2011), '"La langue de Baudelaire." Une approche de Baudelaire et du langage poétique avec Benveniste', *Le français aujourd'hui*, 4 (175): 4754.
Lechte, J. and M. Margaroni (2005), *Julia Kristeva: Live Theory*, New York: Bloomsbury.
Mechelen, M. van (2017), 'Julia Kristeva's Semanalysis and the Legacy of Émile Benveniste', in K. Bankov (ed.), *New Semiotics: Between Tradition and Innovation. Proceedings of the 12th Congress of the International Association for Semiotic Studies (IASS/AIDed)*, 1473–80, Sofia: NBU Press.
Nikolchina, M. (2004), *Matricide in Language: Writing Theory in Kristeva and Woolf*, New York: Other Press.
Nikolchina, M. (2017), 'Revolution and Time in Kristeva's Writing', *diacritics*, 45 (3): 79–80.

Nikolchina, M. (2020), '*Signifiance* and Transubstantiation: The Returns of the Avant-garde in Kristeva's Philosophy of Literature', in S. Beardworth (ed.), *The Philosophy of Julia Kristeva*, 265–81, The Library of Living Philosophers, 36, Chicago: Open Court.

Sollers, P. (1968a), *Logiques*, Paris: Éditions du Seuil.

Sollers, P. (1968b), *Nombres*, Paris: Éditions du Seuil.

Spassova, K. (2018), 'Authentic and Heterogeneous Mimesis: Reflection and Self-reflexivity in Todor Pavlov and Yuri Lotman', *Slavica Tergestina*, 20 (1): 81–9.

Stoyanov, E. (2019), 'The Political Dimensions of Mikhail Bakhtin's Bulgarian Reception: Between Structuralism and Impressionism', *History of Humanities*, 4 (2): 365–75.

'Synopsis of Alain Badiou, "La subversion infinitésimale"', *Concept and Form: The Cahiers pour l'Analyse and Contemporary French Thought*, http://cahiers.kingston.ac.uk/synopses/syn9.8.html (accessed 2 November 2021).

Tihanov, G. (2019), *The Birth and Death of Literary Theory: Regimes of Relevance in Russia and Beyond*, Stanford, CA: Stanford University Press.

Vuillemin, J. (1993), *La Philosophie de l'algèbre*, Paris: P.U.F.

Watkin, W. (2003), 'Melancholia, Revolution and Materiality in the Work of Julia Kristeva', *Paragraph*, 26 (3): 86–107.

Watkin, W. (2014), *Agamben and Indifference: A Critical Overview*, London: Rowman and Littlefield.

Watkin, W. (2017), *Badiou and Indifferent Being: A Critical Introduction to Being and Event*, London: Bloomsbury.

4

Modernist trajectories in time: Kristeva's *The Enchanted Clock*

Carol Mastrangelo Bové

Julia Kristeva's novels, especially her most recent, *The Enchanted Clock*, criticize American pragmatism. An examination of this critical stance in its connections to her thinking on abjection and the maternal, components of her work that are most often discussed, enables a fuller understanding of psychoanalytic fiction's contributions to questions of national identity, history and gender. Kristeva's novels, in their careful representation of time and place, also explore knowledge about the material and historical conditions that critics often find lacking in psychoanalysis.

While some of the best writing on literature and film often engages with her psychoanalytic theory, Kristeva's novels merit more attention. They constitute significant fiction in their own right and deepen the understanding of her theory. *The Enchanted Clock* (2017), for example, raises questions relevant to life in the twenty-first century, especially how to achieve personal and social liberation in a world excessively pragmatic, often bereft of emotional intelligence and plagued by abjection and violence. An examination of the aesthetic and sensibility of her novels thus illuminates the ways in which psychoanalytic thought contributes to diverse forms of knowledge.

American tendencies of thought and psychic formations I see as excessively pragmatic have contributed to a form of capitalism that has produced imperialist and consumerist behaviour. I am using 'pragmatic' not in the sense in which philosophy uses the term, for example, in referring to the writing of William James or John Dewey, though there are connections to it. Instead, I use it to refer to a central problem Kristeva raises, the reduction of knowledge to causes outside of the self, divine or moral, and increasingly associated with the economic (IR 262). As I read her, such a reduction has led to the dominance of a psychic formation in which one adapts primarily to the dollar. Kristeva consistently argues for the need to understand the psyche more deeply, including unconscious drives, in the face of the onslaught of factors outside of the subject, especially economic and consumerist causes and the thinking on which they are based.

Two notions fundamental to her theory of subjectivity – the early separation from the mother and the threat of abjection – which major literary critics such as Hortense Spillers have engaged are also at the heart of her novels (Spillers 2003: 288–99). This theory is the basis of *The Enchanted Clock*'s critique of the American model of capitalism and the related ideas of liberalism and freedom. These notions remain implicit in *The Enchanted Clock*, primarily in the story of Claude Siméon Passemant, who rejects his mother's abusive, incestuous sensuality as well as her unrelenting pressure to force her son to become a judge. Such a rejection, Kristeva suggests, shapes his separation from maternal, nurturing emotions and behaviours, greatly contributing to his abjection and withdrawal from human ties. Passemant is blind to the reasons for his unhappiness and has been unable from infancy to develop the inner strength needed to function productively, apart from his undeniable knowledge of astronomy and clock-making. Though French, this character becomes in the novel's context an important example in its critique of American pragmatism.

He enters the novel like the robots we increasingly resemble in what Kristeva calls 'the becoming mechanical of the world' (EC 33). Bereft of empathy and emotion, his glance seeks to control others: to make you cringe or even more threatening in the original French – 'vous faire rentrer sous terre': to make you return to dust, to go back down into the earth, in other words, to kill you. He is from the start and throughout the novel fixated on the stars (EC 31), that is, on astronomy as the only source of knowledge and on chronological time, which he believes he is mastering by means of his astrological clock, designed to compute the hours until the year 9999.

In targeting harmful psychological formations like that of Passemant and his excessive pragmatism, Kristeva reimagines modernist fiction. Her novels resemble those of Virginia Woolf and William Faulkner in their density and nonlinear narrative, two characteristics of the best of this literary movement. Her fiction also features an imaginative, confrontational woman struggling for well-being both as an individual and within a group. Such a protagonist appears in much modernist literature and many avant-garde films especially in France.[1] In the finest of these novels, including for example, *The Old Man and the Wolves*, the female protagonist confronts psychological trauma and acquires a tragic dimension engaging the reader in an examination of her plight and its connections to his or her own.

The Enchanted Clock is a compelling novel, narrated by a unique and brilliant woman of a certain age recounting and contemplating her life with focus on the eighteenth-century astronomical timekeeper of the title and its inventor Passemant. The protagonist Nivi confronts the temporal in the form of the clock as she engages in strengthening her relationships and in understanding the world as she speaks. Her well-being, physical, emotional and intellectual, derives from interaction with her son, Stan, whose fascination with the clock leads to her own; with Theo, who saved her life while she was swimming in the Atlantic and becomes her lover; and with Marianne, her friend and colleague. Committed to her work as a psychoanalyst, much like Kristeva herself in this semi-autobiographical narrative, Nivi examines especially psychoanalysis and astrophysics, the latter primarily because of Theo's work and Stan's fascination with the eighteenth-century astronomical clock.[2] That is, she engages with others and examines scholarship across the disciplines, including the sciences. In doing so, she discovers a theory that brings excitement and coherence to her life, one that underlies a project to combat the contemporary world's excessive pragmatism, as well as the consumerism, chaos, violence and abjection to which it often leads or worsens.

Kristeva's discussion of the development of liberal democracy and its connections to what I see as American pragmatism in her 'Europe Divided: Politics, Ethics, Religion' in *Crisis of the European Subject* (111–62) provides relevant context for my argument on her fiction and Nivi's project in *The Enchanted Clock*. The essay analyses the roots of Christian materialism and its idea of a freedom that is dependent on the market place, citing Max Weber's *The Protestant Ethic and the Spirit of Capitalism* (2001), the foundational text tracing the derivation of capitalistic thought and behaviour to Protestantism (CES 120–1). The tendency towards pragmatic thinking in the United States has roots in Puritan monotheism, that is, in the dominant religion promoting a particular form of work ethic and, more generally, in the American patriarchal state to which it is related.

It is helpful to consider Claude Richard's psychoanalytic reading of American literature in examining Kristeva's neo-Freudian framework and the oppositional tradition from which it arises. For him, the source for this subversive line running counter to the pragmatic tendency of thought in the United States is Epicurus. Richard incisively documents this significant tendency, for example, in his analysis of Nathaniel Hawthorne's *The Scarlet Letter*, in which the Puritan patriarchs fetishize the idea of the absolute spiritual truth communicated in language. In Hawthorne's and Richard's critique of fetishism and reductive ideas of knowledge, both the son/narrator and the woman/Hester become the Other, especially the guilty sexuality latent in language (Richard 1998: 55). The Puritans preached hypocritically against materialism even as they, along with the Transcendentalists who followed, arguably laid the groundwork for capitalism and a work ethic focused on profit and the acquisition of physical comfort.[3]

Like Richard, Kristeva finds a source of oppositional writing in Epicurus. In 'Motherhood According to Bellini' she elaborates her notion of a 'prelinguistic, unrepresentable memory' in terms that derive from the influential Greek writer (DL 239). Furthermore, her essay 'Europhilia, Europhobia' refers to the Greek conception of 'ethos' and hospitality along with the Socratic dialogue in her critique of American freedom, that is, to be free to adapt to the market of production and profit (IR 257–62). She proves that opposition to America's model of liberalism and freedom and its connections to a dependence on external, economic factors has foundations in classical thought. Ethos and the Socratic dialogue as understood by the Greeks, according to her reading, mean an acute awareness of your own subjectivity and opening your mind to that of another. She writes, 'this second conception of freedom, quite distinct from liberalism... is given in the being of speech through the presence of the self to the other' (IR 263).

While the Puritans looked deeply into their relation to God through language, the founders neglected, for the most part, interiority's links to the subjectivity of other human beings, and so have cultivated a tendency towards nationalism and exceptionalism in the United States. Kristeva's thought is quite different from that of many American literary critics, marked by the nationalism of the state as well as of its primary religion, despite the church's apparent autonomy. I am thinking, for example, of the theme of the exceptional in literary studies in the United States. This is the idea that America is uniquely positioned to bring stability to the rest of the world.[4]

While mindful of the need to focus on the histories, strengths and weaknesses of individual nations, especially the positive qualities of France, Kristeva's perspective in her fiction is not nationalistic but fundamentally international, as I understand it. For her, we are not primarily citizens of a nation but rather citizens of the world. She has a background in linguistics; speaks Bulgarian, French and English; and has also authored a novel on Teresa of Avila that illustrates a reach beyond the national and exceptional. In *Teresa, My Love*, Kristeva's narrator Sylvia, based on the author herself, makes frequent reference to the saint's original Spanish texts and examines their cultural and historical contexts in sixteenth-century Spain, including the connections between Judeo-Christian and Islamic Sufi mystical thought (2014).

The Enchanted Clock, my principal focus in examining her novels, opens with the word 'time' and a satiric introduction to life in the twenty-first century, cleverly badgering the reader with the media, popular purchases and technology that, in the context of the rest of the narrative and of Kristeva's oeuvre, conjures up the United States and its impact on other countries:

> products, computers, e-mails, iPhones, trains, planes, videos, markets, supermarkets, hypermarkets, connections, depressions, corruptions, few conversations, miniscreens, giant screens, a few books, fast foods and more or less organic bars... No men, but a mass of chargés d'affaires... Women, a few – more and more – who hold, carry, and transmit.
> (EC 3)

This is the 'mechanical world', which the novel will trace back to eighteenth-century France and to Passemant, the famous clockmaker of that period (EC 32–3). While Kristeva does not use the word 'pragmatic' in the narrative, in the context both here and in her other fiction and essays, 'the becoming-mechanical of the world' (EC 33) in the age of Louis XV and the 'applied research in our time' (EC 266) reveal a common thread leading to an overly pragmatic United States.

The opening of the novel introduces the 'woman question' central to the narrative: France, bombarded by consumer products and technology, has increasingly lost its men, who have become business types. The country has, however, acquired stronger women (EC 3). The comment on the sexes calls attention to Nivi's at times reductive thinking but takes on specific meaning in the context of the novel taken as a whole. Kristeva connects the patriarchal society recreated here, twenty-first-century France and its roots in the age of Louis XV, to that of the United States. Implicit in this novel is the idea that Western governments and religious institutions, founded as they are on monotheistic faiths, shape a set of values which associate men, especially white men, with pragmatic expertise, intellect, power, a business ethic, nationalism and imperialism. These institutions associate women with sexuality, manipulability and fantasy. Therefore, according to Kristeva, women increasingly become vital sources of creative thinking, an other-oriented ethos and a more international perspective.

The Enchanted Clock goes on to explore questions of gender as well as time and memory, mentioning the United States often in connection with its space program and astrophysics, despite the fact that there is not much direct discussion of the country. Indirect references, however, appear in nearly every chapter, most frequently in relation to the work of Theo, a Frenchman who has studied at MIT and UC Berkeley with American astrophysicists and/or in NASA laboratories equipped with telescopes like the Hubble in such places as Harvard, Texas, New Mexico, Arizona, Seattle and Peru. In my reading, these allusions emphasize that the United States contributes in the hard sciences (especially astrophysics), technology (particularly information technology) and more specifically in discoveries of the state of the universe thirteen billion years ago. Represented in the novel as still the strongest superpower with some positive impact on other countries, America provides economic support in many venues, including Apple's subsidies to *PsyMagazine*, which publishes some of Nivi's articles and for which Marianne is grateful, while Nivi's attitude is ambivalent (EC 36). In a more negative light, the novel implicitly criticizes US military research, which has become the principal goal of its space program. Along with information technology, such research neglects fundamental aspects of astrophysics, including the philosophy of science (EC 108–9). In other words, this development is part of the dangerous emphasis in America on the pragmatism underlying contemporary science, technology, and military dominance increasingly in isolation from the contributions of the humanities.[5]

Furthermore, Nivi considers Goldman Sachs's practices as a later version of the eighteenth-century John Law's disreputable behaviour (EC 42), and in this way calls attention to the exploitative nature of American multinational investment banking. Here Kristeva explicitly links American pragmatism to predatory capitalist ventures and eighteenth-century France to twenty-first-century America, connections implicit throughout her novel, as I am arguing.

An additional indirect reference to the United States appears in the religious sect, the Convulsionaries of the French Enlightenment period who attracted a large following among Parisians. The novel relates the Sunday outing of Passemant, an unenthusiastic, temporary participant in his family's visit to the church of Saint Médard to observe the group. In context, it is difficult not to read the Convulsionaries, especially their apparent faith healing and celebrity status, as a covert allusion to American Evangelicals, one of the contemporary American Christian sects deriving from Transcendentalism and Puritanism (EC 92–3). In his book *Études cliniques sur la grande hystérie ou hystéro-épilepsie*, the famous writer on artistic anatomy, also assistant to and collaborator with the neurologist Jean-Martin Charcot, Paul Richer, has linked the threats posed by both the French and American sects in the eighteenth and nineteenth centuries (1885: 884–9). In *The Enchanted Clock*, Kristeva includes the Convulsionaries to indicate the ways in which Passemant escapes from contact with the people and events around him and also to signal the harmful practice – the narrator calls it a 'fad' – not without its similarities to violent Christian fundamentalism. One of the visionaries, for example, 'draws straws to decide who among them will be sacrificed to expiate the crimes of the others' (EC 93).

An example of significant juxtapositions in the novel's portrayal of the United States appears in a more direct and extensive reference. A minor character, Bill Parker, is the American colleague of Theo, Nivi's astrophysicist lover. The scientist visits Paris, expresses interest in meeting a young woman upon her leaving Nivi's office and discusses theories of time with the narrator.

Bill is an unusual combination of sexual licentiousness, intellectual ability and playfulness. Nivi feels affection for him, despite his hurtful tendency to deprecate her discipline, psychoanalysis, and to address her in the capacity of a journalist (EC 154). His behaviour implies, in the novel's critique of certain masculine tendencies, the difficulty many men have in seeing women as intellectually strong, doing important work and attractive at one and the same time. Appropriately enough, in a novel whose introduction highlights strong women while noting the lack of 'real' men, Bill's wife arouses Nivi's unqualified admiration. An American, she may speak little, but is brilliant and shares her husband's passion for astrophysics, examining along with him the telescopic data.

As a representative of the United States, if only of a class/type of American men, Bill confirms that Kristeva's perspective is not reductive. Clearly critical of America's predatory capitalism, revealed in its excessive consumerism and imperialist behaviour, she juxtaposes Bill's more positive qualities – his intellectual ability and playfulness – to the reference to Goldman Sachs and its exploitative multinational investment banking, for example. We recall similar juxtapositions in her earlier novels. *The Old Man and the Wolves*, for instance, portrays the devastating invasion of American consumerism into Eastern Europe after the fall of the Berlin wall. Yet the American jazz singer Billie Holliday's voice, a source of beauty and strength, resonates in the Old Man's head through much of the narrative.

The context provided by Kristeva's portrayal of the United States in her other novels and essays enables a fuller understanding of her insights into American history and institutions including religion and the state. The autobiographical novel depicting her early years in Paris, *The Samurai*, portrays the United States in complex, ambivalent and at times stereotypical/problematic terms, referring to its inhabitants as 'Algonquins crossed with Protestants' (SA 223). One of her two principal protagonists, Olga, is eager to lecture in New York, citing the openness of students who ask constructive questions and engage with her writing (SA 223). She falls in love with an American, Edward Dalloway, an international lawyer, whose name is a conscious reference (NWN 89) to what is arguably the epitome of the modernist novel, Woolf's *Mrs Dalloway*, a significant example of the modernist context on which this narrative draws. At the same time, Olga's colleagues and friends remind her of the unsavoury aspects of America, including its imperialistic behaviour, for example, during the Vietnam War in progress at the time (SA 21).

In the ending of *The Enchanted Clock*, Kristeva mobilizes modernism and its sense of time and subjectivity against what I am defining as American pragmatism. The novel concludes with a quintessentially modernist, Proustian experience. Nivi relives childhood pleasure among the laurel roses – recalling in a darker cherry colour Proust's pink hawthorns – and this pleasure persists in her memory once her cousins have the bushes removed.

She in this way can re-experience the joy in precious moments in the present even as she exists in chronological time. She likens the phenomenon to Theo's perceiving the origins of the universe and its expansion in the gravitational waves he obtains via telescopes along with his Harvard colleagues. He too experiences ecstatic instants of wonder in contemplating the world outside of himself, especially the telescopic images, while at the same time aware of history. His conversations with Nivi reveal an in-depth knowledge of eighteenth-century Paris. Like his partner, he too lives both in the moment and in historical time.

Kristeva draws on rich literary traditions including not only modernism's Proustian moments but also detective fiction. In a plot including possible murders and thefts like that of her three earlier novels, *The Old Man and the Wolves, Possessions* and *Murder in Byzantium*, she also reintroduces Officer Rilsky. Kristeva creates her own version of a modernist sensibility and writing style, making clear that multiple perspectives, including not only that of the detective but especially that of a female psychoanalyst, at times acting the detective herself, enable a profound examination of the human and human relations both local and international. Beyond the elements of detective fiction, the novel makes other references to the worlds created in her earlier narratives, thus having readers consider diverse layers of memory and go beyond the linear time of pragmatic thinking, particularly if they know the previous tales.

Furthermore, albeit indirectly, *The Enchanted Clock* continues to study subjects introduced in her earlier work, *The Old Man and the Wolves*: the exportation of capitalist, predatory values from the United States and their connection to psychic formations of abjection and separation from the maternal. She makes a compelling case to go beyond pragmatic world views, especially that of the very controlling Passemant. Linear time and the isolation of disciplines, particularly astrophysics, characterize his perspective. These characteristics work against hermeneutical thinking across the arts and sciences as well as across national boundaries. Such interpretive approaches employ methods that pragmatic thought rejects, for example, metaphor. The perspectives of Nivi, the third-person narrator, and Kristeva, as understood in the novel taken as a whole, oppose such reductive thinking. The question of pragmatic and empirical thought, components of the hard sciences and technology in the United States and often removed from their context in the human sciences, is in this way an important theme in *The Enchanted Clock* as well as in her other novels and often the target of their critique.

While the criticism on Kristeva's fiction is not extensive, it does provide relevant context and corroboration for my argument that these modernist novels foment constructive debates on pragmatism/consumerism in contemporary life with special emphasis on a gendered resistance in France and the United States. Such resistance, I am arguing, is the lifeline we need in these dark times devoid of a clear and convincing understanding of and commitment to the community, of which we are all a part. It is in this context that I now refer to Benigno Trigo's volume of collected essays on Kristeva's fiction, which notes her references to the 2001 bombing of the World Trade Center, to Christian fundamentalists in the United States and to the use American literary critics and theorists make of her theory of the semiotic (2013). Her allusions to 9/11 as well as to Christian fundamentalism are elements of the critique of the hegemonic presence of American materialism and especially the authoritarian thinking and terrorism it has in part unleashed, as Trigo implies (2013: 8). He also suggests that literary criticism, especially on codeswitching, bilingualism and border literature, calls attention to the political aspect of her theory of the semiotic especially in relation to problems of assimilation and exile in the United States, which are connected to nationalist attitudes (2013: 13).

While the only in-depth analysis of *The Enchanted Clock* of which I am aware does not explicitly mention the American subtext, it does discuss the rise of consumerism and the society of the spectacle, arguably the product in large part of the United States and its influence throughout the world. Miglena Nikolchina focuses on the book as enabling a fuller understanding of Eastern European countries and their attempts to install a rebellious ideology, including Bulgaria, her own and Kristeva's birthplace (2017).

Her 1990 novel *The Old Man and the Wolves* – with 'Santa Barbara' in the original French version a reference to the California city – is, I believe, her best representation of the American threat both to the people of Eastern Europe and to its own. In the wake of the region's failure to achieve revolution, Nikolchina cites as a cause 'the new world order of spectacle and consumerism whose ideological vacuum is continually tempted by varieties of nationalism and religious fundamentalism' (2017: 82). The United States and its capitalist ideology, deriving as I am arguing from a pragmatic, Christian materialism – 'more goods and services for everyone', as Kristeva puts it – have contributed much to this order (SO 195).

American pragmatism and revolution are opposing subtexts in *The Enchanted Clock*, my principal focus in discussing her fiction, as it becomes clear that personal and public crises are imminent in this novel. The private crises include, in especially moving terms, Stan's serious illness (EC 113), as well as doubts about Theo's honesty and behaviour (EC 271, 294). In the first example, when Stan is hospitalized, Nivi goes to great lengths to show that she can deal with her beloved son's precarious health and finally admits that she cannot, as her friend Marianne perceives:

> Nivi has been traumatized. By exile, love, maternity, everything. The tiniest pinprick pierces right through, ravages her like a solar explosion. Isn't that right, Nivi? It's not wrong. Things take hold of me and reduce me to an unnamable state over which I have no power, and that makes

me get involved in other people's traumas. I accompany them; from time to time they accompany me, in spurts, in waves, in as many rebirths.

(EC 116)

In this way, Kristeva adds complexity to her narrator's reliability, engaging the reader in deciphering her degree of lucidity and recognizing her vulnerability to abject states in which she is unable to adequately articulate her story. The passage also reveals Nivi's motivation in treating her patients.

Nivi experiences abjection and struggles to think through her depression and to articulate what she feels with little success. Here Kristeva creates conflicting perspectives in the protagonist to enable us to see that Nivi has her blind spots. In the second instance mentioned above, while she claims to be impervious to jealousy and doubts about Theo, the fact that she excessively ruminates over his presence in Paris when he said he was in Santiago and over his possible involvement in the theft of Passemant's clock demonstrates her blindness. More to the point on the juxtaposition of pragmatism and revolution in the narrative is Nivi's anxiety that her partner Theo resembles, or even *is* the callous and manipulative Passemant. There is also the suggestion that she, too, is vulnerable to his fundamental flaws of indifference to others and the excessive need for control (EC 33, 47, 49, 121).

The worldly crises encompass the attack at the Louvre, the possible murder of a colleague, Loïc, and the theft of the astronomical clock. Thus, via Nivi, Kristeva engages in bridging the gap between the singular and the collective. A strengthening of individual and collective consciousness is taking hold of the narrator, suggesting the best way to deal with such crises. The prose, at its best in its lyricism, for example, in the passage I will describe below, is moving and compels us to empathize with Nivi and to think more deeply about her experience, including her theories and reflections on time, memory, science and love both for her partner and her son. These ideas offer the opportunity to energize a resistance to the pragmatism, lack of order and aggressive behaviour characterizing life in the twenty-first century, including the depression that frequently results, destroying the ability to think creatively. In an interview discussing *The Enchanted Clock*, Kristeva says:

The novel remains the privileged genre in which inner experience can crystalize. Such experience definitely exists in us, at least in those of us who will not submit. It reveals itself, timid but imperious, at the intersection of scientific audacity (biology, cosmology…), virtual realities, hyperconnection, blended families, insecure borders, inexpressible anxiety, and unspoken hope.

(2019, my translation)

Given her commitment to literature and to the novel's accessible language and popularity, it is not surprising that she returns here to the topic of its suitability. In her 'Europhilia, Europhobia', Kristeva points to the imaginary as particularly well-suited to combat a harmful, increasingly pervasive model restricting thought and behaviour to economic causes (IR 267). This reference to the imagination as a resource for resistance – a form of liberation or intimate revolt – to a component of orthodox American thinking clearly applies to her novels, and especially to her most recent.

Kristeva has, however, displayed a balanced interest in essays, poetry and fiction in both her theory and creative writing over many years. The autobiographical narrator of her 1991 novel *The Old Man and the Wolves*, in fact, speaks disparagingly of distinctions among literary forms as 'the frontiers once drawn up between the different genres for the benefit of lazy schoolboys' (62). Kristeva is more interested in describing literature rather than the particular genres included in that category, as I have explained elsewhere in an essay focusing on creative writing and philosophy in her work (2019). Also, in spite of fiction's development as a middle-class phenomenon *within* capitalist culture, her reference in this interview and elsewhere to the suitability of the novel points to its capacity for resistance, especially given its greater accessibility compared to other literary forms. The precision of her analysis of the nature of fiction in the interview cited above makes this clear. Novels have the potential to shape the psychology of the reader, including unconscious drives, in response to those of the author. Fiction can resist – despite its development within capitalist culture – those aspects of the contemporary, including economic factors, that challenge and inhibit opportunities for creativity and loving behaviour.

Kristeva develops a theory of creative resistance in her remarks on the novel's potential, as Maria Margaroni's work shows. She has identified a significant characteristic of Kristeva's idea of a fiction of resistance by calling attention to its visceral character and power to connect with others, to help create a community. According to 'The Vital Legacy of the Novel', *Sense and Non-Sense of Revolt* insists on the need for the literary critic and theorist to go beyond more purely textual questions and to examine narrative's ability to have readers feel the psychic, sensorial experiences the text recreates for both the author and themselves, as my example of the laurel rose conclusion of *The Enchanted Clock* shows (318).

In this context, Kristeva's prose inscribes a form of modernist lyricism. The inscription is, I believe, one of the distinguishing marks of her modernism. In this most recent novel, her protagonist overcomes abjection and regains her ability to think and express herself, enacting a successful integration of body, heart and mind as in the novel's ending:

> Nivi's sadness, always fleeting, lost, on the lookout, has molted into something luminous, unheard of, and fabulous. Not really a destiny but

a unique reality, almost exalting, somewhat like morning, for which a single word comes to her lips: *serenity*.

That vision makes her possible.

In the sun-splattered street alongside the Lux, under her window, she sees a green hedge, the most delicate there is. Vibrating cords caressed by the breeze, foraged by clouds of bees. At the bottom of this cloth of transparent threads, scarcely higher than the height of a little girl of three, a rose laurel. Unique, slim, adorned with smooth dark green foliage, crowned by curly petals of cherry color. Which open to the pure light, the first light of the world.

This is the last paragraph of the final chapter devoted to Nivi's familial life in the apartment above the Luxembourg Garden, a setting that reappears in many of Kristeva's texts including, for example, *The Samurai*, in which she names an entire section of several chapters for the park (SA 291–341). The passage achieves a moving lyricism in its reference to the way in which a delicate laurel rose bush recreates the narrator's joy felt at the age of three in her family's garden. Kristeva uses primarily the visual: 'in the sun-splattered street' but she also evokes the touch and sound the young bush feels and hears ('Vibrating cords caressed by the breeze' [EC 318]) to create Nivi's experience of déjà-vu. In the original French, 'irisée' more beautifully describes the image of the street made iridescent by the sun (HE 440). The anthropomorphizing of the bush, an example of the pathetic fallacy, aptly conveys the strength and beauty of her pleasure.

Beyond the personal precious moment, the passage in context brings together all the components of Nivi's complex personality and rich experience. We recall that her son Stan, unlike Bill, who labels her a journalist, sees her as a mother difficult to categorize, like a Picasso portrait. In the unique personal and filial observations made earlier in the novel, Kristeva has the question of national identity emerge. Stan asks, 'Mama, are you French?' Nivi has made clear in both earlier and later reflections that this question disturbs her: she is and is not French, does and does not want to be (EC 5, 109). Not born in France, like the Bulgarian-born author, she loves the country because, she says, of the bewitching Jardin de Luxembourg and primarily because of her son, Stan, born in Paris. In other words, elements of her personal history, especially her visceral experiences like the sight of the garden and the relationship with her child, have led to her attachment to the Hexagon. Here she implicitly rejects a nationalistic belief in 'my country [France] right or wrong', as she explicitly does in her *Nations without Nationalism* (1993). She makes clear that her experience living in Paris for a long time, 'years of study, reading, music, mostly happy love with Ugo' (the husband and father of Stan who has left them to return to his native Italy) explains the attachment to her adopted country (EC 6). Beyond the gardens, her son and her partners, the intellectual and artistic life in the French capital increasingly arouse love for the city of lights.

The final chapter fittingly calls attention to the main elements of Nivi's life and the links she forges among them including Stan and Theo: she hears the words 'rose laurels' in connection with the noises in her son's bedroom, on the one hand. She understands her memory of the garden in relationship to her love for Theo and the stars, on the other. There are also implicit references in the passage cited to her confrontation with abjection, 'Nivi's sadness'. Kristeva traces this confrontation back to the chaotic, violent environment in Nivi's early years and her traumatization by her cousins' brutal cutting down of the laurel rose bushes in an attempt to install dead flowers in the garden's fountain basin.

The incorporation of the reference to the stars in the conclusion of *The Enchanted Clock*, resonating with the considerable exploration of astrophysics and astronomy in the novel, is a significant characteristic of its reimagining of modernist fiction to include the theme of the production of knowledge. Kristeva is probing many questions relevant to the hard sciences and today's world: for example, among the more straightforward, what exactly is the status of the research Theo undertakes, which commands Nivi's attention? It may appear to be science fiction, as it does to one reviewer (2015). Theo's work, in fact, reveals actual advances in the knowledge and manipulation of the material world, that is, recent developments in astrophysics and technology. He is, for instance, taking pictures that show the state of the universe millions of years ago. The clock which so fascinates Stan and Nivi, and eventually Theo, does exist in the palace of Versailles and is set to tell time until 9999. Though other such timekeepers precede it, they do not portray virility in their form as Passemant's does, with its globe at the top, broad base in the middle and large pendulum hanging below. In other words, Passemant's clock emerges as a patriarchal figure, significant in a novel very much focused on both the woman question and pragmatism.

The relationship between pragmatism and the gendered rationalist traditions of the West matters because Kristeva is exploring the connections between the primarily pragmatic thinking of technology and science, on the one hand, and psychoanalysis and ethics, on the other. She is asking how advances in astrophysics, for example, may influence the psyche, human behaviour and the violent directions it is taking, posing a significant question for science and ethics, even if some readers are unaware of the reality of Theo's research. Here, as in her interview with the physicist/philosopher Étienne Klein, Kristeva underlines the parallels between science, especially discoveries in astrophysics, and psychology, specifically psychoanalysis (2015). The discussion of the multiverse, of foreign matter and of science and technology overall is central in the novel, particularly in the context of their connections to humanist thought, reminding us, in a period when programmes in the United States are destroying the humanities, of Richard's examination of the links between atoms and letters in Epicurus (1998: 18).

Kristeva's most significant question in this novel is how best to resist the abject along with its causes, that is, in my reading, the consumerism, incoherence, conflicts on the planet and American predatory capitalism deriving from its excessive pragmatism. *The Enchanted Clock* proposes that one needs to consider, at least to some degree, all of the disciplines and especially their conceptions of time. Her novel recreates diverse temporal trajectories: shifts between eighteenth- and twenty-first-century Paris, the chronological horizontal paths of pragmatic thought as well as the vertical, synchronic precious moments à la Proust. The narrative thus confronts the danger of believing primarily in the progress made by science and technology alone. Such belief underpins the American tendencies to dominate and to control. This threat, according to Kristeva, derives from the ways such behaviour and thought permeate the globe, especially France. As she makes clear in her allegorical portrayal of eastern Europe in *The Old Man*, the danger is not confined to the United States and France, however. These countries in one sense are not qualitatively different from the rest of the world in their potential for both dangerous and positive developments in the psychic formations that prevail.

The jump cuts back and forth to Passemant and to a lesser extent, the Bill Parker episode, enable Kristeva to put forward a number of different perspectives for the reader to consider. She filters a variety of points of view on the problems of the abject, incoherence and conflict through Nivi's remarks. Passemant understands the most advanced technology of clockmaking and its relation to the discipline of astronomy in mid-eighteenth-century France and succeeds in creating a beautiful timepiece capable of marking every third of a second as well as the movements of our galaxy until the year 9999. His desire, however, is to control time and to escape from relations with others as well as from the material conditions of historical experience.

In this semi-autobiographical novel, Kristeva provides a portrait of not only the clockmaker/astronomer Passemant but also the equally little-known Emilie du Châtelet. She is the physicist who created an intriguing theory on 'the fire of desire and the fire of reason" (EC 231) thoroughly understood Leibnitz, predicted the discovery of bosons and black matter and was also the translator of Newton's *Principia* (EC 142–4, 146–7, 228–33). In Châtelet and her partners, Kristeva offers an example, parallel to Bill and his wife, and primarily to Nivi and Theo, of fascinating male/female pairs. Such duos push against the sexist hierarchies of much history and fiction, which often fail to recognize the 'female genius', both hidden in couples and in more independent formations, as Kristeva documents so well in this novel and in her trilogy, *Female Genius: Life, Madness, Words – Hannah Arendt, Melanie Klein, Colette* (2001–4).

Châtelet's example is different and critical here in that she serves as a foil to the excessively pragmatic character at the centre of this novel. Unlike Passemant, who is nonetheless intelligent and appealing, Châtelet did not strive for control nor did she escape from relationships with others. She was the lover and collaborator of Voltaire, had many close relations, dying soon after childbirth at the age of forty-three.

A more difficult pair to analyse in *The Enchanted Clock* is Louis XV and Madame de Pompadour. Introduced in connection with Passemant, the king is admirable for his cultivation of knowledge, especially his interest and ability in science. His stature diminishes over time, however. Sexual liaisons obsess him (here Kristeva creates another link to the United States in Bill Parker's womanizing), leading to the neglect of his duties and the revolution later in the century. Madame de Pompadour is also admirable for her intelligence in this narrative but, facing more constraints than the king, in part because of her gender and social class, she becomes consumed by jealousy to the point where she attempts to attack Passemant and his invention, the astronomical clock so loved by the king (EC 221).

Most significant, however, in this modernist narrative focused on American pragmatism and resistance, Nivi and Theo together have a remarkable understanding of many disciplines, especially psychoanalysis and astrophysics. They work together for the most part to examine 'truth', without trying to control it, time or each other. Rather than escaping from their situation in the world, they strengthen their 'maternal' ties to others, including each other, Nivi's son Stan, her patients and their colleagues. Notable in this regard is Nivi's indirect advice to Marianne, in the important subplot of the latter's maternity: that she become a good mother by having her daughter recognize her authority, that is, experience faith in her word, which makes the child part of a community (EC 204).

Furthermore, Nivi and Theo nurture others, cultivate precious moments of arrested time, and recognize that one enjoys such instants in the context of history and a chronology enabling an understanding of how the past shapes the present and future, including their ageing and decline towards death. Resonating with Proust and transforming his insights for a very different twenty-first century, Kristeva's novel portrays the two in love with each other and combining their forces to resist submission to abjection and the pragmatism, disorder and violence of contemporary life.

In *The Enchanted Clock*, Nivi and Theo are aware of and willing to acknowledge the increasingly greater obstacles one confronts in contemporary life. These protagonists are more successful in confronting them, however, than those of the earlier *The Old Man and the Wolves*, where both the female protagonist, Stephanie Delacour, as well as the old man, Septicius Clarus, come closer to succumbing to abjection, in part because they are in the throes of attacks deriving from capitalist and consumerist ideology. The principal narrator, the central female character in each of these two novels, is very much like the 'energetic pessimist' Kristeva refers to in describing herself (2016), with the earlier more pessimistic and the latter more energetic, like the respective narratives of which they are a part. The tone of *The Enchanted Clock* is primarily and more uniformly upbeat, as demonstrated in my analysis of its final paragraph.

A vindication of a modernist sensibility and aesthetic, her novel connects the critique of American pragmatism to abjection and the maternal. The connection is central to her understanding of the ways contemporary psychic formations shape a businessman model, that is, capitalism's promotion of the freedom to profit primarily from adapting to the market place.

The novel is at the same time a celebration of elements she considers a source of resistance to pragmatist attitudes, stressing the centrality of a historical consciousness in its representation of eighteenth-century France's blindness to the links between the hard sciences and the humanities. Furthermore, her representing the Paris of both the past and the present so clearly and convincingly belies the apparent weakness of psychoanalytic writing, that is, that it neglects material conditions in its attempt to be universal.

In Nivi's ruminations on France and the United States, Kristeva also distinguishes legitimate national pride from dangerous nationalism, a distinction worth considering in the present age of increasing populism. Finally, her novel compels a rethinking of the politics of sexual identity by creating a strong female protagonist able to decipher the strengths and weaknesses of those around her, along with her own.

Notes

1   See my *Language and Politics in Julia Kristeva* (2006: 122–6) as well as my 'Revisiting Modernism With Kristeva: DeBeauvoir, Truffaut, and Renoir' (2002).

2   It is also relevant to the embedding of science in the novel to point out that Kristeva's mother had read many scientists, especially Darwin, and that the daughter herself, like her protagonist Nivi, had contemplated a scientific career. See Jardine (2020: 40, 59–60).

3   This even though certain Puritans contributed to mystical thought and produced beautiful poetry, for example, Anne Bradstreet.

4   See Pease (2009), in which he analyses the discourse underlying transnational scholarship including both national politics and art.

5   Important exceptions appeared during the Cold War when the United States took the lead in the philosophy of science and the government supported the humanities as part of the war of ideas with the USSR.

References

Bové, C. M. (2002), 'Revisiting Modernism with Kristeva: DeBeauvoir, Truffaut, and Renoir', *Journal of Modern Literature*, 25 (3–4): 114–26.
Bové, C. M. (2006), *Language and Politics in Kristeva: Literature, Art, Therapy*, Albany, NY: State University of New York Press.
Bové, C. M. (2019), 'Desire against Discipline: Kristeva's Theory of Poetry', in R. Ghosh (ed.), *Philosophy and Poetry: Continental Perspectives*, 296–310, New York: Columbia University Press.
Jardine, A. (2020), *At the Risk of Thinking: An Intellectual Biography of Julia Kristeva*, New York: Bloomsbury.
Kristeva, J. (2015), '*L'Horloge enchantée:* Conversation entre Étienne Klein et Julia Kristeva', Kristeva.fr, *Soundcloud*, http://www.kristeva.fr/conversation-etienne-klein.html (accessed 2 November 2019).
Kristeva, J. (2016), 'Je suis une chercheuse d'humanité', *Le Soir*, https://plus.lesoir.be/74435/article/2016-12-22/julia-kristeva-je-suis-une-chercheuse-dhumanite (accessed 2 November 2019).
Kristeva, J. (2019), 'Le Temps du roman: *L'Horloge enchantée'*, Kristeva.fr, *Chroniques-de-la-rentrée*, http://www.kristeva.fr/chroniques-de-la-rentree-litteraire.html (accessed 29 October 2019).
Lasowski, A. W. (2015), 'Alchimie de la science et de l'imaginaire', Kristeva.fr, *L'Humanité*, http://www.kristeva.fr/horloge/LHumaniteMardi28Juillet.pdf (accessed 3 November 2019).
Margaroni, M. (2013), 'The Vital Legacy of the Novel and Julia Kristeva's Fictional Revolt', in B. Trigo (ed.), *Kristeva's Fiction*, 155–73, Albany, NY: State University of New York Press.
Nikolchina, M. (2017), 'Revolution and Time in Kristeva's Writing', *diacritics*, 45 (3): 76–98.
Pease, D. (2009), 'Re-thinking "American Studies after Exceptionalism"', *American Literary History*, 21 (1): 19–27.
Richard, C. (1998), *American Letters*, trans. C. M. Bové, Philadelphia, PA: University of Pennsylvania Press.
Richer, P. (1885), *Études cliniques sur la grande hystérie où hystéro-epilepsie*, Paris: Adrien Delahaye et Émile Lecrosnier.
Spillers, H. (2003), *Black, White, and in Color: Essays on American Literature and Culture*, Chicago: University of Chicago Press.
Trigo, B., ed. (2013), *Kristeva's Fiction*, Albany, NY: State University of New York Press.
Weber, M. (2001), *The Protestant Ethic and the Spirit of Capitalism*, trans. S. Kalberg, New York: Oxford University Press.

5

Sanctity and scandal: Teresa and the challenge of nineteenth-century 'false mysticism'

Martha J. Reineke

Writing on the contributions of psychoanalysis to interpretations of politics and history, Julia Kristeva alludes to the origins of modernity in the Enlightenment, a time during which tradition, custom and law were challenged and reason was elevated as a guide for human activity (KR 305–6). Absent established markers of authority, the human subject increasingly became a question to itself as its efforts to resolve competing claims 'to know' proved elusive. For every demonstrated truth claim emerging from the practice of reason, there were countervailing claims that described a subject in the grip of forces and processes unforeseen and unimagined in the premodern era. As doubts multiplied, key features of the Enlightenment – rationality, identity and representation – fell into crisis (Whitworth 2007: 7).[1] In a world that purportedly had buried God and taken full possession of reason, 'modernism' emerged as an appellation that both captured rising concerns about the status of that achievement and attested to the impact of unseen forces on humans' imaginative and ethical consciousness.

In Julia Kristeva's 2008 novel, *Teresa, My Love: An Imagined Life of the Saint of Avila,* Kristeva focuses on one illustrative crisis that persists: individuals' vulnerability to entrapment by either religious fundamentalism or secularism (TML 587). Kristeva contrasts Teresa's 'amorous faith' with that of a devout young Muslim woman who 'was quite prepared to sacrifice herself – like those female suicide bombers' (TML 8). In doing so, Kristeva creates a perilous association for readers who, summarily dismissing the faith of the Muslim woman or precipitously embracing Teresa's, may be shielded from a disquieting but significant encounter with Teresa. We are alerted to this risk when we notice a tension in Kristeva's own work: unexamined modernist assumptions revealed in Kristeva's telling of Teresa's story are at odds with Kristeva's ethics of analysis, a feature of Kristeva's scholarship in the late 1980s.

I explore this tension by comparing Teresa's faith with a case of 'false mysticism' examined by the Inquisition in the shadow of the 1868 First Vatican Council. My unsettling reading of Kristeva's novel sheds critical light on modernist features of Kristeva's novel even as it locates 'the other', not in the foreigner, exemplified in Kristeva's novel by a female, Muslim suicide bomber, but at the very heart of the Christian imaginary in 'the stranger that is myself'. My argument proceeds in three parts: I review the dialectical structure of the novel, connecting it with Kristeva's major claims about Teresa's spirituality; I challenge Kristeva's conclusions by exposing features of modernism that problematically underlie her claims; finally, I suggest an alternative reading of Teresa's faith grounded in Kristeva's commentary on the figure of the stranger.

Between secularism and fundamentalism: Teresa's third way

Kristeva's quest to understand and describe Teresa's spirituality entails an extended narrative set between two short sections that function as the novel's bookends. A letter at the conclusion of *Teresa, My Love* written to Denis Diderot by the novel's protagonist, psychoanalyst Sylvia LeClercq, serves as one bookend. Diderot is the author of *The Nun*, an eighteenth-century novel about Marie Suzanne Simonin, a young woman who is forced into a convent. Sexually abused and tortured by its prioress, the nun dies at age twenty-eight, her mind still unhinged by what she has experienced (TML 569, 571). Completed in 1780 but not published until after Diderot's death in 1796, *The Nun* is an early exercise in a disenchanted secularism, according to Sylvia (TML 575–6).

The other bookend, at the beginning of *Teresa, My Love*, features Sylvia's encounter with a young Muslim woman. In the midst of sharing initial reflections on Teresa, Sylvia suddenly is distracted by a Muslim hejab. As Sylvia describes attending a meeting of a committee tasked with examining the place of religion in France's secular institutions, she recalls an IT engineer who also was at the meeting. Wearing a 'head scarf', this woman raised her voice to proclaim herself a 'serious person' who always shielded her body from the 'lust of men' by wearing the hejab. So adamant was this Muslim woman in proclaiming that 'she and her God were *one*' and that the hejab 'was a sign of their "union"' that Sylvia sensed the woman was prepared to defend her faith to the point of sacrifice 'like those female suicide bombers on the other side of the world, and soon, perhaps, in our own suburbs' (TML 8).

As analysed by Sylvia, both Diderot and the Muslim engineer display a problematic relationship to modernity. Diderot, in the throes of secular disillusionment with Christianity, no more succeeds in evading the religion he would despatch than the religious fanatic succeeds in embracing it, for both are infected by a 'toxic nihilism' that is a key consequence of the Enlightenment (TML 271). Kristeva's in-depth discussion of nihilism in a 2016 interview insightfully augments Sylvia's claims. Kristeva argues that the 'absence of a theological dimension' in human life is a key consequence of the Enlightenment. People influenced by secularization attest to this lack when they are unable to acknowledge and value 'inner experience'; religious fundamentalists display their attenuated interior lives in the 'toughening of communal identities' (Mock 2016: 79).[2] Both groups reject the impulse that founds the human capacity to create meaning: the 'need to believe' (Mock 2016: 81). With a shared nihilism presumably afflicting the Muslim engineer and the sceptic Diderot, their differences dissolve into each other, revealing the bankruptcy of modernity, that child of the Enlightenment.

Diderot eventually sheds tears for his young nun, which Sylvia takes as evidence of the limits of his caustic narrative. Dismissive of what Kristeva has called 'the incredible need to believe', Diderot has wanted not only to condemn the hypocrisy of a church that functions as an abusive institution but also to expose the bankruptcy of desire in all forms (TML 569). But the religion Diderot would extirpate remains impervious to the weapons he deploys. Diderot does not weep out of empathy for a young woman victimized by a degenerate church; rather, Sylvia suggests, he weeps in sympathy for her passions. Withstanding the corrosive power of his narrative, these passions confront Diderot with this truth: 'The need to believe is inoperable of desire' (TML 575).

The 'scandal' (TML 501) of *The Nun* is not its narrative, lewd for its day. Rather, Kristeva's use of the term brings to mind René Girard's commentary on the Greek *skandalon,* a stumbling block (Swartley 2000: 310). The *skandalon* designates an obstacle, but not one to be successfully avoided after an initial stumble. Rather, the scandal is impossible to avoid. Diderot stands fascinated before his nun: The more repelled he is, the more attracted he is to her; and, the more he finds himself attracted, the more he is repelled. Girard highlights the etymological origins of the Greek *skandalizein*, which means 'to limp' (Girard 2001: 16). Kristeva shows that, colliding repeatedly with his desire, Diderot is hobbled by Marie.

Sylvia includes in her letter to Diderot a statement by Saint Augustine on the nature of God that serves to confirm Diderot's capture by the scandal of desire. For Augustine, God is one 'through whom we discern that certain things we had deemed essential to ourselves are truly foreign to us, while those we had deemed foreign to us are essential' (TML 571). Sylvia suggests that this foreignness, previously assigned to God or the devil, is located within the human, especially in our embodied being (TML 571). Sylvia writes that she understands why, living two centuries after Teresa's death and on the cusp of a revolution, Diderot was determined to 'blow up an ontotheological continent'. Yet his eyes, swimming with tears before a nun whose desire he confronts, attest to an ongoing history of the body to which Diderot testifies without knowing. Pulling open 'sacred drawers of faith', he can see only trash not treasure (TML 578). What distorts Diderot's gaze? Reminding him that she too is an atheist, Sylvia suggests that Diderot would stand as helpless before her nun – Teresa – as before his own nun because he lacks something that is indispensable to acknowledging the cruelties and raptures of the believing body. She exhorts Diderot to make his 'object of incredulity – God – an object of interpretation' (TML 582). If he could, he would not 'abrogate' the mystical experience of the sacred – 'the castle of the soul' – in his campaign to take down God (TML 582).

Between its bookends, the novel features Sylvia's exploration of Teresa's rapturous mysticism, which Kristeva presents dialectically as an alternative to a fanaticism that distorts religion and a secularism that dismisses it. With the character Andrew, an American writer obsessed with threats of terrorism, Kristeva continues to highlight religious fanaticism and contrast it with Teresa's faith. Speaking regularly of Islamic fundamentalism, Andrew attests also to fear of that foreign other. Kristeva relies on Sylvia's psychotherapist colleagues to express religious scepticism. Acknowledging every form of desire *but* the spiritual, Sylvia's colleagues resist Sylvia's sympathetic portrait of Teresa. Set in relief by its contrast to fanaticism and scepticism represented by Andrew and Sylvia's colleagues and supported by the novel's bookends, Teresa's third way is shown by Kristeva not to eschew a bodily desire for the sacred as have Diderot and the young Muslim engineer, he by exposing a dissolute religion and she by believing that carnality separates the human from God. Rather, embracing a new *corpus mysticum*, Teresa makes the body the vehicle by which spiritual life makes itself known (TML 49).

Sylvia uses terms found in Kristeva's non-fiction – *metaphor* and *metamorphosis* – to describe Teresa's third way. Teresa's writings are replete with metaphors – water, a butterfly, a diamond. As understood by Kristeva, metaphors do not create meaning by substituting a complex or abstract idea for one rooted in everyday experience, thereby bridging the unfamiliar and familiar. Nor do metaphors function primarily to awaken us to new possibilities in habitual speech, enlivening the ordinary or hackneyed.[3] Instead, metaphors link by analogy sensation and idea, thereby shifting us to 'the tactile nature of the psyche-soma' (TML 98). Metaphors become metamorphoses when experiences inaccessible to judgement and signification are transformed through metaphor into perceptions that can be grasped. In this way, water plays a central role in Teresa's encounter with God: 'Water, says Teresa, is not *like* divine love; water is divine love, which is water' (TML 98). In a narrative describing four ways of watering a garden (the well, the waterwheel, the rain, the gardener), Teresa explores how she is touched by water/God. She is diluted into God even as God is diluted into her (TML 100). In *The Way of Perfection*, Teresa calls her Sisters to join her: '"Those of you, Sisters, who drink this water and you others, once the Lord brings you to drink, will enjoy it and understand how the true love of God – if it is strong, completely free of earthly things, and if it flies above them – is lord of all the elements and of the world"' (TML 100). With water, as with the other metaphors, Teresa experiences and shares a range of encounters with the divine.

Sylvia also describes Teresa's third way as 'singular'. Teresa's mysticism has 'maximal singularity', her spiritual quest has 'amazing unprecedented singularity', her amorous encounter with her Spouse has a 'singular *jouissance*', and her partaking of the host in the Eucharist offers her 'the most intimate and singular of certainties' (TML 35, 118, 306, 182). 'Singularity' has a significant history in Kristeva's works, which Kelly Oliver helpfully distils (2004). 'Singularity' is not another word for the 'individuality' of a self-determined person who demonstrates autonomous action. Oliver points out that, for Kristeva, the individual stakes out a defensive position and may treat others as threat. By contrast, one who assumes a singular stance is attuned to the deep relationality of being. So also does the singular place limits on the universal. The social context in which we live, prescribing social codes, does function as a source of shared meaning; nevertheless, it is alienating. Embracing singularity, we can at last experience the social as fluid and expansive, facilitating our relationships with others (Oliver 2004: 173–5). Thus, 'singularity' names a robust psychic space in which the human participates in an ongoing process of relational being, constrained neither by the 'individual' nor by the 'universal'. Kristeva explains singularity with reference to music. Dissonant keys and counterpoint are essential to the very existence of music (HA xx–xxi). Likewise, a dissonant 'singularity' points to how humans' unconscious experiences (desires, pleasures, anxieties, traumas) function as tonalities within their lives that neither stand alone (the individual) nor fall under the control of the social context (the universal).

Although singularity is a feature of language, referents of singularity, like music, rest not with signification but with psyche-soma (sound, gesture, rhythm). Advanced practitioners of the singular, saints such as Bernard de Clairvaux (and Teresa), become open to the 'singularity of the Divine', the most intimate reality of Being (PT 209–10). 'Intimacy', supported by metaphor and protected by singularity, is definitive of mystical experience.

For this reason, no closed door bars Teresa from 'access to the Master lodged in the innermost chamber of intimacy' (TML 63). Pointing to an open and dynamic spiritual life, 'metaphor', 'singularity' and 'intimacy' neither discount Teresa's faithful desire via the reductive secularism of psychiatric diagnoses nor tarnish it by categorizing it as religious fanaticism. Rather, these terms support Sylvia's claim that Teresa, through a 'scandalous appropriation of the divine', becomes God's spouse. Likening Teresa to a 'polymorphous creature, indissociable from God Himself' (TML 63), Sylvia describes Teresa as 'playful' in her desire (TML 27, 159, 445).

Notwithstanding Kristeva's compelling treatment of Teresa, she undercuts her efforts to expose as flawed the twin currents of scepticism and fanaticism and commend to her readers Teresa's third way. Teresa does walk a singular spiritual path through early modern Roman Catholicism; however, Kristeva remains at an impasse. 'Bookended', as it were, by the very fanaticism and scepticism she has attempted to surpass, Kristeva is caught in modernism's vice-like grip. Prime evidence is Kristeva's discussion of the devout Muslim woman at Sylvia's committee meeting. Emblematic for Kristeva of the apocalyptic feminine, Kristeva treats this woman as a rigid trope, a theoretical if not literary device, before whom Sylvia stakes out a defensive position. Perceived as a potential threat, not only is this religiously observant woman made by Kristeva to bear the features of the 'individual' but also, in the absence of any acknowledgement of diversity among Muslims, she is cast as the Muslim 'universal'. As a consequence, she is disallowed access to the singularity Kristeva celebrates in Teresa.[4] Most strikingly, Kristeva does not have Sylvia extend to the Muslim woman the protection Teresa is afforded when Sylvia defends her against psychologists' dismissive criticisms. On the contrary, Sylvia treats her faith claims as symptoms of a troubled young woman: A desperate need underlies the Muslim woman's profession of faith which is 'immediately obvious to the rest of us, especially the psychologists' (TML 8). These comments put Sylvia's modernist presumptions on full display: The Muslim woman is the 'other', an individual whose capacity for singularity in her spiritual life is compromised by psychological issues that preclude her from developing a complex interior psychic life supportive of critical, agential thought that is required for vibrant faith.

Confirming that no distance separates Kristeva from Sylvia on this point are Kristeva's comments on Islam in the 2016 interview. Kristeva highlights a 'structural continuity' between Judaism and Christianity that supports the 'interior dimension' of faith which, in *Teresa, My Love*, Teresa displays with such singular power.[5] Acknowledging that Islam is considered the third member of this family of monotheistic faiths, Kristeva nevertheless expresses doubts about that designation: 'One can even wonder – and some theologians do – whether Allah is a true heir of Yahweh or Jesus' (Mock 2016: 82). Kristeva describes Allah as akin to Aristotle's 'unmoved mover', and she bemoans that Muslim practice asks the believer to 'submit to a text' in ways that preclude the believer from interpreting that text or rebelling against it (Mock 2016: 83). The 'psychological complexity' of Judaism and Christianity, which establishes the capacity for a self-reflexive and questioning faith, 'might be muted or perhaps even closed off in fundamentalist Islam' (Mock 2016: 83). Not only does Kristeva separate Judaism and Christianity as kin within the Abrahamic family of faiths from the foreign outsider, Islam, but also, in ascribing positive characteristics to Judaism and Christianity (i.e. life-supporting, psychologically complex, critical, and questioning) and negative features to Islam (nihilistic, psychologically stunted, uncritical, and unquestioning) she comes perilously close to delineating true from false faith. Recognizing an intimate relationship between humans and Allah only in Sufi mysticism, Kristeva all but identifies Islam with the fundamentalist Islam she decries (TML 37–40). Elsewhere, Kristeva takes that step, declaring that 'Islam has become stuck in the fundamentalist mire' (PT 258).[6]

As Diderot took on Christianity, Kristeva takes on Islam. Kristeva has suggested that Diderot, who Peter Gay explicitly names a 'proto-modernist' (Gay 2007: 5), was confounded by unexamined presumptions about the Christianity he sought to challenge. But Kristeva does not see how her cursory treatment of Islam aligns her with Diderot. Drawing on a distorted, tendentious, and largely unfounded view of Islam, Kristeva seemingly would bar observant Muslim women from joining their Christian and Jewish sisters in the family of monotheistic faiths. Having fallen prey with her discussion of the Muslim woman engineer to modernist tendencies she has noted and criticized in Diderot, Kristeva has closed off access by Muslim women to a third way, beyond fanaticism or scepticism. She cannot imagine they can walk a path to singular faith as did Teresa. But more compelling evidence exists to confirm how powerfully modernism confounds Kristeva and, perhaps also, the readers of her novel. Turning from an intrareligious rather than interreligious perspective, I reflect on a debate about true and false mysticism within nineteenth-century Christianity in order to shed more light on Kristeva, modernism, and the limits of her achievement in *Teresa, My Love*.

Foundering in false mysticism

Kristeva's problematic relation to modernism comes more clearly into view when *Teresa, My Love* is compared with *The Nuns of Sant'Ambrogio* (Wolf 2016). Written by a leading German historian of Roman Catholic Christianity, Hubert Wolf, and heralded as 'the true story of a convent in scandal', this book examines a late nineteenth-century incident at the convent of Sant'Ambrogio della Massima in Rome at the time of the modernist controversy in Roman Catholicism.[7] Both Kristeva's *Teresa, My Love* and *The Nuns of Sant'Ambrogio* are hefty tomes (630 and 476 pages) published in English in 2015. Both book jackets make a like promise to its readers: Kristeva's is a page-turner; Wolf's is a thriller. Reading Kristeva and Wolf's books back-to-back, not only are we struck by the similarities in the biographies of Teresa and Maria Luisa, the convent mistress at Sant'Ambrogio, but also, and most important, by the centuries-spanning force of scandal. As the protagonists of *Teresa, My Love* and *The Nuns of Sant'Ambrogio* mirror each other, we see how close Kristeva and we have come to being stranded on the shoals of modernism.

Maria Luisa and Teresa are strikingly similar. Both were described by those who knew them as confident, beautiful, and charming women. Both were beset by spiritual ailments: seizures, paralysis, and debilitating headaches. They had visions and experienced ecstatic communion with Jesus (Teresa) or the Virgin Mary (Maria Luisa). Teresa levitated (TML 70, 83, 444). Maria Luisa received miraculous gifts of rings from God (Wolf 2016: 130–1) and letters from the Virgin Mary (Wolf 2016: 136–7), all appearing in a locked box for which Maria Luisa did not hold the key. Both women were subject to suspicions raised about their blatantly erotic spirituality, questionable relationships with their confessors, and rough treatment of young women under their oversight. And, most significant, both women were examined by the Inquisition for false mysticism. Yet in the wake of scandal, as a succession of learned confessors to these women found themselves alternately fascinated by their deep spirituality and suspicious of its heretical, even demonic roots, only Teresa survived to become a saint and one of four female 'doctors of the church' (Eire 2019: 218). Maria Luisa was condemned by the Inquisition and declared a 'false saint'.

Records of the Inquisition Wolf uncovered preserve in detail salacious charges against Maria Luisa. She was accused of engaging in lesbian initiation rites with novices in the convent and of an affair with her confessor Giuseppe Peters (Wolf 2016: 159–60, 301–3). Suspicion fell also on the Marian mysteries of which she was the privileged recipient: the mystical rings were determined to have been purchased locally, and one of the novices penned the letters that Maria Luisa had claimed were written by the Virgin Mary (Wolf 2016: 133–5, 147–9). Moreover, when Princess Katharina von Hohenzollern-Sigmaringen, a devout German aristocrat, appeared at the convent, bringing a jaundiced eye to life there, suspicions escalated into outrage, especially after the princess left the convent, describing her departure as an escape from attempted poisoning by Maria Luisa (Wolf 2016: 35–40). Dismissed as mentally unstable on first report, the Princess eventually got a hearing, resulting in Maria Luisa's trial by the Inquisition.

Secularized readers of Wolf's book may see an open-and-shut case. Surely, in the late nineteenth century, no one could have been taken in by Maria Luisa. Surely they would not have needed terms from a twenty-first-century vocabulary – sociopath, embezzler, sexual predator and pathological liar – to find her guilty of a fraudulent presentation of faith (Wolf 2016: 29, 69–70). But Wolf's commentary does not support facile analysis. Reporting on the physical expression of spirituality among the women of Sant'Ambrogio, he does not categorize it as sexual abuse. He does not label the learned Jesuit confessors dupes, taken in by the wiles of a duplicitous woman. Instead, aligning Maria Luisa's spiritual gifts and that of the young nuns who venerated her with a long history of Christian mystics, including Teresa of Avila and Catherine of Sienna, Wolf stays faithful to his documents which demonstrate that the nuns of Sant'Ambrogio, including its mistress, were not outliers. Indeed, they were the second generation of this order to be led by a woman whose miraculous powers led to an investigation. Early in the nineteenth century Maria Agnese Firrao also was charged with false holiness; however, her conviction was insufficiently confirmed by church leaders, resulting in a consistent and fairly widespread belief that she had been vindicated. None other than Pope Leo XII was convinced of her spiritual authenticity and miracles associated with her convent. He actively promoted her order (Wolf 2016: 98–102).

Late in the nineteenth century, as suspicion fell on the order once again, belief in miracles persisted among the second generation's nuns and their learned superiors. Although Karl von Reisach, the cardinal who advocated for Princess Katherina when she claimed she was poisoned, condemned Maria Luisa on that count, he was not suspicious of miracles, for he believed in them. Maria Luisa's Jesuit confessors, Giuseppe Leziroli and Giuseppe Peters, resolutely affirmed her holiness, to which her miracles attested, and actively promoted her veneration. They were, after all, men of their time, and Maria Luisa's special relationship with the Virgin Mary coincided with the Marian cult of the late 1800s (Wolf 2016: 346), which was marked by over a hundred appearances of the Virgin Mary and, in 1854, by Pope Pius IX's papal bull instituting the doctrine of the Immaculate Conception (Wolf 2016: 142–4).

For mystics in every generation, acts of miraculous holiness did not garner uncritical acceptance. If a woman such as Teresa or Maria Luisa fell under suspicion, the Inquisition engaged in careful and rigorous review in order to validate the authenticity of their gifts. So validated, their gifts were welcomed by the church. During Maria Luisa's trial, when confessor Peters emphatically defended her holiness, the spiritual and blessed nature of their physical intimacies, the divine hand of God in the convent poisonings, and Maria Luisa's 'special gifts' (i.e. her relationship with the Virgin Mary), his claims would not have been summarily dismissed with eye-rolling and whispers. The trial transcripts reported by Wolf show that the men trying Peters did not see him as a calculating manipulator of Maria Luisa or as her naïve dupe. Instead, they found him guilty because he had erred in his judgement. He had been wrong to put his faith in Maria Luisa's holiness, not because miraculous gifts are not real but because Maria Luisa, in her specific and particular personhood, was shown not to have received these gifts. He was punished for misjudging her, exiled from Rome and forbidden to exercise spiritual leadership.

As for Maria Luisa, she too was punished when the Inquisition determined that she was not the person those who had witnessed her spiritual gifts had believed her to be. Wolf again remains faithful to his documents when reporting on Maria Luisa's descent into mental illness after the trial and conviction. Rather than engage in armchair psychoanalysis that would discount her spiritual life in its entirety, he cites without editorializing records of her post-conviction hospitalization and eventual disappearance. Whereas her confessor Peters was rehabilitated a few years after the scandal and became a leading voice in the papacy, Maria Luisa was last seen wandering the streets of Rome homeless (Wolf 2016: 348–9).[8]

For scandal not to prove a stumbling block to a scholarly assessment of Wolf's book, comparisons of Teresa to Maria Luisa must be drawn. Was Maria Luisa, like Teresa, a mystic of strong faith unjustly accused by her political opponents? Was she a duplicitous sociopath? How close and how far is she from Teresa? If, attempting to answer these questions, we find ourselves fascinated by what repels us and repelled by what fascinates us, we may find that we have been stranded on the shoals of modernism. We may struggle to navigate between a fanaticism we would deny and a scepticism we would embrace as we try to determine the truth of Sant'Ambrogio and its convent mistress. Although we may want to label Maria Luisa a 'foreigner' and outlier to Christian faith, Wolf's account suggests that if we do so, we may force Teresa out with her. And, if we claim Teresa as our own, as Kristeva would want us to do, we may have to claim Maria Luisa as well. The Enlightenment promised clean calls on matters of faith. Miracles such as levitation and visitations from the Virgin Mary were supernatural phenomena that modernism was supposed to expose and put out of play. The challenges the Inquisition faced in the sixteenth century in determining whether Teresa was a false mystic should not still have been faced by the Inquisition that examined Maria Luisa on the cusp of the twentieth century. And yet that happened. Wolf has shown that modernist scepticism did not take Maria Luisa down; rather, persons who believed in miracles found her wanting as a mystic and cast her out.

Recent studies of the miracle of levitation in the early modern era, one of Teresa's gifts, can help put some distance between ourselves and the persistent and problematic lure of modernism. Galileo, Descartes and Leibniz, who are among those who set us on the path to Enlightenment, left records of their scientific accomplishments for us to examine. But we also can examine from that same era detailed flight records of levitating saints and flying witches (Eire 2009: 321). Although Protestants and Catholics divvied up the turf of miracle differently, categories of the natural, supernatural and preternatural they shared enabled Protestants and Catholics alike to sort the spiritual gifts of those who flew, delineating the faithful from the demonic (Eire 2009: 323). The persistence of magic simultaneously with the development of empirical sciences shows that the Enlightenment did not put us on a glide path to disenchantment, as Weber claimed (Eire 2009: 322). As Teresa and Maria Luisa's stories likewise confirm, humans have retained an incredible need to believe that does not balk at miracles. There were and are no clean and easy calls on false and authentic faith. Christianity in the past and now contains within it its own strangeness. We can explore how the faithful account for that strangeness, making space for faith and setting up as well a monitoring capacity interior to the faith. But, contrary to what modernism promised, we cannot stand above the fray of belief, there to adjudicate the truth or falsehood of beliefs or calibrate them so as to uphold moderation and bound off fanaticism. The underlying strangeness of our incredible need to believe cannot be outrun, whether we stand within a religious tradition or assume a position outside where we can make comparisons among religious traditions.

We are all strangers

At the end of *Teresa, My love*, Sylvia commends to Diderot Saint Augustine's remarks about God, suggesting that the way out of the scandal of desire in which Diderot is caught may be found in claiming foreignness, not as a feature of God or the devil but of human nature itself specifically in places where 'flesh overlaps with word' (TML 571). Sylvia's advice is reminiscent of Kristeva's discussion of foreigners in *Strangers to Ourselves*. Attending to this text, we can reframe the modernist impasse at which we have arrived, along with Kristeva, for we have more options than our modernist inclinations suggest. We need not trace 'the other', before whom we stumble, to the nun we dismiss as a crazy woman from Sant'Ambrogio. Nor are we obliged to find 'the other' in the foreigner, exemplified in Kristeva's novel by the female, Muslim engineer who wears the hejab and summons suspicion. Instead, we can discover the other closer to home: The other is 'the stranger that is myself'.

Sketching an ethics of strangeness, Kristeva challenges modernism's approach to truth. Analysis shows that the truth of the stranger is entertained by a human subject in process. That in me which seeks the truth returns me to that from which I have become estranged: the negativity of my own life-process. Writes Kristeva:

> My discontent in living with the other – my strangeness, his strangeness – rests on the perturbed logic that governs this strange bundle of drive and

language, of nature and symbol, constituted by the unconscious, always already shaped by the other. It is through unraveling transference… that, on the basis of the other, I become reconciled with my own otherness-foreignness, that I play on it and live by it.

(SO 181–2)

The human subject, formed in the wake of what Kristeva calls a thetic break, is always in process, always bounded by exclusions, always absent from the place where it would be, always found only in a place where it is not. The subject's labour is never final, never reaches its goal. Instead of perceiving the subject to be in possession of truth proffered by modernism – the tidy outcome of a life shaped by fanaticism or scepticism – analysis invites the subject to entertain a strangeness before the truth.

Kristeva aligns strangeness with the uncanny, the *unheimlich*. The uncanny attests to aspects of our being that we have bounded off as alien and proper to another: the stranger. According to Kristeva, the uncanny marks primary repression and is proper to the constituting work of the proto-subject in infancy. Later, as a subject in the world, when confronting the strange uncanny, the subject feels dread. Dread is always a border phenomenon. As a consequence, we do not only experience strangeness when we project alterity on to the other who we objectify on behalf of resecuring our own subject status. More radically, if we feel our very existence is under threat, we revisit the uncanny with bodily memories of our vulnerable existence as protosubjects new to the world of childhood (SO 184). On whatever terms we encounter the uncanny, we can dwell in its catastrophic effects, suppress its symptoms and eliminate its strangeness by attaching it to scapegoats. Or we can articulate its strangeness in order that we no longer feel compelled to throttle difference but can live with it. Kristeva states that only if we learn to detect strangeness in ourselves will we obtain the courage not to see it everywhere but in ourselves (SO 192).

Kristeva, the author of *Teresa, My Love*, would agree with Kristeva, the author of *Strangers to Ourselves*, on this: the stranger is not a truth to be known and placed outside myself, but is a symptom of my desire. Yet differences in their views abound. The word 'uncanny' appears only once in *Teresa, My Love* (TML 445). Kristeva, the author of *Strangers to Ourselves*, would remind the novel's author that she once called on us to find the 'courage to call ourselves disintegrated in order not to integrate foreigners and even less so to hunt them down, but rather to welcome them to that uncanny strangeness, which is as much theirs as it is ours' (SO 192). That advice could have a salient impact on Sylvia, who, in *Teresa, My Love*, possesses expert knowledge, enabling her to expose and dismantle the faith claims of the young Muslim engineer. By contrast, in *Strangers to Ourselves*, Kristeva removes the psychoanalyst from the seat of authority. No one occupies that space; instead, analyst and analysand circle unrepresentable alterity, elaborating on risks they encounter in ways that suggest reciprocal promise rather than threat (SO 182–3, 189). As Kristeva affirms elsewhere, the analyst's task is 'to record the *crisis* of modern interpretive systems without smoothing it over, to affirm that this crisis is inherent in the symbolic function itself and to perceive as symptoms all constructions, including totalizing interpretation, which try to deny this crisis; to dissolve, to displace indefinitely, in Kafka's words, "temporarily and for a lifetime"' (KR 319; emphasis in the original).

An ethics of strangeness, revolving around the capacity of the human to be posited by and assume a position in relation to others, requires embodiment. The ethos of this ethics attends our habituation to others, the practices of self-formation that we take up in light of others, as Kristeva acknowledges in her reflections on singularity. But our ethics is always lived in the in-between. The scandal of human existence is this: we are caught between need and desire, bound and unbounded materiality, other and self. That which makes us human and provides the occasion for ethics is an alterity that we never assimilate. It is an other that is always other in the same. In her love story for Teresa, Kristeva has highlighted the sanctity of the interior castle in which Teresa dwells with her beloved; however, she has forgotten that which lurks in the shadows of that home: the *unheimlich*. Uncanny strangeness 'sets the difference within us in its most bewildering shape and presents it as the ultimate condition of our being *with* others' (SO 192). Only as we embrace this strangeness can we meet others on the borders of being, across the centuries that separate us, in psychoanalytic sessions, between and among our varied religious traditions, and at our national borders as well, not as oddities to be dismissed or as threats to be scapegoated but as fellow strangers with whom we journey.

Notes

1   Attuned to the forces that buffeted men of reason, figures such as Marx, Darwin, Freud and Nietzsche became the great distillers of modernism (Whitworth 2007: 22). As Kristeva affirms, 'All contemporary political thought which does not deal with technocratic administration… uses interpretation in Marx's and Freud's sense: as transformation and as cure' (KR 305). These figures also set the stage for an iteration of the modern that remains contested: no longer attesting directly to the death of God and the triumph of human reason, albeit a reason challenged by the vicissitudes of psychic life, modernism eventually came to identify a division within culture itself, ushering in the postmodern (Cascardi 1992: 128).

2   Kristeva is correct that fundamentalisms (all major world religions include variants of fundamentalism) are communally focused. As Martin Marty, the foremost authority on fundamentalisms and the director of the Fundamentalism Project at the University of Chicago, funded by the American Academy of Arts and Sciences, states, 'While private individuals adhere to

one or another of the fundamentalisms, it is in the communal or collective form that they are acquiring world-historical significance' (1988: 23). But Marty also cautions against subsuming a believer's individual concerns to the collective identity espoused by the species of fundamentalism to which that believer adheres: 'Fundamentalists are intelligent; their perceptions are often accurate, and they are not all paranoid. There really are drastic challenges and threats to what they hold dear; their faith, their families, their community life, their values and practices' (1988: 24). Most significant, Marty states that fundamentalisms emerge as alternatives to modernism, to 'satisfy emergent cultural needs' (1988: 17). Their adherents 'sense the disarray of secularists and humanists' and, in response, counter the 'failure of nerve' they associate with non-believers by questioning the Enlightenment rationalist tradition and decrying it as 'spiritually unsatisfying, not capable of motivating action' (1988: 24). Interdisciplinary scholarly inquiry, exemplified by The Fundamentalism Project, illuminates and furthers understanding of how fundamentalists respond to their adherents' unmet needs. See Marty (1988).

3   An example of the former instance would be 'the information highway of the internet'; an example of the latter would be 'a snowplow works an airport runway with a "yellow grimace"'. This example is from David Tucker, 'Snowbound', in *Late for Work* (Tucker 2006: 26).

4   Kristeva has not examined Islamic beliefs and practices with the attentiveness she has given to Christianity and, in recent years, to Judaism. Invisible to her as she writes about Sylvia's encounter with a devout Muslim woman are the likely details of this woman's faith: her rich prayer life; her immersion in the astounding aesthetics of sight and sound found in Islamic architecture, art, and music that forge within her a deep sensory connection to the sacred; her complex and nuanced attention to the practice of Islam in daily life guided by an interpretive tradition of law with powerful parallels to Jewish Halacha; and her increasing attunement to and maturation in relationship with Allah (Lapidus 1976). These features of faith counter stereotypes of Islam: mindless 'submission' to an unyielding God, an uncritical embrace of key tenets, and stunted emotional development.

5   Kristeva repeatedly aligns Teresa with both faiths, pointing out that Teresa's paternal grandfather was a forced convert (converso) from Judaism to Christianity and her father is therefore a converso (TML 139, 147, 239–40). For recent scholarly commentary on Teresa's Jewish heritage, see Eire 2019: 1–8.

6   In a lecture included in *Passions of our Time*, which covers the same ground as the 2016 interview, Kristeva says that determining whether Islam is a member of the monotheistic faiths is 'sensitive'. She suggests that 'specialists can deal with this at another meeting' (PT 256). Rather than draw on recent scholarly research to supplement her psychoanalytic readings of Freud, as Kristeva regularly does when writing about Christianity and Judaism, in offering her views on Islam, in this lecture Kristeva founds her psychoanalytic interpretation of Islam on Freud's statements about Islam, notwithstanding his paucity of knowledge (PT 257). Moreover, she asserts that 'it behooves anthropologists, sociologists, and psychoanalysts, with or without specialists of religion' to continue to study Islam (PT 258). With specialists in religion

treated as an optional rather than required resource for scholarly engagement with Islam, Kristeva cannot be surprised that hurdles stand between her and dialogue with Muslims about Islam. These barriers are easily removed: http://www.columbia.edu/cu/lweb/img/assets/5495/Islamic_Studies_bibliog.pdf.

7   Truly groundbreaking in Wolf's scholarship, and the focus of most interest among historians, is not his account of the erotic lives of nuns – a tired trope if ever there was one – but his investigation of high-stakes Vatican politics spanning the end of the nineteenth century and the beginning of the twentieth during which two wings of Catholicism, one progressive and the other traditional, vied for the ear of Pope Pius IX. The Maria Luisa story is a backstory to this larger struggle for control. 'Modernist' was the term assigned in Roman Catholic history to the progressive wing, a movement among biblical scholars and theologians to promote historical biblical scholarship and reflect systematically on the role of human experience and emotion in religious belief. They were at odds with proponents of New Scholasticism, who viewed the authority of scripture in a traditional way and prioritized reason, guided by God and the church, as the arbiter of all things faithful. In the story of the convent of Sant'Ambrogio, a key advocate for Princess Katerina, Gustav Hohenlohe-Schillingsfürst, was associated with the modernist movement (Wolf 2016: 337ff.); Giuseppe Peters, Maria Luisa's confessor, was a proponent of the New Scholasticism (Wolf 2016: 363ff.). But modernists in this period were not yet prepared to dispense with gifts of holiness, including miracles. The division between the two movements featured other disagreements, most centrally, the nature of papal authority. Interestingly, the terms 'modernism' and 'modernist' are not found in literary analysis until the 1920s and 1930s. Whitworth states that, although one may wish to ponder whether these terms' use in the Roman Catholic modernist controversy in the decades preceding inhibited their adoption in the humanities, evidence for this hypothesis is lacking (Whitworth 2007: 39).

8   Maria Luisa's trial began in December 1859 and concluded in February 1862. Wolf's book offers a close reading of trial transcripts which rested unnoticed in the Vatican Archives until 1998, when Pope John Paul II opened the archives for researchers (Wolf 2016: 76). Highly respected among his colleagues before the publication of *The Nuns of Sant'Ambrogio*, Wolf's standing as an historian has, if anything, grown since the publication of this book. His careful and dispassionate reporting on the trial transcripts brought to light a key moment in Roman Catholic history and, however belatedly, held Giuseppe Peters accountable for complicity in murder. As Maria Luisa's confessor, Peters had known of her poisoning plans and did not stop or report her (Wolf 2016: 307). He claimed to have believed her when she attributed questionable deaths in the convent to divine intervention. He was sentenced to prison; however, he was recalled to Rome after two years, where, fully rehabilitated and, with a new name, Joseph Kleutgen, he became a towering figure in late nineteenth- and early twentieth-century Roman Catholic theology. He exerted a strong influence on the papacy of Pope Pius IX. He drafted the crowning document of the First Vatican Council in 1870 – the doctrine of papal infallibility – and became an esteemed scholar of the New Testament (Wolf 2016: 362).

References

Cascardi, A. J. (1992), *The Subject of Modernity*, New York: Cambridge University Press.
Eire, C. (2019), *The Life of Saint Teresa of Avila: A Biography*, Princeton, NJ: Princeton University Press.
Eire, C. M. N. (2009), 'The Good, the Bad, and the Airborne: Levitation and the History of the Impossible in Early Modern Europe', in Marjorie Elizabeth Plummer (ed.), *Ideas and Cultural Margins in Early Modern Germany: Essays in Honor of H.C. Erik Midelfort*, 307–23, New York: Routledge.
Gay, P. (2007), *Modernism: The Lure of Heresy*, New York: W. W. Norton.
Girard, R. (2001), *I See Satan Fall like Lightning*, trans. J. G. Williams, Maryknoll, NY: Orbis Books.
Lapidus, I. M. (1976), 'Adulthood in Islam: Religious Maturity in the Islamic Tradition', *Daedalus*, 105 (2): 93–108.
Marty, M. E. (1988), 'Fundamentalism as a Social Phenomenon', *Bulletin of the American Academy of Arts and Sciences*, 42 (2): 15–29.
Mock, K. (2016), 'The Need to Believe and the Archive: Interview with Julia Kristeva', *Dibur Literary Journal*, 3 (autumn): 77–94.
Oliver, K. (2004), *The Colonization of Psychic Space: A Psychoanalytic Social Theory of Oppression*, Minneapolis, MN: University of Minnesota Press.
Swartley, W., ed. (2000), 'Response by René Girard', in *Violence Renounced*, 308–20, Telford, PA: Pandora Press.
Tucker, D. (2006), 'Snowbound', in *Late for Work*, 26, New York: Mariner Books.
Whitworth, M. H., ed. (2007), *Modernism*, Malden, MA: Wiley-Blackwell.
Wolf, H. (2016), *The Nuns of Sant'Ambrogio: The True Story of a Convent in Scandal*, trans. R. Martin, New York: Vintage.

6

Kristeva's traumatic real: Securing the symbolic nation through the law of the veil

Tina Chanter

What constituencies or communities are assembled under the sign of Kristeva readers, and how do these communities constitute themselves? How contingent or necessary are the borders that define such communities? How stable or unstable are these borders, how solid or permanent, how fragile or permeable? What are the possibilities of challenging and reconfiguring those borders, and the possibilities of such challenges opening up transformative moments for subjects, communities and foundational discourses? What might it mean to do justice to Kristeva's work? Would it be to read her work alongside, with and against, a diverse body of work, which might entail reading her against herself in some ways? Might it require reading her alongside texts which do not align with her own texts in order to make something new of them?

The sheer scope and proliferation of Kristeva's work is awe-inspiring, eliciting my continuing admiration and respect, not least for her dexterity in weaving into her work diverse influences from linguistics, literature, psychoanalysis, art and philosophy, and for the psychic acumen her work can display. On the other hand, certain political aspects of her work inspire in me a good deal of unease, discomfort and disenchantment, and in some instances, strong disagreement. It is out of the tension produced by these conflicting impulses that the current chapter is produced.

Kristeva's corpus has facilitated thinking about how boundaries function, how permeable or impermeable they might be, how pure or impure the regions they ostensibly separate might be, how much and in what ways these regions might be contaminated by their supposed antitheses, and how the breaking down of form, or formlessness, can precede the configuration of new forms. Her work has shed light on the ways in which metaphor and metonymy play into and traverse signification. Kristeva's investigation of semiotic *chora*, of affective investment in an economy of drives, describes a process of sensible and corporeal conditioning that helps to shape objects and subjects, and as such feeds into and constitutes subjectivities and communities. In understanding meaning not purely as a function of the symbolic but as a result of the intertwining of the symbolic with the semiotic, Kristeva moves beyond construing meaning merely as a symbolic function of the law, enjoined by prohibition.

As is well known, rather than assume, along with classic phenomenology, a transcendental ego as the origin of meaning, Kristeva's emphasis on the material, affective, semiotic conditioning of signification, which builds on Freud's understanding of condensation and displacement in dreamwork, provides a conception of subjects that are continually undergoing production. The propositional, syntactic, referential, symbolic meanings that produce subjects are therefore beset with fluctuating investments in sites of pleasure or displeasure, regulated by a maternal archaic ordering and orchestrated by functions such as expulsion, rejection and projection. Such investments do not so much precede the referential meaning that Saussurean analysis conceives in terms of signifier and signified, as both enable it, and create sites of resistance, revolutions of meaning and displacements within the free play of signifiers.

The question, then, is not so much how discrete subjects produce discrete meanings but rather how subjects situate themselves in and are made possible by the wider networks of investment and meaningful contexts they inhabit, contexts that facilitate and exceed them in ways that are not entirely circumscribed by any rational account. As Stacy Keltner puts it, 'semiotic conditions produce and yet remain foreign to meaning and the subject' (2011: 27). Subjects can and do intervene in systems of meaning in order to influence what can count as meaningful, disrupting and redirecting habitual paths of meaning, even as they are acculturated in and by semiotic textures, flows, tonalities, rhythms and so on, which play into and condition the meanings they produce, symbolic meanings which in turn condition the semiotic.

Jacqueline Rose, in an early assessment of Kristeva's work, suggests that we should not 'be surprised' that Kristeva falls 'at various points throughout her work, into one or other side of the psychic dynamic which she herself describes', either by 'rac[ing] back into the arms of the law' (1986: 151), or by placing 'the mother at the source and fading-point of all subjectivity and language – a point which, as Kristeva herself has argued, threatens the subject with collapse' (1986: 155–6). Neither, perhaps, should we be surprised, despite Kristeva's stringent advocacy of continuing to think through the impact and meaning of images, to 'revive the development of thinking' (SH 104) – a task that becomes all the more urgent as we are continually bombarded with a proliferation of images in a digitized culture – that the foundational fantasies that govern Eurocentric provincialism too often fuel her own reflections in ways that suggest there are aspects of this culture that Kristeva herself leaves unthought.

In the face of this, what would it mean to point to a 'discursive retrieval' analogous to the one Hortense Spillers calls for when, quoting Fred Moten, she suggests that 'the subject of "social death" becomes… objects that "can and do resist"' (2018: 29)? If Spillers' concern is with '[h]ow one views black others' (2018: 26), a project she undertakes in part by rethinking the Lacanian idea that the 'unconscious is "structured like a language"' (2018: 28) in the context of the alternative paternal genealogies articulated by Richard Wright, James Baldwin and Ta-Nehesi Coates, my specific focus here is how to respond to a series of problematic equations Kristeva performs between the idea of femininity and castration, decapitation, masking and veiling (SH 106, 110, 116–17, 124). I proceed by taking up the question of art in relation to abjection. If art has, in one way or another, been a constant theme for Kristeva, since the publication of *Powers of Horror: An Essay on Abjection* in 1980 she has also revisited the question of abjection periodically, for instance in *Hatred and Forgiveness* ([2005] 2010) and in *The Severed Head* ([1998] 2012). The former text, while featuring an illuminating reprisal of some of the central themes of *Powers of Horror*, also includes some disturbing pronouncements on the subject of veiling, statements that I read together with Kristeva's consideration of the question of veiling in the context of her discussion of art in *The Sense and Non-Sense of Revolt* and *The Severed Head*. I do so in part in order to offer an alternative reading of Kristeva's own problematic conclusions regarding women and veiling.

Alison Jasper, who raises the question of Kristeva's 'orientalis[m]' (2014: 179), would not be the first to do so. Over the years, other critics of Kristeva have also raised the issue, although without making this their primary focus. Rather, earlier critiques problematized Kristeva's appeal to the semiotic maternal as a celebration of an allegedly prediscursive, natural, realm from which Kristeva claimed to retrieve a revolutionary potential, but whose subversive force could only ever be temporary and unsustainable. Kristeva has been taken to task for being too structuralist (Butler 1992: 163, 167; Fraser 1992: 180), and for being not structuralist enough (MacCannell 2003: 75); for being too Lacanian (Butler 1992: 173), and for not being Lacanian enough (MacCannell 2003: 75).[1] Critics who disagree over whether Kristeva strays too far from Lacanian orthodoxy or not can agree, however, that she is at fault for othering non-Western cultures. Judith Butler judges her as falling short when it comes to espousing a form of orientalism (Butler 1992: 172), while Juliet Flower MacCannell sees her as implicitly sympathizing with fascism while at the same time casting cultures such as India as less civilized than cultures that foreground monotheistic religions (MacCannell 2003: 87).

After reviewing Butler's and MacCannell's earlier critiques of Kristeva, I build on certain aspects of these critiques, but also rework other aspects of them. I do so by suggesting a parallel between Kristeva and Levinas, and by situating Kristeva's work within the context of work by Falguni Sheth, Sara Ahmed and Meyda Yeğeneğlu. Finally, I suggest a way in which Kristeva's own discussion of art might inform a more nuanced appreciation of the way in which wearing a veil can signify.

For Butler, by associating the poetic, rhythmic aspect of language with the child's pre-Oedipal, non-syntactic interactions with a maternal body, not only is Kristeva said to deprive the semiotic of any meaningful political challenge to the symbolic aspect of language from which she distinguishes it; Kristeva is also seen to reaffirm the normative authority of the symbolic law of the father that on the surface is interrogated by her return to the lost territory of the mother's body, thereby undermining any transgressive promise her emphasis of the semiotic might have heralded. Moreover, Kristeva is seen as naively endorsing an appeal to a biological conception of sex, as if it makes sense to maintain a conception of sexual difference as grounded in biology. Bringing into question any such appeal to biological sex as a natural phenomenon that somehow remains outside of history, and demystifying any causality or generativity Kristeva's maternal *chora* might have, Butler draws on Foucault's understanding of sex as one of several terms to have been grouped together and posited as a '"fictitious unity"' which was then invested with the meaning of a '"causal principle, an omnipresent meaning"'. Sex was '"thus able to function as a unique signifier and as a universal signified"' (1992: 174), when in fact it is merely a symptom of discourse.[2] While Kristeva's notion of the semiotic might have appeared to offer some kind of challenge to Lacan's symbolic order, in fact it merely reinvoked its authority. Thus, for Butler

> the discursive production of the maternal body as pre-discursive is a tactic in the self-amplification and concealment of those specific power relations by which the trope of the maternal body is produced... [A]ny theory that asserts that signification is predicated upon the denial or repression of a female principle ought to consider whether that femaleness is really external to the cultural norms by which it is repressed. In other words... the repression of the feminine does not require that the agency of repression and the object of repression be ontologically distinct. Indeed, repression may be understood to produce the object that it comes to deny.
> (1992: 174–5)

The focus of Butler's critique is Kristeva's 'view of the psychotic nature of homosexuality' which Butler attributes to her 'structuralist assumption that heterosexuality is coextensive with the founding of the symbolic' (1992: 167). In fact, suggests Butler, Kristeva's pathologizing view 'tells us more about the fantasies that a fearful heterosexual culture produces to defend against its own homosexual possibilities than about lesbian experience itself' (1992: 170). Along the way, Butler also criticizes the methodological duplicity, or incoherence of Kristeva's articulation of the relation of the semiotic to the symbolic, faulting her for her 'orientalism' (1992: 172). Butler says that the 'opposition between the semiotic and the symbolic' amounts to a

> metaphysical quarrel between the principle of multiplicity that escapes the charge of non-contradiction and a principle of identity based on the suppression of multiplicity. Oddly, that very principle of multiplicity that Kristeva everywhere defends operates in much the same way as a principle of identity. Note the way all manner of things 'primitive' and 'oriental' are summarily subordinated to the principle of the maternal body.
> (1992: 172)

If for Butler, Kristeva is, we might say, duplicitously, a methodological formalist, MacCannell also has concerns about what she sees as Kristeva's refusal to be open about her theoretical and political commitments, characterizing her as 'straddling' a 'borderline' between identifying with abjection and identifying 'with the Logos' (2003: 86).[3] MacCannell posits Kristeva as not structuralist enough. '[A]nxious to examine that which has been left out of the system – the feminine' (2003: 72), Kristeva, according to MacCannell, wages 'hopeless guerrilla warfare against what, ultimately, is for her an enormous, a monstrous, yet normative system that can neither be shaken down nor shaken up', namely, 'structures that repress, oppress, suppress' (2003: 71). These structures are informed by 'the normalising work of the Oedipal triangle (subject-object) relations' (2003: 72–3), a normalizing that remains in tension to certain states and conditions, such as that caused by the 'failure of complete separation [from the mother]... a condition she calls abjection' (2003: 72). Such a failure produces a 'tension... between the abject, fragmented subject in its relation to the Other' (2003: 73) and in relation to the normalizing Oedipal structures that McCannell thinks Kristeva inherits from Freud rather uncritically (see 2003: 74). Kristeva thus performs a kind of 'phenomenology' (2003: 73, 75) of 'a subject who has not achieved separation, ego identification, a subject for whom consciousness is not of an object, is not correlated with an object, but with an abject: this subject that is not an ego actually results from the inability to correlate the ego with an object' (2003: 73). In the normative, Freudian scenario, 'The ego forms a desire for the object *instead of* the mother' due to the 'Law of Father', which 'insists that desires continually take stand-ins, tokens or signs rather than the mother as their object, or means of satisfaction' (2003: 74). The 'fate of the subject for whom the Oedipal triangle fails to do its work of normalisation (ideal gender identification via the castration complex leading to heterosexual desire) and integration into the Symbolic order (via the rules of language)' (2003: 73) is to be a 'borderline' subject, one who 'has not achieved the separation of identity provided by access to the symbolic and imaginary forms of existence, ruled by paternity' (2003: 73). Rather than replacing the fantasy of the mother with other objects, rather than abiding by the incest taboo, informed by paternal law, the abject subject identifies directly with the Superego. 'To each ego its object, to each superego its abject', as Kristeva puts it in *Powers of Horror* (PH 2).

For MacCannell, Kristeva exhibits an ambivalence with regard to abjection, which holds a certain 'allure' for her, one that MacCannell finds 'chilling' (2003: 86) to the extent that she reads Kristeva's ambivalence as extending to her attitude with regard to fascism. If the mother plays the role of a 'double agent' (2003: 82), the same might be said for Kristeva herself on MacCannell's reading. The child must 'give up [the mother] in order to achieve civilisation' while the mother also 'first serves as direct agent of Symbolic order, forming the child's "clean and proper" sense of itself via sphincter training' (2003: 82). The mother thus comes to stand for that which must be relinquished, the forbidden object of repressed desire, while at the same time facilitating the child's entry into the symbolic order, governed by the paternal law. MacCannell characterizes Kristeva's theory itself as similarly Janus-headed. On the one hand she sees her as a 'linguistic supremacist' (2003: 79), who stands 'firmly with the Logos' (2003: 86), while on the other hand she performs a 'strategic identification with the borderline patient' (2003: 86), celebrating the subject who 'refuses the laws of the Name-of-the-Father' (2003: 86). On the one hand, she is '[o]vertly opposed to fascism' (2003: 86) but, on the other hand, in her discussion of abjection she 'restag[es]' the 'fascist fantasies' (2003: 87) of Céline, claiming to find 'cathartic' (2003: 87) value in doing so. For MacCannell, Kristeva thus wants it both ways. She '"sees" and "hears" the pain of repression' (2003: 86), yet she also essentially remains close to Freud. Like Butler, MacCannell is wary of how Kristeva positions and judges cultures that do not conform to a Western model of repression:

> She extends the anthropological marshalling of evidence for the universality of the pattern of cultural resistance to recognition of the mother by moving outside of the Judeo-Christian paradigmatic confrontation, into those 'foreign' cultures in which the maternal still seems to retain force. She speaks of the Indian case, in which the importance of the mother is so

overwhelming ... hers is still a universalized figural-historical scheme, in which Indian culture is exemplary of a civilisation that is not as advanced in its repressions as ours, based on Jewish monotheism, is.

(2003: 87)

Both Butler and MacCannell, then, while finding fault with Kristeva for different reasons, agree on the problematic orientalist overtones of her work. I endorse Butler's Foucauldian point that any othering of semiotic alterity – whether this is construed in terms of a feminized or homophobic register, or as I will develop, in a racialized register – takes place within an already symbolic field. At the same time, I argue that Kristeva's discussion of abjection introduces a more fundamental challenge, on which Butler's own work on abjection has capitalized, but the implications of which have not perhaps been fully played out in terms of a reading of Kristeva. That challenge is located precisely in Kristeva's insistence on thinking through the sense (and nonsense) of an affectivity or sensibility that resists the resolution into a subject-object relation, which MacCannell sees Kristeva as failing to achieve. Abjection can be thought as the instability that occurs, I suggest, both prior to any stable formation of the subject/object relation between infant and mother, and as the recurrent resurgence of trauma throughout adult experience, which can periodically erupt not merely in borderline subjects, but also for any subject exposed to profound trauma. Here I want to insist upon the significance of what readers of Kristeva have caught sight of under various headings – the 'unnameable' (De Nooy 2003: 121), the 'unspeakable' (Smith 2003: 133), the 'Beckettian not-I' (Ziarek 2003, 153). Kristeva is not the first theorist to have tried to find a way of figuring the unspeakable, the unthinkable, the unnameable, the abyssal – nor, no doubt, will she have been the last. I frame this insistence on the unrepresentable by aligning Kristeva's investigations of the torsions that play out in the wrenching indeterminacy of a (non) relationship between a not-yet-I or a not-yet-subject, and a not-yet-other or a not-yet-object, by reading it alongside Levinas' confrontation of the 'there is' (*il y a*), as the invasion of the night, as the irremissibility of anonymous existence.

MacCannell's tendency is to chide Kristeva for failing to provide a way for the subject to successfully develop a phenomenological subject/object relationship, and thereby failing to install itself properly in the sanctioned, heteronormative positions made available through the castration theory of classic psychoanalytic theory. Butler reads Kristeva as (problematically) precisely endorsing the heteronormativity of psychoanalysis. Yet as I see it, Kristeva's elaboration of an affectivity that does not conform to the strictures of the subject/object relation provides purchase for a potential reworking of the sedimented meanings of a symbolic system, even if Kristeva herself does not always develop this potential, by falling back into endorsing patriarchal, heteronormative or racist fantasies of wholeness, where some individuals are pressed into service primarily as objects, while others operate primarily as subjects. It is here that I think a parallel with Levinas' reflections on the 'there is' (*il y a*) is productive. For both Kristeva and Levinas there exists a sensibility that cannot be fully recuperated by the language of a subject-object relation, or by meaning understood as constituted by an 'ego' in the world. For Kristeva this sensibility or affectivity is abjection, while for Levinas it lies in the encountering of the 'there is'. In both cases, any stable distinction between subject and object, inside and outside, activity and passivity is inoperative.

Differentiating himself from classical phenomenology, for which the relation of the ego to the world is fundamental, Levinas focuses, in *Existence and Existents*, on the appearance of a substantive in anonymous being:

> Our investigation did not start with the ancient opposition of the ego to the world. We were concerned with determining the meaning of a much more general fact, that of the very apparition of an existent, a substantive in the heart of this impersonal existence, which, strictly speaking, we cannot give a name to, for it is a pure verb.
>
> (1978: 82)

For Levinas, there is an indeterminate reference of '"something is happening"' which does not indicate that we do not know who the subject, substantive or author is, but rather that 'action itself... somehow has no author' (1978: 57). Levinas designates this action without an author the 'there is', a murmuring 'in the depths of nothingness', which 'resists a personal form' and which 'transcends inwardness as well as exteriority; it does not even make it possible to distinguish these' (1978: 57). The 'subject-object distinction' is not the 'starting point' (1978: 58) for understanding the impersonal, anonymous being of the 'there is'. Levinas characterizes the world of intentions, where there is a subject and an object, as a world of light, where we grasp objects and thoughts according to their forms. The 'there is', however, resists the distinction between subject and object, and resists forms. Here there is a dissolution of forms, an invasion of presence by darkness. Thought cannot grasp the 'there is'. 'There is no discourse' (1978: 58). There is no fixity. This impersonal existence is not a world, which is 'no longer given' (1978: 58). There is a 'disappearance of all things and of the I', so that all that is left is 'the sheer fact of being' which returns 'in the midst of the negation which put it aside' (1978: 58).

For Levinas, then, like Kristeva, there is a way of signifying that is not captured in concepts, knowledge or thought. Prior to the distinction between a stable ego and the world, language has a way of signifying that is not captured by the formal meanings of words. While they 'cannot be separated from meaning', words nonetheless have a 'materiality' for Levinas, and can operate as sensation. A word is capable of having rhythm, rhyme, meter, alliteration, etc. And a word detaches itself from its objective meaning and reverts to the element of the sensible in still another way inasmuch as it is attached to a multiplicity of meanings, through the ambiguity that may affect it due to its proximity with other words. It then functions as the very movement of *signifying* [*signifier*].

(1978: 54; 1984: 87)

This way of signifying is the 'musicality' of a poem, which is 'behind' the signification of the thought to which the poem directs us. When we 'lose ourselves' in musicality – in the rhythm or metre of a poem, or in the echo of alliteration or assonance, whereby words relate to one another, rather than to objects – there is no longer an inside and outside, no longer a subject and an object. This 'new element' does not refer to any substantive. Here sensation produces 'things in themselves' (Levinas 1978: 54) that no longer have any reference to objects. A painting is 'deeply stamped with exoticism' and 'extracted from its reference to an "inside" – that is, as having lost its very character of being a world' (Levinas 1978: 54). The similarities between Kristeva's understanding of the semiotic, and Levinas's understanding of the musicality and poetry of language are striking. Like Levinas, Kristeva sees art as a site in which this non-syntactic, non-conceptual way of signifying establishes itself.

For both Kristeva and Levinas it is a question of pointing to the manner in which the subject/object distinction is gone beyond, exceeded, put into question, rendered unstable, without being nullified or negated. In art, there is both a figuring and a disfiguring, a putting out of play of the conventional subject/object relation, where mastery, clarity, freedom, sovereignty are operative, and a re-engaging of the substantiality and materiality of language, such that matter is not mere content in the service of a preconceived form but rather the materiality of language, or paint, is allowed to signify in a way that disrupts form, by reorganizing conventional meanings. Kristeva says,

The power of horror... *figures* but it *disfigures* as well: the source of a resurgence in our representations that cut through the forms, volumes, contours to expose the pulsing flesh... [t]hat stubbornly pursues 'economy' and 'figuration'... [as] a challenge directed at the horror, through the invention of an unprecedented form, which doesn't shrink from abjection but reshapes our vision so that we see it with new eyes.

(SH 103–8)

By aligning Kristeva's understanding of abjection with Levinas' understanding of the 'there is', we can revisit Butler's characterizing of the relation of the symbolic and the semiotic as a clash between identity and multiplicity and her calling Kristeva to account over her primitivism/

orientalism. If in the abject there is an approach of dissolution, the threat of disintegration, fragmentation or formlessness, of psychically merging with another or being obliterated, there is also the possibility of rebuilding or reshaping the all but disintegrated subject through a realignment of boundaries. This can take place through a realignment of the borders that separate one subject from another – a renegotiation of the defence mechanisms through which the fragile ego navigates its relationship both with its own sites of trauma and its relations with others (see HF 185). The realignment of boundaries can also take shape in the challenging and reconfiguration of socio-symbolic, normative, boundaries, which can (among others) have gendered and racialized implications. These two levels (interpersonal and socio-symbolic) are always intertwined with one another; how their transformation is put into play will differ in each case, and how they are understood, whether as a personal revolution or as a political transformation, is perhaps a matter of emphasis.[4] By insisting, along with Levinas, on a level of meaning that is not subject to the law of contradiction, Kristeva is not merely being inconsistent or incoherent: she is acknowledging how literature and art can work to undermine, rework, re-signify and transform conventional, symbolic meanings, by dissolving them and reforming them. Nor is she failing to understand the need to perform a phenomenology in which a subject is constituted in relation to an object; she is undertaking a 'phenomenology of abjection' (HF 185), in which the stability of the subject-object relation is undone, where the borders between inside and outside are disrupted, where 'the abject invades me; I become it' (HF 188). There is a loss of boundaries between 'I' and 'other'.

> As an intertwining of affect and meaning, abjection has no definable object, strictly speaking. Between an object not yet separated as such and the subject I have yet to become, abjection is one of those violent and obscure revolts of the being against what is menacing it and what appears to come from an outside as well as an exorbitant inside, an 'abject' cast beside the tolerable and the thinkable: close, but inassimilable.
> (HF 184)

Kristeva, like Levinas, sees art as a site in which sedimented relations between form and content can be reworked, as can the instability of subject and object. Art can facilitate an 'anamnesis' (HF 184), and in doing so can give access to the all but unsayable.

Nicholas Chare suggests that 'Kristeva perceives the symbolic aspect of language, the syntactic structures that act as guarantor for specific significations, to be in the ascendant under normal circumstances' (2016: 57) and that 'It is possible to produce forms of language that exploit the semiotic to contest the signifying structures, challenge the preferred meanings set in place by the symbolic' (2016: 57). Yet, what constitutes normal circumstances, and who is qualified to challenge preferred meanings? What happens when the intertwining of the semiotic and the symbolic is interpreted in such a way as to uphold conventionally symbolic meanings, while failing to recognize how some subjects are struggling to re-signify those hegemonic meanings? What happens when the hegemonic cultural meanings that dominate in some contexts remain invisible as sites of domination for some subjects? What happens when orientalism is invoked? Mythologies perpetuated by Eurocentric thinking abound. It is critical to contest them, especially when those perpetuating them are looked up to as authoritative voices in feminist theory. Despite Kristeva's distancing herself from feminism, her work nonetheless continues to be invoked in its name.

Citing the progress in attaining rights made by those 'rejected because of race, social origins, or religious difference', Kristeva suggests that it now 'seems obvious to us to resist racism as well as religious persecution or disparagement based on class' (HF 43). Yet how far this apparently obvious resistance to racism is consistently exhibited by Kristeva's own work remains unclear to me. In *The Severed Head*, Kristeva asks whether a 'veiled woman' is 'a sacrificed, decapitated, immured woman?' (SH 123). I want to pose the following question: do Kristeva's views on veiling amount to a performance of castration anxiety with regard to those who practice it? While answering affirmatively, I will also indicate the resources offered in Kristeva's work to suggest an alternative answer.

Before elaborating, in order to situate Kristeva's remarks on the veil, I turn to the analysis theorists Falguni Sheth and Sara Ahmed employ in their considerations of the dynamics of race and nationalism. The language we use and the metaphors and images we invoke in distributing agency, and in allocating vulnerability and blame, trade in the patrolling and policing of borders. The assumptions informing the imagery we employ help to constitute how we construe the relation between individuals and collectivities, subjects and their contextual histories, in ways that can either stabilize and enshrine as permanent the mythologies in which these participate or destabilize, disrupt, challenge and help to rework such mythical investments.

Metaphorical language can work to accomplish closure and containment; it can also establish the porosity and permeability of borders (Ahmed 2004). Communities keep out certain members of their polities, while keeping others in their place – or moving them out of their places, resituating them, imposing on them in the process some preconceived ideal as to how they should live their lives. The incessant, ongoing, relentless naturalization of our self-representations requires us to constantly renew our efforts to wrench ourselves free of the terms into which our very bodily desires so readily settle, so that we are able to recognize normativity as normative, and to put it into play. What is at stake is to be able to recognize our assumptions *as* assumptions, and to reformulate our natural interpretations of the world as questions.

Thanks to race and postcolonial theorists, we have become familiar with certain tropes that frequently arose as part of the colonial effort to bring native peoples into line. Such gestures were performed in the name of ostensibly universal, humanist, cosmopolitan values, in the name of 'civilizing the natives', allegedly for the sake of rationality. What this turned out to mean was an incessant recapitulation of the essential irrationality of those who were to be subjugated. Sheth takes up this argument and gives it a new twist. According to the demand that everyone be like 'us', 'within reason', whatever does not appear to fit in with Western norms, she suggests, is considered offensive, strange and transgressive. Hence the veil becomes a sign of cultural strangeness that cannot be tolerated by nations that take themselves to be characterized by an open, democratic and transparent society. The 'so-called choice' of Muslim women to cover themselves up is seen in and of itself as defiant of Western values, as 'unreasonable' and 'unruly', as Sheth puts it (2009: 108). In elaborating this point, Sheth remarks upon the tendency of the Western world to make the veil stand in 'for the worst, nonrepresentative, but most notorious practices of all of "Muslim culture", ranging from polygamy, sexual slavery, terrorism, suicide bombings, the systematic oppression of women, political repression, female mutilation, and perhaps the worst of all – the stark refusal to accept certain quintessential principles of Western liberalism' (2009: 101).

The logic at work here is that not only is the veil taken as synecdoche for the whole of Islam, becoming embroiled in a metonymic slippage from veiling to terrorism, but also that, in Sheth's words, the veil 'itself becomes the naturalized target of the state's hostility' (2009: 108). Sheth continues, 'Islam is perceived as a culture whose principles and visual significations are fundamentally transgressive to Western liberal norms. As such, Islam (and Muslims) imply a radical heterogeneity and a cultural ontology so distinct from the prevailing political culture that it (and they) are naturalized under the banner of "irrationality", "unreason", or "madness"' (2009: 108).

The generic demand that people discard customs that make them stand out from Western norms is stipulated further by Sheth in terms of Western, liberal feminist assumptions that the West is simply better than non-Western cultures, an idea that is perpetuated by a highly selective and idealized interpretation of Western cultures as free and autonomous. From these assumptions proceeds the belief that covering up one's body must be a product of patriarchal oppression. To wear a veil can only be construed as 'a response to coercion from a patriarchal authority or in submission to attempts to control one's sexuality' (2009: 102). To assume that there can only be one reason a woman would wear a veil, and to articulate that reason in ways that are continuous with tenets that derive from a particular version of Western feminism, namely liberal feminism, is, argues Sheth, problematic at a number of levels. It ignores the diverse array of specific contexts in which and reasons for which particular women in particular cultures and situations decide to veil. Far from capitulating to male control, these include precisely the opposite, since some women find that wearing the *chador* or the *niquab* puts them in control of their sexuality, by 'liberating' them 'from prying gazes' (2009: 104). To assume that veiling can only be construed as submissive – whether to religious ideology or male power – is to attribute to a highly diverse and multifarious set of women the same lack of agency, thereby participating in the supposition that they couldn't '"possibly" be doing this of their own accord' and that they 'must be subject to external constraints or pressures' (2009: 102). To deny women agency in this way positions them as powerless and infantile, when in fact veiling has been a resource of resistance for women.

The wider point that Sheth makes is that we should 'understand veiling as a part of a set of customs and decisions that are negotiated in relation to one's ever-dynamic circumstances', which, far from simply signalling a blanket capitulation to authority, include negotiating 'personal and professional autonomy from elders and family' and invoking 'a stance of political resistance to a national administration rather than a symbol of religious commitment' (2009: 104). In short, the reasons women decide to veil are as varied as the women themselves. To identify veiling purely and simply as a product of coercion is to refuse to grant women the autonomy that they see themselves as practicing. It is also to endorse the liberal ideals that 'subjects are fully formed' (2009: 104) irrespective of their contexts, while at the same time it is to imagine that 'the contexts in which one finds oneself are either fully formed or ideal or completely independent from the subject in question' (2009: 105).

Let me pause to review some of the major points Sheth makes. First, she remarks the elision of differences between a range of practices taken to be symbolic of Muslim culture (2009: 101), such that the veil, polygamy and suicide bombings become more or less synonymous with one another in a Western imaginary that reads wearers of the hijab as 'potential terrorists' (2009: 108). The hijab inhabits the role of synecdoche, as it comes to stand for a series of outrageous and incomprehensible practices to which foreign cultures subject their women. Second, veiling thereby becomes instrumental in signifying the fundamental irrationality or madness of a culture that refuses to be assimilated into the ostensible transparency, autonomy and freedom that are represented as key values in a western culture, which, however, is presented only in a highly idealized version. This idealized version, which becomes the pretext for condemning the infiltration of Islamic symbolism into the public realm, presents the separation of state from religions as fundamental to the West, for example. Yet it can only maintain this fictive myth of separation by ignoring the extent to which Western calendars, holidays and so on, in fact continue to be organized by a Christian agenda, and as such betray the alleged religious neutrality that is nominally so dear to Western states. Third, in failing to contextualize the practice of veiling, there is a failure to read the actions of Muslim women as autonomous agents in a variety of situations, and a reduction of veiling to a product of coercion, which attributes an essential lack of agency to all Muslim women, as if they were devoid of power, individuality and specificity.

Turning back to Kristeva, we find a remarkable synchrony between her observations on the topic of veiling and Sheth's analysis of the tendency to reduce veiling to coercion by patriarchy, its consequent imputed lack of agency, its equation with if not madness then psychical instability and its implication in a metonymic slide that elides its difference from violent practices that then become representative of the whole of Islamic culture. Kristeva suggests that a young girl is 'pushed by her father and brothers to wear the veil', that veiling is practiced by those who suffer from 'dual personalities' or 'psychical split[s]', and that 'There is not such a wide gulf between... Palestinian [suicide bombers] and our young girls in veils' (HF 26). It is difficult not to discern vestiges of French colonialism in such characterizations. If we turn back, along with Yeğenoğlu, to Fanon's essay, 'Algeria Unveiled', in which he articulates what he takes to be the political doctrine of French colonialism in relation to Algeria, this point can be illuminated, precisely along the lines of castration anxiety. Frantz Fanon identifies the penetration of the veil as key to colonialist logic, which he characterizes, in a passage Yeğenoğlu quotes, as follows: '"If we want to destroy the structure of Algerian society, its capacity for resistance, we must first of all conquer the women: we must go and find them behind the veil, where they hide themselves and in the houses where the men keep them out of sight"' (Yeğenoğlu 1998: 40).[5] As Yeğenoğlu unpacks it, the impenetrability of the veil that the colonial impulse construes itself as having to break through is also the impenetrability of the Orient as such. The veil, then, becomes castrating. It prevents penetrability of the Orient; it stands in the way of the colonial drive, the desire to conquer, to know and to control. As such, colonialism figures the veil as intolerable, because it resists that which takes itself for the light of reason, confronting the colonial master with a screen of darkness, beneath which he imagines to reside the true Orient, if only he could rend the veil that hides it, the veil prohibiting his gaze. It resists the will to know, the will to power – it refuses to yield. The encounter with the veil then, which marks the limits of this mastery, constitutes a traumatic encounter. It blocks the ostensible progress of knowledge that the colonizer would claim. It constitutes an ineradicable, untameable, recalcitrant alterity. It stands in the way of the ideal of transparency to which the will to dominate appeals. 'With modernity', says Yeğenoğlu, drawing on Foucault, 'comes a new form of institutional power which is based on visibility and transparency and which refuses to tolerate areas of darkness' (1998: 40).

It becomes clear that banning the veil is less about any empirical threat posed by the women who choose to wear it than it is about securing the subject of representation in the mythology of transparency and openness that is so dear to western narrations of so-called democracy. The veil is castrating because it signifies the impenetrability of the Orient. It impedes the will to know. To penetrate its unyielding darkness is to secure the penetrability of women, which, in the all-too-familiar trope of figuring the mastery of land in terms of female sexuality, in turn becomes symbolic of the conquerability of the mysterious lands of the Orient.

Western imaginaries have become invested in the symbolism of the veil as threatening, as castrating, as a placeholder for the traumatic real – that which holds in place systems of meaning but which itself can only be indicated as somehow unimaginable, unrepresentable, the *object petit a*. The logic that is installed here involves, then, yet another (counter-transferential?) displacement, a projection in which the trauma of colonization for the colonized is denied or disavowed, displaced on to the colonizer, who finds himself or herself traumatized in the face of the veil. I am not responsible for traumatizing the other; the other is responsible for a trauma that affects me, by stopping in its tracks the will to mastery, knowledge and control. The colonizer thus avoids taking responsibility for invading the land of the colonized, for prohibiting native peoples the right to speak their language, the right to orchestrate their lives in the ways they see fit and to inhabit their lands in the ways to which their cultures have habituated them. Instead of acknowledging invasion, oppression and coercion, it is the colonizer who construes himself as the one who is wounded, affronted, afflicted, by the blockage of the gaze that the veil comes to signify, standing in for, as it does, the disciplining of immigrants, interlopers, whose alterity confronts Westerners with a past they will not own for themselves. My suggestion is that such a disavowal structures the reaction of those who align themselves with the 2010 French law that prohibited the wearing of the full-face veil in public. They partake in a similar displacement or disavowal, as when Kristeva suggests '[a] ban on wearing the veil might be… necessary' (HF 26). The question is: necessary for whom, and for what purpose? Perhaps not so much for the protection of those who would wear it as for the protection of those for whom the confrontation with it covers over or veils the trauma of colonialism. Even in countries that have not instituted a similar prohibition, it is certainly the case that plenty of anxiety has been fuelled by those who wear the veil, as is indicated by instances such as a judge requiring a defendant to remove her *niquab*.

The anxiety provoked by the veil is fuelled by a fear of alterity, which – according to the affective pull in which this image trades – must be counteracted in the name of preserving national security, sealing our borders, borders which are imagined to have become too permeable, too leaky, too indeterminate. We can thereby illustrate the metonymic displacement or slippage (to which Sheth alerts us) that occurs between the veil and multiple potential threats that are marked by their association with Islam, according to 'stereotypes that are already in place' (Ahmed 2004: 75), and which facilitate a 'slide', for example, between asylum seekers and terrorists (2004: 80). Ahmed draws attention to the

> structural possibility that the terrorist 'could be' anyone and anywhere. The narrative of the 'could be' terrorist, in which the terrorist is the one that 'hides in shadows', has a double edge. On the one hand, the figure of the terrorist is detached from particular bodies, as a shadowy figure, 'an unspecifiable may-come-to-pass.' But it is this could-be-ness, this detachment, which also allows the restriction on the mobility of those bodies that are read *as associated with terrorism.*
> (Ahmed 2004: 79)[6]

Nationalism functions, in Cecilia Sjöholm's terms, as a site of libidinal investment, in what is imagined to be a sphere of transparency, illuminated by Enlightenment values, which must secure itself against what is imagined to be the darkness of those who threaten our integrity and must therefore be kept securely outside (2005: 31). None of this can be explicit. It must remain veiled, lest it interrupt the myth of equality that Enlightenment thinking pedals in.

Commenting on Clérambault's *Morphology of the Draped Suit*, Kristeva says: 'Let us consider a veiled woman: is she a venerated, protected woman, as the chador indicates and claims? Or a sacrificed, decapitated, immured woman?' (SH 123; VC 144). Answering her own question, she goes on: 'I see... a casket. I really want to believe there's a woman there, but buried alive' (SH 124). Kristeva sees Georges Seurat's *Veil*, which reminds her of the 'fluid veils' of Corradini, while being very different. It is, she says, the 'absolute imaginary head, in a class of its own, beauty playing with the boundaries of forgetting' (SH 124). In *Sense and Nonsense*, Kristeva refers to the Italian sculptor Corradini. Having discussed the 'veiling and unveiling of the phallus' in connection with sacred mysteries, she suggests that it is not just the phallus that is veiled but that 'all sorts of... desirable objects' are veiled and 'become desirable by being veiled/unveiled' (SNS 89). She understands the baroque sculptor Corradini's 'Purity' in terms of a phallic displacement, suggesting that it is not merely that the veil renders the entire body phallic but rather that the veil puts into question 'the entire body of representation itself; culture is a representation that unfolds representation' (SNS 90). Through the motif of 'allegorical women who conceal [or veil] themselves by exposing themselves in a subtle displacement', we witness, Kristeva suggests, 'a veritable revolution of thought' (SNS 90). Kristeva goes on to suggest that through the baroque sculptor's veiling/unveiling or presence/absence, art puts on trial representation itself. The phallus, says Kristeva, is 'displaced' on to the bodies of Corradini's allegorical women in an 'exquisite gesture' that 'invites us to seek ways to veil/unveil the key values of a culture in crisis to transmute them' (SNS 90).

If Kristeva can recognize a revolt in the 'exquisite gesture' of veiling in the realm of art, what prevents her from transferring this insight on to the public/political realm, which in France has deprived women of the right to wear the veil? If art, along with psychoanalysis, is understood as a site of expression for singularity, why is the singularity of each woman's decision of whether to wear a veil not appreciated? If in art the veil can 'make the visible appear through that which obscures it' (SNS 90), if Kristeva can suggest in the context of art that 'mystery and revolt are the same thing' (SNS 90), thereby focusing on art that raises the question of respresentability as such, can we understand women who wear the veil not as burying themselves alive but as exercising the freedom to dress as they choose, a freedom that can signify not acquiescence to authority, but precisely revolt?

We might think of this in terms of flipping the veil, such that prohibiting the veil in France can be read as a displacement of colonial trauma. It seems to me that women's appropriation of the veil as a site of resistance/revolt is at the same time an insistence on being taken seriously as the agents and authors of their own meaning within the specific contexts against which veiling must be read. In reading the veil, in some circumstances, as a site of subversion of the very authority Kristeva takes it to represent, should we not read it as also contesting representation, not merely in the aesthetic realm but also in the political realm? Such a reading would not ignore the fact that every action constitutes an intervention in pre-existing social and cultural realms; as such, in Kristeva's terms, it would constitute phallic displacement. To acknowledge that this is the case is to interpret the wearing of veils as capable of signifying resistance, by taking up, challenging and re-signifying norms that perpetuate the myth that only the fathers and brothers whose authority Kristeva imagines to be behind the decision to wear a veil are capable of effecting symbolic meaning. As such, perhaps women's resistance in France to symbolic/legal dictates stripping them of the freedom to wear the veil should indicate both the need to envisage a space for a revolt that is not confined to art and psychoanalysis and a space for art (and psychoanalysis) that is not subsumed by politics.

Kristeva's support for the prohibition on the wearing of the veil constitutes a stark and uncompromising statement that amounts to a demand that, if non-Westerners want to live in France, they have to abide by rules which fail to respect diversity, laws that require them to abandon sartorial practices that might signify a plethora of cultural, religious or personal commitments, and which require them to pay homage to a version of nationalism that imitates a highly specific image of what it means to be French.

The very analyses that theorists such as Sheth and Ahmed provide around the metonymic and metaphorical ways in which something like a nation comes into being are themselves facilitated, however indirectly, by precisely the kinds of thinking Kristeva's work itself has made possible. In the words of Sjöholm, the 'revolution of the semiotic does not challenge or change norms for any given reasons, or with any given goals in mind... But it is precisely its unwillingness to simply replace one norm instead of another... which makes the semiotic into such a powerful political concept' (2005: 32). Rather than this constituting a limit of Kristeva's thinking, the refusal of the semiotic to assimilate itself to any particular politics constitutes its very productivity. It is up to us, in each instance, to trace the conceptual, affective and political consequences of semiotic incursions into the symbolic, and their symbolic ramifications. Can the very avenues of psychic and personal survival some subjects are able to develop for themselves – including gendered struggles against drowning in 'loss and separation' (SH 117) (as Kristeva observes, '[w]oman' is '[a]lways somewhat a *stranger* to phallic ordeals' [SH 117]) – be etched in symbolic and imaginary economies premised on the social/ psychic death of others: on their being 'buried alive'?

Let me conclude by taking up the words of a French woman wearing the tricolour flag: 'The veil covering your eyes is much more dangerous than the veil covering my hair.'[7] The veil is intolerable because it reminds the West that there is another way of seeing things, another point of view. The veil is traumatic because it is a sticking point, stopping up the seamless narrative of equality, universality, rationality that flows from the stories that celebrate Habermas's ideal spectator, which presumes the world can be analysed in terms of, and democracies have lived up to, rational communication. The veil interrupts the clarity of Enlightenment narratives; it slices into, cuts up, traumatizes the stories we are so used to hearing and retelling, tales that are told from the point of view of the able-bodied European master, the one with whom Hegelian self-consciousness identifies. The veil blocks the supremacy of the white European vantage point that has established itself at the centre of both philosophical theories of the modern state and the orientalist gaze. It insists on the murkiness of such views. If the veiled women of Corradini and Seurat put into question representation itself by performing phallic displacement, perhaps Clérembault and the protestor who draws attention to the veil covering the eyes of those who object to veiling highlight the need to displace Western assumptions about who has a right to view and represent what and the authority they call on to do so. They thereby demand that we attend to other stories, stories in which the veil becomes a site of resistance, which hides not weakness, or submission to authority but re-signifies authority differently. When veils, encrusted with tradition, lose their translucency, when veils before one's eyes solidify into new dogmas (see SH 104), it is necessary to lift such veils, to see them as veils. Reading Kristeva alongside Levinas, Ahmed, Sheth and Yeğenoğlu allows us to elaborate such re-signifying not so much outside communication but as resounding within the fabric of communicative and not so rational discourse, inhabiting metaphorical reiterations and metonymical displacements that dictate the rhythmic orchestration of our very existence, its ebb and flow. An ebb and flow to which we accommodate ourselves so easily, unless we continually interrogate its seductions, which might be thought as *chora*, as quasi-transcendental, awash with affects and with compacted, socially saturated, memories.

Notes

1 It is perhaps worth noting that despite Butler's early critique of Kristeva, some of the positions she endorses in her later work bear more than a passing resemblance with Kristeva's elaboration of the semiotic pre-history of infancy. While Butler invokes the work of Jean Laplanche and Christopher Bollas, the account she provides in *Giving an Account of Oneself* (2005) also resonates with Kristevan themes.

2 Butler quotes Foucault, *The History of Sexuality*, vol. 1 (1980: 154).

3 MacCannell says, 'The choice [Kristeva] leaves us with (be rational, repressed and a victim, or irrational revenge taker; be a Jew or be a Nazi; two faces of the same thing) is not an aporia but a call to an either/or decision. This is the decision she, as an analyst and thinker, refuses to make openly, straddling as she does a borderline that "sees" and "hears" the pain of repression while standing firmly with the Logos. As a *writer* I am afraid the rhetorical weight is on the side of the victimiser, to whom, in the case of the fascist, she gives so much space' (2003: 86).

4 I do not mean here to suggest that trauma 'can be good for you' or that what does not kill you makes you stronger. I mean that to have survived trauma, to have been able to find a way to survive, to live, is to have confronted the impossible, and to have reconfigured oneself in order to keep going. In the process, one will also have rethought, and repositioned oneself in relation to symbolic and imaginary resources; one will have reimagined what it means to be a subject, what it means to live. This can have political ramifications: how one lives, what one does, how one thinks, the change one calls for, what one writes (both theoretically and creatively), how and what one teaches, how one articulates, and understands the world, the difference one might make.

5 Yeğenoğlu is quoting Fanon (1965: 37–8).

6 Ahmed is quoting Massumi (1993: 11).

7 'Le voile devant vos yeux est bien plus dangereux que le voile sur mes cheveux.' See the photograph by Almay accompanying Angelique Chrisafis, 'France's headscarf war: "It's an attack on freedom"', *The Guardian*, 22 July 2013, https://www.theguardian.com/world/2013/jul/22/frances-headscarf-war-attack-on-freedom (accessed 2 November 2021).

References

Ahmed, S. (2004), *The Cultural Politics of Emotion*, New York: Routledge.
Butler, J. (1992), 'The Body Politics of Julia Kristeva', in N. Fraser and S. L. Bartky (eds), *Revaluing French Feminism: Critical Essays on Difference, Agency, and Culture*, 162–76, Bloomington: Indiana University Press.
Butler, J. (2005), *Giving an Account of Oneself*, New York: Fordham University Press.
Chare, N. (2016), 'Manet's Abject Surrealism', in R. Arya and N. Chare (eds), *Abject Visions: Powers of Horror in Art and Visual Culture*, 51–70, Manchester: Manchester University Press.
De Nooy, J. (2003), 'How to Keep Your Head When All about You Are Losing Theirs: Translating Possession into Revolt in Kristeva', in J. Lechte and M. Zournazi (eds), *The Kristeva Critical Reader*, 113–29, Edinburgh: Edinburgh University Press.
Fanon, F. (1965), *A Dying Colonialism*, trans. H. Chevalier, New York: Grove Press.
Foucault, M. (1980), *The History of Sexuality. I: An Introduction*, trans. R. Hurley, New York: Vintage.
Fraser, N. (1992), 'The Uses and Abuses of French Discourse Theories for Feminist Politics', in N. Fraser and S. L. Bartky (eds), *Revaluing French Feminism: Critical Essays on Difference, Agency, and Culture*, 177–94, Bloomington, IN: Indiana University Press.
Jasper, A. (2014), 'Taking Sides on Severed Heads: Kristeva at the Louvre', *Text Matters*, 4 (4): 174–83.
Keltner, S. K. (2011), *Kristeva: Thresholds*, Cambridge: Polity.
Levinas, E. (1978), *Existence and Existents*, trans. A. Lingis, The Hague: Martinus Nijhoff.
Levinas, E. (1984), *De l'existence à l'existant*, Paris: Vrin.
MacCannell, J. F. (2003), 'Kristeva's Horror', in J. Lechte and M. Zournazi (eds), *The Kristeva Critical Reader*, 67–97, Edinburgh: Edinburgh University Press.
Massumi, B. (1993), 'Everywhere You Want to Be: Introduction to Fear', in B. Massumi (ed.), *The Politics of Everyday Fear*, 3–38, Minneapolis, MN: University of Minnesota Press.
Rose, J. (1986), *Sexuality in the Field of Vision*, London: Verso.
Sheth, F. (2009), *Toward a Political Philosophy of Race*, Albany, NY: State University of New York Press.
Sjöholm, C. (2005), *Kristeva and the Political*, London: Routledge.
Spillers, H. (2018), 'Time and Crisis: Questions of Race and Psychoanalysis', *Journal of French and Francophone Philosophy – Revue de la philosophie française et de langue française*, 26 (2): 25–31.
Smith, A. M. (2003), 'Transgression, Transubstantiation, Transference', in J. Lechte and M. Zournazi (eds), *The Kristeva Critical Reader*, 130–8, Edinburgh: Edinburgh University Press.
Yeğenoğlu, M. (1998), *Colonial Fantasies: Towards a Feminist Reading of Orientalism*, Cambridge: Cambridge University Press.
Ziarek, E. (2003), 'The Uncanny Style of Kristeva's Critique of Nationalism', in J. Lechte and M. Zournazi (eds), *The Kristeva Critical Reader*, 139–57, Edinburgh: Edinburgh University Press.

7

Kristeva on Arendt: Politics and the subject

Robin Truth Goodman

Precarity: The subject-in-politics

In her book on Hannah Arendt, Kristeva faults Arendt for her incomplete assessment of modern literature. For Kristeva, Arendt's neglect meant that she had insufficient tools for demystifying the standardization and technologization of society that in her own analysis led to the authoritarian crises of the twentieth century. The basis of this disagreement resides in a conflict between Kristeva's process of the subject and the body ('*sujet-en-procès*'), on the one hand, and, on the other, Arendt's focus on political plurality. These differences between Arendt and Kristeva lead to differences about how narratives work, what type of human action storytelling entails and how narratives form bridges between the subject and political possibility. Such differences in their views on political action also testify to differences in how they describe the political retrenchments of modernity: dogmatisms, fascisms, bureaucratizations, conformisms, terrorisms and fatalisms as well as how they explain the form the subject takes within these modern modes of being, speaking and acting. In this chapter I argue that the incommensurability between Arendt's and Kristeva's perspectives, despite Kristeva's attempts to mirror her own critique in Arendt's work, exposes a political impasse constituting our present.

The divergence between Kristeva and Arendt points to conceptual vocabularies that are currently undergoing radical shifts, that have not yet been settled and that underlie our relation to the political. Tensions and contradictions arise in Kristeva's applying her conceptual vocabulary – words like *subject, heterogeneity, experience, violence* and *sovereignty* – to Arendt's analysis, as landmarks of the political, because Kristeva's vocabulary does not necessarily cohere to Arendt's concepts. For example, Kristeva's subject is drawn from Lacanian psychoanalysis, divided or destabilized by a pre-subjective fragmentation that disrupts symbolic language or as coming into existence by disgustedly expelling part of itself as object. On the other hand, Arendt, steeped in twentieth-century phenomenology, seeks to steer philosophical inquiry away from the subject-object split and its reliance on transcendence that, in her view, has led the tradition astray, where the thinking subject is isolated from the world of action. Instead of restricting all philosophical thinking away from the disrepute of the 'visible, tangible, palpable' (1971: 12), she focuses on words like *contemplation, action, speech, plurality* and *beginning* that blend subject and object or avoid them altogether as referential categories. Even so, Kristeva turns to Arendt to work out her ideas of the primacy of the social bond and what happens when the social bond is endangered or split.

The philosophical orientations of Kristeva and Arendt are bifurcated to the extent that it looks *odd* for Kristeva to choose Arendt as her intellectual antecedent, foil or interlocutor. Indeed, Kristeva laments some of Arendt's choices, concluding that 'Arendt the philosopher did not delve into the style of modern literature with its crises, conflicts, and discoveries' (HA 43), remarking that her sense of Arendt's faults stems from Arendt's 'hostility to psychoanalysis' as well as her neglect of sexuality and 'the psychic realm' (HA 42) as it frames the subject's 'passageway between *zoe* and *bios,* between physiology and biography' (HA 47). Arendt, she continues, reads Kant against his critics and contemporaries, appreciating him for the relentlessness of his critique but not cognizant of his interior melancholia underlying his work, noticed by other philosophers. Neither, says Kristeva, was Arendt sensitive to 'a theory of the unconscious' (HA 230) that might be discerned in Kant's treatment of the imagination, of judgement or of common sense. Kristeva traces the formation of subjectivity as life process, and praises Arendt for recognizing life as important to retrieve when modern power mechanisms are making it superfluous: 'It is precisely the questioning of this fundamental value [of life] – its formation in Christian eschatology as well as the dangers that it faces in the modern world – that quietly unifies Arendt's entire work' (HA 8). Yet, Arendt is looking for constructions of the political that are not determined by pathways of growth or development in life, biological cyclicality, psychical origins or necessity. For Arendt, natality is a non-metaphysical conceptual lapse or uprooting, almost like an aporia or an absence, which promises that concepts do not determine the outcomes of their action and do not develop according to some foundational or preconceived plan. When politics is bound up with the life process, she writes, political freedom is reduced to security – 'a security which should permit an undisturbed development of the life process of society as a whole' (1961: 150) – and freedom gets defined as freedom *from* politics, or survival: 'The life process is not bound up with freedom but follows its own inherent necessity; and it can be called free only in the sense that we speak of a freely flowing stream' (1961: 150). Whereas Kristeva wants to know how the subject comes to be as a life, Arendt sees the subject as a philosophical fallacy and an obstruction to thinking politically even about life. Kristeva's reading of Arendt exposes their points of disagreement as particularly vexing in this historical moment, when the political is under increasing stress as the democratic institutions that have been the traditional avenues of democratic participation, expression and redress are challenged by authoritarian tendencies, global violence and the increasing reduction of civil society to the vying of economic interests, technological mechanization and corporate accumulation.

Framed in a spirit of alliance, the dissonance between the two philosophical directions suggests that contemporary debates about what constitutes political life may be mediated by disputes over the legacy of modernism and, in particular, over the status of the subject. What the two philosophers both acknowledge is that modernity ushers in precarity. Precarity arises from a loss of authority due to religion, community and morality all diminishing as regulators of conduct, language and feeling. As both Arendt and Kristeva acknowledge, confrontations with foreigners, strangers and radical others, who may seem to threaten a shared sense of reality or common sense, also give rise to feelings of precarity in an increasingly mobile world. In her work on Melanie Klein, for example, Kristeva remarked on 'the renewed loss of a settled way of life that humanity experienced during the twentieth century' (MK 195) because of new technologies ('satellite television or the internet', MK 195) and forms of persecution and uprootedness, detaching us 'from our natural habitats' and turning us 'into nomads once again' (MK 195), assaulting 'maternal support' (MK 195) and 'threatening to destroy identity itself' (MK 195). Both thinkers, refugees and stateless for part of their lives, attribute precarity to a loss of connection between the individual and the community of political action. Yet, whereas Kristeva understands this precarity playing out inside the subject, as presubjective fragments disrupt subjective stability and language forms, Arendt perceives a loss in political possibility linked to a decay in the authority of the nation state and an increasing split between thinking and action – historical or contingent events that human beings can change. As precarity has become an increasingly prevalent condition and distressing concern with the twentieth century morphing into the twenty-first, the disparate accounts of modernism resonate within today's climate where precarity has reached again a crisis situation because of, for example, terrorism, violence and militarism but also forced migration due to social breakdown and war, employment insecurity, decline of social safety net provisions and climate change, among other threats of modern life.

The two philosophers come to these different understandings of precarity, in part, through their different understandings of language, Arendt hesitantly considering philosophy's communicability while Kristeva critiques the Symbolic as always failing in its communicational function due to its structure in loss and lack. In this respect, Arendt interprets Kafka's language as communicating and 'style-less': that is, 'clear and simple, like everyday speech' (2007: 94, 95), whereas Proust, says Arendt, 'perceived reality only as it is reflected' (1968: 80), meaning that he 'enlarged... inner experience until it included the whole range of aspects as they appeared to and were reflected by all members of society' (1968: 80). Where, for Arendt, inner experience is thus aligned with perception and broadens with more perception, for Kristeva, inner experience is constantly at war with perception, diluting it, dissolving it and distorting it. As for Céline, who is central to Kristeva's account of the precarity of the modern subject,[1] for Arendt he is pure and transparent ideology, expressing a hatred of the Jews in all its 'bluntness' (1968: 335) that both the elites and the bourgeoisie are happy to hear. Arendt's modernist literary taste provokes Kristeva's roundabout explanations. She says for example that for Arendt, Kafka 'sketches out models for thinking' (HA 88) which produce 'truth' (HA 88), when the philosophical tradition that pursues unified truth is exactly the opposite of what Arendt would want to model. Even as Arendt wrote widely on revolution and revolt, Kristeva alleges regretfully that Arendt, because of her interest in what Kristeva calls 'classical narrative structure', 'did not recognize the need for rebellion – an intrapsychic need but a historical one as well – that led the century's avant-garde to an unprecedented reevaluation of narrative structures' (HA 93). In other words, Kristeva interprets Arendt's stance towards modernism, language and the subject as errors – caused by Arendt's insufficient grasp of precarity – when they are crucial factors in Arendt's perspective on the decay of politics in modernity.

Kristeva takes up Hannah Arendt as a study in subjectivity because of Arendt's focus on natality and the centrality of beginning to her project. Kristeva's book on Hannah Arendt is the first in a trilogy about female 'genius',[2] which, in her rendering, is linked to the creation of a life but not reduced to its 'natural' sense. Kristeva's main concerns in the female genius trilogy are with the phenomenological themes of life and love:

> [H]er first piece of abstract, purely philosophical writing seeks to question... the diverse bond that unites people in the world. The aims of her later work begin to take shape here: the theme of life, presented through the theme of love, structures this inaugural text and allows us to read Augustine in the light of Arendt's subsequent body of thought.
> (HA 31)

For Kristeva, 'life constitutes the world' (HA 34) – in other words, as she later explains, the baby's entry into the world is a singular mark, a spontaneous bonding with the world that also opposes and revolts against it. The volumes following the one on Arendt – whose selection Kristeva attributes to personal choice rather than objective criteria – are extended discussions of the life and works of Melanie Klein and Collette, one a psychoanalyst and the other a modernist novelist, who are thinkers that Kristeva frequently references in other works. 'Genius', as Kristeva herself admits, is not usually a role attributed to women, because their perceived differences from men give them 'substantial obstacles to realizing their genius' (HA xiv). At the same time, however, mothers can inhabit 'genius' not only of 'love, tact, self-denial, suffering' (xv) but 'also of a certain approach to living the life of the mind' (HA xv): life equates to creation.[3] Women's capacity to give birth and make something new individuates them, releasing them from 'groupthink' (HA xiv) or chatter. In the introduction, Kristeva justifies her choice by outlining an impasse in feminism, where the excessive focus on motherhood in the post-1960s context has led to a discrediting of 'any notion of feminine specificity or freedom' (HA xiii), whereas the three 'geniuses' of her trilogy give birth to innovation and creativity 'to remake the human condition' (HA xv) by expressing 'the singularity of every woman' (HA xiv). Yet, was not Kristeva's use of 'natality' (if it is borrowed or modified from Lacan) still invested in the maternal relation figured in infantile need? Kristeva wants to situate experience as in a metaphoric but essential relation to biological life processes that produce subjectivity – *le sujet en procès*, as she says (in process/on trial) – when Arendt's whole project, her very idea of natality is to break out of the thinking of thinking as life process because, she insists, when life is defined in relation to need, it cannot escape from mechanization; that is, it is bound by its pre-conditioning and its teleology rather than radically opened to contingency.

Though Arendt was concerned with thinking in solitude – as thinking 'removes itself from what is present and close at hand' (1971: 199), having 'a destructive, undermining effect on all established criteria, values, measurements... customs and rules of conduct' (1971: 175) – her principal worry was over politics. As Margaret Canovan writes in her groundbreaking defence of Arendt as a political philosopher, 'the central preoccupation of Arendt's political thought is the revaluation of politics and political action' (1992: 275). Arendt was concerned that philosophy's traditional separation from politics influenced a contemporary sense that politics was based on the will – on choosing command or obedience – rather than on people coming together to speak and to act. Arendt wanted to peel the political away from what philosophical traditions and historical forces attached to it, unbinding it from necessity or determinism. For her in a nutshell, politics consisted of a plurality of free citizens revealing themselves as unique in public through speech and action: 'The *polis*, properly speaking', she observes, 'is not the city-state in its physical location; it is the organization of the people as it arises out of acting and speaking together, and its true space lies between people living together for this purpose' (1958: 198). Though each participant has a particular story, the story is disclosed only through spectators narrating the actions of others, and so what makes someone unique is revealed by their appearance in public.

The primacy of the political, for Arendt, is therefore contradictory to Kristeva's formation of the developmental subject as it enters into language. Kristeva's interpretation of Arendt through the lens of her own framework marks a stalemate and raises the question of the contemporary subject's articulation in the political. This is important because in the current climate, neoliberal power tends to push the subject out of the political, creating disassociations, dissonances and, indeed, precarities between politics and the individual citizen's self-identification with it. In other words, neoliberalism's 'democracy' is a politics of raw power that does not need to invite individuals inside, that actually leaves the subject dangling with no political space of action, a type of power that Arendt would identify as contrary to politics and call it 'violence'. In the rest of this chapter, I address two areas of apparent intersection – singularity and plurality – where the two writers diverge, and I discuss what this divergence can tell us about the contemporary split between politics and the subject that neoliberalism is orchestrating.

Singularity/natality

Kristeva's approach to her analysis of Arendt's politics contrasts sharply with the standard approaches of Arendt's critics. Most critics frame Arendt's turn to political theory as a response to her experiences during the Holocaust and, subsequently, as the response of a stateless refugee, so they build their descriptions of her positions as emergent from *The Origins of Totalitarianism* and the Eichmann trial. Margaret Canovan, for example, dates Arendt's thinking on politics from the 1951 publication of *Origins*, and explicitly states that most of her original reflections 'have their roots in her experience of the overwhelming political catastrophes that she summed up under the heading of "totalitarianism"' (1992: 7). Canovan faults most of Arendt's commentators for launching their analysis from Arendt's 1958 *The Human Condition*, so that they miss how Arendt centralizes a basic contradiction in the modern nation state: the assumed exclusive racial basis of community on which the modern nation state was built was undermined by the idea of the nation state as a guarantor of rights, especially under an expansionist and territorial imperialism, demanding a revised sense of political connection that *The Human Condition* would then go on to formulate. Richard J. Bernstein's recent study positions Arendt as 'an astute critic of dangerous tendencies in modern life' (2018: 3) and goes on to assert that the statelessness forced on her by the Nazis is the lived experience that grounds her thought; this experience led to her realization of the human need 'to belong to some kind of organized community' (2018: 27–8) that would counter the increased superfluity and marginalization of those expelled from the nation state. Judith Butler acknowledges Arendt's early work slightly, as an allusion to religious influence, but quickly moves on to her main interest in Arendt's idea of 'heterogeneity' that Butler attributes to her experience in exile and her reporting on the Eichmann trial, leading to her scepticism about the nation state and her search for another mode of political belonging. 'Her critique of German fascism and nationalism', concludes Butler, 'led her to a politics centered not on a Jewish homeland but on the rights of the stateless' (2012: 149). Such critics read Arendt as responding to a mid-twentieth-century crisis in the nation state, where she sees modernity itself as ungovernable under its terms and wants to imagine other modes of political life.

Kristeva's analysis, on the other hand, poses the nation state as a second-order belonging and politics as demanding to be thought outside of the relations constructed through the nation state and citizenship. Unlike these other critics, Kristeva begins her commentary with an interpretation of Arendt's pre–Second World War dissertation on Saint Augustine but *marks this as the beginning of Arendt's thinking on the political*.[4] The point of this study was to interrogate the Christian mandate 'to love thy neighbor as thyself' as a modern premise, particularly as a critique of what Arendt understood as Heidegger's solipsism and his emphasis on the primacy of 'Being towards death' in modern experience. For Arendt according to Kristeva, Heidegger's focus on death limits Being to the interval between birth and death that cannot be reversed; she thinks 'it is important not to limit thinking to its solitude' (HA 153) in this bracketing of the life process. Heidegger, says Kristeva, 'assigns death as a "shelter" for Being' (HA 151). In contrast, at no point 'does Arendt subscribe to the notion that death is the muse of philosophy, if not the only indispensable condition for thought' (HA 151). Instead, 'Arendt ceaselessly returns to birth... for a way of thinking about joy' (HA 151). So, the stranger – the thinking subject previously unknown to the world and born without necessity – for Arendt becomes philosophically significant as part of a contestation of her teacher.

This is significant: in a sense, Kristeva is theorizing Arendt as positing a modern individual who is politicized, prior to its advent in the modern nation state, through its relation to the other. Arendt's dissertation on Augustine, in some kind of parallel to Kristeva, poses life as a craving, and more precisely, a craving for an object that the infant fears to lose and that actually must be lost, that is, the happiness of everlasting life itself. The fear of loss spurs a constant need for security and, therefore, a desire for a worldly other. 'Man' [*sic*], she says, 'desires to belong to something outside of himself' (1996: 18). This figure of 'Man' demanding an other to satisfy his needs resonates with Kristeva's infant before the mirror stage. Additionally, Kristeva reads

Arendt as appropriating from Augustine a spirit of rebellion or a 'desire for rupture' (HA 34) based in this craving for eternal life, the idea that something new must always be arising and breaking through in order to make the everlasting continue on.

In both Arendt's account of the stranger in Christianity and in Kristeva's account of subjective emergence in the maternal relation, the nation state does not play a central part. In Kristeva the individual is made up of language fragments mediated by the maternal body, whereas for Arendt he or she comes to existence as a singularly minded appetite that precedes socialization – this is a problem that he or she must transcend through bonding. 'Natality', as 'the fact that we have entered the world through birth' (1996: 51), for Arendt, is the condition for our worldliness, our connection to the other, which 'is characteristic of the human condition as such' (1996: 52). Life, as the need for the other that is 'characteristic of the human condition', that 'exists in a mode of relation' (1996: 53), is 'transformed into a future possibility' (1996: 55), that is, something unconditioned, that does not yet exist, a question to itself, a story told to others. Rosalyn Diprose and Ewa Plonowska Ziarek point out that attempt to control the unpredictability or openness of human affairs that would result from a new life is, for Arendt, a 'degradation of politics' (2018: 2). Instead, they outline the effects of natality as distinct from biological birth as well as from established political forms and institutions, often as the capacity of action to disclose something unique. Referencing the stranger or the immigrant as much as the creative principle of life itself, 'natality' describes a type of human agency whose speaking and acting disrupts time to start a different, unpredictable, unconditioned temporality tied to a 'plurality of distinct others' (2018: 5). In this way, natality politicizes the political.

To readers of Kristeva, Arendt's formulation may sound familiar. Kristeva appropriates the spontaneous birth of the 'not-yet', the unpredictable and the undetermined that Arendt upholds as the basis of political action and freedom to explain what she calls in *Revolution in Poetic Language* a theory of signification, where the primary drives experienced in pre-subjective pieces of language and gestures 'connect and orient the body to the mother… The mother's body is therefore what mediates the symbolic law organizing social relations' (RPL 27). Similarly, for Arendt, 'it is through love of the world that man explicitly makes himself at home in the world' (1996: 67), where love and desire create the web of relations that is the world (or politics). Divergently, Kristeva faults Arendt for not taking into account psychoanalysis, and particularly the role the mother plays in the 'dawning of the bond with the Other' (HA 46) that the lover will then rediscover[5] as the seeds of the political bond. Kristeva's newborn enters into the already existing world of language through a bonding with the mother who must be rejected, often violently, and the attachment to her repressed because of the paternal prohibition. In *Revolution,* the 'no[m]' (the no/name) of the father takes the form of the social imposition of the Symbolic which, she says, 'introduces, through categorial intuition, both *semantic fields* and *logical* – but also *intersubjective* – *relations,* which prove to be both intra- and trans-linguistic' (23). Kristeva's subject-in-process is developmental in its challenges to symbolically established power.

Kristeva is, therefore, interested in the subject and its life as the site where politics begins. Her turn to psychoanalysis coincides with her critique of a phenomenological tradition that 'brackets' an account of where the subject comes from, and she affirms 'the insurmountable necessity of *positing* an ego' in order to locate 'the positionality of the speaking subject' (RPL 32). Before the phenomenological subject that is bracketed, the pre-linguistic guttural spurts, pre-grammatical sound and corporeal tics encounter the commonsense world of the Symbolic in response to biological need. This encounter she sees as underlying the relation to the other that projects the subject as political. The 'shattering of discourse', she writes in *Revolution* (meaning, the pre-Symbolic utterance's assault on the Symbolic), 'reveals that linguistic changes constitute changes in the *status of the subject*' (RPL 15); also, such changes to signifying practice, which modernist literature exemplifies and which are evident in an intersubjective bonding with the other, attest 'to a "crisis" of social structures and their ideological, coercive, and necrophilic manifestations' (RPL 15) which include the capitalist mode of production as well as totalitarian tendencies.

Though Kristeva specifies that capitalism 'has stratified language into idiolects and divided it into self-contained isolated islands' (RPL 14), she is less clear on how an acknowledgement of proto-linguistic fragmentation might destabilize its systems of extraction and exploitation, or how her sense of the subject would introduce a revolution in governing forms. The heterogeneity of primary experience butts heads against the unifying power of the Symbolic, but the Symbolic eventually wins out when the subject matures, without any fundamental transformations, even though the pre-linguistic heterogeneity sometimes disrupts its repression through psychosis, religion, and art. For Kristeva, the infant's pre-Symbolic utterances make its entry into language singular every time. The infant's corporeal, gestural vocalizations enter into permanent conflict against established enunciatory codes, with the Symbolic trying to impose order and control on the unsubmissive instinctual drives, and the instinctual drives trying to destroy the Symbolic but failing time and again as the Symbolic succeeds in re-establishing its dominance. In other words, Kristeva's interpretation of the subject as a problem for political relations leaves open the question of how her heterogeneous sense of the subject, aware of singular drives and individual pre-symbolic sense-experience, might – empirically – reactivate political practices against domination.

Where Kristeva's emphasis on beginnings wants to interrogate phenomenology's brackets on subjective emergence in relation to the Symbolic, Arendt's is about the constantly regenerative process of the political, that is, situating the political as always beginning again in action, what-has-not-been-before – the political bond – constituting the world anew.[6] As Diprose and Ziarek elaborate, Arendt's notion of natality illustrates a de-essentializing and 'non-biological understanding of the human condition and of democratic plurality' (2018: 22): 'democratic plurality in general' (2018: 18), while depending on 'women's reproductive self-determination' (2018: 18), also, in a broader sense, surfaces again inside of diverse political speech and new beginnings that modernity has buried under administration and other forms of normalization, conformity, totalitarian tendencies, and sovereign expression. In view of natality, a person or power cannot choose with whom to share the world (the way the Nazis wanted to decide with whom to share the earth) because the political – coming to be through natality – cannot follow a pre-generated plan. For Arendt, the philosophical tradition's imagining of historical action as work on the world, culminating in Marx, assumes that the outcome of an action is prefigured, as History is prefigured in the Hegelian subject making the world by transforming material objects based on a mental blueprint. According to Margaret Canovan, Arendt disagreed with 'Marx's concept of man (subject of History) as a craftsman who can be in control of his material, and can "make history" as he makes a table' (1992: 73), because thinking of politics in terms of work or biology means confining political action to satisfying human needs, surrendering freedom to necessity and giving up the potential of politics to make something out of nothing, to form a web of relations that never existed before. As Arendt writes in *On Revolution*, 'The less we are doing ourselves, the less active we are, the more forcefully will this biological process assert itself, impose its inherent necessity upon us, and overawe us with the fateful automatism of sheer happening that underlies all human history' (2006: 49). 'Nothing', she writes in *The Human Condition*, 'ejects one more radically from the world than exclusive concentration upon the body's life, a concentration forced upon man in slavery or in the extremity of unbearable pain' (1958: 112). Arendt here is issuing a warning against a crisis of the political that she attributes to the total instrumentalization of life itself. The body shields us against politics and diminishes what we might have in common, closing down freedom, unleashing accumulation and turning history into a tool.

As the basis of the political for Arendt, natality is drawing from Kant's 'reflective judgment' (linked to the imagination). In this, it contrasts with a traditional philosophical idea of action as instrument, work, or the means to biological survival where 'the actual fabrication is performed under the guidance of a model with which the object is constructed' (1958: 140). In this type of judgement, the non-conceptual particular cannot be prescribed or subsumed in general categories of thought, has not yet been experienced, is not rule-bound and has yet to be systematized.[7] Politics is the formation of a community that has not ever existed, that is, a world shared by people (strangers) and ideas not pre-selected or pre-conceived but 'born'. Arendt's account of natality uses the fact of birth to reflect upon a politics without foundations, or, as she says, a politics without bannisters – the imperative of a being together, a community belonging or a territorial sharing with those who are not already inside one's prior conception of the world. Not 'Being towards death' or responding to a death drive or answering to Oedipus but rather in avoidance of all of it, the other, for Arendt, because it is born, is the yet-unknown, the precarious.

In eliding a psychoanalytic account of relations towards others within Arendt's natality, Kristeva may be reading Arendt against herself and against her positing of the political as its own origin and its own rule – as 'something altogether new' (2006: 11). Kristeva may be burying what Arendt calls the concept of freedom under a contrary concept of freedom attributable to the body and its drives and the unbracketing of subjective experience. In her influential 1981 essay 'Women's Time', for example, where Kristeva outlines three different phases of feminism, the third and most helpful phase is 'the singularity of each woman, her complexities, her many languages at the cost of a single horizon' (WT 197), where each woman born, outside of cyclical or linear chronological temporality, indicates the failure of prior representation and therefore the rejection of the sociosymbolic contract. Connected to the splitting of the subject in 'physiology and speech' (WT 197) as in Modernism, the type of freedom or creativity that Kristeva envisions depends on a pre-political attachment (in Arendt's perspective) and biological process that Arendt would see as endangering the political, mechanizing it and confining the individual and its action to a drive for security and survival, or necessity. Action, here for Kristeva, can happen in dialectical contention with the order of the social. For Kristeva, freedom is a site of new, singular expression that infringes on established expression, whereas for Arendt, freedom is politics resulting from an individual's entry into it, as this individual forms human relations anew by bearing witness, in speech, to an action that has not happened before.

Kristeva's re-reading of Arendt may be responding to a trend in feminism that Nancy Fraser has identified with a critique of 'state-organized capitalism' and that Kristeva's early work may have impacted: second-wave feminists, Fraser writes, 'rejected the bureaucratic-managerial ethos of state-organized capitalism' (2009: 105) as defining what constituted the political. For these thinkers, the state was organized according to an androcentrism which guaranteed inequality and relegated certain areas – like the domestic – as not under its jurisdiction or regulatory arm, even in the case of violence. Unfortunately, continues Fraser, neoliberalism has used such liberal critiques of the state to support its free-market policies and transformed it to serve the interests of accumulation. Neoliberals, says Fraser, have remade this second-wave feminist critique of politics in the nation state as 'grist for schemes aimed at reducing state action *tout court*' (2009: 111), demanding austerity and faulting welfare-state policies, for example, for high deficits, even while granting subsidies to big business especially in agriculture, pharmaceuticals, technology and defence. Neoliberalism has turned the attributed shortcomings of the state as a mode of political organization into an ideological platform for redistributing wealth upwards. Rather than recomposing the political from a tradition of political theory of the state that has been forsaken, Kristeva's use of the mother-child dyad marginalizes a consideration of the state as what organizes the political while building a theory where language acquisition is always in revolt against a world constituted by language. Her affiliating with Arendt, then, could be considered as an acknowledgement of the need for the 'relation to the other' to reclaim politics *tout court* when the nation state has been maligned as expressing the interests of the rulers or of always operating within a logic of exclusion. With this in mind, Kristeva is suggesting that Arendt's political sphere – rather than critiquing the mid-twentieth-century crisis of the nation state – unbrackets the subject in its heterogeneity and posits the ego in revolt.

Plurality/heterogeneity

Throughout her discussion of Arendt, Kristeva traces a psychoanalytic heterogeneity at the heart of the plurality of Arendt's public spaces that Arendt herself does not explicitly concede. After her discussion of Augustine's influence, Kristeva turns to talk about Arendt's next book, *Rahel Varnhagen: The Life of a Jewess*,[8] another text usually skirted by her critics. Kristeva states clearly that this text, a biography of an assimilated Jewish woman who hosted a salon frequented by Romantics in Germany at the turn of the nineteenth century,[9] is an 'example' (HA 50) of Arendt's political thought, a 'particularity' (HA 50) that produced her concept of the political in her subsequent career. Kristeva identifies in *Rahel* Arendt's political concept of the spectator: in this biography-like study, Arendt begins to develop the thesis that she more deeply explores later in *The Human Condition*, where political action takes the form of a life appearing before a plurality of spectators who witness it: the speech of the witness discloses the 'who' that performs the action 'as a distinct and unique being among equals' (1958: 178). For Arendt, the storyteller/witness recognizes that '[l]ife in its non-biological sense' (1958: 173) is a life made new in a type of artistry or narrative action that can be shared.

While Kristeva detects the 'veritable *history* of [Arendt's] political thinking' (HA 54) in *Rahel*, she does not concede the 'non-biological' aspect that Arendt attributes to Rahel's *bios*, instead tracing Rahel's desire as a type of counter-transference, where her own love (for Heidegger) gets woven into her account of the other (Rahel) and the other's loves. Kristeva faults Arendt for never discussing pathology or emotions: 'not once, in fact, does Arendt mention hysteria, depression, or paranoia' (HA 53), even though women psychanalysts of the era like Joan Rivière and Helene Deutsch were already starting to analyse the 'hysterical personality' (HA 57). She also mocks Arendt for including a section on Rahel's dreams, where Kristeva claims, she psychoanalyses with 'pleasure... thinly veiled acts of sexualized exclusion and humiliation' (HA 65) that reveal her inner conflicts. One of Rahel's dreams is about Athens; Kristeva revels in this as Arendt portrays herself as '[i]ndifferent to the sexual... meaning of dreams' (HA 66) even while using the same material as her model of political action. Arendt, Kristeva continues, misses Heidegger's point that poetry and its language underpin the city state. She also misses Aristotle's point that an action can only be made into an accomplishment and an individual can only be made unique and distinct if memorable. Yet for Kristeva, memory, like the Unconscious, is interruptive and dangerous to speech in the disclosure of the 'who' that makes action public, as a beginning.

Kristeva, then, reads Arendt's study of Rahel Varnhagen as developing the constituent parts of what would later become her philosophy of political action, making explicit the components of Arendt's public practice that fall close to Kristeva's own psychoanalytic story of subjective emergence. Yet, in contrast, Arendt treats the history of the assimilated Jew as marking a crisis of the political related to antisemitism that culminated in the Holocaust. Rahel's assimilation, she notes, testifies to a secular Enlightenment engaged in universalism through Reason, but, at the same time, Reason only brings the liberation of private thinking – 'it appears that it can free isolated individuals only, can direct the future only of Crusoes' (1974: 10). Similarly, in her later (1951) study of Marcel Proust in *Origin* (whom she deems as, for the most part, a 'contemplator of inner experience' [1968: 80]), Arendt criticizes Proust's assimilation in salon society as demonstrating 'the decomposition of politics', making evident the 'victory of bourgeois values over the citizen's sense of responsibility' and a society that 'had emancipated itself completely from public concerns' (1968: 80). Proust's post-Disraeli, post-Dreyfus Parisian society, says Arendt, accepted Jews as exotic exceptions expressing 'Jewishness' as long as they were seen as separated from the cultural group, 'dejudaized', as having 'lost that measure of political responsibility which their origin implied' (1968: 83). So, even though Arendt does link Jewish being to birth,[10] a move that Kristeva underlines as revealing 'a prepolitical attitude' exposing a 'newness at the heart of plurality' (HA 67), Arendt criticizes Jewish being in its Enlightenment reconstruction as too privatizing (as not political, not bonding with others).

Kristeva, then, fails – she fails to show her own view of the subject as heterogeneous in the same terms as Arendt does in her reconstruction of the political as an alternative to the nation state's turn to totalitarianism and exclusion. In other words, the singular subject Kristeva describes is still alienated from the political bond that Arendt is theorizing even though she (Kristeva) is making a heroic effort to align them. Nevertheless, even though Kristeva ultimately does not locate the point of correspondence between her heterogeneous subject and Arendt's politics of plurality, her train of thought is provocative. In looking to connect her psychoanalytic critique – with its attention to emotions, mothers, pathologies, drives, language and sexualities – to Arendt's early works (those prior to rethinking philosophy's traditions of the political in the wake of the crisis of the nation state propelled by the Holocaust), Kristeva is broadening Arendt's sense of the political. She is also broadening the field of application of Arendt's insights into politics beyond the contingencies of Arendt's time. Kristeva's insinuation that Arendt's political action is but an exemplary instance, a historically particular appearance of the heterogeneous subject, connects Kristeva's critique of Arendt to the next volume of the 'female genius' series, the one on Melanie Klein.

In this volume, Kristeva defends Klein's turn from the overtly political – even during the same political turmoil as Arendt faced – and towards the analysis of private psychosis, as proving to be 'the most pressing political characteristic of our day' (MK 15), for, she continues, it furthers 'our understanding of our being as an endemic state of ill-being' (MK 15). Klein's psychoanalytic studies foreground envy, depression, isolation, primary aggression, greed, paranoia, destruction, sadism and the death drive in the social bond: 'states of battle and retributive justice dominate the universe of primary violence imposed by the death drive, even more ruthlessly so when that drive is excessive' (MK 160). The motivating factor behind this prototypical anxiety and alienation is not an Oedipal crisis but rather birth and separation. The breast, which is the internalized ideal projection of the mother's closeness, is also persecutory and punishing and splits the subject. The pre-subject internalizes external objects (like the breast) to keep from losing them but still loses them similarly to the way the stateless, in Arendt, lose their political community, where citizens try to make up for loss by clinging to the authoritarian strongman.

Klein's divided and clashing subjectivities expose another difference that Kristeva has with Arendt's political. In Kristeva's descriptions of Klein, there is no rest – the external world of objects and relations is always out of order with the subject in history, and the subject cannot find its place in the shared world. '[I]f', Kristeva notes,

> this future subject readily grants himself a 'presence' of other people that he internalizes as much as expels, he is not facing an object but, in fact an *ab-ject*... It is a subject and an object that, as such, are crystallized only through what Klein calls the 'depressive position'.
>
> (MK 72–3)

In other words, Kristeva is proposing a 'fix' to Arendt's philosophy of being with others and sharing the world where that being together in politics is constantly in the process of being lost or destroyed or constantly imperilling or rejecting the subject who wants 'in'. As Peg Birmingham describes Kristeva's intention, 'immemorial violence (the sadomasochistic or death drive) that is part of primary natality is always already in a relation to the object' (2003: 66). For Kristeva, Klein's psychoanalytic subject exposes the political as full of antagonisms and vehement aggressions that torment and alienate political existences when traditional political institutions fracture or de-form. As Peg Birmingham concludes, 'Kristeva suggests that while Arendt develops the psychological virtue of excellence at the foundation of our pleasure in the company of others, she ignores completely... our desire to dominate and inspire fear in those to whose company we bring nothing but grief' (2003: 56–7). Where Arendt argues that violence instrumentalizes power and so *is not* political, Kristeva uses Klein to return violence to the political as constitutive of it, to show that the political is much more embattled than Arendt's theory of action, revelation of the 'who', and narrative recognition admits.[11] Kristeva's affiliating with Klein pinpoints that the subject unravels and thus *becomes heterogeneous*, with the breakdown of the nation state appearing in sexuality, affects, language and pathologies: the broken political is inside the subject, devouring it, splitting it, alienating it and endangering it, most often violently, and not only at the historical moment that Arendt witnessed. Kristeva is suggesting, in her descriptions of Klein's studies and theories, that the structure of the Unconscious through the separation with the mother is already inside (but repressed by) Arendt's political philosophy which is centred on a separation from tradition, a devastation of political avenues in the nation state, and a general uprootedness of community belonging.

Through Klein's theory of this embattled embodied subject, Kristeva links the crisis of the nation state that led to the Holocaust – and led Arendt to want to rethink politics around the idea of natality – together with the crisis of the nation state that neoliberalism orchestrates.[12] Kristeva's retrofitting of Klein's heterogeneous psychoanalytic subject into Arendt's politics of plurality stands out as Kristeva's analysis moves into what the critics have recognized as Arendt's more overtly political philosophical works. Arendt's analysis of the 'crystallization of totalitarianism' results from the nation state's inability to recognize the minorities in its midst as lawful persons, expelling them, and then exterminating them, just as Klein's subject is split by loss. The repressed or expelled heterogeneity of the Symbolic (alongside the repressed or expelled plurality of the political field) appears even more as 'a reality only upon the fall of the Berlin Wall in 1989' (MK 134), Kristeva writes, and is still 'occurring today', witnessed in 'the status of undocumented aliens' – those who have lost their primary identification – and so has 'lost none of its urgency' (MK 135). Just as the language fragments, drives and instinctual corporeal motions disrupt the Symbolic that holds together social reality, such movements of stateless populations disrupt and break up 'national, political, and religious bonds' (MK 136) due to the loss of common sense that is 'tantamount to madness' (MK 137). In other words, the madness of the subject is reflected in the madness of the political because it is discordant with it.

Yet, ultimately, what Kristeva is identifying by trying to match her divided subject to Arendt's ideas of political action and natality is that the two do not match: in other words, Kristeva's modernist subject cannot find a home within Arendt's pluralism just as Arendt's pluralism is unrooted from the subject that Kristeva so meticulously describes. This is the neoliberal condition: the subject set afloat, detached from politics and politics unable to come to terms with the subjectivities that, in liberalism, it is supposed to recognize. Our current nation state crisis, in the wake of the fall of the Berlin Wall in 1989 if not before, has been brought about with a surge in identification with the singularity of the market. Like the crisis in the nation state that Arendt attributes to the rise of fascism, this contemporary crisis destroys the social bond and the space between people where speech and action take place, as labourers and superfluous populations are forced into statelessness and cut off from political action. Arendt's statelessness can now be understood as a model or example for a more general absence of political life, as the traditional modes of practising politics – yes, nation states, but not only nation states – do not provide identifications that invite belonging or bonding. In other words, with markets being the dominant and singular paradigm for imagining speech, action, and sharing the world together, people are alienated from thinking about political forms (the nation state or others) as offering a way to connect through speech and action, turning us all into subjects devoid of political possibility which Arendt would call automatons. Kristeva, on the other hand, does not accept that the expulsion of the subject from politics is the final word. She sets out to find correspondences – even if antagonistic ones – between her sense of the subject, on the one hand, and, on the other, the political sphere that Arendt poses in terms that would reject it, catapulting it into precarity. While agreeing that the traditions of politics are unable to respond to the current situation and must constantly seek for new foundations, Kristeva describes a subject who finds its forced separation from the means of speech and action to be ultimately intolerable. This modern alienation, Kristeva tells us, is the condition of life's rebellion; that is, the subject's brokenness is so great as to disrupt the social conditions that lead to its expulsion, opening still unmet pathways for its birth in the political.

Notes

1 'When reading Céline we are seized at the fragile spot of our subjectivity where our collapsed defenses reveal, beneath the appearances of a fortified castle, a flayed skin; neither inside nor outside, the wounding exterior turning into an abominable interior, war bordering on putrescence, while social and family rigidity, that beautiful mask, crumbles within the beloved abomination of innocent vice. A universe of borders, seesaws, fragile and mingled identities, wanderings of the subject and its objects, fears and struggles, abjections and lyricisms. At the turning point between social and asocial, familial and delinquent, feminine and masculine, fondness and murder' (PH 135).

2 Trilogies and, as well, tripartite groupings are common in Kristeva's oeuvre, from her detective series to her dialectics.

3 Arendt herself was not all that enthusiastic about the category of genius. She faults the tradition of genius for its solipsism. 'What is important in our context', she notes, 'is that the work of genius, as distinguished from the product of the craftsman, appears to have absorbed those elements of distinctness and uniqueness which find their immediate expression in action and speech' (1958: 210). In addition, as an expression of the artist's identity in what they have done, the genius artwork turns the artist into a maker of things like the worker, governed by a violence that shapes things, rather than an actor engaged politically: 'the idolization of genius', frequent in the modern age, therefore 'harbors the same degradation of the human person as other tenets prevalent in commercial society' (1958: 211).

4 The dissertation was overseen by Karl Jaspers in 1929, before Arendt's flight from Germany, and revised for publication between 1958 and 1965. The revisions were never completed by Arendt.

5 Kristeva reiterates this point in a 2014 essay 'New Forms of Revolt': 'Through a narrative of free association in the rejuvenating revolt with and against the old law... one's singular autonomy emerges, along with one's renewed link to the other. But this other "Freudian palace of memory" that psychoanalysis revisits and transforms was not perceived by Hannah Arendt, who praised Saint Augustine's palace of memory but dismissed psychology and psychoanalysis, which in her eyes were sciences of "the general"' (7).

6 '[T]he constituent principle', Antonio Negri describes Arendt's thesis, 'is grounded on nothing more than its own beginning and takes place through nothing but its own expression. The radical quality of the constituent principle is absolute. It comes from a void and constitutes everything' (1999: 15).

7 'At stake', notes Linda Zerilli of Arendt's use of 'reflective judgment', 'is trying to be at home in a world composed of relations and events not of our own choosing, without succumbing to various forms of fatalism or determinism' (2005: 128).

8 Written in 1938 as her second dissertation (that would eventually qualify her to teach) and first published in 1957.

9   She lived from 1771 to 1833.
10 'Arendt returns here to the Augustinian theme of birth, but for the first time she casts it as a definition of Jewish being. As she later put it, Arendt considered herself a Jew not by virtue of her belonging to a religion, but "by birth"' (HA 67).
11 In the same way, she uses Colette in the next volume to illustrate why language is less concordant than Arendt might concede when, in her account, the storyteller is the one able to match up the 'who' with identity.
12 Kristeva therefore understands Arendt's thinking to be 'no longer historical but historicizing' (MK 134).

References

Arendt, H. (1958), *The Human Condition*, 2nd edn, Chicago: University of Chicago Press.
Arendt, H. (1961), *Between Past and Future: Six Exercises in Political Thought*, New York: Viking Press.
Arendt, H. (1968 [1966]), *The Origins of Totalitarianism*, San Diego, CA: Harcourt.
Arendt, H. (1974), *Rahel Varnhagen: The Life of a Jewish Woman*, rev. edn, trans. R. and C. Winston, New York: Harcourt Brace Jovanovich.
Arendt, H. (1978 [1971]), *The Life of the Mind: The Groundbreaking Investigation on How We Think*, San Diego, CA: Harcourt.
Arendt, H. (1996), *Love and Saint Augustine*, ed. J. V. Scott and J. C. Stark, Chicago: University of Chicago Press.
Arendt, H. (2006), *On Revolution*, New York: Penguin.
Arendt, H. (2007), *Reflections on Literature and Culture*, ed. S. Young-Ah Gottlieb, Stanford, CA: Stanford University Press.
Bernstein, R. J. (2018), *Why Read Hannah Arendt Now?*, Cambridge: Polity.
Birmingham, P. (2003), 'The Pleasure of Your Company: Arendt, Kristeva, and an Ethics of Public Happiness', *Research in Phenomenology*, 33: 53–74.
Butler, J. (2012), *Parting Ways: Jewishness and the Critique of Zionism*, New York: Columbia University Press.
Canovan, M. (1992), *Hannah Arendt: A Reinterpretation of Her Political Thought*, Cambridge: Cambridge University Press.
Diprose, R. and E. P. Ziarek (2018), *Arendt, Natality and Biopolitics: Toward Democratic Plurality and Reproductive Justice*, Edinburgh: Edinburgh University Press.
Fraser, N. (2009), 'Feminism, Capitalism and the Cunning of History', *New Left Review*, 56: 97–117.
Negri, A. (2009 [1999]), *Insurgencies: Constituent Power and the Modern State*, trans. M. Boscagli, Minneapolis, MN: University of Minnesota Press.
Zerilli, L. M. G. (2005), *Feminism and the Abyss of Freedom*, Chicago: University of Chicago Press.

PART TWO

Kristeva and aesthetics

8

Modernism unleashed and restrained: Joyce, Céline and Arendt in Kristeva's tale of the century

Marios Constantinou

Modernity's metaphysics of motion and the earthy zeroines of maternity: Transposing Joyce, Arendt and Kristeva

Some of the vital implications of this chapter have already been anticipated by Raoul Vaneigem, one of the most manifest and poetic embodiments of the spirit of 1968. One peak illumination of Vaneigem's quick thinking is that the modern bourgeoisie epitomizes the acceleration of world transformation while increasing the weight of dead time in everyday life. The bourgeois image of modern politics is that of a 'driver pumping the brake while his accelerator is jammed fast to the floor: the more his speed increases, the more frenetic, perilous and useless become his attempts to slow down' (Vaneigem 1983: 120). Bourgeois power valorizes a sense of short-lived, ephemeral, transitory modernity which 'seeks to imprison men within this transitoriness':

> To replace the old theology of *stasis*, the bourgeoisie sets up a metaphysics of motion [...] an ideology of change in the service of what does not

change [...] thus in our universe of expanding technology and comfort we see people turning in upon themselves, shriveling up, living trivial lives, and dying for details. It is a nightmare [...].
(Vaneigem 1983: 121)

Like Stephen in *Ulysses*, the 1968 generation – to which Julia Kristeva belongs – appeared on the public stage of history as if awakening from a nightmare. Yet Vaneigem in the above passage reiterates manifest symptoms of political abjection whose strains had already been discerned by Hannah Arendt in the 1950s.

Arendt writes at the onset of the space age which has found a way to 'act on the earth', 'as though we dispose of it from the outside'. As Arendt notes, 'at the risk of endangering the natural life process we expose the earth to universal cosmic forces, alien to nature's household' (1958: 262). The atomic age that yields 'the onslaught of speed', a 'conquering process' of 'taking possession of the earth' comes at the price of a 'decisive shrinkage of the earth' and a climaxing crisis of worldly sense (Arendt 1958: 250, 251). Encircling and circumscribing the earth amounts to expropriation of lands and humans alike, generating a momentum of world alienation and inner world stultification. The eclipse of the public world, the crisis of the memorable word and deed co-evolve with the process of the earth's imperial encirclement. These crises are coextensive with the endless accumulation of carbon-driven capital and techno-fossils along with the nuclear fallout of atomic acceleration – now geologically formalized as the Anthropocene. Deprived of public world, intimate life and natural sense, the political animal vanishes in an age which escalates extinction rates in general. Arendt's care for the word and the world was ominously presaged by James Joyce. Joyce's intuition is both wordly and worldly in the Arendtian sense, bringing all the afflictions of the age of acceleration home to roost. The discussion that follows lays the groundwork for rethinking Kristeva's tale of the century through her encounter with Joyce, Céline and Arendt.

In Joyce the word is literally in flux. It flows in liquid form. The text emerges from thought streams and word motility. Deeply implicated in modernity's metaphysics of motion, Joyce wavers experimentally over Stephen Dedalus and Leopold Bloom, between a tormented solipsistic ideal and the ambivalence of recomposed nothingness. Unrooted and prospectively modernity's *homo sacer*, Bloom is a living hell of meaningless stasis within the banality of constant change, epitomizing modernity's fallen public space – noman, adman, free-floating 'anythingarian' and unsurprisingly freemason. A 'misbirth with a trailing navelcord' (Joyce 1986: 32, verse 36) – that is precisely the nightmare Stephen is trying to awaken from. What wears Stephen's mind down is the fatigue of 'painless, patient consciousness', the twilight limbo of 'specterlike symbols of force and velocity [...] the old professor was an atheist free-mason. O the grey dull day!' (1976b: 456). Neurasthenic modernity in a nutshell – burned out, banal, excessive, depleted and frenzied at once.

Interestingly, psychoanalytic modernism intervenes, in its own turn, in the thick of a stultifying, superegoic, ferociously socialized public consciousness that mystifies the impoverished ego, while hystericizing its intimate life with the combined pressure of the id. Arendt was apprehensive of modernity's steamrolling transition from republican citizen to stultified bourgeois. On his antipodes, she extolled exceptional illuminations of psychic life as they concurred in happy – though tragic – coincidence with creative political impulses, while equally acclaiming those unifying impulses of personality that defied the social conformism of the mass individual. Indeed, Arendt lamented the twilight of political spontaneity and of pulsing intimacy – both coming increasingly under the precipitous pressure of cultural philistinism and docile publics. Adjoining Arendt's generation, Joyce's bourgeois, the *stulti homines* in *Dubliners*, were rehearsing not only the social reduction of the political into pullitics but, besides, they were drowning intimacy in abject marriages. Expectedly, the onrush of such social tyranny of stultifying weakness, dependence and conformism magnifies the paternal rescue fantasy of 'papal infallibility... the greatest scene in the whole history of the Church' (Joyce 1976a: 184). In effect, modernity's metaphysics of motion comes to span a veiled sideshow of abjection – 'in collision with man and collusion with money' (Joyce 1976c: 433).

It is the obscurity of an edgeless and politically uneventful modernity wasted in convulsive spasms of mutable nihilisms that Arendt's horror discloses. Read from this perspective, Joyce's 'Ivy men' in *Dubliners* sustained by 'secret satieties' are crouching shadows of the city-boss (1976a: 129–48; 1976c: 435). They are figures of modernity's mystified bourgeois ego languishing on the rocks of *vita privata*, drained of intimate life but quite skilful in public relations and pullitical science. Arendt was stunned by the spreading dryness of words-in-action, the growing sterility of the poetic springs of the political and its constituent acts, owing to modernity's stultifying cast of mind – too many illusional beginnings and phoney callings, too few thoughts. I have evoked the term *pullitics* from the *Wake* where the 'brain of the Franks, hand of the Christian, tongue of the north' play 'pulicy-pulicy' (1976c: 127, 414). Read backwards, it reflects an acute sense about what stultified Ireland's public life – the Ivy mob's backstage rule profiled in *Dubliners*. Read in forward motion it affords a prophetic glimpse into the coming of the 'dirigible man' – 'Lead kindly fowl! They always did: ask the ages.' Joyce foretells ironically Arendt's horror – modernity outpaced by the deluge of the social: 'What bird has done yesterday man may do next year, be it fly, be it moult, be it hatch, be it agreement in the nest... automutativeness right on normalcy... born to lay and love eggs... palmy date in a waste's oasis...' (1976c: 112). In the Circe chapter of *Ulysses*, Bloom – the bourgeois avatar of social implosion – spells a mixomasonese

Esperanto vision of 'universal language' and 'universal brotherhood' with 'no more patriotism' but with 'free money, free rent, free love and free lay church in a free lay state'. It sounds like a free money market with a free fox in a free hen roost (1986: 399, 1690–4). The *Wake*'s prophetic bird steers modernity into travestied beginnings and misbirths, guided by the pullitics of imperial favouritism, patriotic opportunism and Roman 'Patholicism' (1976c: 611).

Instead, Stephen's covenant with his aching conscience conveys his *nostos* for a saving grace reflected in the face and form of Mary – 'Guide us home'; 'not like earthly beauty, dangerous to look upon, but like the morning star, which is thy emblem, bright and musical…' (Joyce 1976b: 396). Stephen's nostos is activated by Mary-cum-foundress and *initiatrix*, not by syndromes of castrating Patholicism. Rather, it is a way out of it. As we shall see, this motif reappears in *Ulysses*, attending the spasms of an awakening consciousness that is groping for a new form of life.

We may afford a keener sense of Stephen's breakaway *nostos* if we consider more closely the worldly bearings of the Homeric notion of *nostos* which involves an initial movement of epic expansion as well as a return-cum-renewal. *Nostos* is the embedded truth of Homer's homebound epic – always redirecting, testing and transposing offensive expansion. In the spatial structure of Homer's epic, Odysseus is the poetic hero of this second conception of homeward movement – an eventual recovery of a mortal form of life from the imperial hubris of unworldly expansion. In Joyce's mock epic the nostalgic impulse of this counter-imperial motion is keyed not to modernity's 'wandering Jew' – the bourgeois persona of the rootless cosmopolitan Bloom cum Ulysses – but to colonized, plebeian and worldly muses of embodied forms of life.

For instance, Molly is by half of Jewish origin. But when Molly finally seduces Bloom in proposing to her, she does not answer promptly. Rather, she transposes to earthly surroundings – spacing out over the sea and the sky, 'thinking of so many things he didn't know'. Unrooted, Bloom didn't know of sailors playing; of all birds flying; of 'washing up dishes on the pier', of 'the sentry in front of the governor's house with the thing around his white helmet, poor devil half roasted'; of 'the glorious sunsets and the figtrees in the Alameda gardens'; of 'all the queer little streets and the pink and blue and yellow houses and the rosegardens and the jessamine and geraniums and cactuses and Gibraltar as a girl where I was a flower of the mountain' (1986: 643, Penelope 1580–1602). Molly's nostalgic *jouissance* for her living roots in colonial Gibraltar not only strikes a sharp contrast with Bloom's groundless universalism but also effects a tormented yet powerful sublimation of the traumatic loss of her son Rudy at infancy. *Amor matris*. Moreover, it is irreducible to narrow nativism. Molly's climaxing monologue is concurrent with the singularity of the particular-universal of the earth's gynecic rotation. Joyce timed Molly's ultimate 'Yes' so as to coincide with the daybreak's first vision of light – from the East. Missing a right emphasis or harnessing *nostos* in one direction rather than another may certainly authorize a double hubris either in the form of *translatio imperii* or in the form of nationalist mystification.

In this light, Kristeva's omission of the stirring movements of worldly *nostos* in her overall approach to Joyce does poetic injustice to what Joyce identifies as the 'noughty zeroines' of modernity and maternity (1976c: 261). Although I am aware of the esoteric and Kaballistic undertones of the concept, I emphasize instead its less mystifying nuances. I consider Joyce's female zeroines in terms of their anticolonial and counter-imperial resonance, as odd muses embodying varying degrees of abjection, marginality and dispossession, of resilience and resistance – yet inviting deep non-bourgeois and earthly affirmations. Zeroines then are treated as political omphaloi, as too obvious, hence negligible synecdoches that awaken to an omitted sense of the political. Gibraltar and Molly are interposed as such cutting points, as awakening *omphaloi* – navel chords. They link back words, affects and actions to the lowest initiatory point, to a cipher of zero value. And yet, that zerocipher's orality and vitality enables the formation of a new psychic space with embattled illuminations that echo the loss anew.

Consider in this light the omphalic tale of Anna Livia Plurabelle (ALP) in *Finnegan's Wake*. ALP is raped by the invading conqueror 'brave son of Scandiknavery' (1976c: 47) and dogs alike. Being an imperial trophy and prey to 'Northmen's thing' (215), she is a metonymy of Dublin's river Liffey and a parody-mother to 'a hundred eleven wan by wan by wan' (201). A zerocipher of fullness and nothingness, ALP epitomizes folk archetypes of living nature, feasting fertility and gift economy, mocking bourgeois reason, etiquette and family patterns. A Rabelaisean geomater, ALP parodies earth, birth and modernity's grave crisis of regenerative potential beyond its interloping wars of expansion – a joyful truth of a folk carnivalesque *nostos*. Interestingly, ALP comes to be known only under the rule of social 'gossipocracy' (476). Yet, we are able to reconstruct the semiotic flows of the political at the tail of Anna Livia's earthly tale.

The washerwomen's nocturnal slumber by the river banks – just like modernity's mental fatigue induced by the outpouring of excessive publicity – transposes by juxtaposition back to another earthy figure of anti-colonial awakening. Joyce's description of the selfless, no money-seeking milkwoman in 'Telemachus' – the initiatory chapter of *Ulysses* – is indeed a morning tale of waking, an epiphany of renewal: 'Old and secret she had entered from a morning world, maybe a messenger [...] silk of the kine and poor old woman, names given her in old times. A wondering crone, lowly form of an immortal serving her conqueror and her gay betrayer, their common cuckquean, a messenger from the secret morning. To serve or to upbraid...' (1986: 12, verse 398–406). Stephen lays the coin in the uneager hand of the mystical envoy, coming 'from the secret morning', registering his debt: 'we'll owe twopence'. 'Time enough, sir, she said...' (13, verse 457–60). *Amor matris* – 'the lowly' but nourishing folk 'form of the immortal' reasserts itself abundantly as a second, anti-colonial maternity. It catalyses a self-conscious mother-son bond against the background of a barren country viciously bound by the pact between 'conqueror and gay betrayer'. *Amor matris* is not necessarily a pre-Oedipal fusion. Similarly, Molly Bloom's intimate revolt that amorously embraces Stephen receives its bearings from the rebounding *jouissance* of *nostos*, of earthly rootedness – Gibraltar. In 'Scylla and Charybdis' Joyce foregrounds defiantly the animate aura that withstands modernity's metaphysics of motion, intimating that 'the movements which work revolutions in the world are born out of the dreams and visions in a peasant's heart on the hillside. For them the earth is not an exploitable ground but the living mother' (1986: 153, verse 104–7).

It is in the light of such maternal figures that Kristeva's 'Stabat Mater' needs to be reappraised. Succinctly put, Kristeva presents Mary as a conformable figure of stultified pietas – a standard cliché of the Catholic symbolic economy – emptied out of any self-reliance or historical and genealogical context. Mary as an empty shell simply carries out God's command in her womb – a 'maternal receptacle purified as it might be by the virginal fantasy' (SM 176). The reduction of Mary to Mater Dolorosa confines her to a woeful masochist mourner of a corpse, obsessed with death and pain at the foot of the Cross. Kristeva weaves in and out of Catholic stereotypes of the virginal-maternal, arguing that the Virgin 'assumes the paranoid lust for power', elevated from woman to Heavenly Queen and the Holy Mother of the earthly Church. The trick is that 'she succeeds in stifling that megalomania by putting it on its knees before the child-god' (SM 180). Still, the Virgin bears the paranoid fantasy of being exempted from time and death thanks to 'the very flattering representation of Dormition or Assumption'. Thus, she is set apart as a 'Unique Woman, alone among women, alone among mothers, alone among humans since she is without sin'. Only nuns and martyrs may accede to this ideal – masochistically – receiving as their bonus 'the promised jouissance' (SM 181).

All the same, Kristeva's balanced sadomasochistic approach to Mary veils the profound. Once we traverse the Catholic gallery of Mary's streamlined representations, we may risk re-reading Mary's poetic verse, her own ode to birth – just to glean out some historically bound earthly subjectivity. First, let us duly register Mary's radical doubt addressed to Gabriel as to the news of bearing the Son of the Sublime: 'How can this be since I am virgin?' (Lk. 1.34). Mary – a more or less twelve-year old girl – is utterly mystified, alarmed in horror by the perplexed greeting of Gabriel. This most reasonable of misgivings thrusts Mary into a canonically hysterical subject position of radical doubt and abject ambiguity – 'But why me?' 'What's all this?', 'How could this possibly come to be?' and so on. Hence Mary alternates between abjection and *jouissance* before coming to terms with the sublime. Her spirit magnifies and rejoices in the shadow of the most high (Lk. 1.46-7), as if that episode was a prerequisite for Mary's move to the poetic plane of epic history and the tracing of divine justice. What has gravely been missed by Kristeva is young Mary's abridged version of the emancipatory subject that 'has scattered the proud in the thoughts of their hearts, has brought down the powerful from their thrones and lifted up the lowly; has filled the hungry and has sent the rich away empty' (Lk. 1.51-3). In fathoming the social, psychoanalytic and political truth of the ages, Mary partakes of the becoming-God of the abjected. Thus, the maternal in Mary's ode to birth fertilizes a political sense of what an anti-imperial subject on trial could possibly be. Shouldn't this be treated as an improbable affirmation of Kristeva's early orientation? Mary ultimately conceives the sublime Word, risking a bloody and abject birth. On the brink of an administered infanticide which forces her into exile, Mary becomes both a refugee life-giver and trustee of the coming sublime.

To further consolidate Mary's status as a 'naughty zeroine' let us consider her involvement in the wedding incident at Cana as recounted by John in 2.1-11. Wine – the milk of earthly joy – runs out, becoming a possible source of embarrassment that may end the wedding feast. Mary, as a guest, simply says to Jesus, 'They have no wine.' Jesus then – inexplicably quick-tempered – turns to Mary and says: 'Woman what concern is that to you and to me? My hour has not yet come.' Still, Mary tells the servants to do what they are told by Jesus. And water jars are converted into wine. But what did actually happen? Apparently, Jesus works through his initial reservations, his sense of uncertainty about rising into the public prospect of *vita activa*. The anxiety of assuming a public calling is pronounced and entails a break with family norm and bond. And yet it is Mary's prudential power that prompts Jesus' move into the public world of grounded History as defined by lasting words and deeds. Mary's discretion is a motivating force that puts a hesitant Jesus on the tracks of historical motion. This transition cannot be facilitated by the sadomasochistic persona depicted in Kristeva's 'Stabat Mater'. In fact, Mary-cum-initiatory-subject was already poetically prefigured in her own ode to birth. Her innocuously descriptive remark provides the ground for ending Jesus' abstention from public life. It ends his political invisibility. He appears as a doer under the auspices of maternal *auctoritas* in the Arendtian sense. Thus, a quite distressed Jesus discloses the first signs of notable public action by rescuing a worldly festivity from disaster. Here, Mary's subject position is one between a Roman-Arendtian initiatrix and a Joycean noughty zeroine rather than one between a pathetic Catholic Queen and a Patholic Mater Dolorosa – as assumed by Kristeva. Mary – a zeroine of beginnings, a nothing in earthly becoming, not just an empty vessel – awakens Jesus into a second birth that founds a public world. Mary is the worldly ground of immortality.

Zerological *mordernism*: Epiphanies of abjection and the powers of abstraction

Absent of a moment of foundation and beginning, of a moment of revolutionary *jouissance* bound to a durable constitution able to sublimate the birth trauma of the new, modernity in that legendary Arendtian sense lapses into the apocalypse of counter-revolution and total war. This is a messianic zero-degree of the same, or the same as an invalid exception, so to speak. What I am hinting at is modernity as the accelerating condition which annihilates *auctoritas*, Arendt's neo-Roman concept intended to mediate between power and violence due to its reliance on dependable foundations and authoritative beginnings. What it degenerates into is what Joyce in the *Wake* had intimated as *awethorrorty* (1976c: 516). More precisely, modernity conveys the abiding crisis of *auctores imperii Romani*. Europe could no longer augment its world-historical role without thrusting itself into a permanent crisis of auspices, gravitas and foundations. Writing after overlapping apocalyptic ends of God, of the Reich, of Europe's empires, of literature and ultimately of reason, amounts to writing posthumously about death at the vanishing point. Céline's war chronicles call up just those ghosts of Europe's zero-hour. They pulse with the modern subject's visceral spasms, echoing an insider's insight who is at the same time a vanquished outsider. Writing about the Reich's messianic now-time and its vertiginous disappearance through the eyes of a disgraced collabo cannot come about except as a refusal of writing itself, of language and narrative. Modernity's fall time is repeated by a vanquished language, neutralized as if to exorcize its self-erasure, abjectly stripped even of elementary pretensions.

Born of an invalid body and a war-induced brain injury, invented or not, Céline's vertiginous perspective abides by loss and pain cum style. It re-inscribes disaster in panoramic terms, inside-out, lingering over modernity's zero-hour. A living dead, a zero-subject subsisting on excess liminality through Europe's imperial implosion from Verdun to Stalingrad, a blatantly defeatist Céline gives up gleefully not only on what he considers a dead language, literature and France – which are coincidents – but is also resistant 'to revive anything at all!... Europe died at Stalingrad... the Devil has its soul! he can keep it!... the stinking whore!' (2008: 19). Indeed, of all the occupied countries, only France could have spawned such an intrepid species of rustic and Socratic collabo. Emptied out of all contextual specifications such as being victim and victimizer, betrayed and traitor, which bound him to a loop that intertwined the carnage of two imperial wars, Céline labours revoltingly with the abjections of modernity's signifiers: language, France, Europe, America, all variably rigged by academicism, technological nihilism, racial anxiety, phoney messianism, masonic plutocracy, Judeophobia and militarism: 'If you like delirium, fine – but look out! – do it right! To do it right, it has to come from a man's core – from his soul. Not from his head... today our delirium is pretty well confined to political fanaticism – even more ridiculous. Oh I know! I got caught up in it too!' (1989: 312, 314).

Céline's sarcastic gusto delights in mischievous hallucinatory abjection. But however gutsy and spirited, Céline's style of abjection is deeply conscious of its undertaking. It outlives the devastation of all that were held sacred up until Europe's zero-hour. And effectively draws itself apart from the rampant conformism of the social in its post-totalitarian form. As such, it confounds modernity's degree-zero of self-destruction with the zero-degree of writing, becoming a non-writing of diffuse orality. In transposing the form of spoken exuberance from modernity's underworld into a restlessly leaping syntax, with swerving affect flows verging on psychotic delirium, Céline re-accents the living impulses of popular orality, converting them into a written slang. The hiccupped syntax re-enacts the undulating rhythms of rails, train cars and bridges after bombing raids. True or induced, recursive fits of trauma and coma occasion an aesthetic justification of the jump-cut syntax of the war chronicles: 'I can make you hear the booms...' (2008: 209). The long shadow of the First World War trauma recasts its spell upon the coma of the Second: 'is it fate?... or just to amuse you?... I'm really out!... they try to wake me up... they even shake me... Oh, no intention of moving!... you visualize the cataclysm?', 'elements unchained...' (2008: 196, 191, 193). Modernity unleashed.

Through re-reading Céline, my hope is to elucidate Kristeva's frame of abjection by relocating its scope in the context of persistent imperial processes. Necessarily, this entails removing some dust from Kristeva's consolidated perspectives on key figures and moments of modernism, while opening new windows that will allow her approach to abjective modernism to obtain the political relevance it now lacks, welcome or not. My argument foregrounds opposing visions and forms of the modern, which not only articulate convergent abjections of the social but also occasion semeiotic epiphanies of the political – long forgotten, yet necessary by any means. To this effect, I will treat Joyce, Céline and Arendt as modernist contemporaries, inducing critical juxtapositions and mutual illuminations that cut across Kristeva's reading apparatus.

What is in question is not Kristeva's emphasis on the power of horror but the becoming of this horror as commonplace as Céline's blasé crossing of Germany's infernal hinterland. It weighs upon the vanishing train-travelling viewer who literally merges with non-space, coinciding in motion with a fading bomb-shelled nothingness. Indeed, Kristeva's book-length study on Arendt was sufficiently extensive to occasion such a shift of perspectives, most notably by rethinking not just an all-encompassing abjection but the banality induced by an accelerated and vertiginous version of it. Céline was unfortunately not considered relevant in that context, which is why Kristeva's original concept of abjection risks mystification if not obsolescence; more so, because Céline's frantic syntax, precipitous ellipses and shifting affects keep boiling down to a contemporary, presumably post-totalitarian loop of motorized appearances, stuttered speech, syncopated writing, non-stop transmission and overstimulated screen perception. Céline remains an early explorer of an intriguing déja-vu fascism with explicit postmodern prospects whose theoretical apex have been annotated by the likes of Baudrillard and Virilio. What the implosion of the fascist form has rendered to the post-totalitarian order was a terminal process whereby – in the absence of perceived causes – the speed of unprecedented effects snowballed into contagious de-subjectification. On my reading, this is precisely what Kristeva's study on Céline lacked at the time she was writing, that is, a concept of motorized surplus abjection which uproots by de-earthing the planet, proletarianizing and in effect desensitizing before the power of horror.

Céline epitomizes bourgeoisiephobia in terms of a submissive racial revolt. His revolting abjection of modernity's demonic progression is pointedly illustrated by his figure of the 'social robot' (1937: 183). Streamlined, rationalized and shiny 'according to the tastes of the day', the mannerist parvenu is fully equipped with 'plutocrap dictionaries' – 'a cadaver with no tomorrow, lifeless, ghostly without color or horror' – 'more dead than death, infinitely' (1937: 182–3, 188, 189). The soporific bourgeois mentality encapsulates modernity's 'perfect progression toward the robotic' (1937: 188). 'The man of means is as dead as credit' – that is Céline's verdict about modernity's fate (1937: 98). If Arendt's most radical hope for redemption was political revolution graced with a Constitutional Assembly, Céline's nightmare was 'dissembly' (182) and 'stultification' (160–1) – the 'crushing law of the pendulum of stupidity' (120) which make impossible any revolt in favour of 'the prerobotic individual' (198). Céline despairs in the impossibility of retrieving the prerobotic condition from the 'modernist junk-heap' (1937: 198). Denuded of direct emotion, bourgeois clowns are incapable of 'awakening or releasing anything dangerous among the masses' (198). Céline overcomes the social insanity of robotic modernity by faking its derangement with a posthumous sense of savage humour. The 'social sort' – that comedy of salons of good taste and refinement – 'needs no more than ten minutes to come up with more oddities and horrors of taste than the entire French Cavalry could do in ten years...' (1937: 265).

In her treatments of Céline, Joyce and Arendt, Kristeva plays down emphatically their shared anti-bourgeois impulse. The perspective schematically outlined above is attuned to this unexplored possibility. It seeks to foreground Céline's hostility to the social arabesques of modernity, which for him is not simply bad verse but a bourgeois fairyland of endless abjection. It is, therefore, discrepant with Kristeva's philobourgeois leanings, her explicit discomfort with the implications of Arendt's critical account of the salon culture, as well as with her condoning smile upon the dismantling of the political. As I shall argue, Kristeva's framing of modernism is bluntly indisposed to the creative élan and political edge of the anti-bourgeois impulse that affords more worldly illuminations of abjection.

Kristeva's is an altogether different conception. Abjection in *Powers of Horror* is defined as 'horror and suffering in their libidinal surplus value, which has been tapped, rationalized and made operative by Nazism and Fascism' (PH 155). At variance with Kristeva's narrowly psychoanalytic approach, Céline's labour of abjection bears on a surplus of motorized and uncompensated uprootedness, experienced as depaganization, as an assault on Nordicism, its corporatist guild system and so on (1937: 254). In a psychoanalytically restricted sense, abjection is indeed what Kristeva suggests, a 'precondition of narcissism' (PH 13). But Kristeva adds that it is also 'a narcissistic crisis' which I gather bears on Céline's 'reproachful jealousy' or to be more precise, Judeophobia (PH 14). Abjection thus 'shatters the wall of repression and its judgements', retracing the ego back to its revolting origins 'from which in order to be, the ego has broken away' (PH 15). Here, Kristeva stops short of explaining that Céline's is expressly a case of Nordic abjection, that is, ancestral resurrection of communal racialism that underwent uprootedness and ego death. This condition of de-earthing acts as an imaginary solvent that transmutes the death drive into a trumpet call for Nordic renewal, for a life restored to its racial meaning. And indeed, Céline articulates abjection with modernity's self-propagating fate of endless wandering and plundering. Céline's eyes sparkle with a residual Frankish aura of the Crusades:

> transpose!… poetically if you can! but who tries?… nobody… look at Goncourt!… that was the end!… 'they ceased to transpose'… what were the crusades for?… the crusaders transposed themselves!… now they get themselves ejected from their sixteenth floor in Passy by air conditioned super-jet direct to Golgotha… seven minutes… get their pictures taken on the Mount of Olives […] home again for cocktails… now that every man and his wife has a motor on his ass and can go wherever he likes without legs, without a head, he's nothing but a balloon, a half portion of air… he won't even pass away, he's done it already…
>
> (2008: 144)

Already dead, in high-tech trance, postmodern pilgrims are barely different from the dazed, God-holic medieval crusaders! Be that as it may, Céline's motorized abjection hinges on what forces life itself and the Nordic spirit into the loophole of delirious militarism and futile imperial strife among the French and Germans – both members of the *Populus Francorum*. Frankish people remain, to recall a prominent Jewish-turned Catholic anti-fascist of the stature of Simone Weil, 'geographically stationary' but 'morally uprooted, banished and then reinstated' (1952: 45, 47). These 'mock people' are at long last affronted by two equally abjective options: 'either to fall into a spiritual lethargy resembling death, like the majority of slaves in the days of the Roman Empire; or to hurl themselves into some form of activity necessarily designed to uproot, often by the most violent methods, those who are not yet uprooted, or are partly so' (Weil 1952: 45, 47). Céline's rogue abjection mocks the value that modernity has placed on this loopy enterprise. And indeed, his abjection subsumes tauntingly modernity's fascist flipside too. Still limited by liberal and moral preconceptions about fascism, Kristeva overlooks its genealogical force which is not exceptional but convergent with Nordic Europe's age-old imperial culture.

In her analysis Kristeva argues that Céline's abysmal abjection shares 'the horror of hell without God' (PH 147), 'the post-Catholic destiny of a mankind bereft of meaning' (PH 173), and wonders: 'is it not obvious that for Céline scription and style fully occupy the place left vacant by the disappearance of God, Prophet and Faith?' (PH 187). Kristeva's implied answer to her own doleful question is manifestly plain, but remains a far cry from Céline's scandalous response, 'and worse, I'm a doctor – a pagan for my complete worship of physical beauty, health. I hate sickness, penitence, anything morbid. Completely Greek in that respect. I admire the wholesomeness of childhood' (1989: 315). By the very tone of its address and implications, Kristeva's question betokens an intolerance of paganism which is connoted as a post-Catholic void. What remains muted in Kristeva's metaphors, teeming with Catholic fullness as they are, is Céline's Nordic crossing of the posited void. Céline sarcastically relishes biblical fruits such as good and evil, except that he tastes them as simultaneous truths. In book, body and mind, he incarnated a paganist *coincidentia oppositorum*, with accelerating intensity, to the end. A modernist Nordicism gone astray? No doubt. Both as fate and entertainment.

What then is the intricacy which, in hindsight, strains Kristeva's pivotal project in *Powers of Horror*? In my view, it absorbs Céline's abjection in excess rather than transpose it, keeping generally clear from any sustained political abstraction of the tidal flows that spilled into visceral modernism. Yet that is a necessary risk if Kristeva's valuable work on abjection is to have any contemporary resonance. For instance, her short treatment of Joyce in *Powers of Horror*, unduly formalist as with Céline, focuses on the singular 'catharsis' of the 'pure signifier': 'the abject lies, beyond the themes, and for Joyce generally, in the way one speaks [...] it is the Word that discloses the abject [...] the Word alone purifies from the abject' (PH 23). I take this as 'viceversounding' (Joyce 1976c: 355). Besides taking pleasure in parodic catharses and vicarious word illuminations, Joyce also thinks and actually *thinks through them*, calling forth their realization in practice. It is only by the complete omission of this possibility that Kristeva can exclaim: 'How dazzling, unending, eternal – and so weak, so insignificant, so sickly is the rhetoric of Joycean language' (PH 22).

Further below it will be indicated that this 'sickly rhetoric' could very well be politically insightful and inspiring for those willing to *transpose* sufficiently. For now, it suffices to note that yes, seemingly inconsequential, unreadable and endless repetition of meaningless sequences do indeed purify language as Kristeva argues – except that they also yield ephemeral but strongly epiphanic moments of evocative politics. The real in Joyce comes under the sign of obscure epiphanies – vibrant with political resonance.

Equally, in Céline, the real appears through outwardly dull and recurrent lapses into fathomless abjection just to punctuate, as in Joyce, conversational bagatelle and hallucinatory trifles. Spinning off aberrantly in the void of surplus futility, Céline neutralizes both modernity and writing while seizing hold of them. We can, and we must, imagine wit into that as well as a truth that went wrong. Just consider Céline's joke in *North* where he remarks on Germany's 'innate sense of order' right after RAF's bomb raids which reduced Berlin to rubble:

> I saw men and women of seventy and eighty... some of them blind... bringing everything back to the sidewalk, piling it up in front of every housefront, putting on numbers... bricks here... yellow tiles there! broken glass in a hole... no goofing off!... If Paris had been destroyed you can imagine reconstruction crews!... What they'd build with the bricks and beams and drain pipes!... may be two three barricades?
> (2006: 36–7)

Beyond doubt, an always seasonable idea. And still a diehard counter-revolutionary joke. Only that its singular form transposes the real of history in a way that baffles and outwits any linear account.

Kristeva's lasting legacy on Céline will certainly be remembered for its challenge to gingered liberal observances and taboos, but, more importantly perhaps, for another reason. Kristeva foregrounded rhythms of pre-Oedipal *jouissance* and abject excess which unsettled neat subject-object dichotomies and was therefore resonant with new subversive hybrid positions. Especially her early work has even conceived of an anti-imperial subject-in-process, never named as such but forcefully implied and subsequently suppressed with equal force. In the wake of the tempestuous global '68, Kristeva comes to a reckoning with *le sujet zerologique*, signifying the annihilated subject of Eastern Buddhism, which remained – with the exception of Heidegger – unidentified within the mainstream of Western culture (Ffrench 1995: 172). As a subject beyond the sign, the zero-subject is rendered as a paragrammatic inscription by the text, which nevertheless de-inscribes the subject in question. This process was previsioned in *Finnegans Wake* both as warning and as promise. Joyce's 'abnihilisation of the etym' announces the elimination of meaning set in delirious motion by the Anthropocene Century of 'North Armorica' and the 'mordern atems' of the atomic age (1976c: 353, 3). Here, the parasyntactic word recreates out of nothing the possibility of a world as a subject-in-process. Joycean parasyntaxis echoes the spasms of the 'empyreal Raum' – modernity's 'penisolate war' (1976c: 3), an intimate foreboding of the earth's debasement in the homicidal age of atomic nihilism. What is revealed through parasyntactic epiphanies is indeed the worldly scope of an anti-imperial subject in process – Kristeva's early desideratum in *Revolution in Poetic Language*. Joyce is never alluded to in this context but Kristeva's zerological subject is, despite other influences, Joycean in the sense that the very notion of the text nullifies the subject who is, at the same time, its condition and possibility. Kristeva, however, reads this possibility directly, wildly and rightly into Marx: 'the development of imperialism's forces of production brings about a relative relaxation of the relations of production and reproduction', enabling the subject-in-process to break through into the stable apparatus of linguistic structures (RPL 105). Enduring the 'social and cultural shackles' that other ages had forged by a forced schizophrenia, human experience gets broadened

> beyond the narrow boundaries assigned to it by old relations of production, yet connected to those relations, which will consequently be threatened by it. Marx believed that capitalism had produced its own gravedigger: the proletariat. Imperialism, however, produces its true gravedigger in the non-subjected man who sets ablaze and transforms its laws, including – and perhaps especially – those of signifying structures.
> (RPL 105)

'The productive process of the text', she boldly concludes, 'thus belongs not to this established society' but to the signifying process that 'lies outside the sphere of material production'; it 'transforms the opaque and impenetrable *subject of social relations*', into 'a subject in process/on trial' (RPL 105, emphasis added).

Now, who really remembers that anti-imperial zerocipher, 'the true gravedigger' that outlives imperialism's *dementia praecox*, recovering sufficient strength to poke holes into the 'opaque and impenetrable' laws of the social? Who with presence of mind dares to recall that abject, rodent, subterrestrial persona that undercuts imperial delusions about earth and space conquest? Not just forsaken, but cast out of Kristeva's subsequent thinking, it still haunts its progression – an unconscious force, a power of political abstraction. This probing, abject subject retrieves forgotten earthly impulses of revolution and under-stands crack by crack, scoop by scoop, blow by blow – being moreover funny, a joy(ce)ful Rabelaisean monstrosity.

However bold *Powers of Horror* was, it lacked precisely those powers of abstraction that *Revolution in Poetic Language* transposed resourcefully from Marx to Mao and Freud. What Kristeva had thought conjointly, namely the anti-imperialist power of the political as a semeiotic process of 'gravedigging', 'inseparable from instinctual and linguistic change' which breaks through the dull conventions of the social and its pathological legality, eventually regresses into the re-sacralization of the social at the expense of the political. It is fatefully stabilized by the re-Oedipalization of modernity, past and present (RPL 105). Kristeva works no longer with a concept of the political to say nothing of 'revolutionary practice', which although located within the social, produces 'landslides', sets off explosions and 'unstoppable' breakthroughs that 'change all signifying structures' (RPL 104). Now the necessary work of transposition that elucidates the accelerating landslides of the modernist detritus which rocked the nuclear century becomes inessential. The effects of textual flows and all the illuminative abjections underlying semiotic anti-imperialism become superfluous. It is these effects that dwindled in *Powers of Horror*, which fell short of what Sontag in her approach to Godard described as quintessential to the latter's method, namely, the 'abstracting treatment' (2001: 160). Badiou in our own time has effectively called that experimental method a 'traversal of impurity' (2013: 230). This possibility remained unrealized and overshadowed by the reception of her work on abjection. It could have been a critical backdrop or necessary supplement to Kristeva's own reading of Céline. All the more so because Céline in *Wake*'s terms is a 'bagateller' in the form of 'awethorrorty', writing 'thothfolly' about 'mortinatality', using 'sinscript slanguage' (1976c: 415, 516, 447, 421).

In the light of *Wake*'s semiotic anti-imperialism, Céline's writing may sound like 'a redivivus of paganism' (Joyce 1976c: 50). But no, it is more than a sophistical withdrawal into paganism. It comes before, goes through and far to the end of Europe's orgiastic apocalypse. It is fascinatingly, a past, a passing through and a post-disaster literature which enacts with bizarre joy the symbolic, the imaginary and the real of the century at once. It defines a literature that signals epochal shifts and overwhelming transitions from a state-of-siege situation to all-out blitzkrieg and total war. It is a writing style which renders differing mindsets, senses, moods and perspectives with one stroke. In effect, it prefigures the information blitz of our age. It is a literature of landslide abjection that accompanies the century's loop of uprootedness. That is simply too much for either a critic or an analyst to cope with without formal operators able to disentangle its messianic knots, its crypts of ambivalence, its war trauma, its treasonous collaborationism or its Nordic withdrawal as open-ended signifying processes. Kristeva herself was literally overpowered by the work on abjection, owing precisely to this glaring lack of formal operators of political abstraction.

The social secret of the coming terror: Arendt's political sense of abjection and Kristeva's containment of the political

Kristeva's contentment with an impotent concept of the political is summed up in her avowedly post-metaphysical reading of Arendt. I will, therefore, attempt a necessarily hermeneutic analysis of Arendt's conceptualization of the political which may provide a vantage point for elucidating the political scope of abjection in her work while illuminating the limits of Kristeva's reading of Arendt's take on the political.

The main thrust of Kristeva's critique concerns Arendt's mournful jeremiad against the social 'which destroys the freedom of the polis' (HA 162). Kristeva assumes that Arendt's preoccupation with the fate of political freedom in modernity neglects 'the plural and possible economies of prepolitical freedom' that disclose the social in a new agreeable light. In consequence, modernity's undoing of the 'purely political' along with the emergence of civil society and its attendant freedoms should be considered as integral to the dismantling of Western metaphysics (HA 162). Kristeva's social sublime is therefore a haven of yet undisclosed freedoms. The bottom line of this analysis is the fall of the Berlin Wall in 1989: 'Did that mark the end of imperialism? Or at least its totalitarian strains? Probably so' (HA 134). Kristeva valorizes emphatically false endings and post-metaphysical beginnings which, however, are still propelled by modernity's climactic loss of political sense.

Disagreements with Arendt aside, a rare lesson one may still keep learning from her work is being alert to the impending danger of such a civil social sublime, namely, its looming conformism. Welcoming the dismantling of the political falls in quite well with the unequivocal proprieties and commonplaces of the neoliberal age of governance. Why is this so? Because it stitches too much on the canvas of respectable society whose complacent clichés 'make judgement superfluous and devoid of all risk' (Arendt 1994a: 297). Conformism troubled Arendt immensely for being the outstanding feature of the post-totalitarian mind. In this section I will unpack Arendt's take on conformism in relation to Kristeva's congenial reception of the end of the political, the end of imperialism and so on. My concern is to demonstrate that Arendt's thinking is much more complicated than it appears to be in Kristeva's account and that, despite its contradictions and ambivalences, or may be because of them, it retains its relevance in our time. Instead, Kristeva's promising and pioneering works *Revolution in Poetic Language* and *Powers of Horror* have not, in my view, sustained their momentum due to the waning significance of the political in her later work.

Kristeva's acumen, however, could not fail taking notice of what was critical substance in Arendt. Although her study of Arendt was written from the standpoint of a supportive and appreciative orientation to the social, Kristeva acknowledges that 'Proust's masterpiece, the most insightful of all on this point, illustrates Arendt's analysis of the sociological and one might say psychological crystallization that transforms economic and political elements into absolute evil' (HA 128). Indeed, Proust's age was not simply a springtime of the social. The social was inexorably sacramentalized by elite assemblies convoked in stylish guest salons. These salons enshrined the bourgeoisie's witty solemnity, rank and patronage power. But, besides revelling in glamour and talented perversion, they excelled in subtle cruelties, quixotic meanness and Romanesque vanitas that proved to be an ominous secret of hackneyed terror. These mini-bourgeois holocausts of the social were very much rehearsing Arendt's concept of the banality of evil. The social-Darwinist quasi-madness of the salon assemblies was precursive of a modern brand of world carnage. It was a cue to the real of the century to which Céline's abjective labour was a singular response and to which Kristeva was by all means propitiously alerted. What was emphatically foregrounded by Arendt was the conversion of the republican citizen into a complaisant, fashionable bourgeois who thus lays the groundwork for social totalitarianism, political gangsterism and the unleashing of imperialism. Consequential and tyrannical aspects of the social undergo positive sublimation in Kristeva, hence her eulogies to 'prepolitical freedom'. Succinctly put, what is that which, when Kristeva thinks about Arendt, either thins out to mere irrelevance or is unjustly inflated to the point of becoming a metaphysical threat to cherished pre-political freedoms?

What are vitally depreciated are a couple of palpable distinctions. One such distinction is that between sheer politesse and the promising moments of the political with its convocational sense of the council form. Another is the sharp contrast between the phoney civility beaming with the social exhibitionism of a spoiled and clannish bourgeoisie mimicking the mores of factional aristocracy and the self-restrained civic publics of revolutionary republicanism. Both distinctions lose their scope and significance for a politically viable and emancipatory modernity. The difference being that, while Arendt specifies the geosocial condition which unleashed the totalitarian drives of modernity, she is, all the same, concerned with restraining them. Kristeva, by contrast, condones both the social groundwork that prefigured the intensity of totalitarian mobilization and its post-totalitarian spillover into Americanist conformism, against which Arendt was shaping her inchoate concept of the political. That which Kristeva undertakes to contain is the effect of the political in Arendt. And that is a marked difference between the two. It suggests divergent perspectives on Proust, who intimates that the social organization of salons discloses the martial arts of a decomposing bourgeoisie. Bourgeois salons came to pass as a social war machine, armed with assimilation filters and cold-blooded ostracisms, regulating social descent and ascent, and specializing in tactics of counter-assault that created zones of smothering influence, prestige, attraction and repulsion. Theoretically, the biopower of bourgeois salons in the belle époque was sustained and propelled by finely detailed codes of fastidious politeness and outward geniality. Practically, it was steered by iron-fisted lifestyle elites engaging in routine rituals of banal cruelty. Those flawless war machines of the social exposed by Proust broke into modernity as mini-holocausts of social bubbles presided by impeccably futile, guardian races of ephemeral status, kill-happy valetudinarian dandies of stylization and sly connoisseurs of the laws of snobbery. Conditioned to the methodical sacrificing of useless valets – and Jews – they operated under the command of Arendt's unwritten laws of the social. This was, indeed, the secret of the coming terror. Whatever the limitations of Arendt's perspectives on modernity, she was deeply in touch with the real of the century. Her outstanding study of Rahel Varnhagen bespeaks volumes of her political disgust at the horror of the social.

Plainly disaffected, Kristeva attempts an apparent feminist rescue of Varnhagen from the grip of a manipulative and sadistic Arendt, who, she claims, is unable to appreciate the pre-political sphere of intimacy and inwardness. But that was precisely what agitated Arendt, namely, the operationalization of intimacy into private vices and egoistic moods, transpiring in turn into public concerns – as if political questions were trivial matters of a gossipy salon. After all, Varnhagen herself dropped parvenu illusions of arrivisme towards a more self-conscious pariah position. That was Arendt's perceptive insight – wishing to turn the fate of the outsider and outcast into a political possibility. Though Kristeva regrets Arendt's 'neglect' of the need for intrapsychic rebellion (HA 93), Rosa Luxemburg was an Arendtian exemplar in that sense. In her portrait of Luxemburg, Arendt details a wholesome but vulnerable life of authentic intimate revolt, of self-conscious outsider femininity and intellectual originality, credited with a communist reinvention of the political (Arendt 1968). At issue here is not only Kristeva's lulled sense of the political but also her failure to fathom the implications of Arendt's earnest responsiveness to Luxemburg's 'intrapsychic rebellion', articulated as it were with a historical sense. A lapse which forces unfairly the unwarranted conclusion about Arendt's intellectual biography of Varnhagen: 'lovingly cutting into the flesh of another woman' (HA 55). Moreover, Kristeva's oversight was reinforced by sensational gossip about Arendt's affair with Heidegger which thus transfigured Hannah into Rahel through a reverse psychoanalysis of her correspondence.

It is disappointing to realize how much a first-rate thinker like Kristeva fails to draw the implications or even to appreciate the stakes of the social as a complex apparatus that put pedal to metal, so to speak, stepped up totalitarian pressures, precipitated conformism and reinforced antisemitism, leaving the European Jewry politically defenceless. Instead, Kristeva pinpoints an ostensible inconsistency in Arendt's philosophy, namely, the politically self-conscious valorization of her particular identity as a German Jewess – not realizing that her stance was a necessary response to the false and failed promises of the European Enlightenment and its universalist pretensions that largely justified colonialism and imperialism. In this light, Kristeva's recourse to Enlightenment humanism and universalism sounds overconfident and cavalier, ignoring the entire corpus of critique from de Sade through Nietzsche and Heidegger, to Wittgenstein, Adorno and Horkheimer. But it also sustains the equally untenable presumption that the Enlightenment itself should be treated as the unimpeachable sanctum of a model, schoolmasterly modernism, which is sentiously pronounced in her late work. In fact, her own theological perspective on Eastern Orthodoxy manifests all the aggressive and imperious symptoms of an unleashed modernism, with the Enlightenment priesthood on the background and papal infallibility on the foreground.

A pivotal question remains: why did Kristeva not take up the challenge of redeeming Arendt's epitomized abjection of the social, namely, that monstrous condition of 'vices surrounded by riches' (1984: 105)? After all, Kristeva's engagement with Céline was, I believe, a correlative experiment on the literary and political value of abjection. Arendt's earthy sense of anti-bourgeois abjection, akin to that of Proust, Benjamin and, yes, even to Céline's, afforded her a deeper insight into the stakes of the political, après le deluge; that is, after awakening to the consciousness of a momentous disintegration of the sense of public judgement. Arendt was shocked by the accelerated annihilation of elementary justice. She was equally alarmed by the phenomenal loss of that minimal elegance which defines self-restrained public power. Mindful of her own thriller-like, last-minute escape from Germany, having to negotiate with the limit experience of uprootedness and the social traffic between caste, race, class and outcasts, Arendt emerged into a new mode of consciousness. After the fatal implosion of European modernity, Arendt retraced its double: America.

The acceleration of the transpolitical: Fascist abjection and Madison Avenue Americanism

What is remarkable about fascism as a generic form is that it is commonly approached by taking for granted its own self-descriptions as bottom lines. Either it is, therefore, categorized under the rubric of biological obsession underpinned by a mixture of national destiny, cultural supremacy and racial purity or it is signified by adopting Carl Schmitt's friend-foe distinction, with national socialism being the exemplary embodiment of the political intensity that defines their necessary opposition. No one can disregard the quality of scholarship that has followed one of the two or both interpretive frames.

What emerges from the context of this chapter, however, is another submerged possibility, occasionally overlooked, but no less striking or thought-provoking. The possibility I am evoking is something of the order of the *transpolitical* that overdetermines the fascist form and which Baudrillard calls the 'swept away effect'. This refers to an 'aleatory giddiness' that feeds on itself (1987: 114). In Baudrillard's delireal schema, the effects of fascism accelerate faster than the stimulation they receive from its causes, thus devouring them. Arendt, writing in the 1950s, was already considering this possibility – facing up a resistant reality whereby the Jewish question and antisemitism, though small and unimportant phenomena in terms of global politics, became causal or catalytic factors for the Nazi movement and a world war. Hence, 'the grotesque disparity between cause and effect which introduced the era of imperialism' (1979: viii). What is inferred is that, insofar as fascism thrives on the acceleration of the transpolitical, it is forced by its movement and speeding drive to devour its own reality principle, that is, the German Völk itself, whose annihilation it pursued blindly to the end, thus achieving the absolute loss of meaning and perspective. In that sense, the fascist apocalypse revealed its own emptiness and utter insubstantiality despite its essentialist self-definition. Its deadly novelty aside, fascism's true calling was this doubling back on itself which catapulted modernity into the nothingness of an utter banality. Even more gravely, however, fascism disclosed in advance the black hole of the century's post-totalitarian order. Heidegger suggested as much about the outcome of the Second World War – it resolved nothing! Except that it accelerated the Anthropocene.

For Baudrillard, the sinister genius of the fascist form was in some sense uncannily repeated by May 1968. His verdict about the elusive '68 is that 'it remains indecipherable. It was the forerunner of nothing' (1987: 115). What I glean from Baudrillard's overstatement is that May's deep power manifests something of an invariant motif which is inherent in modernity's forward thrust – a pure inconsequentiality. Having swept France like an avalanche, the May movement's success was 'to absorb its own continuity, swallowing its own energy and disappearing' (Baudrillard 1987: 105). In Barthean terms, the May movement had removed bourgeois impurities without any real harm incurred by the bourgeoisie itself – except the initial shock. Modernity's nuanced modes of eliminating impurities were conceptualized by Barthes along the lines of chemical engineering. Hygienic revolution and chemical warfare advanced in partnership, implicating the drive of abjection and purification in a self-referring modernizing loop. Within modernity's detergent power, Barthes distinguished between purifying fluids like chlorine and ammonia that 'burn and kill dirt', and soap powder which is more selective in its drive, forcing out dirt, but no longer killing it – thus cleaning without making war on it (1989: 40–1). Barthes' distinction recalls the difference between keeping public order and engaging in war – yet modernity's thrust proved this nuance to be quite tenuous.

Modernity's forms of detergent power morphed into an accelerating loop of the transpolitical – a total loss of political bearings.

Rethinking Arendt in the light of modernity's fast drive and its transpolitical effect, I recall her other early insight in 1954 which addresses precisely 'what Europeans dread as "Americanization" – the emergence of the modern world with all its perplexities and implications. It is probable that this process will be accelerated rather than hindered' (1994b: 426). According to her, the rise of the social is 'in constant growth but in no less constant acceleration', thus sweeping away the public realm (1958: 45). Baudrillard seems to amplify Arendt's early foresight. Her intuition was fully attuned to modernity's stampede effect of terror unleashed as an empty form. It was a valid intuition. In the aftermath of war, Arendt readily identified the terminal fear common to both fascist and post-fascist Europe. While the image of America in the past centuries was an image of democracy, the century's central image of America was modernity in itself – the real of Céline's abjection. Post-fascist Europe and America were made after that image of the transpolitical apocalypse of modernity. The political organization of mass society along with the political integration of technological power was an impossible task. The potential for self-destruction which is still latent in these problems keeps an insecure Europe in a state of profound anxiety as to the possibility of coming to terms with modernity. Interestingly, Arendt considers justified such 'fears of Europe for her spiritual identity and her even deeper apprehensions about her physical survival' – which actually concern not specifically Europe or the West but 'all mankind' (1994b: 427). Moreover, she was fully aware that what happened in Europe (totalitarianism) could also happen in America and vice versa. Under the condition of mass society, new forms of totalitarianism may always activate forces of dormant social conformism, the ones that made American 'terror less violent and ideology less insistent' (1994b: 425) – or so it seemed.

Arendt's balance sheet of American modernity must have been a painful blow, first and foremost to Arendt's own fascination with America's political genius. America's exceptional modernity faltered because it had suspended its political *novitas*. Susan Sontag couldn't have summarized Arendt's vision of the American exception more aptly. The ingenuity of America's modernist conservatism was that it extolled the authority of constitutional tradition while celebrating the new, radical, even revolutionary novelty – against old European pieties and hierarchies (Sontag 2007: 200). Arendt's vision that the American exception could sustain the thrust of a viable political modernity and its penchant for *novitas*, owing to the strong and sanctified foundations of the revolution that bind it to *auctoritas*, was shaken by the Vietnam crisis and the eventual disaster – aggravated as it were by the Watergate scandal. Towards the last years of her life, those turning points had indeed created an internal dissonance in her political theory, forcing her to provide further qualifications. Systematic lying, cover-ups and image-making were by now a global policy (Arendt 2003: 264). America's executive elites smuggled conceit and Madison Avenue tactics reminiscent of European corruption, phoney imperialism and world weariness. Still, Arendt entertained a hope that this was only a temporary quirk, though she was deeply aware that the torrents of imperial spectacle that crossed the political were meant to be a lasting fatality, rather than a short-term anomaly. What was coming home to roost at the close of the Vietnam War was a long addictive training in imagery – 'no less habit-forming than drugs' (2003: 274).

When Arendt revisits the issue of modernity's drive in 1975, she makes direct reference to Lewis Mumford's maxim 'the going is the goal' which conceptualizes the non-stop society, the non-stop 24/7 turbo capitalism whereby 'to stop wasting, to stop consuming more and more, quicker and quicker... would spell immediate doom'. The incessant noise of the advertising agencies going on 'at the expense of the world we live in' reinforces the 'runaway economy' and its 'Madison Avenue tactics', the Americanist nemesis of the political (2003: 262, 263). But what exactly is Madison Avenue the name of?

In Arendt's mind, Madison Avenue is a PR euphemism for consumer capitalism. It conceals the deep causes of appearances while speculating on those causes by inducing the forgetfulness of brute facts (2003: 261). *Stricto sensu*, Arendt was no moralist at all. The problem for her was America's wrongheaded, image-driven imperialism, not republican imperialism itself. After all was said and done, Arendt's comprehension of the century was that it intertwined good and evil: 'that without the imperialists' 'expansion for expansion's sake' the world might never have become one; and that without the bourgeoisie's political device of 'power for power's sake', the extent of human strength might never have been discovered' (1979: viii). Thus, the truth of America's abjective war in Vietnam was not imperialist politics per se but Madison Avenue's bizarre patriotism which had split the political into image-making in its first half, and make-believe in the imagery as to the second half (1969: 8). What outraged Arendt's Roman republican realism was that the *ultima ratio* of Madison Avenue's short-sighted Americanism was neither power, nor profit, nor global influence – a reasonable claim to her – but the image itself. Not world conquest – in the sense of Roman imperium – but 'the pursuit of a mere image of omnipotence' (1969: 39). For Arendt, a great power is limited power, pursuing a genuine, qualified imperialism in the void left behind by old European colonial powers. It simply meant – in neo-Roman fashion – adding Vietnam to an imperial string of client-states rather than wasting this possibility in the false cause of image-making. When Ho Chi Minh, Mao and Chu En-lai appealed repeatedly between 1945 and 1946 to Presidents Roosevelt and Truman to obtain US client status, their requests, according to Arendt, were either turned down or remained unanswered because they 'contradicted the image of monolithic communism directed by Moscow' (1969: 28, 29).

Reconsidering Arendt's political thinking from the perspective of Madison Avenue transpolitics enables us to think Kristeva's encounter with Arendt anew. My argument is that Arendt's late quest for containing philistine Americanism – eager in restoring to America a sound Roman sense and a consistent imperialism commissioned by Senatorial authority – is correlative to Kristeva's falling in with *renovatio imperii*.

Re-Oedipalizing modernity – resacralizing Rome: Kristeva's reconceptualization of God and the containment of the East

In order to elucidate this point, however, we first need to explain Kristeva's misplaced critique of Arendt's supposed fundamentalism of the political against which Kristeva weaves her tale of the century. Compared to Kristeva's strictures regarding Arendt's indifference or hostility to psychoanalysis, the point is of primal importance in the following sense. Arendt's Jeffersonian commitment to the revolutionary institution of councils and wards – viewed as elementary republics that crossed party lines – was not meant to advance universal and mandatory political participation. Instead, councils and wards were intended as republican means of containment – as breaks on mass movements driven by the 'swept away effect' of social totalitarianism. In this respect, public spaces are geared to the recruitment of political talent – the best and most natural way for the self-selection of a qualified elite, chosen by no one but constituting itself by its own means (1984: 278–80). A well-ordered republic ought, then, to assure those with the best political talent their rightful place in the public realm – which 'would spell the end of general suffrage as we understand it today' (1984: 279). To Arendt that is not offensive in the least, 'since a political elite is by no means identical with a social or cultural or professional elite', for those who belong to the political 'are self-chosen and those who do not belong are self-excluded' (1984: 279–80). Consequently, Arendt had already acknowledged, as a fact as well as a norm, the necessity of an aristocratic form of republican government that fully respects privacy, individual pursuits, even the 'sterile depressions' of those who are unburdened of public business (1984: 280). Kristeva's assumption concerning Arendt's overemphasis on the political which suppresses her own cherished preference for freedom from politics is a tall tale that needs to be revised. Far from being a whimsical discrimination, self-exclusion from public business 'would in fact give substance and reality to one of the most important negative liberties we have enjoyed since the end of the ancient world... ' (1984: 280). Arendt, then, never devalued the negative freedoms, currently overrated by Kristeva.

Arendt's prudential imperialism, including the aristocratic republicanism of sound sense and taste, along with Kristeva's privileging of an ennobled authority conducive to the polishing of the ego cogito were the optimal alibis of post-totalitarian modernity – allowances for the realm of 'sterile depressions' to fertilize Madison Avenue with republican, psychoanalytic and theological simulacra. Our concern here is to examine the imperial acumen involved in Arendt and Kristeva's tactful taste while pondering the ways of their implied pedagogy. Arendt couldn't have been more explicit in stating that Rome's political and intellectual heritage had passed wholesale to the Christian Church which adapted itself assiduously to Roman thinking – amalgamating 'the Roman trinity of religion, authority and tradition' (1963: 125). It is fair to say that Arendt and Kristeva share at least this common foundation.

In Kristeva's mind, the theological strife which led to the final schism between the Latin West and the Orthodox East ended – rightly and justly to her – with a Roman triumph. Kristeva's argument is that the deserved triumph of the Latin West was made possible due to its conceptualization of the *filioque*, which was more responsive to a 'European' vision of freedom. Why was that so? Because it proved itself more accommodative of modernity's contradictory pulls towards technological advance, social cohesion and subjective freedom – more assenting and conducive to an art of living. The Orthodox East remained theologically unfit to command the contradictory forces of modernization, and much less in tune with 'the basic structural conditions for the advent of an optimal model of free subjectivity' (CES 127). According to Kristeva's conception, the status of the Son in the Orthodox Trinity doctrine of *per filium* handicaps subjectivity as he remains either subordinate to his Father or in fusion with him. Hence the Orthodox rendering of Christ is insufficiently Oedipal.

Instead, in the Roman Catholic revision of the Trinity, the *filioque* stands for a distinct dyad of Father-and-Son, meaning that the Holy Spirit proceeds equally from both subjects. Kristeva claims that the Son in the Orthodox *per filium* fuses masochistically with a predominant Father – in a male, preverbal, semiotic and homosexual *jouissance* – enjoying a passive condition of effeminacy (CES 139, 140, 149). Accordingly, the subject position of the Son is reduced to that of a surrogate daughter – and an admiring wife – which absorbs the feminine. This explains 'the rarity of female sainthood in Orthodoxy' (CES 141) – which may be wrong information, since I have counted at least sixty-two celebrated female saints, sanctified by the Greek Orthodox calendar alone. The issue for Kristeva is that the Orthodox *per filium* forecloses the modernist thrust of anti-Oedipal revolt, thus encumbering the possibilities of subjective freedom and eventual reconciliation in a temporal frame of divine economy. In consequence, the

God of the Orthodox East is inaccessible – 'its negative theology denies any conceptual delimitation of God', remaining a 'bottomless mystery', 'unobjectivizable' (CES 149). For this reason, the Orthodox East betrays utter hostility to modernist freedom, remains indifferent to the public sphere, severing any active ties to the sphere of production, objectivity or the social (CES 152). Of course, such observations constitute a stock cliché scholastically reiterated since Aquinas: *contra errores Grecorum*.

The dilemma between the Roman Catholic *filioque* and the Orthodox *per filium* – a seemingly abstract theological controversy – has profound implications about the fate of *auctoritas* in the West and the East. Evidently, the *filioque* question and the imperial primacy of the Roman See over the East are one and the same question. The Latin West introduces a sharp duality of essences which rationalizes in excess the trialectical ontology of the East. The Latin vision of power made explicit in the *filioque* conceptualizes Christ as an imperial persona of *lex animate* who delegates the constitutional authority of the City of God to an appointed Pontifex Maximus – by way of Apostolic succession. Apparently, the Holy Spirit devolves to the Pope himself – explaining his infallibility vis-à-vis the synodic principle of conciliarity and hence the fallibility of the Eastern Church. In that sense, the living political ecclesia-cum-assembly degenerates into a corporational organization of the social under priestly command. Failing to understand the trialectical nuances of Eastern Greek theology which emerged from a strong philosophical background, Latin theology defined God in essentialist, legalistic and identitarian terms – indulging in simplification, pietism and scholasticism.

The sack of Constantinople in 1204 by Western Crusaders, mobilized and blessed by the Pope himself, speaks volumes in itself. St Bernard of Clairvaux, the holy spindle that weaves Kristeva's *Tales of Love* – ecclesiastic statesman, advisor to popes, counsellor to monarchs, a nemesis to academic heresy and mystic all the same – preached the Second Crusade and supported the Knights Templar, thus accommodating mysticism to the militarism of the dream-and-drum holytrooper nobility. All in all, 'holy violence constitutes love in order to reach the ideal' (TL 166). The crusading spirit of God's courtly lovers driven by holy violence 'confuses stations, disregards manners, knows no bounds. Proprieties, reason, decency, prudence, judgement are defeated and reduced to slavery' (TL 166). Nominally, Kristeva does acknowledge the articulation of amatory and military mystique (TL 152), without ever unravelling the loop between courtly-godly loves and the conquest of Holy Lands that defined the aspirations and strivings of St Bernard's age. Indeed, the driven lover of God was always and already doubled by the marauder – courtship and conquest in 'sollemn nuptialism' (Joyce 1976c: 599). All those holy armies of driven adventurers feasting with God in mystical marriage – an imperial subject in process – were in fact rational subjects of Rome's theological jurisprudence. For instance, besides Virgin Mary's double status as *nata nati* and *mater patris*, that is, as both virgin and mother-daughter of her Son, Kantorowicz points also to Christ's doubleness as both Father and Son of his virginal mother. Impressive doublings, indeed, but all imply an emperor as Father and Son of divine justice, or justice as the inferred mother and daughter of the emperor (Kantorowicz 1981: 144, 100–101). By and large, the Rosicrucian Empire was divined in terms of *ecclesia imperialis*.

Kristeva's tales of the century interlock unmistakably with the grand narrative of the Roman West. In assuring the Orthodox East that she is not crusading anew – 'no use trying to convert you to Catholicism, or even to Protestantism' – Kristeva counsels 'nevertheless to take measure of this great huge fact, namely that in the world of advanced capitalism you want to join up with, God is dead' (CES 182). Pitifully, Nietzsche's testimony that 'God is dead' remains an impossible post-mortem thought in the Orthodox East. Hence, the East can never improve or ride on God's loss. It cannot transvaluate deicide and, for that reason, is unable to re-deify a proximate *auctoritas*, or pursue stand-in values in the void of the deceased God. Obversely, Protestantism reads positive signs of predestination and election in methodical work, professional success and scientific research, thus responding to Nietzsche's pronouncement with a surrogate ideal. For Kristeva, even Masonic or esoteric imitations of Protestantism preserve and transvaluate rather than relativize value – measuring up successfully with the challenges of modernity by seeking sublimation in toil, output, success, fortune and eminence. The whole kit of what Heidegger conceptualized as the 'forgetfulness of being' which led to the Anthropocene is here emphatically affirmed in terms that valorize Western superiority. That is a deicidal subjectivity of freedom, seeking sublimation in personal triumph and the vocational spirit of secular enterprise – 'envisaging other relations to the original Being, to knowledge and to pleasure' (CES 181). In stark contrast, the Orthodox ontology fails to refine the ego cogito of the believer, lacking the diligent sobriety and virtuous reading of the Protestant who seeks redemption in the Scripture as a devotee, as well as in the city as entrepreneur (CES 181). On all scores, Western forms of religiosity, more dualistic and Manichean, are considered superior to the trialectical ontology of the Eastern Orthodoxy. The former can articulate gain and loss into a rational accounting that accommodates the death of God to modernity's drive. The East loses out to the West because it falls dramatically short in reconceptualizing God post-mortem, and hence is unable to resolve modernity's Oedipal crisis with the assistance of psychoanalysis.

In such a closed loop transaction, pope and analyst appear to embody a divine and quasi-divine *auctoritas tutorum* – with the analyst being a secular abbreviation of the Oedipal power carried by the Pontifex Maximus. At long last, Western humanity's hope for redeeming modernity's bill regarding the death of God – while keeping Nietzsche's madman at a distance – lies in rendering God immanent to the temporal power of *ecclesia imperialis*. Here

Kristeva is ironically right. Latin theology was indeed a great modernizing 'take-nique' in Céline's sense: a takeover of lands and souls, of bodies and goods. Catholic, Protestant or Masonic, modernity was unleashed as a moral take-nology appropriate for 'upwardly mobile brothers', 'little beings eager to improve their small stakes', 'their material subsistence', 'to assure and augment their moneybelts' – 'aspiring despotic bosses' (Céline 1937: 194, 195, 291). This is vintage Céline. In contrast, Kristeva reverses authentic anti-bourgeois *ressentiment* into an imperial fantasy of unsublimated French vanity. Identifying with 'the logical landscape of France', she pays tribute to the French who she describes as

> reserved, cynical, impenetrably private, but, on the whole, civilized. They [...] conquered Europe and the greater part of the rest of the world, and then came home because they prefer a pleasure in accord with reality. But because they also prefer pleasure to reality, they go on thinking they're masters of the world, or at least a great power still. The world – irritated, condescending, fascinated – seems prepared to go along with them. To go along with us.
>
> (P 163)

Only Joyce, post-mortem, could tune in with Kristeva's 'tacitempust tongue' – 'strangerous', 'tootoological' and 'panromain apological' (1976c: 457, 625, 468, 469).

In this chapter, I have attempted a conceptual sketch of some of modernism's master sequences. I have proposed an ensemble of exploratory perspectives and transit points which punctuate Kristeva's suave *devotio moderna* while illuminating her final quietus, tagged as it is to logics of *renovatio imperii*. My aim was to bring to light modernism's ambivalence towards what Renato Rosaldo calls imperialist nostalgia, pondering how that ambivalent longing was critically illuminated or cynically affirmed during modernism's high tide (1993). This obscure affect, however, keeps being double-coded down to our days. Then and now, modernism's definitive mood articulates innocent yearnings for authenticity and authority. Yet these swinging yearnings artfully dissimulate the unleashed force by which they were, and still are, fulfilled. Kristeva's early work had promisingly sustained a challenge to the simultaneity of such innocent yearnings and forceful pieties. Could anyone soundly assert that Kristeva's intellectual and psychoanalytic outlook has now been taken in by revival tales and old enchantments – like the lyrical mysticism of Bernard of Clairvaux? After all, wasn't Clairvaux's Christological *jouissance* that drifted into a chivalrous fugue in favour of the Crusades? Is Kristeva's retaling of modernism a transposed romance with the imperial Middle Ages and the eventual conversion of the Knight into the modern gentilhomme of the masonic lodge? Why not consider the thought, indeed, if – at the junction of faith and credit – 'one of the chief functions of the Knights Templar was to serve as forwarding agents and bankers?' (Mumford 1961: 315). Wasn't that the modernizing medieval force on account of which the Orthodox East was discounted by Kristeva? The critical question, then, is to rethink the stakes in the supposed lack of a *devotio moderna* in the East, a disputable virtue credited abundantly to the Latin West by Kristeva. Though far from completed, my quest for an answer to these questions has been in keeping with Joyce's telling cue in the *Wake* – 'A PANOPTICAL PURVIEW OF POLITICAL PROGRESS' in 'THE FUTURE PRESENTATION OF THE PAST' (1976c: 272, capitals in the original).

References

Arendt, H. (1958), *The Human Condition*, Chicago: University of Chicago Press.
Arendt, H. (1963 [1954]), *Between Past and Future: Six Exercises in Political Thought*, New York: Meridian Books.
Arendt, H. (1968 [1955]), *Men in Dark Times*, Eugene, OR: Harvest Books.
Arendt, H. (1969), *Crises of the Republic*, Eugene, OR: Harvest Books.
Arendt, H. (1979 [1951]), *The Origins of Totalitarianism*, Eugene, OR: Harvest Books.
Arendt, H. (1984 [1963]), *On Revolution*, Harmondsworth: Penguin.
Arendt, H. (1994a [1964]), *Eichmann in Jerusalem: A Report on the Banality of Evil*, Harmondsworth: Penguin.
Arendt, H. (1994b), *Essays in Understanding (1930–1954): Formation, Exile, Totalitarianism*, New York: Schocken Books.
Arendt, H. (2003), *Responsibility and Judgement*, ed. J. Kahn, New York: Schocken Books.
Badiou, A. (2013), *Cinema*, Cambridge: Polity.
Barthes, R. (1989), *Mythologies*, London: Paladin.
Baudrillard, J. (1987), *Forget Foucault*, Cambridge, MA: Semiotext(e).
Céline, L. F. (1937), *Trifles for a Massacre*, Dublin, Ireland: Omnia Veritas editions.
Céline, L. F. (1989), *Excerpts from His Letters to Milton Hindus*, in W. K. Buckley (ed.), *Critical Essays on Louis Ferdinand Céline*, 303–20, Boston, MA: G. K. Hall.
Céline, L. F. (2008 [1969]), *Rigadoon*, trans. R. Manheim, Dallas, TX: Dalkey Archive Press.
Céline, L. F. (2006), *North*, trans. R. Manheim, Dallas, TX: Dalkey Archive Press.
Ffrench, P. (1995), *The Time of Theory: A History of Tel Quel (1960–1983)*, Oxford: Oxford University Press.
Joyce, J. (1976a [1914]), *Dubliners*, in H. Levin (ed.), *The Portable James Joyce*, 17–242, Harmondsworth: Penguin.
Joyce, J. (1976b [1916]), *A Portrait of the Artist as a Young Man*, in H. Levin (ed.), *The Portable James Joyce*, 243–526, Harmondsworth: Penguin.
Joyce, J. (1976c [1939]), *Finnegan's Wake*, Harmondsworth: Penguin.

Joyce, J. (1986 [1922]), *Ulysses*, ed. H. W. Gabler with W. Steppe and C. Melchior, New York: Vintage.
Kantorowicz, E. (1981 [1957]), *The King's Two Bodies: A Study in Medieval Political Theology*, Princeton, NJ: Princeton University Press.
Mumford, L. (1961), *The City in History: Its Origins, Its Transformations and Its Prospects*, Eugene, OR: Harvest Books.
Rosaldo, R. (1993), *Culture and Truth: The Remaking of Social Analysis*, Boston, MA: Beacon Press.
Sontag, S. (2001), *Styles of Radical Will*, New York: Vintage.
Sontag, S. (2007), *At the Same Time*, Harmondsworth: Penguin.
Vaneigem, R. (1983 [1967]), *The Revolution of Everyday Life*, St Louis, MO: Left Bank Books, The Rebel Press.
Weil, S. (1952 [1949]), *The Need for Roots*, trans. A. Wills, London: Routledge.

9

The fabric of gothic modernism: Powers of horror in M. R. James' 'Oh, Whistle, and I'll Come to You, My Lad'

Nicholas Chare

Introduction: In the mouth of a mediaevalist

The mediaevalist and writer of ghost stories M. R. James (1862–1936) was not a self-proclaimed modernist, often displaying disdain for modern art and literary modernism.[1] In his letters to Gwendolen McBryde, for instance, he expresses relief that the Royal Academy of Arts 1932 Exhibition of French Art stopped at 1900, meaning 'the lowest depths have not been plumbed' (James 1956: 177).[2] Discussing a 1934 essay about his ghost stories by the modernist writer Mary Butts which was published in *The London Mercury* alongside one about James Joyce and a piece by Aldous Huxley, James refers to Huxley as 'unspeakable' and Joyce as a 'charlatan' (1956: 200–201). James' aesthetic taste was conservative. The contemporary literature he read frequently seems to have been popular detective fiction by authors such as Agatha Christie and Dorothy L. Sayers. The British literary avant-garde of the early twentieth century were not of interest to him, although his work was of occasional interest to them, as Butts' essay demonstrates.

Butts offered a highly complimentary critical engagement with James' ghost stories, praising his style for its concision, precision and elegance.[3] She noted the ambiguous status of ghost stories in general. As manifestations of mass culture, they provided 'a kind of entertainment' and were hence a suspect cultural form (1934: 307).[4] The occult, however, was a subject of some interest to many modernist artists and writers.[5] For Butts, James was noteworthy for his skill at withholding so as to impart: 'when he tells us so little [...] we know so much' (1934: 310). His economy of description opened a space for dark imagining, inviting the reader to fill in the gaps. Another quality Butts identified as important in the stories was detachment. James kept his creations at arm's length, writing of them with a figural sideways glance. Horrors are often reported indirectly rather than confronted head on. James gives the reader experiences of horror 'second hand', affording containment, imprisoning 'things safely for us inside the covers of a book' (1934: 317).

Although James' style and turns of phrase betray the influence of Charles Dickens, the atmosphere of many of his stories is more indebted to another Victorian writer, the Irish author Sheridan Le Fanu.[6] Le Fanu's work encompasses many genres but James was inspired by his gothic tales. James' indebtedness to the gothic tradition is recognized by Penny Fielding, who has used the theme of the library in his fiction works to trace how he explores themes of purity and contamination. Drawing briefly on Mary Douglas' (1991) classic study of the concept of pollution, *Purity and Danger*, and on Julia Kristeva's (1982) essay on abjection, Fielding reads the library in James' stories as 'a site of the impulse towards completeness and classification' that is continually threatened by spectres of deficiency and forces of disorder (2000: 766). Her identification of order and its disturbance as a key theme in James' work is compelling. For Fielding, it is the 'uneasy relationship between objects and their ordering in the cause-and-effect narration of the ghost story' that positions James as a Gothic modernist (2000: 750). Sometimes in Gothic modernism, it is the modern itself which is cast as alien and disruptive, endangering tradition and sowing confusion (Smith and Wallace 2001: 6). In James, however, strangeness in his stories is usually located in art and artefacts – a fabric swatch, a mezzotint, a scrapbook, a whistle, a wood carving – from bygone ages.

The modern is often associated with forces of order, with classifying and cataloguing that impose conformity upon diversity through putatively universal principles of knowledge (Fyfe 2000: 120). James was an enthusiastic cataloguer of mediaeval manuscripts, producing numerous inventories. His work prefigures that of professional librarians such as Brownlee J. Kirkpatrick, who introduced new modes of organization and indexing. As Fielding examines, cataloguing is also a theme in some of the ghost stories. It forms part of a broader concern that James exhibits regarding efforts and failures to preserve order. Zygmunt Bauman identifies the drive to organize and inventory, to order and class things, as paradigmatic of modernity (1991: 5). This drive relies upon disorder for its raison d'être, on chaos as a constitutive outside.[7] In this sense, order as a recurring theme in James' stories renders them quintessentially modern.

Here, drawing on Kristeva's ideas about abjection, about the psychic process by which boundaries of the self are instituted and/or safeguarded through acts of expulsion, I will examine how James' writings embody an arrested sublimation of the abject. In this, they contrast with the writings of Louis-Ferdinand Céline, Kristeva's key exemplar of abject literature, and I will therefore compare and contrast the two authors, the better to articulate the specificities of abjection as it registers in James' fiction. In James' writings, I focus particularly on the significance of fabrics, especially drapery, as they are employed as a motif. Kristeva's discussion of abject materials in *Powers of Horror* accords some importance to skin but does not consider how clothing as a 'second skin' also functions as a boundary and potential locus of boundary breakdown. Using James' celebrated tale 'Oh, Whistle, and I'll Come to You, My Lad' (henceforth referred to as 'Oh, Whistle') as a case study, I argue that drapery in his fiction provides a means by which to express distinctly modern anxieties about the abject.

Journey to the end of the night

James' measured and tidy prose, his conventional literary style, embody a desire for order, even as his tales track its dissolution. In this, the neat elegance of his writings, he is radically different from a modernist such as Céline. Kristeva contrasts the 'discomfort' and 'forlornness' that accompanies reading Céline with the pleasures to be found in Mallarmé's 'serenity' and Proust's 'delightful interlacing' (PH 134). To this list we might also add the joy of Jamesian refinement. For Kristeva, Céline stands out for making writing 'oral', which is to say, 'contemporaneous, swift, obscene' (PH 137). This orality manifests, in part, through a tampering with 'vocabulary and syntax' (PH 134). In Céline's later novels, the use of ellipses strongly contributes to the production of a speaking subject, operating to signal enunciations as unfinished and to cultivate impressionistic melody (PH 198–201). James recognized the use of ellipsis as characteristic of modernist literature, noting disapprovingly: '[d]ots are believed by many writers of our day to be a good substitute for effective writing. They are certainly an easy one' (2001: 473–4). In James, speech is clearly important. He seems to delight in mimicking working class accents but his interest in accent and argot is occasional rather than encompassing. His writing is not overarchingly oral in character.

For Kristeva, Céline's radical literary stylistics enabled him to liberate the semiotic aspect of language, to effectuate an upsurge of affect. James's prose accomplishes the opposite, studiously eschewing stylistic innovation the better to keep affect in check. In his sensitive reading of James, H. P. Lovecraft rightly foregrounds a kind of dispassionate intellectualism and emotional detachment (2000: 70). Despite this, many of the stories were initially written to be read aloud so it is possible the paring of affect may, at least partially, have been undone in performance.[8] James' reading style has been described as untheatrical yet he did read by the light of a solitary candle, by flickering uneven light, in a strongly visually, if not aurally, suggestive atmosphere (Cox 1986: 35). Céline's antisemitic pamphlets were sometimes read aloud by ideologically sympathetic readers, a practice that likely amplified their already highly drive-invested qualities.[9]

Although Céline and James seem polar opposites – the reactionary contrasted with the avant-gardist, tradition pitted against innovation – the reality is more complex. Many of the themes Kristeva identifies in Céline are also to be found in James: 'horror, death, madness [...] outlaws, war, the feminine threat, the horrendous delights of love, disgust, and fright' (PH 137). Only Céline's open delight in sex is absent. Both authors also exhibited misogyny and antisemitism. Rosemarie Scullion describes Céline's woman-hating as swaggering and his antisemitic pamphlets are notorious (1995: 12). James' antisemitic sentiments emerge occasionally in his fiction and in letters to friends. In 'The Uncommon Prayer-Book', the Jewish character Poschwitz (who also uses the aliases Henderson and Homberger), a corrupt book dealer, 'is painted in decidedly uncomplimentary terms' (James 2001: 307, n.14). Writing to Gwendolen McBryde, James observes of William Russell Flint's illustrations for the book *Judith* (Crowley 1928): '[t]he artist had the feeblest idea of illustrating Judith [, there are] about 4 pictures of a nasty almond-eyed Jewess with the fewest possible clothes' (1956: 153). Here his antisemitism is projected on to Flint's works which are similar in style to many erotic prints of the era and exoticize and objectify Judith but do not manifest the caricatural expressions of physical difference associated with antisemitic imagery.[10] James' description of Judith as 'nasty' may also reveal his ambiguous attitude towards women in general.[11]

Céline and James also share a continual concern with boundary breakdown. In Céline, there are frequent scenes of excretion, urination, expectoration, penetration and suppuration. The erotic interests of his male protagonists, their penchant for muscular women, for hard bodies, seem a reaction to the omnipresence of uncertain contours, of corpulence and podge. The Slovak nurse Sophie in *Voyage au bout de la nuit*, for example, is accorded strong praise by Ferdinand Bardamu for her toned physique which he adores:

> Frankly I couldn't admire her enough. From muscle to muscle, I proceeded by anatomical groups... By muscular peaks, by clutches... I never wearied of pursuing that vigour, determined yet willowy, distributed in bundles

that were by turn slippery and yielding to the touch… Beneath her silken, tensed, relaxed, incredible skin…
(Céline 1997: 413)[12]

Bodies such as Sophie's act as a counterweight to the continual boundary dissolutions encountered and experienced by Bardamu, the character who is an avatar for Céline himself.

In James, the abject manifests through instances of decay and ill-definition, of malleability and penetrability. In his 'Twelve Medieval Ghost-Stories', for example, he writes of a woman who lifted up a spectre, her 'hands sinking deep into the ghost's flesh, as if it were rotten, not solid, but an illusion' (James 2001: 463). There are no figures within his stories who function like Céline's hard women but the prose itself, stiff and discreet, incarnates a comparable counterbalance. Whereas Céline's style of writing embodies fracture and breakdown, James' texts are studiously austere, refined rather than scabrous. James also regularly employs direct address and calls attention to the storied nature of the tales. Through actions such as these, he discourages too great an immersion by the reader. In Céline, by contrast, readers are invited to identify with the central protagonists. He encourages the person who reads to wallow in the abject style and content of his novels, whereas James offers only vicarious abjection, the abject encountered as through a glass: darkly, indirectly, obliquely.

James came from a religious background; his father was a clergyman. His mediaeval scholarship included research into the Apocrypha and depictions of the apocalypse. In the published version of his 1927 Schweich lectures, James imagines the mediaeval reception of manuscript apocalypses:

> What remained in the mind of him or her who pored over the pictured Apocalypses was the panorama of tremendous signs in the heavens, heavens which opened ever and anon to show a supreme throne and venerable shapes around it; of monstrous forms of evil looming up to dominate a frightened world; of colossal cavalcades advancing to destroy them; of the blare of trumpets, the voice of thunderings, the ringing of harps; and of one great final convulsion and purging of all things.
> (1931: 80–1)

For him, the manuscript apocalypses were '*picture-books* – the pictures being on the whole the first consideration' (1931: 63). This vision of 'monstrous forms looming up' could readily be applied to some of the apparitions in his tales of the supernatural.

Céline's writing has also been described as apocalyptic. Eric Lorey suggests that his writings offer an 'apocalyptic vision' (1999: 156). This vision can be traced back to *Journey to the End of the Night*, where the character Baryton explains to the anti-hero Ferdinand that circa 1900 he saw humanity 'losing its balance little by little and dissolving in the vast maelstrom of apocalyptic ambitions' (Céline 1997: 371). Later, in *Les beaux draps*, Céline uses fragmentary apocalyptic imagery as he foretells a human catastrophe: 'No need for tickets! There will be enough torment for everyone! [...] All in the same heap! the same carrion! from a slow burn!... to great volcanos! spouts of truths! frosting everything to spray!... thin shrouds... white dust... a breath of nothing' (1941: 26). Kristeva argues that literature such as Céline's 'represents the ultimate coding of our crises, of our most intimate and serious apocalypses' (PH 208).

Céline's and James' shared interest in End Times imagery emerged during a period of increasing secularization. In *Powers of Horror*, Kristeva traces the emergence of the avant-garde's interest in the abject to the waning of organized religion. Previously, religious interdictions had policed European Christian society's encounters with the abject. For Kristeva, in the absence of religion, avant-garde writing offers a possible means of engaging with the abject and purging feelings of abjection. As Sara Beardsworth notes, much of Kristeva's work is dedicated to exploring the role of the aesthetic in 'the secular aftermath of religion' (2004: 118). Kristeva believes art (and, by extension, literature) that engages with the abject may 'purify abjection' (1995: 24).[13] Céline's prose with its abject subject matter and festering style urges readers to enter into a *pas de deux* with abjection which leads them towards meaning's collapse and a loss of sense and self. James, however, merely encourages readers to look on, to observe the abject from safe distance, keeping their feet on *terra firma*.

The fabric of fear

Understanding the dissimilar psychic effects of reading Céline and James is helped by attending to their different approaches to texture. For Céline, as already mentioned, descriptions of hard, muscular bodies seem to offer reassuring firmness in a world prone to collapse and decompose. In James, there is also fear of a lack of solidity: horror is embodied in the hirsute, the soft, the wet. Faced with anxiety-inducing experiences and materials, personages strive to retain their composure. In James' 'The Stalls of Barchester Cathedral', for instance, the archdeacon John Haynes is pursued by a vengeful spirit. Haynes feels the world around him literally giving way, the wooden carvings of some cathedral choir stalls becoming soft and moist to his touch. In the face of this and other trials, he repeatedly confides to his diary the need to be firm: '[t]hese words, *I must be firm*, occur again and again [...] sometimes they are the only entry' (James 2001: 176). Firmness here signals being resolute yet, in the circumstances, an appeal to the solidity of matter also seems intended.

At one point, Haynes describes a carving becoming 'chilly and soft as if made of wet linen' (James 2001: 175). Linen refers to cloth woven from flax but also, more generally, to sheets used for bedding and to tablecloths. In the past, burial shrouds were sometimes made of linen although cotton and wool were common too.[14] Additionally, altar cloths are occasionally called church linens and the word therefore possesses strong religious connotations. Linen and drapery are mainstays in the ghost stories. Textiles provided James with a metaphorical shorthand for registering psychic distress. Fabrics disturb by way of their form: their spoliation, deformation or transformation. Céline also makes reference to linen in his writings but in a qualitatively different way. For him, curtains and sheets are mouldy, musty and damp, contributing to the general atmosphere of putrefaction, moral and physical, in the novels (Céline 1997: 135, 226).[15]

James' 'The Diary of Mr. Poynter' features a sample of textile from a seventeenth-century wall hanging modelled on the hair of a notable libertine. Around two hundred years later, the sample is used as a pattern for new drapes in a house. These drapes come to haunt the chief protagonist, James Denton. The demon that forms the centrepiece of 'Canon Alberic's Scrap-Book', is described as having 'black and tattered drapery about it' (James 2001: 12). In 'Number 13', the head of the fiend that occupies the phantom hotel room of the story is covered 'with some kind of drapery' (2001: 55). A pillow closes over the face of a doctor in 'Two Doctors', suffocating him. He has previously dreamt of a chrysalis that was of 'linen or woollen' material. Upon parting this textile membrane, a head 'in a state of death' was disclosed (2001: 283). This chrysalis is clearly akin to a burial shroud. James discusses the use of a woollen burial shroud in 'There was a Man Dwelt by a Churchyard' (2001: 372).

Cloth has been identified by Claire Pajaczkowska as a liminal material, experienced as neither subject nor object and encouraging 'a curious interplay between maternal and phallic, between distance and proximity, between sight and touch and between sacred and profane' (2005: 224). This renders it especially well-suited to exploring states of abjection, of border troubling. In James, references to drapery are particularly marked. Drapery is a boundary material, often used as a kind of second skin, protecting something from exposure. Gen Doy notes that in the Victorian era, drapery was used in middle- and upper-class households to 'clothe' furniture and windows that were perceived as naked (2002: 11). In the same vein, Anne Hollander writes of Victorian men finding 'their drawing-rooms as decorously clad as their similarly obscured and festooned wives and daughters' (1975: 451). The linking of drapery with decorum, with concealing the indecorous, invites relating James' fascination with fabric to sexual repression.

Freud noted the importance of fabric to fetishism mentioning velvet by name and also referring more generally to underclothing (1928: 21). As Anne Hamlyn notes, fetishes in Freud function metonymically, 'chosen for their contiguity, that is to say, their nearness to the maternal body' (2003: 16).

They can also be used as metaphor. Hamlyn suggests that in the art of Allen Jones, fabrics act to contain and restrain, transforming female figures into phallic symbols. This last reading, indebted to Laura Mulvey's (1973) analyses of Jones' corpus, is compelling in its foregrounding of anxiety about the feminine at work in the iconography of bound and constricted female bodies.[16] Céline's toned women are symptomatic of a comparable disquiet. Their muscular physiques form a hard carapace akin to the second skin that Mulvey believes fetish-wear made of rubber, latex or nylon provides (1973: 15).[17] James, however, represents fabric qualitatively differently. It is disturbed or decayed, singularly failing to conceal or contain what lies beneath or behind it.

In Walter Map's *De Nugis Curialum*, which James translated, tattered clothes register baseness. At one point, Map writes of a character called Eudo, who has fallen on hard times: 'looking on his clothes, he sickened at their raggedness and turned pale at their patches' (1983: 317). Here there is conscious anxiety about what the clothes 'say' of their wearer. Dishevelment shames a person. It is likely because of the negative connotations attached to creases and folds that the artist Norman Blamey 'ironed' Graham Higman's shirt when painting a 1984 portrait of the mathematician. Blamey substituted starch and stiffness for crumpled reality.[18] The resultant portrait depicts Higman seated adjacent to a coset graph on a chalkboard, a graph that expresses the abstract algebraic structure known as a group.[19] Blamey's sartorial intervention may have been motivated by fear that Higman's unkempt appearance would be interpreted as symptomatic of his state of mind. Group theory concerns symmetry and involves mathematical laws, it is about correctness and precision. In this context, the pressed cotton substituted by Blamey becomes a visual register of academic rigour. Creases and folds speak of indiscipline and disarrangement, of mess and muddle.

As signifiers of disarray, drapes and folds run against modernity's desire for order and boundedness. In James, the use of fabric seems informed by anxieties about mess and confusion of this kind. In her article 'Expression in Drapery', Annie Williams suggests drapery acts as a moral barometer and that its study could provide an 'ethical history' of humankind and 'the advances of civilization' (1889: 61). By the early twentieth century, however, drapery in British art was associated with a 'conservative, figurative modernism', with puckered fabric used to shore against the ruin of the classical tradition (Doy 2002: 23). The 'plenteous folds' in drapery can also be suggestive of luxury and excess, a status symbol (Hollander 1975: 455). James' use of ragged textiles and of rumples and folds is very different. It does not affirm refinement or station but rather figures degradation and lapse. In his writings, drapery falteringly veils the abject. This is well-illustrated by 'Oh, Whistle'.

'Oh, Whistle, and I'll Come to You, My Lad'

James' ghost story 'Oh, Whistle', likely written in 1903, centres on an Oxford academic, Parkins, who prides himself on his rationalism and does not believe in ghosts. The title of the story derives from the first line of a poem by Robert Burns.[20] Because of his empirical and scientific outlook, Parkins represents 'the apex of modern civilized man' (Thompson 2001: 193). For an enlightened man such as Parkins, belief in ghosts betrays ignorance and primitivism. On a coastal sojourn at the fictional town of Burnstow, Parkins' scepticism regarding the supernatural is severely challenged when he is plagued by a phantom presence. The haunting is triggered by him engaging in some amateur archaeology at the ruins of a preceptory of the Knights Templar.[21] During some crude excavating of the Templar's church on the site, he uncovers a 'small cavity' in which he discovers a 'cylindrical object', which subsequently turns out to be a bronze whistle (James 2001: 83). It bears Latin inscriptions that translate as 'O thief, you will blow, you will weep' and 'Who is this who is coming?'.[22] After cleaning the whistle, Parkins blows it eliciting a soft note with 'a quality of infinite distance' and causing him to have a vision of 'a lonely figure' (2001: 86). Over the next couple of days, he becomes increasingly anxious, sleeping poorly, disturbed by noises, sensing a troubling presence yet dismissing the feeling as irrational. Finally, he is roused from his slumber and confronted by an entity with 'a horrible, an intensely horrible, face *of crumpled linen*' (2001: 93). Shrieking with terror, he is rescued by another guest. The next day, the whistle is cast into the sea.

The story has generated varied readings, many discuss the whistle and its phallic connotations. In a psycho-biographical interpretation, Maurice Richardson (1959), for example, associates blowing the whistle with masturbation.[23] Links with fellatio are also possible, as the slang term 'meat whistle' for penis implies. The theme of coastal erosion in the story has also attracted attention (Armitt 2016; Packham 2019) as have the references to golfing. The golf course as landscaping has been read as an example of the modern drive for order and stability as it intersects with the natural world (Thompson 2001: 194–5). Here, the neglected role of the abject as it manifests acoustically and visually in the tale will be my focus.

Armitt (2016) and Hayes (2021) have rightly foregrounded James' attention to the acoustic in 'Oh, Whistle'. The whistle produces a sound Parkins registers as quiet, yet unbounded, travelling a vast distance. Hayes refers to it as an 'auditory otherness' (116). In *Sounds*, John Mowitt makes oblique reference to this whistling as a kind of hailing into the dark, a haunting call to the unknown (2015: 57). Lacking a phonemic value, the whistle is vocal noise that parallels other noises in the story. The reference to the shingle that Parkins noisily 'rattled and clashed through', on his way back from finding the whistle, echoes Matthew Arnold's 'Dover Beach', with its 'naked shingles of the world' and 'darkling plain [...] where ignorant armies clash by night' (1867: 112–14). Noises, sounds registered as ambiguous and uncertain, are key to the atmosphere of impending disaster. Noise as a phenomenon incarnates sense unmade, a sonic signifier without a ready signified. Because of its resistance to categorization and definition, it possesses an abject dimension.[24] In 'Oh, Whistle', Parkins' sleep is repeatedly disturbed by rustling which he links with vermin: 'The scraping of match on box and the glare of light must have startled some creature of the night – rats or what not – which he heard scurry across the floor from the side of his bed with much rustling' (James 2001: 87–8).

In the context of a story about a doom-laden musical instrument, this reference to rats and rustling appears intended to connote Robert Browning's 1842 poem 'The Pied Piper of Hamelin'.[25] Based on the famous fairy tale, Browning's piper uses the shrill notes of his instrument to entice all but one of the rats of Hamelin to their watery deaths. When the townspeople refuse to pay him what they had promised, the piper then lures away their children: 'There was a rustling that seemed like a bustling [...] Out came the children running' (Browning 1870: 339). In the poem, a broken promise leads to loss and despair. In the ghost story, it is boundary troubling that invites a malevolent visitation. It is also noteworthy that the expression 'whistle for a wind' was used by seamen when becalmed. A character in the story seems to allude to this superstition (James 2001: 88). To whistle for the wind was to ask aid of Satan and sea-winds were viewed as a manifestation of the devil's power (Hayes 1999: 11).

As well as acoustically uncertain night-time noises, the story also conjures images of visual uncertainty to powerful effect. Soon after finding the whistle, Parkins views a seascape that is dim, faint and pale, indistinct and soft-edged (James 2001: 83). Later, upon blowing the whistle for the first time, he experiences a vision of 'a wide, dark expanse at night' (2001: 86). He will go on to dream of 'a figure in pale, fluttering draperies, ill-defined' (2001: 87). Here psychic anxieties about boundary loss register through a lack of clarity and definition.[26] Horror manifests by way of disrupted and erased borders. The figure as a thing ill-defined also resists hermeneutic efforts. Saying with precision what it is that is being seen is impossible. Parkins therefore falls back on a hermeneutic of vagueness. The phantom presence that assails the scholar is a misshapen force, one that manifests, in significant part, through ruffled fabric. Descriptions of disturbed bedding, of disorder, are used to register the actions of a phantom presence. Repeatedly the spare bed in Parkins' room shows signs of having been slept in. A maid tells him one morning that 'all the things was crumpled and throwed about all ways' (2001: 88). The next day, clothes placed on the spare bed are 'bundled up and twisted together in a most tortuous confusion' (2001: 91).

As part of her exploration of sexual forensics in Victorian and Edwardian England, Victoria Bates includes trial depositions linked to a case of indecent assault brought against a John Martinitzi in which a landlady, Ann Lane, gives testimony about the dirtiness of the bottom hems ('the bottom part of the flap') of the accused man's shirts and remarks: 'I did not notice any thing on the sheets' (2016: 67). Lane is clearly referring to stains (blood or semen). Parkins' disarranged bedding also potentially indexes sexual encounter. In advertising, rumpled sheets sometimes act as a shorthand for sex (Clark 1993: 191). The disordered bedlinen in 'Oh, Whistle', however, is overdetermined. It additionally indicates Parkins' state of mind, functioning as the creases in Higman's shirt might have, had they not been painted flat. The firmly made bed that has been sundered comes to figure order undone. The phantom presence has upset the academic's regimented existence. Here bunched and crumpled fabric stands for a world in revolt, refusing to conform to Parkins' logic of structuring. In a Kristevan sense, they represent a 'destructive happening' (Kapoor 2015). Kristeva uses this term to describe the way Anish Kapoor's artworks installed at Versailles in 2015 exposed abjection as it existed within the 'rational beauty' and 'geometrical charms' of the palace gardens. In the hotel room at Burnstow, the uncertain that haunts Parkins' certitude and sense of order rises to the surface.

Once the apparition is finally revealed, it is literally formed of a furrowed bedsheet (James 2001: 93).[27] An event from James' childhood which he recounts in what is considered his final ghost story, 'A Vignette', is, perhaps, what motivated the description of the ghost's visage. James recalls seeing a malignant figure peering at him through a hole in a gate to a plantation that fronted the garden of the rectory where he lived:

> It was not monstrous, not pale, fleshless, spectral. Malevolent, I thought and think it was; at any rate the eyes were large and open and fixed. It was pink and, I thought, hot, and just above the eyes the border of a white linen drapery hung down from the brows.
>
> (James 2001: 412)

Trick photography of the kind produced by the spiritualist Édouard Isidore Buguet, involving the use of double exposure and draped mannequins or sheeted forms, may also have influenced James' conception of the apparition.[28]

Crumpled linen and drapery embody interplays of light and shadow, of material and its disappearance. Folds act as lacerations in the fabric, cutting into the surface. They cause shadows, patches of varying intensity of darkness. Shadows sometimes act like visual dirt, sullying the uniform colour of an expanse of fabric. Parkins' attention to cleanliness has manifested earlier when, 'tidy as ever in his habits', he carefully cleans the grime-clogged whistle 'on to a piece of paper' (James 2001: 84). In the entity of crumpled linen, he is confronted by a bed unmade, by shadow-riven dirty laundry. This abject thing that bears down on him, like other malevolent forces in James, signifies a challenge to the modern drive to classify and subordinate. Parkins screeches in disgust when faced by the apparition (2001: 94). As it advances, he utters 'cry upon cry at the utmost pitch of his voice' (2001: 94). In essence, he shrieks, no longer capable of speech only of purely affective vocalizations. Parkins' horror is for something that he cannot make sense of, for a force of non-sense, an unthinkable Thing which, in psychoanalytic terms, resonates with the 'weight of meaninglessness' he feels inside himself (PH 2).

'Oh, Whistle', therefore, like Céline's writings, shows the reader something of their own abject beginnings. The furrowed linen reflects the subject before it knows itself as such, the mess in the mirror at the stage before it becomes ordered and defined, 'before being *like*' (PH 13). Gothic fiction frequently manifests a fascination with 'foreign bodies', with the alien that disrupts the familiar (Smith and Wallace 2001: 6). James' Gothic modernism employs the unfamiliar, the out of place, the dirty and the horrible, to speak the abject, the dark underside to enlightened reason. In his interview with Kristeva, Kapoor (2015) describes how the rational leads to 'an irrational object'. In James it is more that the rational as an objectifying force masks the non-objectal, the abject. Through horrible acoustics and visions, James performs a partial unveiling. In this sense, he gestures towards what Maria Margaroni has called 'the beginning before "the Beginning,"' to what lies beyond the reach of 'the structuring principle of the symbolic order' (2005: 79).

This structuring principle, this ordering, involves raising signs into being. Kristeva describes the abject as 'a wellspring of sign for a non-object' (PH 11). The crumpled linen in 'Oh, Whistle' that drapes nothing, that has no object supporting it, names this non-object, this abject on the way to objecthood. James' modernist drapery therefore enables something of the abject to be articulated. In his ghost stories, draperies and other fabrics are contemporary (whatever the historical setting) as they speak for modernity's anxieties about the horrors it has smoothed over through 'purifying, systematizing and thinking', yet which remain as a disruptive potential just beneath the surface (PH 210). The abject persists alongside the modern subject, an ever-present accompaniment, a pressing anxiety.

In some modern literature, such as Céline's, this anxiety is allowed to spill out. James, however, maintains the same precision of speech he accords Parkins and is never reduced to the latter's inarticulacy (James 2001: 79). Unlike Parkins, or Céline, he never cries out (PH 141). Encounters with the abject are staged by James but realized by Céline. Céline's stylistic innovativeness, his rumpling and puckering of syntax so as to push the semiotic (in Kristeva's sense of the term) to the fore in his texts, carries the reader towards an enfolding night. James' supernatural yarns, by contrast, are tightly knit, keeping the powers of horror in check. While Céline's writings are carefully crafted to continually unravel, exposing the reader to underlying dread, James' horrors are studiously draped by his refined prose, charily kept in the dark.

Notes

1. I am very grateful to Maria Margaroni for her helpful comments and edits relating to an earlier version of this chapter.
2. See Constable and Cox, *Exhibition of French Art 1200–1900* (1932).
3. For a discussion of the spectral in Butts' own writings, see Matless (2008).
4. For insights into modernism's fear of mass culture, which was figured as feminine, see Williams (2004: 77–8).
5. For an exploration of modernist writers and the occult, see Surette (1993). In modern British art, for instance, works by Cecil Collins, Ithell Colquhoun and Leslie Hurry manifest occult influences.
6. For an analysis of the influence of Dickens on James and what differentiates the two authors, see Chapter 3 of Thurston 2012. Mark Fisher calls James 'a Victorian figure in the twentieth century' (2016: 81).
7. For further discussion of this, see Williams (1998).
8. Michael Cox suggests that the ghost stories should be understood as contributing to a long-standing tradition of oral storytelling (1983: 149).
9. See Kaplan's discussion of Lucien Rebatet's 1938 review of Céline's *Bagatelles pour un massacre* (1986: 125–6). Rebatet suggests of himself and a group of likeminded readers that saying they have read the pamphlet means nothing: 'We recite it, we proclaim it' (1938: 8). His enthusiastic review is illustrated by antisemitic caricatures.
10. One of the colour plates shows a topless Judith wielding a scimitar in preparation to slay Holofernes, providing a dynamic vision of female empowerment albeit tempered by sexualization. James' (1928) introduction to *Judith* recognizes the story as exemplary of Jewish patriotism but avoids engaging with Judith's decapitation of Holofernes. For a discussion of antisemitic imagery, see Gilman (1991). Gilman mentions women only briefly, believing that it is the representation of the male Jew that 'lies at the very heart of Western Jew hatred' (1991: 5). Representations of Judith in modern art and their relationship to female emancipation are discussed by Dearhamer 2016. Brunotte describes Judith as a modernist icon frequently represented as a 'murderous oriental *femme fatale*' (2019: 177).
11. James' fear of women's empowerment manifested most overtly in his energetic attack upon the scholarship of the classicist Jane Harrison.
12. Translation amended. Philippe Destruel (1987) reads this pornographic fascination with muscular physiques, what would nowadays be described as 'muscle worship', as linked to the interplay of sickness and health, of

durability and decay at play in Céline's writings. The somatotype of the dancer, a lithe muscularity, is regularly referenced in Céline's fiction. The author's second wife, Lucette Destouches (née Almansor), was a professional dancer, suggesting that the muscle fantasies of the fiction were potentially realized in his own sex life. For further discussion of Céline's eroticization of muscle, see Chare (2011: 19–23). For an exploration of the shifting status of the ballerina's body in French culture of the interwar years, see Karthas (2015: 263–302).

13 For a more in-depth discussion of art's cathartic potential, see Chare, Hoorn and Yue (2020).

14 The Turin Shroud, for example, is made of linen (Fazio et al. 2015).

15 James cites Dickens referring to 'mouldy bedclothes' in the 1929 story 'Rats', but fabric is never figured as mouldy by James himself (2001: 375).

16 Mulvey's essay was originally illustrated and accompanied by sub-headings, both of which added additional power to her argument. For Mulvey, Allen's anxiety about the feminine manifests through repeated efforts in his imagery to bind and restrain the female figure.

17 Mulvey writes of Perspex but presumably means latex or spandex which are both common fetish materials. The kink magazine *Skin Two* is so named, in part, because of how fetish clothing assumes the status of a second carapace.

18 Michael Collins, 'Obituary: Professor Graham Higman', *The Independent*, 8 May 2008: 39.

19 For a discussion of the specific graph that appears in the portrait, see Conder and Riley (2014: 129–30).

20 To amuse himself, it is just possible that James might be making an oblique reference to Henry James' *Wings of a Dove* (1902), published in the UK a few months before the story was first read. There, the character Merton Densher observes of the manipulative Kate Croy that: 'She had had but to whistle and he had come' (1902: 199).

21 The name of the fictional town sounds like the word 'bestow', meaning to give or grant.

22 My version of the translation of the first inscription is taken from Patrick Murphy (2017: 48), who offers a compelling argument for how it should be deciphered. Another thoughtful discussion of the inscription is provided by Simpson (1997).

23 The sexual connotations of flute playing (specifically embouchure) feature in 'Elephant in the Room', the tenth episode of Season 3 of the Canadian comedy *Kim's Convenience*, giving a sense of how whistles might be similarly construed.

24 For discussions of noise and the abject, see Chare (2005) and Hainge (2013).

25 It should be noted in this context that James initially referred to the whistle as a 'bronze pipe' in the autograph manuscript (held in the High Walpole Collection, King's School, Canterbury) but then crossed this out.

26 In *The Sense and Non-Sense of Revolt*, Kristeva examines how the multiple folds in the drapery of Baroque sculpture link with the veiling and unveiling

of the phallus in phallic cults (87–93). In Baroque sculpture, drapery does not veil the phallus but involves a similar play of presence and absence. Kristeva reads this diaphanous drapery as providing the sculptor with a means to move beyond figuration, enabling a kind of abstract exploration of representation itself. This exploration of translucency as an absent presence, a representation that refuses itself, is, for her, quintessentially modern. James' tattered and distressed draperies betray literal rather than figurative absences and seem too crudely present in their patchiness to be performing a similar role. He seems more concerned with disfiguring than the veneration of figuration, with the monstrous over monstrance.

27 The common idea of the ghost as a sheeted figure, given recent cinematic expression in *A Ghost Story* (dir. David Lowery, USA, 2017), likely has its origins in linen burial shrouds.

28 For a discussion of Buguet's photographs, see Ardanuy and Csefkó (2018: 487).

References

Ardanuy, J., and M. F. Csefkó (2018), 'Un tipo de document visual descuidado en España: la fotografía espiritista', *Fotocinema: Revista científica de cine y fotografía*, 17: 481–508.

Armitt, L. (2016), 'Ghost-Al Erosion: Beaches and the Supernatural in Two Stories by M.R. James', in L. Fletcher (ed.), *Popular Fiction and Spatiality*, 97–108, New York: Palgrave Macmillan.

Arnold, M. (1867), *New Poems*, London: Macmillan.

Bates, V. (2016), *Sexual Forensics in Victorian and Edwardian England: Age, Crime and Consent in the Courts*, Basingstoke: Palgrave Macmillan.

Bauman, Z. (1991), *Modernity and Ambivalence*, Cambridge: Polity.

Beardsworth, S. (2004), *Julia Kristeva: Psychoanalysis and Modernity*, New York: State University of New York Press.

Braun, A. A. (2017 [1928]), *Figures, Faces and Folds: Women's Form and Dress for Artists, Students and Designers*, Mineola, NY: Dover.

Browning, R. (1870 [1842]), 'The Pied Piper of Hamelin: A Child's Story', in R. C. Trench (ed.), *A Household Book of English Poetry*, rev. edn, 333–42, London: Macmillan.

Brunotte, U. (2019), 'The *Beautiful Jewess* as Borderline Figure in Europe's Internal Colonialism: Some Remarks on the Intertwining of Orientalism and Antisemitism', *ReOrient*, 4 (2): 166–80.

Butts, M. (1934), 'The Art of Montagu James', *The London Mercury*, 29 (172): 306–17.

Céline, L.-F. (1997 [1932]), *Journey to the End of the Night*, trans. R. Manheim, London: John Calder.

Céline, L.-F. (1937), *Bagatelles pour un massacre*, Paris: Denoël.

Céline, L.-F. (1941), *Les Beaux draps*, Paris: Denoël.

Chare, N. (2005), 'Regarding the Pain: Noise in the Art of Francis Bacon', *Angelaki*, 10 (3): 133–43.

Chare, N. (2011), *Auschwitz and Afterimages: Abjection, Witnessing and Representation*, London: I.B. Tauris.
Chare, N., J. Hoorn and A. Yue (2020), 'Re-reading *The Monstrous Feminine*: New Approaches to Psychoanalytic Theory, Affect, Film and Art', in N. Chare, J. Hoorn and A. Yue (eds), *Re-reading* The Monstrous-Feminine: *Art, Film, Feminism and Psychoanalysis*, 1–34, New York: Routledge.
Clark, D. (1993), 'Commodity Lesbianism', in H. Abelove, M. A. Barale and D. M. Halperin (eds), *The Lesbian and Gay Studies Reader*, 186–201, New York: Roultledge.
Conder, M. and T. Riley (2014), 'Graham Higman's Lectures on Januarials', *The Quarterly Journal of Mathematics*, 65: 113–31.
Constable, W. J. and T. Cox (1932), *Exhibition of French Art 1200–1900*, London: William Clowes and Sons.
Cox, M. (1983), *M.R. James: An Informal Portrait*, Oxford: Oxford University Press.
Cox, M. (1986), 'Introduction', in M. Cox (ed.), *The Ghost Stories of M.R. James*, 6–37, Oxford: Oxford University Press.
Crowley, A. E. (1928), *Judith*, London: Haymarket.
Dearhamer, S. H. (2016), 'Exploring the Suppressed Territory of the Third Reich Art World: Judith in the Twentieth Century', *MJUR*, 6: 152–70.
Destruel, P. (1987), 'Le corps s'écrit: Somatique du *Voyage au bout de la nuit*', *Littérature*, 68: 102–18.
Douglas, M. (1991 [1966]), *Purity and Danger: An Analysis of Concepts of Pollution and Taboo*, London: Routledge.
Doy, G. (2002), *Drapery: Classicism and Barbarism in Visual Culture*, London: I.B. Tauris.
Fazio, G., V. Di Leo, F. Curciarello and G. Mandaglio (2015), 'Comparison among the Shroud Body Image Formation Mechanisms by the Linen Fibril Distributions', *The Journal of the Textile Institute*, 106 (8): 896–9.
Fielding, P. (2000), 'Reading Rooms: M.R. James and the Library of Modernity', *Modern Fiction Studies*, 46 (3): 749–71.
Fisher, M. (2016), *The Weird and the Eerie*, London: Repeater Books.
Freud, S. (1928), 'Fetischismus', in Adolf Josef Storfer (ed.), *Almanach der Psychoanalyse*, 17–24, Vienna: Internationaler Psychoanalytischer verlag.
Fyfe, G. (2000), *Art, Power and Modernity: English Art Institutions, 1750–1950*, Leicester: Leicester University Press.
Gilman, S. (1991), *The Jew's Body*, New York: Routledge.
Hainge, G. (2013), *Noise Matters: Towards an Ontology of Noise*, New York: Bloomsbury.
Hamlyn, A. (2003), 'Freud, Fabric, Fetish', *Textile*, 1 (1): 9–27.
Hayes, K. J. (1999), *Melville's Folk Roots*, Kent, OH: Kent State University Press.
Hayes, T. (2021), 'Aural Disturbance in the Stories of M.R. James', *Short Fiction in Theory and Practice*, 11 (1/2): 111–25.
Hollander, A. (1975), 'The Fabric of Vision: The Role of Drapery in Art', *The Georgia Review*, 29 (2): 414–65.
James, H. (1902), *The Wings of the Dove: Volume II*, New York: Charles Scribner's Sons.
James, M. R. (1928), 'Introduction', in *Judith*, xi–xvii, London: Haymarket Press.

James, M. R. (1931), *The Apocalypse in Art*, London: Humphrey Milford.
James, M. R. (1956), *Letters to a Friend*, ed. Gwendolen McBryde, London: Edward Arnold.
James, M. R. (2001), *A Pleasing Terror: The Complete Supernatural Writings*, Ashcroft: Ash Tree Press.
James, M. R. (2005), *Count Magnus and Other Ghost Stories*, ed. S. T. Joshi, London: Penguin.
Kaplan, A. Y. (1986), *Reproductions of Banality: Fascism, Literature and French Intellectual Life*, Minneapolis, MN: University of Minnesota Press.
Kapoor, A. (2015), 'Blood and Light: In Conversation with Julia Kristeva', http://anishkapoor.com/4330/blood-and-light-in-conversation-with-julia-kristeva (accessed 27 July 2020).
Karthas, I. (2015), *When Ballet Became French: Modern Ballet and the Cultural Politics of France, 1909–1939*, Montreal: McGill-Queen's University Press.
Kristeva, J. (1982), *Powers of Horror: An Essay on Abjection*, trans. Leon S. Roudiez, New York: Columbia University Press.
Kristeva, J. (1995), 'Of Word and Flesh: An Interview with Julia Kristeva by Charles Penwarden', in S. Morgan and F. Morris (eds), *Rites of Passage: Art for the End of the Century*, 21–7, London: Tate Gallery Publications.
Lorey, E. R. (1999), 'Louis-Ferdinand Céline's Relation to Christian Thought and Belief', PhD thesis, Boston University.
Lovecraft, H. P. (2000 [1927]), *The Annotated Supernatural Horror in Literature*, ed. S. T. Joshi, New York: Hippocampus Press.
Map, W. (1983 [c. 1182]), *De Nugis Curialium*, trans. M. R. James, rev. edn, Oxford: Clarendon Press.
Margaroni, M. (2005), '"The Lost Foundation": Kristeva's Semiotic *Chora* and Its Ambiguous Legacy', *Hypatia*, 20 (1): 78–98.
Matless, D. (2008), 'A Geography of Ghosts: The Spectral Landscape of Mary Butts', *Cultural Geographies*, 15 (3): 335–57.
Mowitt, J. (2015), *Sounds: The Ambient Humanities*, Oakland: University of California Press.
Mulvey, L. (1973), 'You Don't Know What Is Happening Do You, Mr. Jones?', *Spare Rib*, 8: 13–6, 30.
Murphy, P. J. (2017), *Medieval Studies and the Ghost Stories of M.R. James*, University Park, PA: Pennsylvania State University Press.
Packham, J. (2019), 'The Gothic Coast: Boundaries, Belonging, and Coastal Community in Contemporary British Fiction', *Critique*, 60 (2): 205–21.
Pajaczkowska, C. (2005), 'On Stuff and Nonsense: The Complexity of Cloth', *Textile*, 3 (3): 220–49.
Pfaff, P. W. (1980), *Montague Rhodes James*, London: Scolar Press.
Rebatet, L. (1938), 'Bagatelles pour un massacre', *Je suis partout*, 134 (21 January): 8.
Richardson, M. (1959), 'The Psychoanalysis of Ghost Stories', *Twentieth Century Magazine*, 166: 419–31.
Scullion, R. (1995), 'Introduction', in R. Scullion, P. H. Solomon and T. C. Spear (eds), *Céline and the Politics of Difference*, 1–12, Hanover, NH: University Press of New England.
Simpson, J. (1997), 'The Riddle of the Whistle', *Ghosts and Scholars*, 24: 54–5.

Smith, A. and J. Wallace (2001), 'Introduction: Gothic Modernisms: History, Culture and Aesthetics', in A. Smith and J. Wallace (eds), *Gothic Modernisms*, 1–10, Basingstoke: Palgrave.

Surette, L. (1993), *The Birth of Modernism: Ezra Pound, T.S. Eliot, W.B. Yeats and the Occult*, Montreal: McGill-Queen's University Press.

Thompson, T. W. (2001), 'James's Oh Whistle, and I'll Come to You, My Lad', *The Explicator*, 59 (4): 193–5.

Thurston, L. (2012), *Literary Ghosts from the Victorians to Modernism: The Haunting Interval*, London: Routledge.

Williams, A. (1889), 'Expression in Drapery', in *The Magazine of Art*, 61–5, London: Cassell.

Williams, D. (2004), 'Modernism, Antisemitism and Jewish Identity in the Writing and Publishing of John Rodker', PhD thesis, University of Leeds.

Williams, S. (1998), 'Modernity and the Emotions: Corporeal Reflections on the (Ir)rational', *Sociology*, 32 (4): 747–69.

10

The impact of Kristeva's theory of abjection on modernist art

Rina Arya

Modernism in the visual arts is characterized by experimentalism and the overthrow of order. Visually and conceptually this took many forms, but one key prevalent feature was fragmentation often seen through distortion. This was apparent in the work of Futurism and Cubism, for example, where the image was fractured into planes to convey the flux of the modern world, in the case of Futurism, and to explore a different mode of representing reality, in the case of Cubism. As modernism developed and diversified, the fragment endured as a symbol of the modern condition. The fragment is central to the concept of abjection – the focus of this chapter.

Abjection is a vital and determinative process in the formation of the subject which asserts that, in order to retain a sense of psychological wholeness, we have to refrain actively from engaging with experiences that threaten the boundaries of the self and that remind us of our animal origins. Originating as a psychic process, abjection explains social and cultural codes relating to the emotion of disgust. The most impactful articulation of abjection is by Julia Kristeva, whose theory of abjection was presented pre-eminently in *Powers of Horror: An Essay on Abjection and Literature* (1980).[1] Its translation into English in 1982 brought the concept into prominence in the Anglophone world, especially in the context of the visual arts in significant exhibitions including *Abject Art: Repulsion and Desire in American Art* at the Whitney Museum of American Art (New York, 1993), which was the first formal identification of abject art (Lotringer 1994: 2); *Rites of Passage: Art for the End of a Century* at the Tate (London,

1995); and *L'informe: Mode d'emploi* (*Formless: A User's Guide*) at the Centre Georges Pompidou (Paris, 1996).

In these exhibitions the abject and the process of abjection were used as a theoretical frame with which to look at the body and the bodily in art and aesthetics. As a theoretical frame, abjection can explain paradoxical emotions about horror and death, accounting for why, for instance, we are attracted to and yet repelled by certain things. It has also more recently been deployed extensively to explain attitudes about social rejection. This chapter will present the different but related interpretations of abjection in the work of three artists, Hans Bellmer, Francis Bacon and Maria Lassnig, each of whom present the body as fragmented and in the condition of abjection. Each of the artists use different strategies to reconfigure the body and challenge the boundaries of identity.

Defining abjection: Kristeva's theory

Before we look at the influence that abjection has had on the visual arts and, in particular, in the work of the selected artists, it is useful to offer a definition of 'abjection'. The etymology of the term 'abjection' lies in the Latin word *abicere*, which means to cast away or to rebuff. In contemporary cultural theory the term has become associated with the psychoanalytic theories of Kristeva who defines 'abjection' as the impact that the phenomenon of disgust has on the boundaries of the ego. Defined as central in the formation of subjectivity, abjection is a normal part of psychic development whereby the infant simultaneously seeks and is repulsed by the mother's breast in alternating movements of hunger and satiation. Prior to the infant's misrecognition of itself in the mirror, it must first become estranged from this mother. Kristeva writes, 'Even before being *like*, "I" am not but do *separate, reject, ab-ject*' (PH 13). Abjection therefore occurs before the subject's positioning in language, anterior to the emergence of the 'I'. It is a provisional, transitory sense of differentiation from the maternal: a fragile, unbecoming and unknowing sense of self.

This primary psychic process of abjection recurs throughout life. Being of and about the body, the abject is not something that can be eliminated and looms on the boundaries. Abject materials, such as bodily excretions like menses, urine, faeces, mucus or spit, are capable of triggering memories of this archaic stage of psychic life, of abjection. These materials are abject precisely because they defy categorization as subject or object, and are resolutely in between, threatening the subject with dissolution and preventing the object from objectification. Hal Foster identifies the dual aspect of abjection which involves two distinct senses and operations – *to abject* and *to be abject*; while the operation (of abjection) seeks to stabilize, the condition (of the abject) is inherently disruptive, meaning that there is a constant tension between drives (Foster 1996: 114).

In *Purity and Danger* (1966) Mary Douglas anticipates many of the issues pertaining to abjection. She stresses the vulnerability of the margins, which are the points where dirt collects, and hence are the weakest points of a system (Douglas 2002: 150). Colin McGinn reinforces the revulsion that we have at our unrelenting tendency to 'contaminate' ourselves as a result of our irreducible physicality. Our excretions travel from inside to outside the body, thereby troubling any sense of it having secure borders.

> In order to stave off repulsion we have continually to undergo practices to cleanse the body: the living body is a rich repository – a factory – of dischargeable disgust materials. On a daily, even hourly, basis we must manage and contain the polluting substances generated by our own organic existence, as the body leaks and expels its natural products. The body spews forth its organic materials, what it needs to flourish and survive – and meanwhile we recoil. These vital substances are the objects of our steady revulsion, biologically necessary as they are... We seem as disgusted by the body in the full flight of life, squeezing and pumping, as we are by its quiet dissolution in death.
>
> (McGinn 2011: 19)

The substances in and of themselves may be dubious because of their ambiguous form – they are not quite solid, not quite liquid – but what makes them abject is their position on the boundaries, where they became other and alien to us; what the psychologist Gordon Allport talks about as the 'not-me' – the ego-alien (1955: 43). The following example animates the strangeness evinced by the ego-alien.

> Think first of swallowing the saliva in your mouth, or do so. Then imagine expectorating it into a tumbler and drinking it! What seemed natural and 'mine' suddenly becomes disgusting and alien. Or picture yourself sucking blood from a prick in your finger; then imagine sucking blood from a bandage around your finger! What I perceive as separate from my body becomes, in the twinkling of an eye, cold and foreign.
>
> (Allport 1955: 43, in Miller 1997: 97)

Abjection implies a sense of fragmentation. The clean intact body struggles to maintain its integrity because it is always menaced by the turbulence of the corporeality, which threatens the clean boundaries with contamination. The process of living (and dying) is replete with the cycles of flow which sully the boundaries bringing about fragmentation. And the inability to assure our physical boundaries is supplemented by recognition of the precariousness of our psychic borders, our sense of self. While cultures developed rituals for policing encounters with abject materials – a subject which Kristeva explores in the second part of *Powers of Horror* – artists have sought to create aesthetic conditions that engendered the abject. They do this in a variety of ways including by representing the turmoil of the body and the threat this places on a stable sense of self. In the twentieth century, visual artists started to experiment with the metaphor of the body by breaking it up into fragments or parts which were assembled together in various ways that provoked questions about identity and representation. In his Cubist and Surrealist phases, and particularly in his paintings of figures on beaches executed in 1927 and 1928 in Cannes and Dinard, Picasso distorted the human form by varying the proportions of certain body-parts or by reassembling body-parts in incongruous ways (Berggruen 2003: 76). These strategies were employed for the same ends, which were to defamiliarize the body by presenting it in unusual ways. While he was more interested in subverting strategies of representation (parts and wholes) rather than in the sensory aspect of the body-part and the impact this had on the sundered body, Picasso's seminal studies could be seen to anticipate ideas central to abjection. Integral to the theory of abjection is the idea that the body cannot be reduced to an external static representation. It was instead prone to breakdown, fragmentation and dissolution, as a result, the body-part was used to explore questions of identity, sexuality and death. In its fragmented state, 'lacking its customary wholeness and unity', the body tested our own sense of stability (McGinn 2011: 16).

What follows are three accounts of the work of each of the chosen artists. What is observable in each study is that in their own way each artist wanted to depict the body in its affective state, as *experienced* rather than merely as *seen* (or known). This necessitated depicting the body as *felt*. In their representations the artists reject the instantiation of the body as whole, complete or external, and depict instead the body in its interiority and in a state of fragmentation. Within the civilizing process bodies move from nature to culture, where the former is suppressed through the imposition of boundaries in order to keep the body clean and safe from contamination. This trajectory describes Kristeva's account of abjection, which involves the suppression of the maternal body as the first abject object, essential before subjectivity can be attained in the Symbolic order. As Elisabeth Grosz puts it, 'The subject must disavow part of itself in order to gain a stable self, and this form of refusal marks whatever identity it acquires as provisional, and open to breakdown and instability' (Grosz 1990: 86). In their respective depictions, each of the artists analysed below throws into relief the conflicting impulses of the symbolic and the semiotic where the latter disrupts the overall sense of stability resulting in fragmentation. In brief, the semiotic is associated with the pre-verbal parts of language and is the result of bodily drives. In contrast, the symbolic is the linguistic part of language, and the realm associated with position and order. This is seen most readily in the erosion of the body boundary, which for Bellmer results in the assemblage of body-parts, for Bacon in the overflow of matter from out of the eroded body envelope into the picture plane, and for Lassnig an undoing of the boundary through the power of sensation. Railing against the Symbolic order for each of the three artists had metaphoric ramifications. Each wanted to defy a particular conception of gender normativity. For Bellmer and Bacon this was about a masculine order that partially derived from their respective relationships with their fathers. Lassnig employed abjection to critique conventions of female gender representation, and asserted her right as an older woman to depict her ageing body.

There are consequences for the viewer in looking at abject art, which need to be addressed. Being so accustomed to seeing the body intact and devoid of its materiality, the viewing of the fractured body is both enticing, because the physical presence of the figure is put forward in such an immediate and direct way, and also wounding, because it is a reminder of what we are attempting at all costs to stave off (see van Alphen 1992).

Bellmer's fragmented dolls

Hans Bellmer is best known for his constructions of life-size pubescent female dolls – *Die Puppe* – that were dismembered and distorted in various ways and then photographed. Influenced by the realistic life-size doll Olympia in Jacques Offenbach's final opera *The Tales of Hoffmann* (1881) the dolls directly parody the classical tradition of the nude, and fashion instead an aberrant and corrupt materiality. They can be considered alongside his drawings, etching and books, all of which were part of his 'quest for a "monstrous dictionary" dedicated to the ambivalence of the body' (Semff and Spira 2006: 10).

Bellmer constructed his first doll in 1933, which consisted of a moulded torso, a masklike head and a pair of legs. A few years later, in 1935, he made a second doll, which was less naturalistic, more deformed but also more mobile. He kept the head from the first doll and then added four legs, four breasts, three pelvises, an upper torso and a spherical belly (Taylor 2000: 73). These various body-parts were used interchangeably in assemblages, and the movable ball joints at different points across the body meant that Bellmer could be inventive and increase the grotesqueness of the doll as well as explore the 'fluidity between internal and external properties' (Semff and Spira 2006: 10). Bellmer stated how he wanted to 'construct an artificial girl with anatomical possibilities which are capable of re-creating the heights of passion, even of inventing new desires' (Green 2005: 16).

The doll has been interpreted in various ways: as an alter ego, a fetish and a transitional object 'that protects the artist from an overwhelmingly terrifying maternal imago' (Taylor 2000: 6). The polymorphous configurations of the female body can be interpreted as a harking back to the pre-symbolic abject. Hal Foster comments on how 'each new version is a "construction *as* dismemberment" that simultaneously signifies castration (in the disconnection of body-parts) and its fetishistic defense (in the multiplication of these parts as phallic substitutes)' (Foster 1991: 87).

Bellmer presented the dolls behind the lens of the camera, a device that has several interesting effects. It enables him to be more inventive with the props and backdrops through which the dolls are read, and which he arranges in the manner of crime scenes. The dolls, in their various states of undress, and fragmentation, are featured sprawled on beds, propped up against trees or in other equally disquieting poses that are reminiscent of crime scenes. There are several double aspects to the use of photography. Although at one remove, and hidden behind the lens, the dolls take on an intimacy that they might not otherwise have had if they were viewed as sculptures. The photograph provides a frame through which the viewer can peer, voyeuristically, into their lives and speculate about what has happened to them. There is also a tension between, on the one hand, the doll's artificiality as a mechanical construction, present in sculpture, and the animation of the doll as sentient, which Bellmer facilitates through the soft carving of the limbs and touches such as the shaping of the pudenda, or the clefting of the buttocks. Through photography, the sculptures are transformed into fleshy body-parts that are abject. Although the bodies are clean insofar as they do not contain traces of bodily fluids, the poses they assume suggest defilement. In some instances, the bodies are explicitly sexualized such as in the figurations of two sets of legs around a torso, heightened especially by the presence of paedophilic references, such as white socks and Mary Jane patent black shoes. In other cases, Bellmer partially mutilates the limbs and we are left with the torso laid bare and vulnerable. This restricts the focus to the plump spherical belly and other assembled body-parts, which includes heads. The absence of the face, if indeed a head is present, is depersonalizing and augments the sense of a crime scene. The viewer's gaze falls upon the exposed parts that often point to the most vulnerable points of the body such as orifices or the body boundaries in anticipation of the effluence.

Another common motif is that of the bulbous, fecund stumps, which were more representative of the monstrous maternal. These latter depictions are of spherical torsos, breasts or other body-parts that multiply unpredictably, deforming themselves in the process. They reflect the horror of engulfment at the maternal breast so central to Kristeva's account of abjection and the fear of the unstable body that characterizes the pre-abject stage of development (see PH 12–13).

Bellmer's motivations in his work can be explained in multiple and related ways, all of which consist in attempts to rail against the symbolic order of law and language (see Taylor 2000: 4–5). There are biographical readings that discuss his need to rebel against his overpowering father and to liberate himself from the dictates of 'adult' behaviour, thereby returning to a form of childhood and play, of which the dolls were his companions. Bellmer stood against fascist ideals that expounded particular ideals about masculinity. His dolls represent an anarchic sensibility that went against Nazi values and instead revealed the darker side of human instincts. They represent what is despised and marginalized by society but simultaneously also what fascinates. His work was branded degenerate and he was forced to flee Germany for France in 1938, where he came into contact with Surrealism, and shared its ideology of exploring irrational desires. His mythology of violence conveyed an instinctual need to embrace the abject at the heart of humanity. His language of dismemberment and disfiguration is poignant when considered in the context of the concentration and extermination camps.

Bacon's fluid bodies

Francis Bacon embraces abjection as the métier of his practice. Bacon's depiction of bodies, of the flesh, conveys the consequences of what happens when the boundary, which stabilizes the representation of the body, is marred. The boundaries are blurred in multitudinous ways, resulting in various states of fragmentation and distortion where the body is featured as unstable and anarchic. The boundaries between outer and inner are in tension, as conveyed by the relationship between the structure of the body and the matter, where they are often pulled in opposing directions, which contributes to the effect of torsion (or twisting). Visually this is conveyed by smears and smudges that are wiped across the body. Michel Leiris (1988: 13) uses the term 'liquefaction' to refer to this process of turbulence, which many of Bacon's figures are subject to, and which results in overspill, where the inner contents flow into the foreground, causing confusion as to whether we look at the external or internal, a fact compounded by the overspilled material being more opaque than the boundaries of the body such as in *Portrait of John Edwards* (1988), for example. Bacon's portrayals of the human form are marked by the instability between the body envelope and the force of matter which doesn't respect the boundary. In the previously cited example the spillage from inner to outer is meted out in a controlled way but causes confusion because of the illogic of the overspill being more palpable. More extreme cases show how the 'indefinable form of the figures... seems to lose their bone structure to become strange fluxes or whorls of matter in fusion' (Leiris 1988: 11). The force of his figures causes them to want to exit their bodies through any available aperture or orifice, whether through the mouth or the anus. The spasmodic or paroxysmal potential of the body often manifests itself as a force that cannot be contained and where the body attempts to escape through one of its polyvalent orifices into the outside world. In *Figure at a Washbasin* (1976), the figure clings 'to the oval of the washbasin, its hands clutching the faucets, the body-Figure exerts an intense motionless effort upon itself in order to escape down the blackness of the drain' (Deleuze 2003: 15).

The overflow of flesh (over the body boundary) renders the body out of control and relates to another tension of opposites in Bacon, that is, the merger between the human and the animal. What separates these two entities is an awareness of higher-order existence and purpose. We keep the body clean from material contamination in order to pursue the process of civilization, as sociologists such as Norbert Elias (1978 [1939]) would have it. The transgression of the boundary takes us to the space of the death of god. Bacon was familiar with Georges Bataille's writings and would have encountered the spirit of base materialism presented in the latter's journal *Documents*, which presents the idea of the overlap between the human and the animal. During experiences of extreme pain and suffering, the human is reduced to the position of the animal to express its torment. This often takes the form of a cry or scream, expressions that can be found in the three biomorphic and Picasso-inspired forms in *Three Studies for Figures at the Base of a Crucifixion* (c. 1944). Dawn Ades observes how the figure in the central panel, bearing gritted teeth, and the figure in the right-hand panel, with its open mouth, vent frustration and rage that seems to stem from their inverted positions in the genital region. The displacement of mouth or teeth to the genital area contributes to the bestiality of the imagery (Ades 1985: 16). By merging the human and animal in these forms, Bacon conveys the desperate nature of these creatures and uses these figures to represent the dysfunctional nature of humanity. Their bestial outlets provide channels for the ravening appetites of the figures, which are insatiable and destructive.

One of the reasons that these three figures caused such uproar when first put on show, and still continue to shock even today, is that, in spite of their resemblance to the human form, they are still de facto fragments and not whole bodies, which is enhanced by their placement on podiums. Another example, *Fragment of a Crucifixion* (1950), displays similar tendencies. We are faced with a form that is organic and deeply suggestive of the body without being an actual body-part. In the 1970s and 1980s, Bacon made a number of figure studies that focus on the fragment as body-part. *Triptych – Studies of the Human Body* (1970) consists of three undifferentiated bulbous figures on a rail that resemble the fragmented sculptural forms of Hans Bellmer. *Diptych: Study of the Human Body – From a Drawing by Ingres* (1982–4) consists of two fragments that are like trunks sprouting body-parts – hands and legs that are strapped with cricket pads in the 'male figure', and breasts and legs for the 'female figure'. Not all the fragments are recognizable parts of the body. But what they do in all cases is to evoke the physicality of their part. In their fleshy colour palette and mass, they resemble what Armin Zweite describes as 'the flatlands of shapeless matter' (Zweite 2006: 9), or, to use a Deleuzian phrase, 'a mass of ambulating flesh' (Deleuze 2003: 24).

Bacon's idiosyncratic representation of the body is a reaction against the conventions of narrative representation that were governed by figuration, which he believed distracted from the aesthetic properties of artworks. In a figurative portrayal the viewer's immediate identification of the form, for example, may detract from (or minimize the effect of) paying close attention to the power of the aesthetic. Bacon's figures are instead *figural*, which in its Deleuzian sense refers to a form that pertains to the figurative (but does not resemble it) and is also abstract (Arya 2016: 117). Bacon uses distortion to bring about the *figural*, which involves abstracting from the figure and distorting the figurative appearance of the photograph that he works from in the process of image-making. He approached the human body via the flesh rather than the external figurative form. In his explorations, the body was prone to dissolution, fragmentation and distortion, and he conveyed in powerful terms what it feels like to *be* a body rather than simply *having* a body.

The body fragment takes many forms in Bellmer and Bacon. In some instances, the body is an assemblage of disparate parts that do not form a seamless whole, and where the parts are interchangeable. In other cases, one fragment stands for the whole body, drawing attention to its sentience. Fragmenting the body renders it unstable and vulnerable, both for the viewer, who is uncertain how to read it as it subverts conventional understanding, and also because it takes on an indeterminate form with ambiguous boundaries. Bellmer and Bacon employ fragmentation for different ends, which can be couched in general terms as their assault on the hierarchy of the organic human body. Bacon drew on fragmentation as his strategy of realism. His aesthetic idiom challenged established practices of representing the external body. Bacon turns the body inside-out, thus giving the viewer access to a heightened sensory experience. As well as being inside-out, the body is also fragmented, and this fits in with his desire to dismantle the artificial represented body and to show the lived body which is in motion.

Lassnig's body-awareness painting

There is less documentation about the third artist, Maria Lassnig, as compared with Bellmer and Bacon and, for this reason, a brief historical excursion is useful. Born near the village of Kappel am Krappfeld, Carinthia, in 1919, Lassnig studied at the Academy of Fine Arts in Vienna from the early 1940s and spent much of her career in Austria, with short periods in Paris from 1951 to 1952 and a move to the United States in 1968, where she lived for twelve years before returning to Austria. Her art school training during the war years was politically directed at promoting styles of realism that were devoid of traces of degenerate art.

Lassnig, like Bellmer and Bacon, was motivated to representing the body via the internal rather than the external. All three artists are unconcerned with the external representation of the body, with what the body looks like from the outside or with 'the concept of the "body"... as a reified object of analysis but rather with the sensation of embodiment, that is, what it feels like to be within a body, to be enfleshed' (Turner 1996: xiii). Lassnig coined the term *korperbilder* or 'body awareness' to describe her approach, process and work which were born out of her own awareness of how her body felt; she describes this as being 'in the body house in which I dwell' (Obrist 2009: 28). The condition of embodiment entails the experiencing of pain or of sensory turmoil, and crucially the awareness that the body is always in a state of flux and transformation. Embodiment is conveyed here by the fragile body boundaries that we see, where the skin does not operate as an envelope that contains the body but rather is the point of permeability between inside and outside.

Lassnig places herself at the centre of her creative expression; her paintings record her sensations about being in her body; she is the agent of the perception of sensation and what we have is a record of her experience of being in her body. This process was at odds with her art training during the war years which defied expressionism and sought instead to cultivate a safe aesthetic of realism. The concept of body awareness was developed in her work from 1948 onwards and involved a process of self-reflection on what her body was doing. This was mediated through her expressive use of colour and line.

The foregoing discussion about what body awareness refers to and the degree to which it involves sensation, awareness and reflection articulates something of its richness and complexity. Gottfried Boehm talks about the conceptual slippage that the term has had, not least because of Lassnig's own variations in interpretations (Boehm 2013: 76–87). Understanding coalesces in an overarching sense of what body awareness is, which Boehm defines as:

> firstly not only a situation, but also a turning of the gaze, looking back at one's own body. Expressed more precisely, it concerns another kind of perception, for feelings, especially those which one harbours oneself, cannot be seen, yet arguably can be heard or felt by means of touch, sensation – in short, can be ascertained by all possible means of a physical and affective process of becoming aware.
>
> (Boehm 2013: 77)

In her short essay 'Body-awareness-painting' Lassnig conveys the various ways that she is made aware of her body – 'through pressure, through tension or by straining one part of it in a particular physical position; in other words, awareness is experienced in sensations of pressure or tension, in sensations of fullness or emptiness, etc.' (Obrist 2009: 28). As she was painting she would highlight which body-parts she felt at that time. She 'concentrat[ed] on small feelings: sensations in the skin or in the nerves, all of which one feels' (Hochdörfer 2008: 406). Hans Ulrich Obrist uses the term 'tropism' to conjure up a sense of what Lassnig was attempting to capture. '"Tropisms" are reactions provoked by one's inner movements but they aren't under your control' (Obrist 2009: 9). Painting then became a phenomenological exercise where the artist-as-agent recorded her sensations as they appeared to her and where colour and line were used as sensor. Through this the invisible was made visible (Lassnig 2008: 6). This meant that the body-part in her awareness, which might be an organ, a body-part, an orifice even, was heightened above other aspects rendering the painting incomplete in the sense of fragmentary. Her evocative poems *Self-Portrait in Words I* and *II* of 1958 trace the sensory and synesthetic development of sensations in and around the body: 'Where the flesh has grown fused along the lower edge/it feels like a burn/at the elevation and around the circular part/all this is red/the thickest places bluish red/The nostrils wreathe themselves in flame/and the air is sucked through the high opening' (Obrist 2009: 24).[2]

Lassnig's paintings are experiments that record the sensations of the body as they appear to her. She makes it abundantly clear that she is not drawing or painting the body as an object but instead is intent on painting the sensations of the body. As with any experiment, the control – where certain variables are fixed – enabled the changes that occurred to be tracked. The control in many of her portraits was a stock appearance: a *tabula rasa* presentation of self, seen in a number of portraits, where she appears with blue round piercing eyes, a parted mouth and a cadaverous body. 'I stand, as it were, nude in front of the canvas, without intention, without plans, without a model, without photography, and let things take shape' (Obrist 2009: 75). Her stark expression is intensified depending on whatever else is happening in the rest of the painting. What it actually does is to vary the way we read the body depending on which feature predominates. *Lady with Brain* (c. 1990) shows a misshapen head with a palpable mass of brain sliding down over the left ear. *The Senses* (1996) isolates each of the senses in turn. At times the body becomes reduced to a mere schema on which to support the ailed body-part – whether a breast in *A Kiss for the Whole World/Tathata* (1990) or *The Grim Reaper* (1991), which highlights the grimace of a mouth. Sometimes the body-part that is being fixed on is highlighted by its vibrant and often lurid colour that 'pulse[s] with energy' (Kent 2008: 45). *Figure with Blue Throat* (1961) is an abstract work that intimates a sense of the figurative. The viewer's eye is immediately drawn to the blue that is offset by the red of the face as it throbs with pain. As well as abstracting a particular body-part, Lassnig, especially in earlier work, combines elements of figuration and abstraction, where the image appears abstract but there are strong suggestions of the figure.[3]

In the 1970s Lassnig's sense of body awareness was intensified in her experiments with people under plastic. This was instigated by her observation of fruit and vegetables wrapped in plastic which she came across in grocery stores in the United States. This symbol of modern living, so ubiquitous in the West, came to signify many different sensations, which sometimes worked in opposition. In *Spell* (2006) the plastic functions like an amniotic sac out of which life emerges while the theme that predominates is fear and horror, as seen in *Couple* (2005), who look as if they are set in plastic.[4] In *Self-Portrait under Plastic* (1972) the representation of plastic is multifold. It operates like an invisible barrier that separates her from the viewer, a lens under which we inspect her, and becomes a metaphor for various discourses including vulnerability, the preservation of life and reversing the effects of ageing. Being wrapped in plastic also increases the awareness of breathing, which is something that coalesced with Lassnig's stance of body awareness. Submerged under plastic, the body becomes still and is made aware of its breathing. Then other physiological sensations set in as it moves to a state of suffocation. This extreme measure draws attention to the vital condition of the breath of life as well as the fragility of human functioning.[5]

Conclusion

Civilization is a campaign against abjection. Although we may take great pains to avoid abjection by purifying the body and safeguarding boundaries, it dominates a large part of our existence on an individual and societal level. Kristeva's claims for it are profound. Abjection is foundational to both the production and maintenance of society: '[f]or abjection, when all is said and done, is the other facet of religious, moral, and ideological codes on which rest the sleep of individuals and the breathing spells of societies' (PH 209).

The concept of abjection became of growing interest in the visual arts in late modernism when artists started experimenting with representations of the body and exploring fragmentation and distortion. In the above three accounts we saw how Bellmer, Bacon and Lassnig experiment with the body from inside out, which gives rise to a representation of sensation. In an interview with David Sylvester, Bacon declares one of his aims to be the desire to look behind the veneer that he claims society operates under and to expose the instinctual sensibilities that we are governed by. The overriding animal impulse of the human justifies his ideological formula that places the human on the same level as an animal, neatly conveyed in his phrases 'we are meat', 'we are potential carcasses' (Sylvester 1993: 64). Continuing in this vein, he wanted to 'unlock the valves of feeling' to bring about a more violent and immediate perception of reality (1993: 64). This sensibility is also apparent in Bellmer. In experimental work with his dolls he sought to tap into the 'body's unconscious representations' (Green 2005: 7) in order to 'help people lose their complexes, to come to terms with their instincts' (Taylor 2000: 3). Lassnig's goal was more subjective. She wanted to convey the pain and intensity of body awareness through the phenomenological act of sharing her body as she painted. Painting became an act of awareness, of giving rise to sensation.

Their respective works concern abjection because they are dealing with the fragmentation of the body and the impact that this has on the leaking visceral body, which cannot be comfortably contained. Another way they convey abjection is through the impact that their representations have on the viewer. In all three cases perception and sensation coexist, so the viewer perceives the figure experiencing sensations that are, in turn, experienced by the viewer, which is why viewing becomes a wounding experience.

One of the central purposes of the visual arts (and of the arts in general) from modernism onwards has been to explore sights that are normally hidden from view in everyday life, the exposure of which was regarded by some as distasteful. Kristeva argues for the eccentricity – in the sense of being outside the mainstream (ex-centric) – of the artist who probes the depths of reality:

> We live in a society which is both ultra-conformist – that is perhaps what people will say of our century: that we are hyper-bourgeois, hyper-conformist, we cocoon, are afraid of sex, and so on – and where, at the same time and as a consequence of this, there is a great deal of exclusion, both mental and social. The desire for eccentricity manifested by the artists on show stems from the concern that is at the heart of sacred rites – to take into account that which is marginal to a structure, dirty: 'I am going to concentrate on this dirtiness so as to find a representation of it, and when I have found a representation for this eccentricity, it is a form of harmony.'
>
> (Penwarden 1995: 24)

Kristeva uttered those words in 1995, at the height of the art world's uptake of abjection. But the appeal and relevance of abjection have continued and indeed persist in the contemporary era especially as artists tackle the precarious but ever-increasing urgency of the body – and the bodily – in an age where what is essential about the human has been replaced, or at least eclipsed, by a new vision. Despite the emergence of new paradigms, such as the posthuman, for example, contemporary artists continue to employ the mechanics of abjection on the body as the site of identification of pain and exclusion.

Notes

1. It should be noted that the significant attention paid to Kristeva's theory of abjection has led to the overlooking of Bataille's historically earlier treatment of abjection – in 'Abjection and Miserable Forms' (1934) – which had the socio-political as its focus rather than the psychoanalytic. See Arya (2014: 2) and Arya and Chare (2016: 2).
2. The artist Paul McCarthy cited Lassnig as an influence on his work and wrote an essay 'Flat Polite' for her Serpentine show of 2008, which reflected the viscerality and even disgust-inducing quality of Lassnig's works.
3. The metaphor of a tightrope is used to describe Bacon's relationship between figuration and abstraction.
4. In making these pictures, she gave her models plastic sheeting to work with and wrap themselves in. To add to the spectral effects, she painted these figures in the basement of her house. See Hochdörfer (2008: 406).
5. Entrapment under plastic becomes an extended metaphor to signify the institution of marriage. In *Lady in Plastic* (2005) and *The Illegitimate Bride* (2007) the plastic covering doubles up as a wedding veil, and in *Couple* (2005) couples are represented under plastic.

References

Ades, D. (1985), 'Web of Images', in D. Ades and A. Forge (eds), *Francis Bacon*, exhibition catalogue, 8–23, London: Tate Gallery and Thames and Hudson.

Allport, G. (1955), *Becoming: Basic Considerations for a Psychology of Personality*, New Haven, CT: Yale University Press.

Arya, R. (2014), *Abjection and Representation: An Exploration of Abjection in the Visual Arts, Film and Literature*, Basingstoke: Palgrave Macmillan.

Arya, R. (2016), 'The Fragmented Body as an Index of Abjection', in R. Arya and N. Chare (eds), *Abject Visions: Powers of Horror in Art and Visual Culture*, 105–18, Manchester: Manchester University Press.

Arya, R. and N. Chare, eds (2016), *Abject Visions: Powers of Horror in Art and Visual Culture*, Manchester: Manchester University Press.

Bataille, G. (1970), 'L'Abjection et les formes misérables', in *Écrits posthumes, 1922–1940*, vol. 2 of *Œuvres completes*, 217–22, Paris: Gallimard.

Berggruen, O. (2003), 'Picasso and Bacon: Painting the Other Self', in W. Seipel, B. Steffen and C. Vitali (eds), *Francis Bacon and the Tradition of Art*, exhibition catalogue, 71–83, Milan: Kunsthistorisches, Skira Editore.

Boehm, G. (2013), 'Body and Life: The Pictures of Maria Lassnig', in *Maria Lassnig: Der Ort der Bilder*, exhibition catalogue, 76–87, Graz: Neue Galerie Graz in Universalmuseum Joanneum.

Deleuze, G. (2003), *Francis Bacon: The Logic of Sensation*, trans. D. W. Smith, New York: Continuum.

Douglas, M. (2002 [1966]), *Purity and Danger: An Analysis of Concepts of Pollution and Taboo*, London: Routledge.
Elias, N. (1978 [1939]), *The Civilizing Process: Vol 1, The History of Manners*, Oxford: Basil Blackwell.
Foster, H. (1991), 'High/Low Art: Art and Mass Culture', *October*, 56: 64–97.
Foster, H. (1996), *The Return of the Real: The Avant-Garde at the End of the Century*, Cambridge, MA: MIT Press.
Green, M. (2005), *The Doll*, trans. M. Green, London: Atlas Press.
Grosz, E. (1990), 'The Body of Signification', in J. Fletcher and A. Benjamin (eds), *Abjection, Melancholia, and Love: The Work of Julia Kristeva*, 80–103, London: Routledge.
Hochdörfer, A. (2008), 'Maria Lassnig Talks about her Exhibition at the Serpentine Gallery', *Artforum* (summer).
Kent, S. (2008), 'Maria Lassnig: Baring the Soul', *Art World*, June–July: 45.
Lassnig, M. (2008), *Maria Lassnig*, exhibition catalogue, London: Serpentine Gallery/Koenig Books.
Leiris, M. (1988), *Francis Bacon: Full Face and in Profile*, trans. J. Weightman, London: Thames and Hudson.
Lotringer, S. (1994), 'Les Miserables', in S. Lotringer (ed.), *More and Less*, 2–7, New York: Semiotext(e).
McCarthy, P. (2008), 'Flat Polite', in M. Lassnig (ed.), *Maria Lassnig*, exhibition catalogue, London: Serpentine Gallery/Koenig Books.
McGinn, C. (2011), *The Meaning of Disgust*, New York: Oxford University Press.
Miller, W. I. (1997), *The Anatomy of Disgust*, Cambridge, MA: Harvard University Press.
Obrist, H. U., ed. (2009), *Maria Lassnig: The Pen Is the Sister of the Brush, Diaries 1943–1997*, trans. H. Fine with C. Schelbert, Göttingen: Steidl.
Penwarden, C. (1995), 'Of Word and Flesh: An Interview with Julia Kristeva', in S. Morgan and F. Morris (eds), *Rites of Passage: Art for the End of the Century*, 21–7, London: Tate Gallery Publications.
Semff, M. and A. Spira, eds (2006), *Hans Bellmer*, Ostfildern: Hatje Cantz.
Sylvester, D. (1993), *Interviews with Francis Bacon: The Brutality of Fact*, 3rd edn, London: Thames and Hudson.
Taylor, S. (2000), *Hans Bellmer: The Anatomy of Anxiety*, Cambridge, MA: MIT Press.
Turner, B. S. (1996 [1984]), *The Body and Society: Explorations in Social Theory*, 2nd edn, London: SAGE.
Van Alphen, E. (1992), *Francis Bacon and the Loss of Self*, London: Reaktion.
Zweite, A. (2006), 'Foreword', in A. Zweite (ed.) in collaboration with M. Müller, *Francis Bacon: The Violence of the Real*, 9–27, London: Thames and Hudson.

11

Androgynous and a foreigner: Orlando's revolt

Christina Kkona

Uprooted irony: Revisiting Kristeva's theory of the feminine

Early in her career, in an interview published in *Tel Quel*, Julia Kristeva reformulates the Lacanian 'La femme n'existe pas' as 'La femme, ce n'est jamais ça', translated into English as 'Woman can never be defined'. Claiming first that woman is not an ontological category ('it is something which does not even belong in the order of *being*'), Kristeva moves to the representational level to argue that in 'woman' there is something that exceeds representation (WND 137). Thus, neither the representation nor the definition of woman can be accurate: woman is never *that*, because woman cannot *be*. In the patriarchal linguistic paradigm of the symbolic order, woman appears as a formulaic negativity.

What is theorized in Kristeva's work is less 'woman', as such, than 'the feminine', as a constituent of psychosexual identities. Although this distinction is not always clear in Kristeva's writing, the conceptualization of the feminine is more apt to contribute to an understanding of human singularity beyond binaries. Transformative in its nature, the feminine is firstly constructed in what she calls the two-sided Oedipus phase – a scheme that subscribes to the Freudian/Lacanian phallic monism that points to 'the universality of the phallic reference, which is manifested in both sexes, though in different ways' (SNS 96). As a response to the fear of castration, phallic monism can be understood as the infantile illusion of the absence of sexual difference transformed into an unconscious reality structuring one's psychosexual life.

Kristeva's contribution to the oedipal theories is mainly situated at the level of the twofold oedipal phase of the girl. *Oedipus 1* refers to the archaic period of incestuous desire for the mother, a phase of primary homosexuality, until she reaches *Oedipus 2*, whereby she is supposed to change object by redirecting her desire towards the father. However, the attachment to the archaic mother is not exempt from a desire of expulsion: attraction for the mother alternates with repulsion for what is yet neither 'subject' nor 'object'. Abjection is more violent between daughter and mother than between the latter and the idealized boy. Therefore, the girl's *phallic Kairos* (encounter with the phallus as signifier of both lack and law) turns out to display 'a structural dissociation between the *sensible* and the *signifier*', insofar as the phallus is 'figured in the imaginary by the penis and is, therefore, perceived/conceived by the girl as something *extraneous*, and as radically heterogeneous' (EPE 33). However, the girl's passage to Oedipus 2 is eased by the investment of what Freud calls the 'father of individual prehistory', a pre-objectal father reuniting both maternal and paternal traits, with whom the girl can identify. The maternal part of this bisexual father facilitates the phallic Kairos.

Yet the extraneousness of the phallus reactivates the *hallucination* of the extralinguistic sensuous experiences of both satisfaction and frustration within the previous mother/daughter relationship. The discrepancy between past and present experience

> marks the being of the female subject with a negation: 'I am not what is', 'I am, nonetheless, if only by sheer force of not.' The extraneous or illusory character of the phallus is perhaps another way of designating *this double negation of 'nonetheless' and 'not'*.
>
> (EPE 33)

Experiencing this heterogeneity translates into the *belief* that 'the phallus, as well as language and the symbolic order, are illusory yet indispensable' (SNS 100). For the girl, becoming a subject of language and law is therefore experienced as play. The homophony *Je/Jeu* depicts the disillusionment of women: I is a game because *la femme, n'est jamais ça*, 'the woman' is beyond subjectivation. For Kristeva, this belief in the illusoriness of the phallus constitutes the proof of female psychical bisexuality, insofar as it relies on the disjunction between sensory experiences and significance, that is, on a never abandoned adherence to the semiotic as the codification of the mother/daughter osmosis.

The extraneousness of the phallus, according to Kristeva, may invigorate the girl's adherence to the social; however, it may also trigger depressive regressions by drawing the girl towards the pre-objectal relation to the mother and away from the extraneousness of the symbolic. Moreover, the overinvestment of the illusionary phallicism engenders the 'girl-phallus' 'exemplified by the beautiful seductress', aware of her masquerade, which becomes the source of both provocation and disappointment. Finally, the denial of psychical bisexuality accounts for the denial of the illusoriness of the phallus entailing an identification with the phallus as such: 'The result of this is the female paranoiac: the boss, director, or virile lesbian, partisan of power in all its more dictatorial forms' (SNS 102).

Despite the psychotic dangers, psychical bisexuality is a structural constituent of all female subjects, irrespective of sexual preferences. Feminist critics, who aim to discuss Kristeva's work within the debate around the possible resistance to the hegemonic order, direct their arguments against her embracement of phallic monism, the androcentricism of the symbolic or the heteronormativity of the oedipal trajectory. Kristeva does not theorize homosexuality as such and even less non-binary identities. As Judith Butler among others suggests, a problematic association between sapphism and psychosis seems to unfold in her work (Butler 1989: 109). Unsurprisingly, as a psychoanalyst, Kristeva provides different clinical cases to support her argument. However, diagnostic generalizations lead to the radical claims of her early works. In *About Chinese Women*, Kristeva claims that the lesbian 'wages a vigilant war against her pre-oedipal dependence on her mother, which *keeps her from discovering her own body as other, different, possessing a vagina*' (ACW 29). If in this case the lesbian identifies with the phallus, in *Tales of Love*, lesbianism is relegated to the pre-objectal fusion with the mother:

> lesbian loves comprise the delightful arena of a neutralized, filtered libido, devoid of the cutting edge of masculine sexuality.... It evokes the loving dialogue of the pregnant mother with the fruit, barely distinct from her, that she shelters in her womb. Or the light rumble of soft skins that are iridescent *not from desire* but from that opening-closing, blossoming-wilting, *an in-between hardly established that suddenly collapses in the same warmth*, that slumbers or wakens within the embrace of the baby and its nourishing mother... Relaxation of consciousness, daydream, *language that is neither dialectical nor rhetorical*, but peace or eclipse: *nirvana, intoxication, and silence.*
>
> (TL 81, emphasis added)

Kristeva's homophobia is obvious in such a passage where lesbian sexuality is constructed as intrinsically unintelligible (Butler 1989: 111),[1] as foreign to tropes and rationalization, as 'silence' or intoxication. There is no desire between women, as far as their bond is constituted in the pre-symbolic realm where need, desire and demand are not yet distinct. Veering towards sameness, female homosexuality is protected from otherness. However,

Kristeva's homophobia is no less ambiguous than female sexuality itself, especially when it comes to creativity, given that she has several times been criticized for emphasizing the feminine in terms of male writers' identification with the mother, which takes the form of 'fetishism or homosexuality, depending on whether they adopt the masculine or the feminine position' (Hermann 1989: 19).

> ... female creators need at least some degree of female homosexuality, whether it exists in reality or in fantasy. In order for my mother to become an erotic object that I can eventually master, abandon, and replace with other objects, I must somehow assume a phallic and manly pose that imitates a father or an authoritarian male figure. At that point, I can participate in another mimetic system and another *identificatory game involving falseness* and an identification that is impossible, yet manifested as an imitation, a supplement, and a fetish used as a substitute.
> (I 67, emphasis added)

Here again, the actual or imaginary lesbianism of the writer or the artist is no more than an acknowledgement of the female bisexuality that condenses the feminine propensity for the semiotic modality and the illusoriness of the phallus. The emphasis on the 'identificatory game involving falseness' underlies the je/jeu of the becoming subject of a woman, while at the same time the female homosexuality in question becomes a play. From this point of view, sapphism is, as Miglena Nikolchina has already observed (1999: 39), close to Woolf's understanding of androgyny.[2] In Pamela Caughie's words with regard to *Orlando*, androgyny is a 'metaphor for the dramatic, the role-playing self' (1989: 48). In her interview 'Unes femmes', Kristeva revisits the question of female homosexuality without addressing this time its necessity for female creativity, but rather its limits with a reference to Woolf. This time female homosexuality is even more explicitly reduced to an 'identification with virility'.

> Female homosexuality or identification with virility can come to a woman's rescue, for *she is exiled* forever from a maternal territory that she must lose in order to become heterosexual. These are two ways for female libido to satisfy this frustration, but *they are weak and do not make up for the basic deprivation*. This is perhaps what one could call *castration* for the woman.... It seems to me that artistic 'products'... and praise are less gratifying and carry less weight for women than for men. Virginia Woolf may have been very intrigued... by the positive response her work received, but this response did not give her enough narcissistic gratification to eradicate the permanent anguish that *led her to decompose language and to destroy her identity to the point of madness and suicide.*
> (I 111, emphasis added)

Anne Hermann certainly has this passage in mind when she comments:

> Since for a woman literary production cannot provide the narcissistic gratification it does for a man, the disruption of language leads to madness rather than innovation. And since female homosexuality can be conceived of only as virilization of 'the feminine', women writers' lack of access to a maternal figure leads to premature death.
> (1989: 19)

Women are doubly exiled: first, from the maternal territory and second from language. However, several inconsistencies complicate Kristeva's argument. Identification with the phallus did not suffice to save Woolf from madness and suicide; yet, it 'led her to decompose language'. This statement seems to contradict Kristeva's infamous dismissal of Woolf's writing in 'Oscillation between Power and Denial':

> In women's writing, language seems to be seen *from a foreign land*; is it seen from the point of view of *an asymbolic, spastic body*? Virginia Woolf describes suspended states, subtle sensations, and above all, colors – green, blue – but *she does not dissect language* as Joyce does. Estranged from language, women are visionaries, dancers *who suffer as they speak*.
> (OPD 166)

Either Woolf 'decomposes' language to the point of suicide or she does not 'dissect language' to the degree that Joyce does. Or is it, perhaps, that Woolf, speaking her suffering, decomposes language from the outside (foreign land), while Joyce decomposes language from the inside? On the one hand, psychosis prevents Woolf, despite her success as an author, from becoming Joyce; on the other hand, Woolf as a woman remains a foreigner to language, to the symbolic. Reading this passage along with a *Room of One's Own*, Nikolchina pertinently states:

> Kristeva interprets Woolf in terms of exile, estrangement, stasis... and painful asymbolia, that is precisely in the terms that underlie her own theoretical stand and that give rise to the division between the revolutionary, true to 'mother', semiotic-oriented male artist... and the silent sister of philosophy with her hidden face. This division, however, *repeats*, a certain figure in Woolf herself, the *figure of the androgynous Shakespeare and his mute sister*.
> (1999: 31)

In fact, Kristeva interprets not only Woolf but women writers 'in terms of exile, estrangement, stasis'[3] and indeed silences Woolf within her own speech.

Diagnoses of the author or generalizations more or less abandoned in Kristeva's later work establish the limits of Woolf's literary merits. It is as if Kristeva, who never dedicated an essay to Woolf but used her as an evident intertext in *Samurais*, needed to keep Woolf at a distance as an exemplary case of the copresence of homosexuality and melancholia, and thus of both an overwhelming return to the archaic mother and the collapse of the paternal image. If she opts for Colette, it is because the French writer's work, contrary to those of Dickinson, Woolf or Akhmatova, celebrates feminine *jouissance*. More recently, writing about Simone de Beauvoir, she finally recognizes Woolf's 'genius' explicitly by emphasizing that the author of the *Deuxième sexe* does not have the literary talent of Colette or Woolf (HF 112).

Her generalizing tendency with regard to women or to female authors, her homophobic affirmations or vague diagnoses are far from faithful to the spirit of Kristeva's 'rejection' of feminism in favour of *ecceitas* – Duns Scotus' concept for one's absolute and ungraspable singularity – hidden behind her refusal to define 'woman' and her understanding of 'unes femmes'. More recent claims seem to be more aligned with queer understandings of otherness rather than feminist or gender demands for social inclusion.

> [W]hat interests me when I listen to someone in the psychoanalytic session is not to know that Jean is homosexual and Marie is not, but *what kind of particular homosexuality* he is living, not to put an etiquette on it, homosexual or heterosexual. Because there are sometimes more resemblances between one homosexual and one heterosexual than the people considered to belong to the same group.
> (PK 337, emphasis added)

The acknowledgement of a plurality of sexualities or homosexualities as well as the singularity of every sexual being is what actually distinguishes psychoanalysis in its evolution from other approaches, despite its quasi-dependence on universalizing principles like the oedipal trajectory of subjectivation. The most significant revolt is the linguistic emergence of a double singularity. In other words, being 'une femme' is to acknowledge femininity as much as the kind of *particular femininity* one is.

Kristeva's understanding of femininity is founded on her reading of *The Future of an Illusion*. As Ewa Ziarek suggests, Freud's work emphasizes 'the fetishistic function of the fixity of the law, which, in order to protect the subject *against the radical contingency* of existence, seeks its legitimation either in the theological or national *necessity*' (2005: 33). In other words, the symbolic establishes an illusionary reassurance against the contingency and finitude of the death drive. The feminine revolt is located in the 'ironic adherence and non-adherence to this new form of authority, with the refusal of the fetishistic fixity of the symbolic and the psychic protections against finitude and contingency it offers' (2005: 34). Therefore, the extraneousness of the phallus occurs 'at the moment of hegemonic articulation when the excluded, feminized particular lays claim to universality through an identification with the new form of paternal authority' (2005: 34). This adherence/non-adherence to the phallic universal inherent in feminine subjectivation is experienced as we have seen as *je/jeu*, as *play*, and therefore as a 'conjunction of chance and necessity, that is, the acceptance of contingency inscribed within the symbolic' (2005: 38). From this point of view, the feminine *jeu* bears similarities with the Lacanian Real as *tuchê*. In Seminar XI, Lacan retraces the interrelation between Symbolic and Real in Aristotelian terms: automaton designates the signifying chain, whereas signifiers are linked according to certain determining rules; tuchê is the ungraspable Real that lies beyond the chain and functions as its external cause. Tuchê is both what causes the automaton and what interrupts its regularity. The deterministic nature of the symbolic allows for a certain predictability, while tuchê designates the absolute unforeseeability of the Real, the unanticipatable event for which we are never prepared. 'The tuchê manifests itself when something disrupts the working of the automaton, something unforeseen that cannot be traced back to or explained in terms of the symbolic laws of the automaton' (Bistoen 2016: 87).

This is not to say that the feminine corresponds to the Lacanian Real or that it is the bearer of the death drive. Kristeva does not subscribe to the tradition of Lacanian politics of the Real (Žižek, Laclau, Stavrakakis), that is, inaccessible to symbolization and therefore resistant to normative sociality. Rather, the feminine is a disruptive force from within the symbolic and not from the outside. Maintaining open the hiatus between particular and universal, tûché and automaton, the feminine 'opens the symbolic to ongoing transformation' (Ziarek 2005: 69). Thus, feminine negativity, the disillusionment (I am not this) and ironizing of the symbolic (nevertheless I am), by revealing the contingency in the heart of necessity, the aleatory nature of the representational realm, open possibilities for counterhegemonic action.

It is not coincidental that feminine negativity is theorized in terms of strangeness, extraneousness or exile. The ambivalence of the feminine is similar to the foreigner's – the uprooted subject of race, class, gender and so on. In *Strangers to Ourselves*, Kristeva focuses exclusively on the question of the national foreigner; however, when she talks about the two kinds of foreigners, she refers to the 'uprooted of all countries, occupations, social standing, sexes...' (10). Depending on how they experience their 'attachment to a lost space', the uprooted are divided into 'ironists' and 'believers' (SO 10). It is as if these two categories corresponded to the feminine and the masculine parts of the subject. The ironists are those who 'waste away in an agonizing struggle between what no longer is and what will never be-the followers of neutrality, the advocates of emptiness' (SO 10). The translation here leaves behind an important sentence: 'durcis ou larmoyants, mais toujours *désillusionnés*' (hardened or tearful, but always disillusioned) (E 21). Attached to a lost space (the archaic mother) and disillusioned (not), the uprooted ironizes the hegemonic order, in the same way that the disillusioned feminine ironizes the symbolic. As for the encounter with the locals, the ironist 'expects *nothing* from it, but he slips in *nevertheless*, convinced that even though everything melts away, it is better to be with it' (SO 11). Furthermore, the uprooted ironist is 'feminized' insofar as he or she is not a believer. As Kristeva suggests, 'structurally... a woman is better placed than anyone to explore illusion. I am not sure "atheism" means anything more than taking the Other and exploring it' (SNS 106). The feminine, the structurally bisexual and uprooted part of the subject, 'is a being that never adheres to the illusion of being, any more than to the being of this illusion itself' (SNS 106). The ironist-foreigner is therefore psychically a woman, in her structural bisexuality, and therefore in revolt.

In what follows, I aim to demonstrate that Kristeva's theory of the feminine/foreigner as a disruptive force, as a perpetual irony of the society, can remediate her own dismissal of certain female artists, and of Woolf in particular. As a writer and as a feminine male/female figure, Orlando seems to engage in a journey of constant self-reinvention, 'whereby happiness exists only at the price of a revolt' (SNS 7).

Orlando in process: Play and revolt

'I am growing up,' she thought, taking her taper at last. 'I am losing some illusions,' she said, ..., 'perhaps to acquire others.'

(Woolf 2003: 85)

Mocking nineteenth-century biographical conventions, *Orlando* is, as its title suggests, a 'biography' mapping the works and days of its protagonist from the Elizabethan times to the book's publication in 1928. The infamous beginning of Woolf's parodic satire depicts a multifaceted play: 'HE for there could be no doubt of his sex, though the fashion of the time did something to disguise it – was in the act of slicing at the head of a Moor which swung from the rafters' (Woolf 2003: 5).

Clothing, disguise, gender identity and doubt form a multilayered ambiguity that runs across the entire narrative. A sort of antiphrasis (Orlando's game is meant to prove his undoubtable masculinity possibly hidden by the 'fashion of the time', Woolf 2003: 5) introduces the reader to the hidden link between gender and race: Orlando slices at the head of a Moor, taken for an old football, as it swings from the rafters. Left behind because of his young age, the sixteen-year-old Orlando would 'steal away' from his mother to find refuge in the attic room, where he would 'lunge and plunge and slice the air with his blade' (2003: 5). Seeking independence from his mother while trying to master the 'art' of his ancestors, Orlando stages an imitation of their atrocities by engaging in what could be understood as a masturbatory experience with sadomasochist undertones. This sadistic moment is followed by a 'chivalrous' gesture, when after having cut the cord, he strings up again the skull 'fastening it… almost out of reach so that his enemy grinned at him through shrunk, black lips triumphantly' (2003: 5). Orlando seems to ceremoniously surrender to his triumphant enemy, by arranging, in a sort of ironic reversal, to be laughed at sardonically by the unchanged skull. Thus, Orlando's je/jeu follows the scheme of double negativity of the feminine subjectivation: *he is not* like his ancestors insofar as he cannot find refuge in the national necessity of imperialism. Yet, *he* is insofar as his play, by transforming the colonial atrocities into antics, gives to the skull – the figure of the abjected foreigner – the possibility to laugh at British racism. Therefore, Orlando's game enhances the ironic denial of the doubt around his sex that inaugurates his story. His vain effort to identify with the figure of the father will be further jeopardized by another phallic figure, the queen herself.

> when she saw his legs she laughed out loud. He was the very image of a noble gentleman. But inwardly? She flashed her yellow hawk's eyes upon him as if she would pierce his soul… named him her Treasurer and Steward; next hung about him chains…. He was about to sail for the Polish wars when she recalled him… she pulled him down… and made him bury his face in that astonishing composition – she had not changed her dress for a month – which smelt for all the world, he thought, recalling his boyish memory, like some old cabinet at home where his mother's furs were stored.
>
> (2003: 10–11)

The queen 'who knew a man when she saw one, though not, it is said, in the usual way' (2003: 11), laughs at the gaze of Orlando's legs, covers him with jewellery and protects him from dangerous masculine expeditions, such as wars. However, the narrative does not elaborate on gender restrictions before the Victorian era. If the looseness of Elizabeth I's reign is marked by the semiotization of the symbolic, as Christopher Brown suggests (2013: 19), it is less because of the queen's ambiguity (she 'neither gives up nor assumes a prohibition', PH 15), but rather because of Orlando's narcissistic crisis due to the queen's failure to satisfy his desires.[4] If the phallic queen pretends to Orlando's lawful possession, it is because he responds to her personal feminized ideal about what a 'noble gentleman' is, or to her incestuous confusion between a lover and a son. However, Orlando experiences the corruptive behaviour of Elizabeth less as royal favour and more as abjection: her dirty dress recalls the musty smell of his mother's stored furs. The extraneousness of the foreign scent[5] repulses Orlando, who, 'buried' in her lap, feels as if he would be swallowed by the 'domineering tenderness' of the queen (Woolf 2003: 11). If the beautiful 'lady in green' (2003: 6) is Orlando's sublime mother, the queen is the abject one. This feeling of suffocation translates the danger of death and decay that would ease Orlando's change of object which Elizabeth would notice, as if coincidentally, through her mirror. If the queen's mirror reflects Orlando kissing a young woman, Orlando's infidelity goes beyond the betrayal of royal illusions. He or she is always attracted by the racial/sexual other, by the foreigner insofar as he recognizes himself as a foreigner. Orlando's first love, the Russian princess Sasha, is no less androgynous than himself: 'Legs, hands, carriage, were a boy's, but no boy ever had a mouth like that;... She was a woman' (2003: 17). Sacha's occasional remoteness, though suspicious, does not strike the young man as a sign of betrayal but rather as one of sociocultural difference. Woolf does not miss the occasion to mock prejudices: 'he had heard that the women in Muscovy wear beards and the men are covered with fur from the waist down; that both sexes are smeared with tallow to keep the cold out, tear meat with their fingers and live in huts' (2003: 22). If the princess's hairless face and luxurious attire belie the racist rumours, her deceptive departure ironically feminizes Sasha, in the sense of ascribing to her a stable gender identity: 'he hurled at the faithless woman all the insults *that have ever been the lot of her sex*' (2003: 30, emphasis added). Loving Sasha leads to Orlando's exile from the court – her departure to his first seven-day trance.

Orlando's almost voluntary exile to Constantinople results in him becoming a duke. The conferring of the dukedom takes place on the eve of a Turkish insurrection against the Sultan, during which foreigners are under threat. Orlando is meant to have escaped only because, falling in trance, he is mistaken for dead. The biographer relies on the unverifiable testimony of a washerwoman who depicts a male figure 'in a cloak or a dressing gown' and 'a woman, much muffled, but apparently of the peasant class' entering Orlando's room from the balcony (Woolf 2003: 64). However, the gender and identity of both figures are questionable given that Turkish coats 'can be worn indifferently by either sex' (2003: 64). The social status of the supposedly female figure could identify her as Rosina Pepita, the Spanish dancer of unknown parents and a 'reputed gipsy' whom Orlando marries on the sly. Thus, Orlando's imminent genital transmutation is intertwined with different forms of resistance: a violent uprising; a disgraceful interracial, interclass marriage; a bodily reaction to the time of the clock that causes a seven-day trance; and an accidental survival.

Before analysing Orlando's defiant actions, let us stop for a moment at what could ironically appear as their outcome. As if punished by divine wrath like Tiresias, Orlando wakes up a woman: 'he was a woman' (Woolf

2003: 67). This sudden narrative denial of sexual difference (*he* is *she*) is followed by a plural pronoun: 'The change of sex, though it altered *their* future, did nothing whatever to *alter* their identity' (2003: 67, emphasis added). The anatomical transmutation does not affect Orlando's identity, who remains unruffled in front of the mirror. If anatomy is Orlando's destiny and thus alters her future, it does not alter her (sexual) identity, inasmuch as Orlando's sexual undecidability does not derive from her body change. The ironically definite statements on Orlando's gender identity before or after her transformation[6] reflect the incompatibility between stable identity categories and Orlando's singularity. Her singular way of inhabiting the world veers, I argue, towards Kristeva's feminine, understood as a process of acknowledging her innate bisexuality, the 'promised land' of inventing one's own sex, that for Kristeva amounts to the 'end' of one's psychoanalytic therapy (SNS 105).

Orlando's pronounced femininity, irrespective of gender transmutations, stems from his or her ironic adherence/nonadherence to the different eras and sociocultural spaces he or she lives through, revealing contingency within necessity. For as deviant in terms of gender, sexuality and longevity as he or she may be, Orlando's adaptability constantly challenges the margin/centre or the outside/inside oppositions. Definitional questions, such as 'What's an "age," indeed? What are we?' (Woolf 2003: 100), remain unresolved and definitive answers to the question of sexual difference remain suspended.

Writing *The Oak Tree* across three centuries, Orlando creates a plurivocal palimpsest that not only reveals the arbitrariness of historical divisions (Caughie 2013: 503) or the play of different selves, genres, sexes and rhetorical stances but mainly creates a text in the image of herself, a subject-text that unravels the simultaneous multiplicity of the different singularities that compose the subject in process. Even if her sojourn within a gipsy[7] tribe forces her to 'overscore the margins and cross the lines', the manuscript hides its edges, its trans-movement across different boundaries and limits, and recalls a meticulously fabricated 'darning':

> She had carried this about with her for so many years now, and in such hazardous circumstances, that many of the pages were stained, some were torn, while the straits she had been in for writing paper when with the gipsies, had forced her to *overscore the margins and cross the lines* till the manuscript looked like a piece of darning most conscientiously carried out… She had been working at it for close on three hundred years now… She had been a gloomy boy, in love with death, as boys are; and then she had been amorous and florid; and then she had been sprightly and satirical; and sometimes she had tried prose and sometimes she had tried the drama. Yet through all these changes she had remained, she reflected, fundamentally the same.
>
> (Woolf 2003: 116–17, emphasis added)

This 'sameness' within difference reflects that Orlando's ongoing transformation cannot be understood as the succession of different selves in the progressive flow of historical time. Rather, 'Orlando had inclined herself naturally to the Elizabethan spirit, to the Restoration spirit, to the spirit of the eighteenth century, and had in consequence scarcely been aware of the change from one age to the other' (2003: 120). Orlando's adaptability is the result of the ironic stance of the feminine particular that lays claim to universality through an adaptation to the different new hegemonic orders. Orlando's happy position demonstrates that Woolf's character, like Colette, succeeds where she fails: 'Hail! natural desire!... In whatever form it comes, and may there be more forms, and *stranger*' (2003: 145). Woolf reminds us of the Lacanian ethics of psychoanalysis as not ceding on one's own desire ('*ne pas céder sur son désir*', Lacan 1986: 368), that is, preserving an openness to the unexpectedness of one's desire beyond defined categories, the risk one should take in her ongoing redefinition. No matter how 'antipathetic' the Victorian era is to her,

> [s]he had just managed, by some dexterous deference to the spirit of the age... to pass its examination successfully.... Orlando had so ordered it that she was in an extremely *happy position*; *she need neither fight her age, nor submit to it*; she was of it, yet remained herself. Now, therefore, she could write, and write she did.
> (Woolf 2003: 131, emphasis added)

In the words of Caughie,

> Orlando, as a writer and as a woman, is both *within* the common language and *apart* from it. *She need not submit to the tyranny of symbolic systems nor insist on another opposing system.* Hers is not such a simple choice. As the novel makes evident, sexual identity, historical periods, and literary styles *are all constructs*. Each is structured like a language and as such has no fixed or natural relation to anything outside itself. We cannot discover the appropriate form or the true self or the innate differences between the sexes, for there is nothing stable to measure them against.
> (1991: 8, emphasis added)

This oscillation between sexes, moods, contrasting points of view is the result of the double negativity performed by the feminine, of this neither/nor that triggers creativity. Woolf represents the clash between the sociocultural and linguistic categories to which Orlando's unreliable biographer needs to refer and her protagonist's invention of different paradigms. The inadequacy of language or different binary frameworks to do justice to Orlando is translated into contradictory theories with regard to sexual difference, as Caughie observes (1991: 44). Either Orlando remains essentially the same because there is no substantial difference between the sexes or 'the difference between the sexes is, happily, one of great profundity' (Woolf 2003: 92). Despite what sounds like a feminist discourse, the biographer will opt rather for *ecceitas*: 'Of the complications and confusions which thus result every one has had experience; but here we leave the general question and note only the odd effect it had in the *particular* case of Orlando herself' (2003: 93). The question is not to decide on Orlando's sex but rather focus on how Orlando inhabits her masculinity and her femininity.

From Sasha to Shelmerdine, the androgynous person she decides to marry, Orlando is attracted to sexually ambiguous figures, either foreigners or travellers. The racial, sexual or social other accommodates Orlando's own strangeness. I have stressed from the beginning how the questions of sex and gender intersect with that of race; nonetheless, the oscillation between belonging and non-belonging is expanded on all levels of her life, including nationality and rank. Orlando's difference, however psychosexual it may seem, generates politico-legal complications insofar as she poses a threat to the authorities. Upon her return to England, Orlando finds herself deprived of every possibility of citizenship due to the bewildering charges she faces: the charge of being dead, of being a woman 'which amounts to much the same thing' (Woolf 2003: 82) and of being a disgraced English duke. If Orlando goes through her transformations as if almost nothing has happened, it is the turn of the legal authorities to put her 'in a highly ambiguous condition, uncertain whether she was alive or dead, man or woman, Duke or nonentity' (2003: 82). Woolf's humorous feminist critique of British society translates the feminine double negativity in the face of the phallic order: I am not that, but nevertheless I am, where 'that' does not only describe the structuring of power relations in terms of gender, race and rank but the necessity of categorization, of the binaries that allow the building of these power relations. Outside these arbitrary categories due to the very uncertainty around her person, present from the very beginning of the novel, Orlando points to the contingency within necessity, to the arbitrariness of binary schemas and the artificiality of legal categorizations.

Orlando's ambiguity about her desired origins or her longing for hybridity is reflected on her dark hair and complexion: while in Constantinople, he fantasizes about his possible Turkish origins: 'one of his ancestors had taken up with a Circassian peasant woman' (Woolf 2003: 59). As a woman among the gipsies, her dark features 'bore out the belief that she was, by birth, one of them' (2003: 69). In an ironical reversal, Woolf's gipsies attempt to other England: 'this barbarous land where people live in houses because they are too feeble and diseased to stand the open air' (2003: 69). They even intend to help Orlando, 'in many ways inferior to them... to become more like them' (2003: 69). Orlando's adaptability is again at work: unexpectedly, there is no real tension between the wandering life of those without nation, property or rank, and the luxuries of British aristocracy. Yet her singularity is *neither* against *nor* for inclusion. The excitement of experimenting with anonymity and new forms of life coexists with a longing for home: 'Orlando had contracted in England some of the customs or diseases (whatever you choose to consider them) which cannot, it seems, be expelled' (2003: 69). Not only can her past not be denied but Orlando's irony dissociates the gipsy mentality from the merits of nomadic life. Disillusioned, she expects nothing from them, but she opts for experiencing freedom within their tribe rather than returning to her old life. Yet contrary to Orlando's adaptability, the gipsies become concerned about her difference. Belonging amounts to adopting the same ethical principles and reasoning, for 'no passion is stronger in the breast of a man than the desire to make others believe as he believes' (2003: 73). For them, a duke, 'was nothing but a profiteer or robber who snatched land and money from people who rated these things of little worth' (2003: 72). Although her effort to reverse their argument by 'finding the gipsy life itself rude and barbarous' is not efficient, it is impossible for her to adjust to their mentality. However, she silences her disagreement, 'through lack of having the right to state it. No longer knowing what one truly thinks, except that "this is not it"' (*ce n'est pas ça*) (SO 17).

Leaving behind the gipsies means abandoning 'those Turkish coats and trousers which can be worn indifferently by either sex' (Woolf 2003: 68). Dressed for the first time as a woman, Orlando is forced to compare the powers and limits of the sexes: 'she pitted one sex against the other, and found each alternately full of the most deplorable infirmities, and *was not sure to which she belonged* – it was no great wonder that she was about to cry out that she would return to Turkey and become a gipsy again' (2003: 78, emphasis added). Becoming a gipsy amounts to be freely ambiguous in Turkish trousers, for 'the gipsy women, except in one or two important particulars, differ very little from the gipsy men' (2003: 75). From this point of view, being stateless does not mean as much to be sexless, but rather genderless. Faced with the necessity to adapt to strict gender roles – unless one improvises different masquerades – the gipsy becomes the embodiment of a perpetual resistance to the binaries of the British society prohibitive of hybridities and transgressive desires. Returning home equals a return to fixed gender roles that, as I have tried to demonstrate, Orlando ironically defies through the double negativity of the nevertheless and the not: 'if it meant conventionality, meant slavery, meant deceit, meant denying her love, fettering her limbs, pursing her lips, and restraining her tongue, then she would turn about with the ship and set sail once more for the gipsies' (2003: 80). Orlando's 'happiness' at the end of the novel is her capacity to 'become a gipsy *again*', but this time within British society (2003: 78).

When the Victorian era presses upon Orlando the need to get married, she decides to become 'nature's bride': 'I found my mate… it is the moor' (Woolf 2003: 122). As the double signification of the word 'moor' suggests,[8] Orlando veers towards the orient following the gipsy's advice: 'it's better that I should lie at peace here with only the sky above me' (2003: 123). This is the moment when she unexpectedly falls in love with Marmaduke Bonthrop Shelmerdine. This person, who is meant to make out of Orlando 'a real woman at last' (2003: 125), is no less ambiguous than herself, composed of a series of differently gendered selves each of which awakes a different Orlando. The dialogue between these lovers who seem so perfectly to reflect each other recalls nonetheless the tension between belonging/unbelonging, sharing/not sharing within the gipsy tribe. Orlando is anxious about whether her marriage to Shelmerdine – an alternative marriage that does not pertain to traditional understandings of engagement, fidelity and gender obligations – is approvable by the spirit of the age:

> but if one's husband was always sailing round Cape Horn, was it marriage? If one liked him, was it marriage? If one liked other people, was it marriage? And finally, if one still wished, more than anything in the whole world, to write poetry, was it marriage? She had her doubts.
> (2003: 130)

Orlando's doubts translate the ironic distance that separates each singularity from belonging to an established order. Isn't marriage a linguistically, legally and socially specific institution? No, when it comes to Orlando's silent revolt.

Orlando's ambiguity calls for a constant redefinition of words, a reinvention of language, a redistribution of categories at the intersection of sex, race, gender and rank. Her feminine/foreigner's ironic stance towards the different established orders, her androgynous body, her journeys, her demeanour and her ordeals constitute a perpetual revolt, in Kristeva's sense, against the blindness of strict identificatory processes and immutable definitions. They are an incessant effort on the part of Woolf's protagonist to invent herself without ceding on her singularity. The plasticity of this plural singularity is an ongoing *play* (je/jeu) with words and norms. Orlando's only unchangeable energy across the centuries is by definition transformable and transformative: her writing poetry. Like *The Oak Tree*, a palimpsest/poem, a poem in process, a poem that oscillates between illusion and disillusionment, Orlando's work could be a form of successful Kristevan psychoanalysis.

Notes

1 For a detailed analysis of homophobia in Kristeva's work, see Gambaudo (2013).
2 See Woolf (2015: 71): 'Coleridge perhaps meant this when he said that a great mind is androgynous. It is when this fusion takes place that the mind is fully

fertilised and uses all its faculties. Perhaps a mind that is purely masculine cannot create, any more than a mind that is purely feminine, I thought. But it would be well to test what one meant by man-womanly, and conversely by woman-manly, by pausing and looking at a book or two.'

3 See also ACW 39: 'Woolf, who sank wordlessly into the river… seized by a sort of bizarre gaiety that brought on the fits of strangles, hooting, uncontrollable laughter.'

4 See PH 15: 'Two seemingly contradictory causes bring about the narcissistic crisis that provides, along with its truth, a view of the abject. *Too much strictness on the part of the Other*, confused with the One and the Law. *The lapse of the Other*, which shows through the breakdown of objects of desire' (author's emphasis).

5 Here, I would disagree with Christopher Brown, who associates the queen's scent with the biblical abomination of menstruation, for the age of the queen seems to prohibit such an interpretation.

6 'He-for there could be no doubt of his sex'; 'we have no choice left but to confess – he was a woman'; 'Orlando had become a woman there is no denying it'; 'My sex… is pronounced indisputably, and beyond the shadow of a doubt…, female' (Woolf 2003: 5, 67, 126).

7 For reasons of consistency with Woolf's text, I shall continue using the term 'gipsy' to refer to the Romani tribe. Woolf does not use it as a slur, though her depiction of the Romani tribe is somewhat indebted to the Occidental tradition of thought Edward Said has defined in his *Orientalism*.

8 The word 'Moor' designates both an 'open uncultivated land' and an African, such as the one whose head is hanging from the rafters of Orlando's house at the beginning of the novel.

References

Bistoen, G. (2016), *Trauma, Ethics and the Political beyond PTSD. The Dislocations of the Real*, Basingstoke: Palgrave.

Brown, C. (2013), 'Mystical Gibberish or Renegade Discourse? Poetic Language According to *Orlando*', in A. Martin and K. Holland (eds), *Interdisciplinary/Multidisciplinary Woolf*, 196–200, Liverpool: Liverpool University Press.

Butler, J. (1989), 'The Body Politics of Julia Kristeva', *Hypatia*, 3 (3): 104–18.

Caughie, P. (1989), 'Virginia Woolf's Double Discourse', in M. S. Barr and R. Feldstein (eds), *Discontented Discourses: Feminism/textual Intervention/psychoanalysis*, 41–53, Urbana, IL: University of Illinois Press.

Caughie, P. (1991), *Virginia Woolf and Postmodernism. Literature in Quest and Question of Itself*, Urbana, IL: University of Illinois Press.

Caughie, P. (2013), 'The Temporality of Modernist Life Writing in the Era of Transsexualism: Virginia Woolf's Orlando and Einar Wegener's Man into Woman', *Modern Fiction Studies*, 59 (3): 501–25.

Gambaudo, S. (2013), 'Julia Kristeva, "woman's primary homosexuality" and Homophobia', *European Journal of Women's Studies*, 20 (1): 8–20.
Hermann, A. (1989), *The Dialogic and Difference. 'An/other woman' in Virginia Woolf and Christa Wolf*, New York: Columbia University Press.
Lacan, J. (1986), *Le Séminaire, Livre VII, L'éthique de la psychanalyse*, Paris: Le Seuil.
Lacan, J. (1997), *The Seminar of Jacques Lacan: The Ethics of Psychoanalysis*, VII, New York: W. W. Norton.
Lacan, J. (1998), *The Seminar of Jacques Lacan: The Four Fundamental Concepts of Psychoanalysis*, XI, New York: W. W. Norton.
Minow-Pinkney, M. (1987), *Virginia Woolf and the Problem of the Subject. Feminine Writing in the Major Novels*, New Brunswick, NJ: Rutgers University Press.
Nikolchina, M. (1999), 'Born from the Head: Reading Woolf via Kristeva', *diacritics*, 21 (2/3): 30–42.
Woolf, V. (2003 [1928]), *Orlando: A Biography*, Hertfordshire: Wordsworth Classics.
Woolf, V. (2015), *A Room of One's Own*, ed. D. Bradshaw and S. N. Clarke, Oxford: Blackwell.
Ziarek, E. (2005), 'Kristeva and Fanon: Revolutionary Violence and Ironic Articulation', in T. Chanter and E. P. Ziarek (eds), *Revolt, Affect, Collectivity, The Unstable Boundaries of Kristeva's Polis*, 57–75, New York: State University of New York Press.

12

'Let it end, this cold insanity. Let it happen.' Kristeva's melancholic modernism and the Parisian novels of Jean Rhys

Rossitsa Terzieva-Artemis

> *For those who are rocked by melancholia, writing about it would have meaning only if writing sprang out of that very melancholia.*
>
> KRISTEVA, *BLACK SUN*

Much has been written about the difficulties of exact periodization of major art and literary movements, and one notoriously difficult period to pinpoint is modernism. Theoretical discourses variously stretch it back to the mid-nineteenth century and the publication of Baudelaire's *Les Fleurs du mal* (1857), or to the end of the nineteenth century and the major work of Ibsen and Strindberg in drama and Zola in fiction and criticism, or else to the beginning of the twentieth century when music, the fine arts, theatre and literature witness significant changes across Europe. It is clear that modernism still defies strict temporal definitions; yet, if we follow the frequently quoted statement of Virginia Woolf that 'in or about December, 1910, human character changed' (1971 [1924]: 320), we should be conveniently setting a chronological marker for the start of a very idiosyncratic period in the history of European culture reaching well into the period of the Second World War.

As a temporal slash in the epochal, on a much personal level, the year 1906 in particular marked the arrival in England from Dominica of an eternal foreigner, a talented writer to be, who, at the time, had hardly any inkling about the future or about the literary career she was to embark on soon – Jean Rhys (1890–1979). Trust as we may Woolf and her specific temporal reference, this chapter proposes a much narrower reading of modernism and, more specifically, a look at the interwar modernism, a period comprising the prime of high modernism in the 1920s and the literary production of the giants Joyce, Woolf, Yeats, Pound and Eliot, but also the less prominent, somewhat 'subdued' Rhys and her so-called Parisian novels – *Quartet* (1928), *After Leaving Mr Mackenzie* (1930) and *Good Morning, Midnight* (1939). While not conceived as a trilogy in the precise meaning of the term, these three novels trace a specific development in Rhys' female protagonist – a bohemian outsider entangled in the rubble of the everyday – in the context of her oeuvre, but also in the larger context of modernism.

To make the reading of modernist melancholy and liminality possible in Rhys' novels, I will have recourse to the work of Julia Kristeva and her discourse of love and melancholia, as well as the insights of the philosopher Walter Benjamin into the melancholic modernity of the twentieth century. As Sánchez-Pardo points out, interwar modernism stands for 'an endemic *mal du siècle* that under the guise of melancholia, depression, or manic-depressive illness came to the fore in the period between the two wars' (2003: 7). The uncanny, the operation of language and the structuring of the subject, the repetitive traumatic return to loss and the melancholic discourse are some of the elements that connect the literary and the psychoanalytic fields in the particular context of interwar modernism, but they also refer to the larger discourse of human existence always oriented towards death as modernity's ultimate end point.[1] Thus, if modernism is traditionally conceived as a rupture with the past and a break with the old, my reading of Rhys, and of Kristeva for that matter, offers a linguistically informed interpretation of the production of the self and melancholia as represented in these three novels.

As I will move on to argue, Rhys demonstrates in her works that a discourse of becoming is possible not despite, but *in* melancholia. In other words, I read the obsessive return to and repetition of traumatic experiences on the part of Rhys' female protagonists as symptomatic of a melancholic modernist sensibility and infatuation with the discourses of love and death rather than with the Enlightenment's discourse of reason. In the place of the optimistic Enlightenment view of the unified thinking subject, in the aftermath of the First World War especially, modernist writers focus on the fragmented, chaotic human existence directed by irrational forces and the disintegration of cultural values. Such an ominous existence, such a unique cultural melancholia, therefore, can be embodied only in a language that goes well beyond the limits of the symbolic to touch upon the shadowy domain of the psychic. Rhys' expressive needs guide her in that same direction: an economy of linguistic expression that signifies deep melancholic currents in the characters, continuously resisting narrativization, in an ongoing crisis, yet always in the process of becoming.

In a 2001 interview for *New York Arts Magazine* Kristeva points out that art examines types of 'fragility', the fragility of 'perversion, that is, all sorts of sexual transgressions'. Literary production is a strong material testimony for the existence of such transgressions made public through the aesthetic use of language and narrativity. This in itself is a significant move to divest these transgressions of the taboo and prejudice with which they are approached traditionally by society. Two major factors that could motivate a writer to create such works are the gratifying element of exposing long-standing bigotry, as well as the liberating effect of the writing process that can produce changes in the somewhat stagnant social discourses on the transgressive. In the same interview, Kristeva pinpoints a surprising aspect that makes writing an important factor for social change:

> This is ever the case with literature and when it does not try to treat perversion, it deals with psychotic states, that is, the states of identity loss, the loss of language, the borderline cases which cohabit and coexist with delirium and violence, but all of this does not have to bear the imprint of something negative.
>
> (2001)

It seems that Kristeva refers here to a common feature between psychoanalysis and literature: namely, that both are non-judgemental approaches to perversion, a probing into the existential difficulties entailed in the precipitation of the subject.[2] This, in my mind, has much to do with the attempt of the modernist writer to break with the trivial and the routine found in realism, and to explore the dubious, incoherent aspects of the human mind. Writers as diverse as D. H. Lawrence, Ford Madox Ford, Joyce and Woolf would demand such a break in their fiction, not simply as a gesture of severing links with the past but as a significant expressive move to depict that subject-becoming which so much fascinated them in the first place. Rhys, by virtue of her own outsider's positioning in a traditional English society, must have experienced first-hand the need to break up with the social and aesthetic conventions expected from a female writer in order to portray the indubitable melancholic existence of the interwar bohemian woman: out of place, out of luck, altogether out of order.

Unambiguously for those who have followed closely her writing through the years, Kristeva's research in subjectivity is embedded into two important discourses, namely, the discourses of love and melancholia. If in her early work, *Revolution in Poetic Language* (1974), Kristeva analyses the linguistic aspect of human interaction from a particularly structuralist approach, her books in the 1980s, *Powers of Horror* (1980), *Tales of Love* (1983), and *Black Sun* (1987), turn to the affective aspects of human existence and bridge the linguistic with the psychic economies of the self. Kristeva recaptures in the latter texts this double bind of language and affect that structures the process of becoming:

> We are no doubt permanent subjects of a language that holds us in its power. But we are subjects in process, ceaselessly losing our identity, destabilized by fluctuations in our relations to the other, to whom we nevertheless remain bound by a kind of homeostasis.
>
> (PSF 9)

Literature and the analytic situation are connected in an important way in Kristeva's work via the discourses of love and melancholia, since in her view these discourses can provide effective ways of dealing with the unsymbolizable chaos found in the Real and the entrapments hidden in the Imaginary that overwhelm the modern self.[3] The same discourses can bend even the limits set by the Symbolic register, to which language belongs as a system, through the unveiling of the unconscious in the literary writing and the analytical situation. In other words, at the intersection of these two practices, in the operation of the discourses of love and melancholia, we can find recurrent 'crises in meaning, value, and authority' that are embodied in language or else arrested in silence (Beardsworth 2004: 13). It seems that modernism accepts those instances of crisis and works out ways to frame them in poetic and narrative forms in order to give 'body' to the eruptions of the unconscious. For Rhys, this involves embracing crisis altogether and working it in the texture of her narratives; linguistic, impressionistic narratives that do not, cannot, simply tell a story, but touch upon existence in its often tentative, non-descript nature: the paragraphs turn into sentences, the sentences into phrases in which numerous ellipses rupture the rhythm of language to the point of a crash in communication.

Rhys must have related completely to the general cultural diagnosis proffered by Kristeva's observation that we are subjects in process. She too experienced herself as a subject of and subjected to the language of the dominant culture: a white Creole in an imperial metropolitan society that engulfs, judges and expels the one who does not submit. Marya in *Quartet*, Sasha in *Good Morning, Midnight* and Julia in *After Leaving Mr Mackenzie* are similarly examined as specimens of a fading/faded femininity that is liminal, dispensable and easily expelled from the discourse of utility dominant in their society. In other words, as Mullholland argues in relation to the liminal positioning of these protagonists,

> her [Rhys'] work is indicative of the social and economic situation for a much wider group of women living alone in European cities in the

interwar period, who conducted their lives in the precarious threshold spaces between the traditional public and private identities designated for women.

(2012: 446)

Living in such threshold spaces, Rhys' heroines are not simply existing on the margins – they are ceaselessly searching, temporarily finding and losing their way in the Parisian metropolis; they are enigmatic, bohemian, as if having no roots in one particular society, but relating to people and places through the images of the men who have misused them over time.

But is this liminality a space marked by despair? Not so for the writer, not so for the analyst. The Lacanian Unconscious is embodied in the knot between the Real, the Symbolic, and the Imaginary, but unlike the pessimistic Lacan who despairs at the eternally barred subject and the failure of communication, Kristeva sees a productive reconfiguration of the subject possible via a return to its semiotic origins. Those semiotic origins are found scattered, not centred, in language and its margins: into the rhythm, the repetition, the displacement, the substitution, the elision where the unconscious is embedded. Language and its obverse or marginalized 'other' are the two aspects that merge into the semiotic and disrupt the symbolic status quo. This inherent duplicity of language is advantageous rather than detrimental for the precipitation of the subject, for it opens up possibilities to step in and out of the Symbolic, and go back – even temporarily – to the semiotic. Such a linguistic crisscrossing captures instances of the unconscious in order to make the other, 'shadowy' aspect of the subject visible. That is why Kristeva is preoccupied in her work by 'the heteronomy of our psyche' made flesh in language:

> I am interested in language [*langage*], and in the other side of language which is filtered inevitably by language and yet is not language. I have named that heterogeneity variously. I have sought it out in the experience of love, of abjection, of horror. I have called it the semiotic in relation to the symbolic.
>
> (1998: 8)

The other side of language is also to be found in Rhys' novels and takes the form of the misunderstood, the unacceptable, the silenced or the transgressive. Here, in an example from *Quartet*, the protagonist is overwhelmed by her recurrent sense that she is being engulfed by the 'dark waters' of Montparnasse or, probably, by the dark waters of her own life:

> As she walked back to the hotel after her meal Marya would have the strange sensation that she was walking under water. The people passing were like wavering reflections seen in water, the sound of water was in her ears. Or sometimes she would feel sure that her life was a

dream – that all life was a dream. 'It's a dream,' she would think; 'it isn't real' – and be strangely comforted.

(2000a: 96)

The repetitive use of 'water' and 'dream' in the excerpt produces a frame for the heterogeneous experience of being yet not belonging in a place and living yet daydreaming that Marya faces daily. The unhomely effect of the emblematic Parisian locale on the protagonist is expressed in a language which hints and ever-so-gently touches upon experience, rather than communicates precise meanings. For the modernist writer, the expressive aspect of the text is loaded with meaning as if by proxy: the reader is to infer, to deduct, to modulate variable possibilities among the narrative offerings, before she is to ever find a meaning or a set of meanings that, comparably, stand for the obscure signification of the text.

Language, however, is a symbolic practice and a specific medium especially prominent in literature, so it has to do with the poetics of becoming, of building up a communicative system and sharing it with others. Having memories, histories and stories, speaking about oneself, to someone, are viable ways to heal what Kristeva calls a 'shattered narcissism' or, simply, a shattered sense of self (1998: 11). This shattered self is displayed ever so well in the analytic situation, but equally well in literature too: both analysis and literature suggest a gap, or a 'chasm in the very subject' that needs attention (BS 52). While there is no tangible 'solution' to the subject's lack, as Lacan has made clear in his seminars, Kristeva works in the direction of a return to the semiotic and the opening up of the discourses of love and melancholia as ways to embrace and renew subjectivity. Beardsworth understands the social conundrum which Kristeva analyses here and further clarifies: '[t]he modern Narcissus, encountered in the therapeutic setting, reveals that modern Western cultures lack the kinds of discourses of love, loss, and separateness that are necessary for symbolic life, connections with others, and the social bond' (2004: 12). Probably this is why late modernist writers try to focus on the chasm in the very subject as experienced in the interwar period and chase after its adequate literary expression. This might be also why Rhys's protagonists are continuously searching for love – beyond erotic love, towards the amatory – even though the search turns disappointing, silly, and futile most of the time:

> Love was a terrible thing. You poisoned it and stabbed at it and knocked it down into the mud – well down – and it got up and staggered on, bleeding and muddy and awful. Like – like Rasputin. Marya began to laugh.
>
> (2000a: 96)

The narcissistic bind, where the ego is unproductively centred on itself, supports essentially a strict subject/object opposition which juxtaposes one self to another. Freud, for example, has paired love and hypnosis in his *Group Psychology and the Analysis of the Ego* (1921) because of 'the idealization, subjection, compliance, and sapping of initiative that they are capable of inducing in the subject', as Rose contends (1993: 41). Unlike Freud, Kristeva sees a way out through the production of a new discourse of love which, in tandem with melancholy as the response to the lost object, can reposition the subject vis-à-vis the other players on the social scene. The discourses of love and melancholy make the precipitation of the subject possible through an affective return to the semiotic language which is there to fill in the gaps in the symbolic language. This process welcomes the manifestation of the Unconscious in the subject rather than negating its socially disruptive aspects. Rhys, undoubtedly, embraces such a return to the semiotic throughout her work too: the semiotic is a viable way for the discourse of love and the expressive potential for the precipitation of the subject. It does not dispense with pain and disappointment, yet it fleshes out the shattered sense of self. In this way, rather than interpreting the typical Rhys protagonist solely as the victimized other, we are able to see the potential, even the threat, to the traditional social discourse in these women's relentless attempts at finding love even in the wrong places.

This potential is enhanced by the fact that the problem of subjectivity, in both Kristeva and Rhys, is inseparable from the question of sexual difference. In particular, Kristeva examines these two issues in conjunction with the operation of the Unconscious and semiotic language. Very frequently in her writings, Kristeva pairs the concepts of 'woman' and 'materiality', and in this way she opens herself to criticism on the grounds of choosing essentialism and imperative heterosexuality.[4] However, she upholds a much broader view of woman, often as the abject other, isolated in the social discourses, and clearly argues in favour of the idea that the concepts of woman and the feminine are still a vast, contested territory.[5] Kristeva approaches sexuality and the feminine with utmost care for she, like Rhys, recognizes that the feminine is hospitable to the proliferation of the discourses of love and melancholy.

For Rhys, by virtue of being an outsider, a foreigner in a very rigid gender and class system, a white Creole woman who 'pollutes' the English speech with her intrusive accent, language is a battle ground to establish oneself and to accept the inevitable defeats along the way – the sense that she will never belong completely, that she will never merge. Even for the fluent speakers of French and English in her novels – Marya, Sasha and Julia – the language of the Other is constantly disrupting the stability and the sense of self, yet, at the same time, such disruptions also fuel the tentative steps towards manifest subjectivity. There is no sentimentality in the process, though: Julia, for instance, cannot remember precisely her own story and each tiny memory turns into 'a disconnected episode to be placed with all the other disconnected episodes which made up her life' (1977: 41). Sasha, on the other hand, listens attentively to a couple of young compatriots of hers, winding their way through a casual conversation with the patron of a café and successfully managing to 'stab' her – the ageing beauty of no economic standing and support – in that same pitiful French. Despite its disruptive aspect, the intrusion of the Other is a means the female protagonist uses in her search for the identification that might settle the sense of shattered self. Against the colourful, tattered battleground of the café, boulevard and salon of interwar Paris, the cross-linguistic disruption[6] and regress are potent tools for the precipitation of the female protagonist, and of Rhys herself, as the biographers readily note.[7]

The regress to the semiotic and the eruptions of the unconscious are undermining the subject's position as a unified agent on the social scene, but, at the same time, they permit repositioning of the self in a 'revolutionary' way.[8] It seems to me that here Kristeva touches upon yet another concept that she analyses extensively in her more recent work, namely, the concept of 'revolt'. For her, the possibility to rethink the 'mental disposition' that makes us carry on with our daily lives, a disposition which is not a cliché, but an active re-examination of our interior life, is a viable form of revolt. As Kristeva further dwells on the concept of revolt, she explains that

> it is neither an expression of simple existential anguish nor contesting a socio-political order, but re-establishment of things which we start again. And, in this sense, revolt which engulfs the psychic space is a form of life, be it the state of being in love, or an act of aesthetic creation or a project that could imply a very modest activity but which allows you to re-examine your past, that is, to interrogate it and to renew it.
> (2001)

It is interesting to see the connection between love and revolt that Kristeva makes here. There is an accent on hope and recuperation rather than on impossibility, and this makes love a valuable source for the precipitation of the subject. Naturally, as a practicing psychoanalyst and a scholar, Kristeva cannot endorse a solely optimistic script that will lead one into subjecthood, as works such as *The Sense and Non-Sense of Revolt* (2000) and *Intimate Revolt* (2002) have shown. Yet the possibilities hidden in the discourse of love to promote the process of becoming provide a reasonable dose of hope, a hope which cannot gloss over the difficulties ahead. On a personal level, the function of love as revolt and transgression in melancholic modernity accounts for the modernist writer's access to semiotic language. In Kristeva, but very much in Rhys too, the close complicity between the discourses of love and melancholy set the stage for the examination of both life and self in a 'revolutionary' way.

In most studies on Kristeva, love has often been examined briefly for the sake of more appealing discussions, for example the discussions of the semiotic, the symbolic, the *chora*, the feminine, and revolt.[9] However, Kristeva's entire work emphasizes the importance of love for her theory of the subject as she has shown in her books *Tales of Love* (1987), *In the Beginning Was Love* (1987), *New Maladies of the Soul* (1995), to name just a few. Love could be 'translated', or put in words, but there is always something gone amiss in the process, and often this something, this 'it', is the most important thing.[10] Because love is a metaphor, which means thriving on condensation as Lacan has shown, it is often felt as something impervious, or opaque, which resists analysis of the analogy 'part-to-whole'. Like its sister desire, love is not to be bound by a definition or a parameter, but rather makes one roam the psychic space in search of that one lover who will (hypothetically) complete us. This lover is what the ancient Greeks called the *atopos*, the unclassifiable. As Roland Barthes writes, '[t]he other whom I love and who fascinates me is *atopos*. I cannot classify the other, for the other is, precisely, Unique, the singular image which has miraculously come to correspond to the specialty of my desire' (1990: 34). A fascinating game between the sexes, or between members of one sex, love is not to be understood and defined, but to be practiced, despite the inevitable losses it entails. Such 'losses' are measured sometimes in terms of personal space, freedom, immediacy, but still love offers an unexpected gift – the gift of speech – that appears as an excess in the array of social discourses. As Kristeva admits wisely, as if echoing Diotima who also tells a story about love in Plato's *The Symposium*, 'Love is something spoken, and it is only that' (TL 277).

The aphoristic simplicity of Kristeva's statement emphasizes the importance of putting into words, in language, that which structures the precipitation of the subject. If love is only spoken, it means that it functions in a linguistic medium that is governed by an affective element, the latter pointing towards the work of the unconscious as the realm that knots together the Real, the Symbolic, and the Imaginary registers. To put it differently, love provides the narrative frame that one needs to relate to the others and to her own fragmented subjectivity. The work of the writer, in this case of Rhys, testifies to the need to speak about love: her protagonists Marya, Sasha, and Julia are all overwhelmed by the need to speak and search for love among a varied, though poor (both psychically and financially) mass of people – Frenchmen, expatriates, low life, and middle-class people of dubious position, etc. The women are the ones to despair about the lack of a discourse of love, one capable of grounding them somewhat into the crude reality of interwar Paris. The lack of such discourse, not of individual sexual partners, causes these women to drift into the opposite direction of victimhood and incapacitation. But, as Charles Shepherdson rightfully asks in connection to the discourse of love,

> Are we only telling tales when we tell tales of love? Is the narrative therefore a fiction, a myth, a web of words designed not simply to describe

or document but rather to contain and make more tolerable a narcissistic wound that accompanies the subject through all the various historical formations that mark its symbolic life?

(2000: 96)

So, how shall we speak about love and what tales do we tell about it? Or, to rephrase the question in Kristevan terms, how do the tales of love help one tolerate the self-inflicted wound of narcissism? Rhys seems to have found a very specific way, a tone that matches the melancholic voicing of insecurity and doubt that imbues late modernist writing. Her tone expresses a disbelief in the ideals of communion and understanding in a world which faces a lack of love discourse, and, at the same time, a doubt about whether these ideals are easily attainable in the wake of the First World War and just before another great war descends upon Europe.

If, as Kristeva implies, to speak means to believe, then to speak about love means to believe in love, despite the knowledge that it is bound to fail. As Kristeva demonstrates years later, in *Tales of Love*, for instance, the pure optimistic belief in the world of possibilities that love opens cannot simply replace the necessity to study the conditions that make love possible in the first place, starting with the structure of primary narcissism. Thus, Kristeva analyses the archaic 'first abjection' as a 'presymbolic moment in subject formation, necessary for separation', in which the maternal figure is abjected in the process of primary identification via the transference to the imaginary father. The psychic correlation between the abjected mother and the imaginary father is what feeds primary narcissism and precludes love (Beardsworth 2004: 76–7). On the other hand, if we simply say that love is impossible because of the primary narcissism, we ignore the more important question of how to make it possible at all. In a Lacanian reading, the labours of love are always already lost or wasted due to the lack in the barred subject, but then again why does Lacan devote *Seminar XX* to the question of love, and remain preoccupied with such precarious topics in the rest of his work too? Lacan seems to be intuiting the value of systematizing the issue of love, despite numerous instances of his exasperation with such a slippery problem. One colourful example of this is his ominous verdict that, 'Love rarely comes true, as each of us knows, and it only lasts for a time. For what is love other than banging one's head against a wall, since there is no sexual relation?' (1982: 170). Rhys's protagonists would readily testify about that: variously entangled in fruitless relationships with men of questionable morality, Marya, Sasha and Julia are to find out the hard way, through 'banging their heads', that love is escaping them. Their experiences, as well as Lacan's diagnosis, ultimately tie love with the lack of truth, with temporal insecurity and with the 'non-existence' of the sexual relationship.

The lack of truth that Lacan discusses above is not to be understood in epistemological terms; the lack of truth refers to a state of uncertainty and disorder where the subject is kept helplessly hovering, and love can hardly guarantee existential stability. Temporal insecurity is against the state of permanence and balance that the subject ideally needs. Although it might sound paradoxical, the third aspect of Lacan's statement, the lack of sexual relation, could be explained by the fact that, in his theory, woman exists only as a fantasy to man. The myth of the sexual relation veils the real division in the subject, hence the related and opposite formula 'There is something of One' which refers to that fantasy of unity 'We are as one.' And again, as Lacan admits, 'That's what the idea of love starts out from… the problem then being how on earth there could be love for another' (qtd in Mitchell 1982: 46). Kristeva, though, has an altogether positive answer to this rhetorical question, since she writes that the 'effect of love is one of renewal, our rebirth' (TL 15). She contends that there is a possibility to overcome difference by embracing it; to love, in her view, is to accept difference and to build productively upon it. If, *contra* Lacan, for Kristeva love for another *is* possible this is not simply through the recognition of differences but also through a return to a maybe old-fashioned but useful term – 'respect', respect for someone I will never be or I will never totally know.

To a great extent this kind of mutual recognition is what is missing in the encounters that Rhys's female protagonists have: Marya, Sasha and Julia encounter individuals who do not see them as selves, but as more or less available bodies, not even as prestigious sex trophies, least of all as intellects. The women are manipulated and abused by the men, in many cases by other women too, like in the case of *Quartet* and the strange *ménage* between Marya and the Heidlers. The abuse, either physical or psychological, is channelled to a certain level where only hunger and alcohol seem to work on their bodies and minds, thus providing a minute respite from the depravity of the everyday rubble. As foreign bodies, Rhys's protagonists have become foreign minds too, to a degree they become foreign to their own selves.

The need for recognition of differences, and not for smoothing them away, seems to be what Kristeva proclaims as the minimum requirement for an encounter between individuals. However, while the recognition of differences is something commendable, the practice of it is quite difficult to achieve in reality. If in love we find at work the first instances of the positive recognition of differences, it turns out that it is one of the most difficult acts too. Often, love finishes with the failure to recognize those differences which have made love possible in the first place when an ideal object was found. In other words, when the ego in-mixes the subject and the object, the one and the other, there is no possibility for getting away with the shattering effects of the trauma of narcissism, as Kristeva argues. The trauma of narcissism for her is not a singular event, but the traumatic return of the first encounter with another before subjectivity has been put in place. However, the very structure of the subject has a peculiar traumatic dimension, resulting from giving up the other and accepting the essential lack in one's self. The trauma is usually experienced over and over, but a subject dispels its effect by virtue of 'finding out' about another. The problem is when the subject gets caught into the trauma and re-lives it to the full via a return to the sameness, the identical. Such a giving-in to the Imaginary entrapment of the same means that the ego, metaphorically speaking, sees only itself and misses even the fact that there is a mediating element, the water which reflects its image, as the original myth of Narcissus portrays. In other words, the ocular and the imaginary drown the discursive realm which always presupposes the relation between two at least.[11] According to Oliver, this means that,

> [I]t is the negative in the sense of the phrases 'I cannot know you,' 'I cannot be you,' 'I will never master you,' that allows for relationships beyond domination, beyond recognition. As soon as I am sure that I know you... I have stopped having a relationship with you and instead have a relationship with myself, with my own projection onto you. When I think that I know you, our relationship is over.
>
> (2001: 64)

Very much so in the case of Rhys' female protagonists who stagger to find love in the everyday as Marya struggles with poverty and the despair of being unloved by any of the men in her life. These men are 'sure' they 'know' how to manipulate Marya to achieve only very basic gratification of their needs without reciprocating her love. However, Paris of the sordid hotel rooms and cheap cafés alludes that *another* life is possible too, and the melancholy of Marya's existence merges with the desire to love and be loved. Desiring as she is to find and give love, Marya gets mastered by men who, instead, have relationships with themselves in the most narcissistic possible way. In *Quartet*, Heidler is a narcissistic handler, not a lover, who cannot relate to her, but even her own husband, Stephan, cannot either. The failure to love another results also from a total subjection to the Symbolic order which, in Lacan, thrives on differences and juxtapositions like 'man/woman', 'black/white', 'right/wrong', 'order/disorder' and so on. Kristeva uses the term 'symbolic' to indicate one of the modalities within the signifying process that constitutes language. While for Lacan there is an imperative need for the separation from the mother in order to secure the advent of the Father who introduces the Law, Kristeva argues in favour of the importance of the symbiotic mother-child relation before the Father, when the child's ego comes into being and love for another is initially introduced. Remnants of the mother-child symbiosis are to be found in the semiotic modality of language where signification is broken into two, as has been discussed earlier. Genuine love makes such a return to the semiotic possible since the obstructive boundaries of the symbolic are broken, and vice versa: the semiotic makes love viable by offering a special language to speak about love. However, such an account cannot make us believe that the transgression into the semiotic is totally unproblematic, so that love can easily flourish. Thus, I certainly agree with Kristeva that the labours of love are not lost if, and only if, they are taken out of the strictly symbolic modality of language and targeted at the subject's psychic economy in a time of crisis. As she points out,

> I am thinking of humanity as it suffers from a 'crisis of values,' a humanity that no doubt remains a child, but a child that feels itself to be an orphan. For that humanity, the Other is Me: I am an Other. This humanity lives in, and on, separation.
>
> (PSF 55)

Such a 'crisis of values', moreover, is manifested in the new maladies of the soul we experience in modernity ever so strongly, which range from 'autism to psychosomatic affections, and to borderline cases, "false Selves," "as-if personalities" and other narcissistic disturbances', as Kristeva says in an interview (1996). For her, then, the analytic experience and art – as a venue of exploring the psychic space through an aesthetic use of language – are the two ways in which love could be productively emancipated through the symbolic in order to tame these maladies of the soul. The access to speech and language, therefore, and most importantly to these 'nameless recesses of meaning', is what permits the subject to come to terms with her love. Rhys is very clear that her writing is such an exploration of meanings and expressive ways, all in an attempt to find viable access to the discourse of love both on a personal level and as a modernist writer. Her female characters, though deprived of visible literary talents, share into her search for such a discourse in the difficult landscape of interwar Paris. Rather than being simply victimized females, there is a sense that Marya, Sasha and Julia are collecting the pieces of their selves that have been dissipated by numerous failed relations with men who do not see anything else but their own reflections. This is probably why the women in Rhys' novels ultimately do not find recourse to actual love relations and their discourse of love is ultimately a melancholic one.

What is love's function if not to help cure that shattered narcissism that makes us 'as-if' cases and 'as-if' people? There is an opening-up through language that allows for an unexpectedly productive configuration of self and other to appear, where language acts as an intermediary between bodily perception and logic, between private and public, between need, demand, and desire. If speech is a language that materializes in the encounter with the other, it is 'a moment of truth' for the subject who announces her own vulnerability to an equally vulnerable other. In other words, as Salecl aphoristically emphasizes, as if summarizing both Lacan and Kristeva on the link between love and speech/language,

> There is no love outside speech: non-speaking beings do not love.... Love emerges out of speech as a demand that is not linked to any need. Love is a demand that constitutes itself as such only because the subject is the subject of the signifier. As such, the subject is split, barred, marked by a fundamental lack. And it is in this lack that one encounters the object cause of desire. This object has a paradoxical status: it is what the subject lacks, and at the same time what fills this lack. The enchantment of love is how the subject deals, on the one hand with his or her own lack, and, on the other hand, with the lack in the loved one.
>
> (2000: 17–18)

The lack in the subject and the loss of the object give rise to a discourse of melancholia, which is ever so perceptible in the modernist literature of the interwar period. The discourse of love and the discourse of melancholy could be found symbiotically existing in the works of modernists such as Virginia Woolf, Katherine Mansfield, Rebecca West and, as this chapter argues, in Rhys too. However, it is the work of the German philosopher Walter Benjamin which both Rhys and Kristeva recall in their literary and theoretical works. Benjamin is the quintessential explorer of the relation between melancholic discourse and the *Zeitgeist* of interwar Europe. In *Black Sun*, Kristeva repeatedly refers to the work of another 'foreigner',[12] Benjamin, in relation to his work on melancholia as explored in his groundbreaking book on baroque mourning, *Ursprung des deutschen Trauerspiels* (1928) translated as *The Origin of the German Tragic Drama*, but also to his observations in later works such as *Passagenwerk* (1927–40). In this work Benjamin examines the poetry of Baudelaire in order to establish a vocabulary of melancholia through which poetry relates to the 'newness' sensed in the late nineteenth century and the arrival of the new century. Kristeva, on the other hand, focuses her discussion in *Black Sun* on the poet Gérard de Nerval as the prime exponent of the arrival of literary modernity in Europe. Baudelaire's and Nerval's treatments of modernity are perceived by Benjamin and Kristeva respectively as representative of idiosyncratic theories of writing which merge phantasms and even deliriums of the past, and witness the chasm in the times and also in the modern self.

Benjamin interprets Baudelaire's poetry as an ultimate exercise in interruption, in the application of a shock method of discontinuing a flow or a tradition that renders modernity's melancholia tangible. In his view, such an interruption of tradition displayed in literature has an important function beyond the merely expressive use of language; when masterfully applied, the interruption creates an insightful opportunity for the subject to brace up the power of the melancholic spirit beyond its sad, mournful façade and to achieve a higher level of historical thinking:

> Even though melancholia is a subjectively experienced phenomenon for Benjamin, its source of (potential) value is not the individual or solipsistic creative tendencies or abilities it might bring with it but the way it might allow one to gain access to the historical origins of one's suffering, and indeed to the logic of historicity itself.
>
> (Flatley 2008: 65)

The revolutionary potential that the melancholic experience of modernity offers, therefore, is embedded in the sudden arrest of speech, images and affectivity. Figuratively speaking, Benjamin reads Baudelaire as quintessential maker of 'amber nuggets' in which time is arrested and a possible, even if illusory, future progress crystallizes. As such, melancholy is not one pathological mood among others for the subject but a fundamental attunement as Benjamin calls it, or *Grundstimmung*. According to this early text, Benjamin sees the task of philosophy as allowing melancholy to be linguistically presented, a task which literature has already creatively embraced. In Benjamin there is no promise of a future and the sense of melancholy is created by the recognition that the moment of crisis is in fact a standstill rather than an incentive to progress. Very much in line with such a perception, we might consider how Rhys creatively embeds in language such a standstill in the psychic world of her female characters. It seems that nothing much is happening in her Parisian novels; rather, a sense of constant yearning and contemplation are expressed as a form of revolt and transgression in melancholic modernity. While the contemplation of life is easily identifiable as an instance of a specific standstill, the crisis such a standstill marks refers to the development of a surprising historical sense in the female protagonists. Although compacted by the lack of physical resistance, the awareness that society works against women through various forms of gender and class oppression is clearly connected with the sense of spiritual revolt to be found in the tension between their yearning after love and the lack of such a discourse, between establishing their identities and fighting off meretricious yet socially acceptable models of womanhood. In *Good Morning, Midnight*, Sasha has a kind of 'out of body experience' when contemplating herself: 'Who is crying? The same one who laughed on the landing, kissed him and was happy. This is me, this is myself, who is crying. The other – how do I know who the other is?' (1969: 154). Julia, in *After Leaving Mr Mackenzie*, will answer: 'And then I was frightened, and yet I knew that if I could get to the end of what I was feeling it would be the truth about myself and about the world and about everything that one puzzles and pains about all the time' (1977: 41).

Kristeva, *pace* Benjamin, reads Nerval's poetry as symptomatic of a modernity in which the surface of representation breaks up with reality, the images become fragmented and the coherent poetic 'I' dissolves altogether. As such, these elements are indicative of modern changes that already imbue the poetic language and the texture of the literary work. The revolutionary moment of connecting literature to the larger domains of the social and the political is achieved, then, by extension, through a critical meditation on the transhistorical and cross-cultural values of such literature. In other words, the connection between modernity and literature is not just a relation between a temporal medium and a literary work as an end product but a sharpening of awareness and critical perception in writers and readers which has transformative dynamics via the use of the semiotic modality of language. Based on this comparison between Benjamin and Kristeva, it is only fair to note the potential doubt Kristeva feels for such a successful bonding of literature and society overall. The sense of doubt we get stems from the experience of modernity and the positioning of people who are to bridge critical meditation with the experience of the present via the language of the purely Symbolic in Lacanian terms. The access to the semiotic language and its 'burst' into the literary, with its power to bend the law of the Symbolic order and express affective states, is what moments of crises call for. Literature and art, in general, offer a venue for the temporary ordering of broken-down images and a failing Symbolic order, a provisional taming of what is a 'nameable melancholia' in modernity (BS 100).

Rhys seems to share Kristeva's interpretation of melancholic modernity, especially in interwar Europe. Hers are literary works which do not dwell on a promise for a future change or on a language of freedom. As her Parisian novels show, the language Rhys explores is already disruptive in its semiotic quality and its persistent return to trauma and melancholia. There is no evasion of the lost Thing, 'the real that does not lend itself to signification, the centre of attraction and repulsion, seat of the sexuality from which the object of desire will become separated', but an attempt to phrase in words the lack in the subject (BS 13). This is how Marya fills in the gaps in her life, between cafés, encounters with men, and her shabby hotel room:

> She spent the foggy day in endless, aimless walking, for it seemed to her that if she moved quickly enough she would escape the fear that hunted her. It was a vague and shadowy fear of something cruel and stupid that had caught her and would never let her go.
>
> (2000a: 28)

Quite in line with Kristeva's ideas explored in *Powers of Horror*, Rhys depicts, or tries to approximate, the permanent crisis of self that her female protagonists experience; the crisis of minds arrested in the grips of desire for the elusive Thing that is not a particular object even (as in mourning), but an abject, maternally-connoted non-object. This non-object has to do with the fact that her female characters are cut off from their origins, literally from their mothers, from their mother-country, and, ultimately, the maternal as in the case of Anna Morgan, the central character in Rhys's 1934 novel *Voyage in the Dark*, a victim of a botched abortion.

Marya, Sasha and Julia do not yearn after a future in which the present hardship will dissipate miraculously. The possibility of change itself, of a future which might hold another object of desire, is transformative, if not revolutionary, in Benjamin's terms, although it is 'revolutionary' in the Kristevan sense of turning and re-turning to a discourse that searches for expression and the response of the other. As Kristeva argues, therefore, both the abject and the object of desire hold special places in the subject's economy of becoming:

> If the object settles me with the fragile texture of a desire for meaning, which, as a matter of fact, makes me ceaselessly and infinitely homologous to it, what is *abject*, on the contrary, the jettisoned object, is radically excluded and draws me toward the place where meaning collapses.
>
> (PH 1–2)

The desire for meaning and the abject coexist in Rhys' female characters and this tension leads towards a collapse of meaning and existential crisis which could be interpreted as a victimhood or incapacity by some, yet it is a crisis which has a transformative value for the individual in the long run. Her Parisian novels strangely bridge the philosophies of both Benjamin and Kristeva by embracing the discourses of love and melancholia, and embodying them in a language and form that evoke a dishearteningly anxious European modernity between two world wars.

If interwar modernism, and Rhys's *oeuvre* in particular, try to make psychic fragility visible, how do we negotiate the distance between the individual and society as depicted in such works as *Quartet*, *Good Morning, Midnight*, and *After Leaving Mr Mackenzie*? Isn't Rhys supposed to be longing after a more accommodating society to the misfit and the foreigner, instead of 'saving' the individual soul of her much bruised and beaten by life heroines? Kristeva's simple answer is that, in the long run, literature targets the subject, the individual, as the sole guarantor of a possible change in society. Her project is thus to demonstrate that literature (and psychoanalysis) can produce first a change in an individual, and then in society, which will be able to invent the 'amatory code' which has been missing for so long from our discourses. For example, Kristeva interprets the biblical verse 'Love your neighbour as yourself' as one of surprisingly modern urgency:

> To become capable of loving our neighbour as ourself, we have first of all to heal a wounded narcissism. We must reconstitute narcissistic

identity to be able to extend a hand to the other. Thus what is needed is a reassurance or reconstruction of both narcissism, personality and, of course, the subject for there to be a relation to the other.

(1998: 11)

Although for many this sounds ultimately individualistic, as opposed to an all-encompassing political programme for social reform, Kristeva's writing is on the lookout for a change that will initiate the subject-in-progress, *sujet-en-procès*, into subjecthood. The cure, therefore, is still 'talking', but talking to someone who needs to work hard in order to be able to hear her own voice and to internalize the form of revolt inherent in language against the Symbolic. The revolt, in this sense, will be the re-examination of attitudes and the understanding of the subject in a way that will further cure what has been an ailing society. As she has argued earlier, the revolt will necessarily pass through a re-interpretation of and a renewed engagement with the Symbolic, and also with the seemingly less problematic discourses of love and melancholia, for these discourses always manage to disrupt the symbolic modality of language through their reinvestment in the semiotic.

Rhys' female protagonists, therefore, cannot be read as isolated examples of socially ill-fitted, mistreated women in interwar Paris. Bohemian and emblematic as they might be, they are rather symptoms of modernity as it lives through a period of ultimate crisis. The transformative power of these critical times is inherent in the affective texture of life through the rubble of the everyday that sets obstacles to self-understanding and growth more often than not. Rhys is experiencing the *jouissance* of the writerly text embodied in the semiotic language which she often employs to narrate her protagonists' stories and, undoubtedly, her own life story. In the depiction of the debris of modern urban existence, in the sordid sexual encounters and the spiritual poverty that dominate Rhys' work, we are to find the remnants – and the beginnings – that nod towards possibilities of finding a new object of love in the future that will ease the melancholia of the present.

Notes

1   See Jonathan Flatley's book *Affective Mapping*, for example, where he points out that 'The very origin of the word "modernity," from *modernus*, meaning "now" or "of today" (as opposed to "of yesterday") implies a problematic sense of anteriority, the sense that the past is lost and gone' (2008: 28).

2   I use the rather technical term 'precipitation' here instead of 'development' or 'growth' because in my mind it emphasizes accurately the process of becoming as if in a step-by-step mode, without the nuance of a positive evolutionary direction. In a way I am trying to match what Kristeva terms the 'subject-in-process'.

3 The Real, the Imaginary and the Symbolic refer here to the three Lacanian registers (see Lacan's *Seminars*).
4 See, for example, Butler's critique of Kristeva in *Gender Trouble* (1990), *Bodies That Matter* (1993) or Grosz's *Volatile Bodies* (1994).
5 See, for example, her early essay 'Woman Can Never Be Defined' (1974). The title and the essay as a whole echo the famous Lacanian 'woman does not exist' in *Seminar XX*. Cf. Kristeva: 'On a deeper level, a woman cannot "be"; it is something that does not even belong in the order of being. It follows that a feminist practice can only be negative, at odds with what already exists' (WND 103).
6 I am referring here to the multiplicity of languages in the work of Rhys and the variety of pragmatic occasions for their usage.
7 See, for example, Carol Angier's *Jean Rhys. Life and Work* (1991), Elaine Savory's *Jean Rhys* (1998), Helen Carr's *Jean Rhys* (1996), Alexis Lykiard's *Jean Rhys Revisited* (2000).
8 The cautious use of the term 'revolutionary' here is related to the original notion of 'turning around in a circular motion' rather than to the historically loaded notion of 'upheaval and turning down'. See, for example, Kristeva's analysis and nuanced use of the term in *The Sense and Non-Sense of Revolt: The Powers and Limits of Psychoanalysis* (2000).
9 See, for example, *Abjection, Melancholia, and Love: The Work of Julia Kristeva*, edited by John Fletcher and Andrew Benjamin (2012), John Lechte's *Julia Kristeva* (1990), John Lechte and Maria Margaroni's *Julia Kristeva: Live Theory* (2004), the introduction in *The Kristeva Reader*, edited by Toril Moi (1986), Kelly Oliver's *Reading Kristeva: Unraveling the Double-bind* (1993), among others.
10 Punning again, this time on Freud and Lacan, the untranslatable 'it' is maybe 'the uncanny' kernel of love.
11 In Latin, *relatio* means 'carrying or bringing back'.
12 Benjamin, a German Jew, died tragically in 1940.

References

Ainley, A. (1994), 'French Feminist Philosophy: De Beauvoir, Kristeva, Irigaray, Le Doeuff, Cixous', in R. Kearney (ed.), *Twentieth-Century Continental Philosophy*, vol. VIII, 409–40, London: Routledge.
Angier, C. (1991), *Jean Rhys. Life and Work*, New York: Little, Brown.
Barthes, R. (1990), *A Lover's Discourse*, trans. R. Howard, London: Penguin.
Beardsworth, S. (2004), *Julia Kristeva: Psychoanalysis and Modernity*, Albany, NY: State University of New York Press.
Benjamin, W. (2003), *The Origin of the German Tragic Drama*, trans. J. Osborne, London: Verso.
Butler, J. (1990), *Gender Trouble: Feminism and the Subversion of Identity*, London: Routledge.

Butler, J. (1993), *Bodies That Matter: On the Discursive Limits of Sex*, London: Routledge.
Carr, H. (1996), *Jean Rhys*, Horndon: Northcote House.
Flatley, J. (2008), *Affective Mapping: Melancholia and the Politics of Modernism*, Cambridge, MA: Harvard University Press.
Fletcher, J. and A. Benjamin, eds (2012), *Abjection, Melancholia, and Love: The Work of Julia Kristeva*, London: Routledge.
Grosz, E. (1994), *Volatile Bodies*, London: Routledge.
Kristeva, J. (1996), interview with S. Benvenuto, *Journal of European Psychoanalysis*, 3–4, http://www.psychomedia.it/jep/pages/number3-4.htm (accessed 28 October 2003).
Kristeva, J. (1998), 'interview with K. O'Grady', *Parallax: Julia Kristeva 1966–1996: Aesthetics, Politics, Ethics*, 8: 5–16.
Kristeva, J. (2001), interview with N. Zivancevici, *New York Arts Magazine*, http://www.nyartsmagazine.com/57/juliakristeva.html (accessed 28 August 2003).
Lacan, J. (1982), *Feminine Sexuality*, trans. J. Rose, ed. J. Mitchell and J. Rose, Basingstoke: Palgrave.
Lacan, J. (1988), *The Seminar of Jacques Lacan, Book I: Freud's Papers on Technique*, trans. J. Forrester, ed. J.-A. Miller, New York: W. W. Norton.
Lacan, J. (1999), *The Seminar of Jacques Lacan, Book XX: On Feminine Sexuality, the Limits of Love and Knowledge*, trans. B. Fink, ed. J.-A. Miller, New York: W. W. Norton.
Lechte, J. (1990), *Julia Kristeva*, London: Routledge.
Lechte, J. and M. Margaroni (2004), *Julia Kristeva: Live Theory*, London: Continuum.
Lykiard, A. (2000), *Jean Rhys Revisited*, Devon: Stride.
Moi, T. (1986), *The Kristeva Reader*, New York: Columbia University Press.
Mullholland, T. (2012), 'Between Illusion and Reality, "Who's to Know": Threshold Spaces in the Interwar Novels of Jean Rhys', *Women: A Cultural Review*, 23 (4): 445–62.
Oliver, K. (1993), *Reading Kristeva: Unraveling the Double-bind*, Bloomington, IN: Indiana University Press.
Oliver, K. (2001), 'The Look of Love', *Hypatia*, 16 (3): 56–78.
Rhys, J. (1969), *Good Morning, Midnight*, London: Penguin.
Rhys, J. (1977), *After Leaving Mr Mackenzie*, London: Penguin.
Rhys, J. (2000a), *Quartet*, London: Penguin.
Rhys, J. (2000b), *Voyage in the Dark*, London: Penguin.
Rose, J. (1993), 'Julia Kristeva – Take Two', in Kelly Oliver (ed.), *Ethics, Politics, and Difference in Julia Kristeva's Writing*, 41–61, London: Routledge.
Salecl, R. (2000), *(Per)versions of Love and Hate*, London: Verso.
Sánchez-Pardo, E. (2003), *Cultures of the Death Drive: Melanie Klein and Modernist Melancholia*, Durham, NC: Duke University Press.
Savory, E. (1998), *Jean Rhys*, Cambridge: Cambridge University Press.
Shepherdson, C. (2000), 'Telling Tales of Love: Philosophy, Literature, and Psychoanalysis', *diacritics*, 30 (1): 89–105.
Woolf, V. (1971 [1924]), 'Mr Bennett and Mrs Brown', in *Collected Essays*, vol. I, London: Hogarth Press.

13

The mirror before the mirror: Reflections on Kristeva and Martha Graham's *Hérodiade*

Robert R. Shane

Looking into the mirror, the subject sees their reflection move in perfect synchronicity with themselves. It appears to be completely present in time. But what is the temporality of this experience? Who hasn't faced a mirror and had conversations with others *not* present, for example, recalling a past conversation or imagining a future one, as in Robert DeNiro's famous 'Are you talking to me?' when he played the character Travis Bickle in Martin Scorcese's *Taxi Driver*. Job interviewees are, in fact, frequently given the advice to stand before a mirror in the present as they imagine answering the questions they might receive from their interviewers in the near future. This chapter looks at modern dance choreographer Martha Graham's *Hérodiade* (1944), originally titled *Mirror before Me*, drawing attention to these temporal paradoxes of the mirror and their relationship to subject formation in the work of Julia Kristeva.

In 1944 composer Paul Hindemith, sculptor Isamu Noguchi and choreographer Martha Graham collaborated on *Hérodiade*, a dance based loosely on Mallarmé's poem of the same name (1864–7), whose second of three parts is a dialogue between Hérodiade and her nurse attendant. Hindemith selected the poem even though Graham wanted to create a piece about Medea – which she eventually did in 1946, titled *Cave of the Heart*. Graham premiered the dance under the title *Mirror before Me*, a line from Mallarmé's poem, though Hindemith later asked her to change it to *Hérodiade*. The programme notes indicate that Graham's piece takes place in a woman's antechamber. It is furnished with sculptures by Noguchi: a stool in the centre, an X-shaped stand holding black drapery upstage-left, and the largest and most complex sculpture downstage-right, a vertical bone-like structure which Graham interpreted to be a mirror. As the piece progresses, Herodias – danced by Graham and simply called 'The Woman' in the programme – becomes increasingly tormented, sometimes kneeling before the mirror, pulling away along a diagonal line on her knees as if pleading with her reflection, then lying prostrate before it and finally rolling on the floor in anguish. Throughout the dance she is mesmerized by her otherness – as was Narcissus – to the point she cannot see others, namely the Attendant who tries in vain, like Echo, to regain her attention and bring her back to the present but is rebuked three times. The piece ends when the Woman, standing on the stage alone, shrouds herself in a dark sheet.

Kristeva's work on subjectivity, and her revision of Lacan's mirror stage, is particularly germane to understanding Graham's dance. In opposition to Lacan, Kristeva argues that there is a 'mirror before the mirror', that is, before the subject recognizes himself or herself in the mirror as a subject and then begins moving towards inheriting the language of the father. Kristeva's archaic mirror is the corporeal and facial mirroring between infant and mother as they mimic each other's movements, rhythms and expressions and it sets the stage for subject formation and language acquisition. Graham's mirror, not literally reflective but rather inspired by the bone-like structure of Noguchi's sculpture, is similarly a kind of corporeal mirror expressing archaic psychical and somatic dramas. Mirroring is fundamental to subject formation, but as the subject is always in process/on trial for Kristeva, early mother-infant mirroring operates on an affective register throughout one's life. This temporal ambiguity in which the past is projected on to the present is rooted in the Freudian *Zeitlos*, or the timelessness of the unconscious and the drives. Using Graham's *Hérodiade* as an example, this chapter investigates the temporality of Kristeva's subject-in-process standing before the mirror.

Although the dance is titled *Hérodiade*, the exact identity of the Woman in Graham's dance – as well as in Mallarmé's poem – has been the subject of scholarly debate. This debate itself supports reading the Woman as not having a fixed identity, but as a figure who represents Kristeva's notion of the subject-in-process/on trial. The ambiguity in the identity and ages of the Woman and her Attendant also speaks to Kristeva's account of the unique relationship between mothers and daughters, which I address towards the end of this chapter. Graham biographer and former Martha Graham Dance Company member Agnes de Mille reads the Woman literally as Herodias, the mother of Salomé. For De Mille, an ageing Herodias fearful of losing her youth and desirability was a stand-in for Graham herself, who was aged fifty when she choreographed and first performed this dance. De Mille describes *Hérodiade* as 'the deadly dance between Herodias and her mirror, between Herodias and her [attendant]... Herodias facing an enemy, Herodias facing death: Martha facing old age' (1991: 260). For De Mille the work is ultimately 'a study of the loss of seductiveness and power through age' (1991: 260). She reports that the dance as Graham's farewell to youth created a fracture between the choreographer and the rest of her younger company members (1991: 260). However, as dance historian Stodelle argues, Graham's dances 'were objectifications of emotional crisis' in which theatrical projection was primary over her personal identification with a character (Stodelle 1984: 137); thus, Stodelle resists simply reading the Woman as an autobiographical character.

Stodelle instead focuses on the ambiguity of whether the Woman is in fact Herodias, her daughter Salomé, or a combination of the two (1984: 131). This confusion of identity was already built into Mallarmé's poem. Discussing the character, the poet said Hérodiade is 'a purely imaginary creature entirely independent of history' (qtd in Bannerman 2006: 3). Herodias and Salomé both share characteristics seen in Graham's Woman: 'They were both desperate, demanding women' (Stodelle 1984: 131). Just as she conflates Herodias' and Salomé's identities, Stodelle moves on to conflate those of the Woman and the Attendant as well: 'A prescient, almost eerie moment occurs when the Woman stands in front of the mirror and confronts the Attendant as her own reflection! Now we realized that *Hérodiade* is a soliloquy, not a duet, and that the servant is a projection of the Woman's alter ego' (1984: 131). Stodelle's interpretation is a dialectical synthesis in which she reads the dance abstractly and as concerned with the thoughts of the Woman assisted by her Attendant 'in the painful act of self-confrontation. The illusion in the mirror has to be shattered step by step, or recognized for its potential power to reflect one's true personality' (1984: 130).

However, dance historian Henrietta Bannerman takes a longer view and is not so quick to dismiss the historical roles of Herodias and Salomé in Graham's dance, despite Mallarmé's contention that his poem is independent of them. Although those two historical characters are minimized in Mallarmé's and Graham's versions, their traces do not disappear. Bannerman turns to Kristeva's notion of 'intertextuality', arguing that one cannot banish the earlier meanings of Hérodiade and Salomé in the new text, that is, the dance; rather, the dance has historical resonances with Mallarmé, ancient myth and previous Salomé dances (Bannerman 2006: 14). Graham as a speaking subject, Bannerman argues, takes previous signifying material to re-present it in a new form (RPL 59–60; Bannerman 2006: 14).

By extending Bannerman's intertextual reading into a temporal dimension, we see that Graham's Woman, consciously or not, contains traces of the Herodias and Salomé figures from across time, as well as aspects of

Graham's life in her present. Thus, when considering the Woman standing before the mirror in *Hérodiade*, perhaps the question to ask is not *who* is reflected in the mirror but *when* is her reflection happening? Kristeva's intertwined theories of subjectivity and temporality lend themselves well to a reading of Graham's *Hérodiade*, or *Mirror before Me*. First, I will look at Kristeva's revision of Lacan's mirror stage exploring how the corporal and facial mother-infant mirroring constitutes what Kristeva calls the semiotic modality in language. I argue the physical traces of those early movements are operative in Graham's technique. Then I will look at the temporality of the subject as constructed in Kristeva's work on the Freudian *Zeitlos*, a notion that helps articulate the multiple temporalities of the Woman. Lastly, synthesizing the semiotic and the *Zeitlos*, I will look at Kristeva's account of intergenerational mirroring between mothers and daughters embodied in the ambiguous relationship between the Woman and the Attendant.

The mirror before the mirror: Graham and Kristeva's semiotic

The mirror that figures centrally in Graham's dance has long been a metaphor for subjectivity, from the myth of Narcissus to Lacan's mirror stage. On Lacan's analysis, the child's subjectivity develops in the visual sphere by looking in the mirror and identifying with a specular other; this substitution of the self for a representation (i.e. the reflected image) prepares the child for entry into symbolic language. In symbolic language the subject identifies with his name, an identification with temporal implications. As Kelly Oliver explains, the fragmentation of the imaginary body is given a spatial unity in the mirror, a unity solidified in time by the name (1993: 20). Lacan writes 'the name is the time of the object' (1955: 169; qtd in Oliver 1993: 20). Seeming to anticipate Lacan, Mallarmé too plays with the sound of 'moi' and 'miroir' (Bannerman 2006: 13). 'Moi' or the name gives the ever-changing subject a sense of unity across past, present and future. However, Kristeva's revision of the mirror stage calls into question this temporal unity in ways also performed in Graham's *Hérodiade*.

Kristeva challenges the idea that subjectivity begins or ends at the mirror stage or that it prepares the subject for entry into the Symbolic order. She argues instead that the order, regulation and language of the symbolic are all prefigured in the pre-Oedipal bodily relationship between the infant and the mother. For example, the rhythm and syntax of language find their precedent in the rhythmic, tactile, kinaesthetic and bodily interactions between the infant and the mother, such as holding, feeding and rocking. Thus, there is a *mirror before the mirror* stage, a corporeal mirroring between mother and infant. Kristeva's term for the visceral, corporeal and affective dimension of language rooted in the archaic relationship with the mother's body is 'the semiotic'. Kristeva's classic distinction between 'the semiotic' and 'the symbolic' modalities in language, explicated in *Revolution in Poetic Language* (1974; 1984) and recurring throughout her work, can offer insight into modern dance as a revolutionary poetic language of movement, particularly in Graham's dance which begins to refocus the mirror on the corporeal rather than the specular image. By moving back in time to the archaic infant-mother relationship, we also precede the time of the name.

Poetic language is revolutionary according to Kristeva when it breaks with the phallocentric order of the Symbolic and bears witness to the archaic mother-infant relationships embodied in the semiotic modality of language. Similarly, Graham bears witness to these relationships through the movement language of dance. The semiotic and symbolic modalities are always present in language, but the former tends to be ignored or repressed. Giving form to a pre-linguistic mode that is simultaneously operative within and a challenge to the symbolic order requires pushing the boundaries of language to take on new meanings and syntactical forms. Kristeva shows how this revolutionary language is operative in modern poetry and literature, and her own writing often takes on these characteristics. For example, 'Stabat Mater' and *Powers of Horror* are texts understood not just intellectually, but poetically and viscerally, as the reader encounters Kristeva's folding and division of language. Graham too invents a revolutionary language of movement by defying the conventions of classical ballet. The ballerina dancing *en pointe* with her centre of gravity held high in her chest is often cast in an ethereal role of a goddess or nymph. By contrast, Graham's barefooted dancers, with feet flat on the floor, hold their centre of gravity deep in the pelvis as they engage in her contract and release technique, described in detail below. Graham's grounded dances give voice to feminine desires, *jouissance* and angst, becoming a modern mirror of psychical and visceral dramas outside the lofty realm of ballet. This revolution is most clearly felt as Graham addresses classical mythology, retelling the myths of Medea or Oedipus and Jocasta from psychologically modern perspectives that emphasize and sympathize with the perspective of the women, and specifically maternal, protagonists. *Hérodiade* is, as Bannerman points out, a dance of transition in Graham's work, leading to her modern, gynocentric revisions of ancient myth and legend, typically called her Greek cycle by dance scholars.

Breaking with the symbolic conventions of ballet, yet still working within the mode of concert dance, Graham's work begins to give form to the semiotic, bearing witness to archaic mother-infant mirroring, especially in *Hérodiade*. In one sequence the Woman is sitting on the stool upstage centre, perseverating, and then suddenly leaps forward, chin high, arms in the air, as if frolicking like a child with seemingly no external impetus, but rather, responding to a chain of intrapsychic events. She proceeds to the mirror downstage, but after gazing into it for some time, the Attendant separates her from it by slicing her arm down between them. The Woman kneels on the floor, contracts her core in a rhythm that imitates the movement of maternal eroticism, also closing herself to an infantile almost foetal posture, shrinking and shaping herself to a childlike form. She then rolls upstage, like a child before the ability to walk. No longer able to see her reflection, she takes comfort in the memory of infantile rhythms.

The mirror that is part of the stage décor is not a literally reflective surface but an abstract sculpture by Isamu Noguchi modelled in the biomorphic forms common in surrealist art. This vertically oriented work looks vaguely anthropomorphic and Graham described it as 'a structure in bones of the human body' (qtd in Bannerman 2006: 3–4). Stodelle similarly describes the set and mirror as 'isolated parts of the human anatomy: an empty standing frame spiked with bony extensions not unlike hip joints and ribs' (Stodelle 1984: 132). This bodily mirror, reflecting something physically and psychically interior, invites reflection on the corporeal mirroring Kristeva argues is operative in the establishment of subjectivity prior to Lacan's mirror stage. Although the name offers a temporal unity in Lacan's model, it comes at the cost of separation between the child and mother, as the former adopts the symbolic language of the father. The mirror stage, in which the child both identifies with its reflection and understands it to be other, marks for Lacan the beginning of this separation. But for Kristeva, the separation of semiotic and symbolic which positions the child to enter language and which she calls the thetic break is already pre-figured in the mother-infant relationship (RPL 49).

Kristeva describes the corporeality of rejection reading Freud's *fort/da* game, in which a child throws and retracts a reel of yarn symbolizing control over the separation from the mother by enacting her leaving and returning while uttering childlike speech that approximates 'here/there'. Germane to a study of Graham and modern dance, Kristeva notes that the *fort/da* game is primarily *bodily* and *kinesthetic*, rather than linguistic, and shows how negativity operates on a material level in order to set up the symbolic level (Oliver 1993: 43–4; RPL 170). It is a process of rejection-stasis-rejection-stasis, (Oliver 1993: 45) that is rhythmically repeated, echoing the tactile mother-infant relationship.

The Woman and the Attendant play their own kind of *fort/da* game as the former drives the latter away who keeps returning. But on an even more fundamental level, and as a revolutionary poetic language of movement, Graham's signature 'contract and release' technique capitalizes on rhythms and breath that resonate with the rejection-stasis process within the body and functions as a language of movement giving form to the semiotic. Used in *Hérodiade* and throughout her oeuvre, the importance of contract and release in Graham's technique is analogous to the importance of the *plié* in ballet which is the foundation for other movements. Contract and release is a movement in the body's core and spine. Dance historian Mark Franko describes the bodily oppositions in this technique:

> When the dancer contracts, the concavity of the spine creates the feeling in him or herself and for the observer of retreating beneath or below or into the body's surface structure; the release, on the other hand, reasserts that structure by stretching it outward into space toward its corporeal limits.
>
> (Franko 2012: 114)

The result is what dance historian Frederick Corey describes as 'tensive, percussive, and angular motions' which are 'frequently executed through a contraction/beat/release pattern' (Corey 1990: 204–5), an internalized movement analogous to the rhythmic rejection-stasis-rejection-stasis of mother-infant mirroring. Contracting and releasing, tensing and extending, the Graham dancer's body divides in and against itself, enacting the kind of rhythm and separation of the semiotic. This division of the body provides the foundation for language and resonates with a specifically maternal body. As Kristeva writes, 'A mother is a continuous separation, a division of the very flesh [during pregnancy and birth]. And consequently a division of language – and it has always been so' (TL 254). Since the mother's body forms the substrate upon which symbolic language is built, symbolic language inherits this division in the form of differential meaning, syntactical divisions, grammatical divisions between parts of speech and so on. By highlighting the role these maternal corporeal rhythms from the past play in our present movement and language, both Graham and Kristeva suggest new ways of thinking the subject's temporality.

The *Zeitlos* and Graham's mirror

By taking us back to a mirror before the mirror, Kristeva transgresses the flow of linear time. Furthermore, the semiotic modality of language which is constituted in the mirror before the mirror does not go away after the mirror stage, but is operative in language and subjectivity throughout the subject's life. Graham's conception of the mirror for *Hérodiade* and Isamu Noguchi's 'mirror' sculpture are illustrative of the temporal dramas that constitute subjectivity in process/on trial, as articulated by Kristeva in her reading of the Freudian *Zeitlos* or timelessness in *Intimate Revolt*. In her autobiography, Graham writes about the mirror in *Hérodiade* describing it as foreseeing *future* psychical and physical states: 'When a woman looks into a mirror... and if she's approaching the time when she's no longer young, she sees her skeleton, she sees her bones' (qtd in Jowitt 1988: 209). At the same time, in the programme notes to the dance, Graham also described the mirror as a reflection of the *past* tormenting her in the *present*: 'A mirror provokes an anguish of scrutiny; images of the past, fragments of dreams float to its cold surface, adding to the woman's agony of consciousness' (qtd in Bannerman 2006: 15). Kristeva, following Freud, argues that drives and the unconscious operate outside of linear time – much like the Woman's encounter with the mirror reflecting her future, present, and past selves. Subjectivity is always in process at this temporal intersection of time and timelessness. One of the interminable tasks in analysis is for the analysand to inscribe the timelessness of the unconscious and trauma into the linear time of language, that is, to give it intelligible form, something Graham does through the structure of the choreography.

Mallarmé's 'Hérodiade' already contained the temporal ambiguity seen in Graham's dance, an ambiguity parallel to that surrounding Hérodiade's identity discussed in the introduction. Asking the Nurse to hold up the mirror for her, Mallarmé's Hérodiade says to it: 'O mirror! Cold water frozen by ennui in your frame, / how many times and through what hours, distressed / by dreams and searching my memories, like leaves / under your ice in the deep hole, have I / appeared in you like a shadow far away, / but, horror! In the dusk, in your austere pool / I have known the nakedness of my scattered dreams!' (1957: 31, 33). Looking in the mirror she sees memories, as well as dreams of the future now destroyed. Here the metaphor of frozen water suggests being arrested or stuck in time. These lines about the mirror inspired Graham's original title *Mirror before Me* and their nonlinear temporality lent themselves well to Graham's choreography. In the plots of many works throughout her career she explored the elasticity of time. In particular, Graham often borrowed a convention from Noh theatre, in which the action has already taken place and is recalled as memory (Jowitt 1988: 215, 218), something also seen in Graham's later retelling of the Oedipus myth *Night Journey* (1947), which begins with Jocasta contemplating suicide and remembering the events between her and her son.

The plots for Graham's dances hinged on what she called 'the instant', that is, in the words of Stodelle, 'a moment of extreme emotional crisis as the core of her story... that sudden, blinding realization of one's true role in life... and death' (Stodelle 1984: 128). In the case of *Hérodiade*, the instant is a sudden crisis about ageing. The temporal paradoxes experienced by both Mallarmé's and Graham's subjects standing before mirrors resonate with analytical timelessness spelled out by Kristeva in *Intimate Revolt*. Kristeva notes that Freudian timelessness is a scandalous interruption of conscious linear time by manifestations of unconscious forces: drives, memories, dreams. Repetition and difference play a role in the experience of Mallarmé's Hérodiade and Graham's Woman: in both cases the character recalls the many times she has appeared before the mirror, all felt in the present moment, and also experiences a crisis, a scandal. Taking into account its Latin root *scandulum*, meaning impediment or obstacle – like the frozen water of the mirror which causes Hérodiade to become psychically stuck – Kristeva argues that the Freudian scandal is one of time. The West since Greece has thought of time as coextensive to consciousness and mind and has considered duration as an immediate given of consciousness. But what happens to time when we posit an unconscious? The Freudian scandal erupts when time is freed of consciousness linearity in three manifestations spelled out by Freud as described by Kristeva:

> the specific temporality of the indestructible drive that is manifested first as the pleasure principle aiming for the fulfillment of desires (notably in dreams...); then... in repetition (and the compulsion for repetition); finally, in the favored mode of the archaic, the indestructible and immortal are revealed... [in] the death instinct.
>
> (IR 30)

Those three manifestations quoted by Kristeva run parallel to the narrative arc of Graham's *Hérodiade*. The dance is predicated in desire, as indicated in the programme notes, and then turns to a series of compulsive repetitions, specifically 'the three rebukes', as Bannerman has called them (Bannerman 2006: 9, 13). Bannerman notes that these rebukes follow the structure of Mallarmé's poem which describes three rebukes when the Nurse tried (1) to kiss Hérodiade's hand, (2) offer her perfumes and (3) adjust her hair (Bannerman 2006: 13). Each of these moments in the dance creates a mounting tension before the Woman almost violently recoils from the Attendant discharging the drives (Bannerman 2006: 14). The piece ends in an act symbolic of the 'archaic and indestructible death instinct' when the Attendant helps the Woman remove her dark dress, revealing a light one underneath; the Attendant exits the stage at which point the Woman wraps herself in a dark shroud, briefly extends her arms in a cruciform shape and then curls inward as if in a cocoon.

The dance is a way of working through the death drive. In the analytic situation this is done in part through the dissolution of transference, which signals both the possibility of the analyst's death and one's own. The temporality of the dance was personal for Graham:

> One of the two works Isamu made for me that touched me most deeply is the central image for *Hérodiade*, a dance that came as a great crisis in my life, in 1944. I wanted the images of a woman, waiting, wandering within the landscape of her own psyche, her own bleached bones placed before the black mirror of her fate. When you look in the mirror, what do you see? Do you only see what you want to see and not what is there? If

you are introspective *you see your own death*. A mirror is an instrument of introspection, its use is to search for the truth.

(Graham 1991: 224, emphasis mine)

As a mode of introspection, Graham's mirror reflects on the death drive, but also on the erotic drive, particularly as it was initially a site for remembering youthful desires. It is a place of alienation at times, but not the specular alienation of Lacan's mirror in which the subject identifies with an image external to himself or herself. Instead, Graham's mirror reveals a *temporal* alienation. As multiple temporalities are condensed into one reflection, the subject visualizes in the mind's eye a psychic image of her past youthful self that feels incongruent with the physical reflection before her in the present; simultaneously she anticipates her future death, which is perhaps an even more discordant experience of the subject contemplating the annihilation of her subjectivity altogether.

Reflecting maternal subjectivity

The *Zeitlos* embodied in Noguchi's mirror and Graham's movement points in one direction to archaic mother-infant relationships that form the core of the semiotic discussed in the first section, but it also points to the inevitability of the death drive discussed in the preceding section. These dual directions in time speak to the temporal paradoxes of subjectivity and are intertwined with the ambiguity of the Woman's identity with which this chapter began. Graham's notion of the past was informed by a different psychoanalytic tradition than Kristeva's, namely Jungian analysis and notions of a collective unconscious, as when she speaks of a 'blood memory' passed on for thousands of years, a concept so important to her thinking that it became the title of her autobiography. But Graham also cites the transmission of this memory within an Oedipal family structure that resonates with Kristeva's semiotic: 'For all of us, but particularly for a dancer with his intensification of life and his body, there is a blood memory that can speak to us. *Each of us from our mother and father has received their blood and through their parents and their parents' parents and backward into time*. We carry a thousand years of that blood and its memory' (Graham 1991: 10, emphasis mine). Here I will focus specifically on the corporeal memory between mother and daughter. Reflecting on this temporal mirroring in mother-daughter relationships, Kristeva writes, 'Women doubtless reproduce among themselves the strange gamut of forgotten body relationships with their mothers' (TL 257), and in this final section I will show how those relationships are articulated in the mirrored movements between Graham's Woman and Attendant, whose identities cross generational boundaries.

Graham's *Hérodiade* can be read as conflating not only the subjectivities of a mother and daughter but their respective temporalities. In Mallarmé's poem the attendant or nurse is older than Hérodiade and identified as a maternal figure who literally nursed her as an infant. The protagonist says to her nurse: 'But who would touch me whom the lions spared? / Besides, I want nothing human, and should you see me, / Sculpted, the eyes lost in paradise, / It is when I remember your milk drunk of old' (1957: 37). However, Graham chose a younger dancer, veteran company member May O'Donnell, to play the role of the Attendant. Graham was twelve years O'Donnell's senior and, of course, the leader of the company. And yet Graham's younger Attendant often plays the maternal role in the piece, like the nurse in Mallarmé's poem, tenderly and unconditionally trying to care for the Woman despite the repeated rebukes. Many of the aforementioned interpretations of the characters in the introduction suggest generational and mother-daughter ambiguity: the Woman in Graham's dance and in Mallarmé's poem could be Herodias or Salomé; the Attendant could be an older caretaker who was once the Woman's nurse, as she is in Mallarmé's poem, or she could be younger than the Woman, as the dancer May O'Donnell was relative to Graham. Stodelle has suggested that the Woman and the Attendant are two sides of one psyche – one the alter ego of the other. Read simultaneously from these different subject positions, *Hérodiade* embodies a psychical mirroring between mother and daughter figures, in which they inhabit not only elements of the other's subjectivity but also the temporality of the other.

In the classical psychoanalytic account of the Oedipal phase, the son splits with the mother and identifies with the father. No longer part of a symbiotic relationship, the male subject takes on a newfound sense of unity after separating from the mother. The daughter too splits with the mother in the Oedipal phase, but as Kristeva points out, since the daughter is also female she, in a sense, splits from herself. That is to say, for both the son and the daughter, the mother's feminine sexuality is rendered abject, but the daughter renders herself abject too insofar as she identifies her body with the mother's body (Oliver 1993: 61). Part of what makes the maternal body abject is maternal eroticism, which Kristeva notes is a notion as taboo today as childhood sexuality was in Freud's time. Kristeva observes there is a common tendency in Western society to separate sexuality from maternity, particularly within 'certain superficial interpretations of contemporary psychoanalysis' which assign 'sexuality exclusively to the [female] lover and the unbearable destiny of object relations to the maternal' (R 69). The woman in Mallarmé's poem has an obsession with her virginity, a fact that would at first put her at odds with the figure of Herodias, who was obviously not a virgin by virtue of the fact she birthed Salomé. This obsession also means that as a mother-figure her character resonates with the idealized Western image of maternity: the Virgin Mary. As Oliver points out in her reading of Kristeva's 'Stabat Mater' and *Black Sun*, traditionally the Virgin Mary has functioned as a figure sanctioned by the Symbolic with which a woman can identify after having to abandon her own mother in Oedipal separation (Oliver 1993: 52). Mallarmé, then, desexualizes Herodias, shaping her to the Western ideal.

Responding to the Western Virgin, Kristeva wrote 'Stabat Mater' in two columns, one giving her own account of pregnancy and birth, the other analysing the figure of the Virgin Mary in the West. Fanny Söderbäck characterizes the two parallel columns of 'Stabat Mater': 'one depicting the lived and embodied (three-dimensional) experience of motherhood, the other unraveling and deconstructing an idealized (two-dimensional) image of Maternity' (2011: 82). Graham similarly restores the three-dimensionality to Mallarmé's character in subtle ways, particularly with respect to her sexuality. The contract-and-release technique described in the first section, in fact, originates in the vagina according to Graham. The vagina is so central to her movement that Graham once even dismissed a particular dancer's ability by saying, 'She never would have been a great dancer. She doesn't move from her vagina' (1991: 212). This movement generated in the vagina then resonates and expands throughout the body as tensions and relaxations. The 'tensive, percussive, and angular motions... frequently executed through a contraction/beat/release pattern', recall both orgasm and the rhythms of labour (Corey 1990: 204–5). In the words of dance scholar Katherine Power, Graham's 'movement lexicon, sourced as it is in the propulsive, ecstatic contraction and release of the pelvis, provided the perfect vehicle for a dance predicated on female desire' (1999: 73). Through choreography, that is dance writing or writing with the body, Graham embodies a feminine *jouissance* and bears witness to maternal sexuality.

According to Kristeva, the loss of the mother must be negated in order for the girl to traverse her trauma, that is, she must not only lose the mother but forget the loss itself. This negation of the loss of the mother signals entry into language (Oliver 1993: 62; BS 43). As the girl forgets the mother's body and adopts the symbolic phallus by acquiring language proper, she participates in the familial and cultural devaluation of the mother's body and by extension women, which leads to disappointment, dissociation and melancholy (SNS 100). In her early work, Kristeva conceded that the girl must separate and forget the mother to become a subject, that the girl must in fact kill the mother in order not to kill herself (Oliver 1993: 62): 'matricide is our vital necessity', she writes (BS 27). The psychical drama of loss and matricide plays out in the movement throughout *Hérodiade*, but particularly near its conclusion. A frequently recurring position of the Attendant is to round her back, either while standing or kneeling, letting the curve extend through all the vertebrae in her neck, as she faces down with her arms out and palms down as if shaping her arms and torso around a large spherical void. This shaping is done at moments of separation from the Woman or when the Attendant tries to get her attention. It is as if she holds the emptiness of the loss of the mother. She is affected and aware of the loss and unable to let it go. It is not an actual thing she holds, but an absence. The ability to lose the mother and negate the loss happens only at the end. The Attendant gravely circles around the Woman, unhooking the Woman's outer garment before removing it like a sheath to reveal a light garment underneath that renders her vulnerable. The Attendant removes a dark cloak that had been hanging on the X-shaped sculpture upstage, places it on the Woman's chair and takes the original worn garment with her as she exits upstage behind the screen. Negating the loss for which she had in fact helped the Woman prepare, the Attendant no longer shapes her body around an emptiness, but stands erect as she turns her back to the Woman and walks away, never looking back. The Attendant's gaze no longer meets the Woman's during her final moments on stage, thus denying the possibility of them reflecting each other's subjectivity through facial mirroring. The Woman takes two deep contractions, as if her womb were in pain, before making one final circle centre stage and wrapping herself in the dark cloak, accepting her death.

Since 2011 Kristeva has offered a corrective to her earlier claims about matricide in her work on *reliance* and maternal eroticism. *Reliance* is a word that Kristeva employs, drawing from its many etymological associations from Old French, French, and English; these include: to link, to gather, to join, to put together, to adhere, to belong to, to depend on, therefore to trust, to feel safe, to share your thoughts and feelings, to assemble together, and *to be yourself* (R 79). The first one, linking, presupposes unlinking, that is to say, identification and differentiation operate in a continuous dialectical play between two subjects connecting and separating. In *reliance* one is not doomed to Echo's fate of merely repeating the love object's words, rather the mother inserts her own voice in the pre-verbal dialogue with the infant. In contrast to passive mirroring, or the notion of the mother as a mere receptacle for infantile fantasy, *reliance* articulates the movement of the drive in the corporeal mirroring that is foundational to the semiotic. Kristeva's mirror is a responsive mirroring which allows the mother to witness and facilitate her daughter's emerging subjectivity while simultaneously forging her own. The way in which the infant's subjectivity emerges from her mother's response has long been articulated in psychoanalytic theory, but mirroring and *reliance* allow us to see how the mother articulates her own subjectivity in response to the other, namely, the infant. Prior to the final death scene, Graham's *Hérodiade* contains elements of this emerging subjectivity through the drive energy in the economy of *reliance*.

Before the Attendant removes the outer garment from the Woman, the prelude to the Woman's death, a tender role reversal takes place in which the Woman ceases her hitherto rageful responses towards the Attendant. The Attendant crouches down in a deep *plié*, feet flat on the floor, and laboriously steps backward downstage. With her thighs wide open, the pose suggests giving birth in a squatting position, an identification with the maternal figure. Her head bowed, she no longer makes eye contact and her hands are folded before her face as if in supplication. At first the Woman frantically dances as she had been doing throughout the dance thus far. But as the Attendant stands up, still and almost despondent, with her back to the Woman and her hand cupped over her face, preventing the audience from meeting her gaze, the Woman's demeanour metamorphizes. First, she slides across the ground on her knees almost mocking the Attendant's squatting pose a moment before. She then rises to her feet but keeps her back bent as if in pain as she hobbles closer. Finally, she stands face to face with the Attendant and places her hands on the Attendant's shoulders. The Attendant's hand still blocks her gaze, preventing the face-to-face mirroring, but the Woman seats the Attendant on the stool as if to offer respite. The Attendant drops her hand but her gaze is directed offstage as she sits erect, unaffected by the Woman who continues dancing alone, until finally she holds a standing position, her gaze upward, one arm raised as if shielding her head. Breaking from her self-absorption, the Attendant rises from her chair to comfort her. Circling the stage, then kneeling down with her torso bowed, the Attendant has her arms open, as if again holding a void. The Woman turns around, scoops her hands under the Attendant's upper arms, echoing the shape of the Attendant, and gently helps her to rise – the closest the two come to an embrace. After this moment the Attendant removes the Woman's garment and the latter accepts her fate.

If we read the Woman as a mother-figure, she moves away from the fragmented, disintegrated psychic state performed earlier in the piece to a state where her subjectivity begins to emerge. Paradoxically, her own subjectivity emerges at the point when she begins caring for another. Prior to this, the Woman had been disconnected from the Attendant, absorbed like Narcissus in her own reflection. But working through the temporality and the inevitability of the death drive, she was also able to connect and offer care. The dance thus oscillates between thanatos and eros, offering an ongoing linking and unlinking between them, and ultimately between the Woman/Attendant and mother/daughter.

Dance and mirroring

'Choreography' literally means 'dance-writing' – writing with and for the body – and as Kristeva's work has largely centred on the relationship of the language to the body, particularly the maternal body, it provides tools for understanding not only Graham's *Hérodiade* and the temporal dramas it embodies but modern dance in general as a revolutionary poetic language of movement. Furthermore, Kristeva's revision of Lacan's mirror stage in particular has larger implications for understanding the process behind modern dance. Dancers spend the vast majority of their professional lives not on stage but rehearsing before the mirrored walls of their studios – in contrast with the painter's studio where the mirror appears only for the novelty of self-portraiture. It is before the mirror that the dancer understands herself as a subject and the intimacies of her body on a new level. Graham wrote: 'The next time you look into the mirror, just look at the way the ears rest next to the head; look at the way the hairline grows; think of all the little bones in your wrist. It is a miracle. And dance is a celebration of that miracle' (1991: 5).

It is before the mirror that the dancer understands herself as an other, that is, as an object for the audience. And it is before the mirror that dancers mirror each other as they learn choreography or pass it down from one generation to the next. There is a temporal ambiguity of subjects mirroring one another across time, anticipating future performances. Dancers see not only themselves but each other in the mirror, and as dancers learn a company's repertoire, say, new dancers learning the parts of the Woman and the Attendant, they reflect the movements of the past.

Even more germane to a study of Kristeva, the transmission of choreography from one dancer to the next is enacted not only by looking into the reflective mirror on the dance studio walls but through the corporeal mirroring in which dancers mirror the movement of another dancer. Graham wrote the choreography for *Hérodiade*, both the part of the Woman and that of the Attendant, and then O'Donnell mirrored Graham's movement during rehearsal to learn the latter part. The mirror before the mirror in Kristeva's revision of the mirror stage, that is, the corporeal mirroring between mother and infant that first takes place prior to the mirror stage, is rendered explicit in dance rehearsal. Although mirroring has its precedent in the mother-infant relationship, it is not a terminable event. The semiotic modality in language, operative in the speaking subject in the present, resonates with past mother-infant mirroring, and subjects continue to mirror one another throughout their lives. Like Graham's Woman before the mirror experiencing her present subjectivity as a conflicting composite of memory and future visions, the subject in Kristeva's work is always living at the intersection of conscious time and the Freudian *Zeitlos*.

References

Bannerman, H. (2006), 'A Dance of Transition: Martha Graham's *Hérodiade* (1944)', *Dance Research: The Journal of the Society for Dance Research*, 24 (1): 1–20.

Corey, F. (1990), 'Martha Graham's Re-Vision of Jocasta, Clytemnestra, and Medea', *Text and Performance Quarterly*, 10 (3): 204–17.

De Mille, A. (1991), *Martha: The Life and Work of Martha Graham*, New York: Random House.
Franko, M. (2012), *Martha Graham in Love and War: The Life in the Work*, Oxford: Oxford University Press.
Graham, M. (1991), *Blood Memory*, New York: Doubleday.
Jowitt, D. (1988), *Time and the Dancing Image*, Berkeley, CA: University of California Press.
Lacan, J. (1977 [1949]), 'The Mirror Stage as Formative of the Function of the I', in A. Sheridan (trans.), *Écrits: A Selection*, 1–7, New York: W. W. Norton.
Lacan, J. (1988 [1955]), *The Seminar of Jacques Lacan, the Ego in Freud's Theory and in the Technique of Psychoanalysis, 1954–1955*, II, trans. S. Tomaselli, Cambridge: Cambridge University Press.
Mallarmé, S. (1957), 'Hérodiade', in C. F. MacIntyre (trans.), *Stéphane Mallarmé: Selected Poems*, 20–45, Berkeley: University of California Press.
Oliver, K. (1993), *Reading Kristeva: Unraveling the Double-Bind*, Bloomington, IN: Indiana University Press.
Power, K. (1999). 'Raging Mothers: Maternal Subjectivity and Desire in the Dance Theater of Martha Graham', *Journal of Dramatic Theory and Criticism*, 14 (1): 65–78.
Söderbäck, F. (2011), 'Motherhood According to Kristeva: On Time and Matter in Plato and Kristeva', *philoSOPHIA*, 1 (1): 65–87.
Stodelle, E. (1984), *Deep Song: The Dance Story of Martha Graham*, New York: Schirmer Books.

PART THREE

Glossary

14

Abjection

Dawid Kołoszyc

The concept of 'abjection' was developed in Kristeva's first explicitly psychoanalytic work, *Powers of Horror: An Essay on Abjection*, and remains one of the most widely referenced, though also one of the most elusive, concepts in her thought. Like Freud's notion of the 'uncanny', to which it loosely corresponds, abjection as defined by Kristeva has proven relevant not only to psychoanalysis but also to literary theory, art criticism, cinema studies, cultural studies, gender studies, religious studies, cultural anthropology and political theory.

   Kristeva approaches abjection by way of the original, Latin connotations of the term – the state of rejection, degradation, abasement, of being cast off – in order to posit the abject as the name for a certain 'nothing' at the very limits of the thinkable, the signifiable, the subjective. While echoing Kristeva's conception of the semiotic *chora*, defined as a maternal 'place' or 'receptacle' that marks the emergence of the human being prior to any symbolic meaning, abjection refers to the more archaic event of expulsion which accompanies the newborn's separation from the maternal body: 'In this process, which I have called abjection, the mother becomes the first "abject" rather than [the first] object' (HF 12; see also HF 184). The abject therefore figures, first and foremost, as a non-object (or pseudo-object) that signifies only the absolute absence of meaning or, following entry into the world of symbolic thought, the absolute collapse of meaning – and of coherent subjectivity. 'The abject is not an ob-ject facing me, which I name or imagine … The abject has only one quality of the object – that of being opposed to I' (PH 1). Playing with the language of object relations theory, Kristeva thus affirms the radical alterity of her notion of the abject; whereas objects, regardless of how we define them, help establish an 'equilibrium in the fragile web of desire and meaning, the abject excludes me and pulls me to where meaning collapses. "Something" I do not recognize as a thing. A weight of nonsense that has nothing significant about it and yet crushes me' (HF 184).

While separation from the maternal serves as the prototype for the experience of the abject, food loathing constitutes 'the most elementary and most archaic form of abjection' (PH 2; see also HF 185) for an infant endowed with a basic sense of its material borders prior to any conception of concrete objects. Food consumption introduces an otherness which violates, for the first time in its life, the infant's physical boundaries or, at the very least, injects a sense of uncertainty about such boundaries, ultimately demanding a certain amount of regulation in order to avoid risks to one's bodily integrity – including the risk of sickness and death. Subject to a recurring drive towards nutrition which saves it from starvation, the infant is bound to encounter, on a regular basis, a foreign substance whose very consistency may trigger anxiety or repulsion.

> Spasms and vomiting protect me: I use them throughout my life, in my repugnance – the intermittent retching that will distance me from, and allow me to avoid, objects and extreme situations that I experience as menacing and dangerous: defilement, sewage, sordidness, the ignominy of compromise, in-between states, betrayal.
>
> (HF 185)

As the human subject, encouraged by social conceptions of otherness, develops a more concrete idea of its borders, it also develops a sense of repulsion with respect to substances expelled by the body. Faced with its own 'waste', therefore, the human subject first experiences its body in the process of producing something radically other: a 'nothing' that offers the first hint of the possibility of the subject's eventual return to the state of non-being, to death as the final act of bodily defilement. Recoiling in horror, the subject struggles to erect a physical or symbolic border between herself as a distinct being and that which serves as a troubling reminder of this being's tentative, temporary nature:

> refuse and corpses show me what I permanently thrust aside in order to live. These bodily fluids, this defilement, this shit are what life withstands, hardly and with difficulty, on the part of death. There, I am at the border of my condition as a living being. My body extricates itself, as being alive, from that border. Such wastes drop so that I might live, until, from loss to loss, nothing remains in me and my entire body falls beyond the limit – *cadere*, cadaver.
>
> (PH 3)

Playing with the etymological meaning of 'cadaver' – to fall, decline, perish – Kristeva emphasizes the experience of death as the most radical form of abjection, beyond any possibility of meaningful signification.

> The corpse, seen without God and outside of science, is the utmost of abjection. It is death infecting life. Abject. It is something rejected from which one does not part, from which one does not protect oneself as from an object. Imaginary uncanniness and real threat, it beckons to us and ends up engulfing us.
>
> (PH 4)

As an impossible pseudo-object which both fascinates and repulses, the abject may be said to constitute a 'negative' version of Lacan's impossible object of desire: the object *a*. While the object *a* names something elusive within the other – ultimately, the other's inexplicable desire rather than some inexplicable feature or quality – the abject remains inherently ambiguous in its effect, pointing to a non-existence that threatens to engulf the subject: 'Fascinating and unsettling, it solicits desire, but desire is not seduced: frightened, it turns away; disgusted, it rejects. Not that!' (HF 184). Kristeva's approach indicates, in this respect, that Lacan's discussions of the subject of desire miss the crucial point that subjectivity is not simply sustained (or driven) by the desire for something which, at the intersection of subject and object, is experienced as a 'lack', but also, more fundamentally, by an ongoing effort to affirm its existence beyond the sense of primordial lack which haunts it. Lacan's 'object of lack', according to Kristeva, has become something of a fetish in psychoanalytic discourse, at times preventing rather than encouraging critical reflection on the so-called subject of desire:

> if we imagine ... that the experience of lack, which follows separation, is logically and chronologically prior to the being of the object and correlatively to the being of the subject, then we understand that the only psychosexual significance of *lack* (a noble, ascetic term) is abjection. That is, abjection is the only possible narrative of the experience of lack. Isn't this precisely what literature, religion, and mysticism tell us?
>
> (HF 186)

By the same token, the Other in the Lacanian sense – the other as language, as the symbolic order, as an ideal or demand – is preceded by the Other as the maternal body from which the fragile and egoless human being must first extricate itself. The act of 'rejection' involved in this process serves as a model for every subsequent act of repression: a *primal repression* prior to the emergence of the repressive ego. As Kristeva asserts, 'A pseudo-object, the abject would be the object of original repression' (HF 187). In *Powers of Horror*, she defines primal repression as 'the ability of the speaking being, always already haunted by the Other, to divide, reject, repeat' (PH 12). This definition is echoed, almost word for word, in *Hatred and Forgiveness*, while adding that this ability manifests itself prior to 'the constitution of subject/object (this will occur with secondary repression)' (HF 187). Before the constitution of the unconscious in the formal, subjective sense, something must be disavowed already at a more primordial, psychosomatic level. The split between the conscious and unconscious mind is preceded by a split between 'being' and 'non-being' from which the 'I' emerges, never quite perfectly, on the side of 'being'. And the process of identification associated with Lacan's mirror stage is preceded by the alienation experienced when the first, indistinct boundaries of the infant are invaded or threatened by something not quite definitely *other*.

> Here we are at the borders of human universe in formation. At this threshold there is no unconscious; it will be constructed when representations and the affects linked to them (or not) form a logic. Consciousness has not yet transformed the fluid demarcations of still unstable territories into signifiers, where an I in formation is constantly losing its way.
>
> (HF 187)

This quote, along with several others that precede it, also helps clarify why, despite the proximity between her concept of the abject and Freud's concept of the uncanny, Kristeva insists on their distinction. Although her earliest descriptions of abjection resonate with Freud's language, they do so with a noticeable difference:

> A massive and sudden emergence of uncanniness, which, familiar as it might have been in an opaque and forgotten life, now harries me as radically separate, loathsome. Not me. Not that. But no nothing, either. A 'something' that I do not recognize as a thing. A weight of meaninglessness, about which there is nothing insignificant, and which crushes me.
>
> (PH 2)

Freud's 'uncanny' describes the experience of something familiar (or seemingly familiar) yet eerie or unsettling, which the subject encounters in the form of an object, a person or a situation. As such, it introduces a sense of estrangement in the very midst of an otherwise familiar reality composed of concrete subjects and objects. Abjection, on the contrary, involves the 'return' of a primordial 'nothing' – or, more precisely: nothing recognizable or familiar in the strict sense – which threatens to dissolve the subject's essential, if partly imaginary, sense of existing as a distinct body/mind within a more or less meaningful, more or less stable reality. Infusing the subject with a recollection of its own, former 'non-being' – of its emergence into 'being', '[b]etween an object not yet separated as such and the subject I have yet to become' (HF 184) – and, simultaneously, with the impossible to assimilate sense of the inevitability of its eventual return to non-existence – abjection at its most extreme is captured effectively in Kristeva's explorations of depression in *Black Sun*. In this text, Kristeva describes the experience of an unnameable *Thing*: a nothing, a wound, a black hole (BS 87), which figures at the core of the depressed subject yet remains beyond his or her capacity for symbolization which is to say, too, beyond any *meaningful* distinction between the familiar and the unfamiliar. The Thing names, as it were, the ultimate symptom in the life of the speaking subject: the invasion of the subject's body and language by what feels like a foreign, dead entity. Kristeva's understanding of abjection thus reconfigures not only Freud's understanding of the uncanny but also his understanding of the return of the repressed. Whereas, in Freud's thought, the repressed primarily revolts against the ego as the agent of repression, Kristeva emphasizes the return of the abject as a threat to the ego's narcissistic assumption of clear psychosomatic borders, and of its mastery over the territory they contain. 'Abjection is therefore a kind of *narcissistic crisis*' (PH 14), even if it also figures as 'the precondition of narcissism' (HF 187) – marking the infant's primary sense of becoming a separate entity. Moreover, Kristeva reconceptualizes, in this context, Freud's understanding of sublimation as the transformation of repressed drives and affects into subjectively and culturally meaningful, productive or *sublime* activities. In Kristeva's theory of abjection, sublimation describes, first and foremost, the subject's capacity to name the unnameable non-object at the core of his or her being. 'In the symptom, the abject permeates me, I become abject. Through sublimation, I keep it under control. The abject is edged with the sublime' (PH 11; see also HF 187). Sublimation thus provides the most effective means of reconstituting the abject beyond the radical ambiguity that threatens to return the subject (and society) to 'those fragile states where man strays on the territories of animal' (PH 12).

Insofar as such radical ambiguity destabilizes the borders between the material, the subjective and the social, abjection as a subjective experience remains inherently linked with various aspects of Kristeva's cultural theory. In terms of Freud's psychic topography, Kristeva describes the abject as both the product and the troubling adversary of the superego: 'To each ego its object, to each superego its abject' (PH 2). Similarly, in cultural terms, the abject figures as an essential threat to social conventions, regulations and ideals. Abjection, in the extended sense, therefore constitutes anything that 'disturbs identity, system, order. What does not respect borders, positions, rules. The in-between, the ambiguous, the composite' (PH 4). For this reason, every social, cultural, moral, political or religious system struggles with abjection from the very beginning; the abject must be concealed, disavowed, expelled or kept at a safe distance in order for the social order to come into existence – and remain in order. Be that as it may, abjection tends to assume the form of a radical 'perversion' or corruption of the social order, rather than a direct refusal of it, as though to remind it, all the more effectively, 'that the impossible constitutes its very *being*, that it *is* none other than abject' (PH 5). Indeed, Kristeva considers this sort of 'transgression' to be the most explicit form in which the abject manifests itself within any social order: what has been cast aside through prohibition defiles that prohibition through the very means set up to maintain the semblance of a world of proper, acceptable, coherent subjects and objects. The basis of Kristeva's analysis, in this regard, is formulated around a theory of religion which resonates with aspects of George Bataille's and Mary Douglas' thought. Every religious order is constructed around explicit or implicit taboos – whether sexual, dietary or spatial – and every taboo sets up the conditions for a return of the abject within a transgression. Thus 'any religion is in fact a way of purifying the abject' (HF 13). One of the earliest and most powerful examples of this may be found in the Hindu caste system, which, assuming a radical split between purity and impurity, relegates an entire social group to the status of 'untouchables' and assigns to it the task of looking after abject aspects of human existence, such as the removal of human waste and the burial of the dead. The Christian doctrine of original sin, which sets up a principle of corruption both at the beginning of human history and at the very core of every individual human being, embodies, in Kristeva's view, the most elaborate attempt to contain abjection in Western religious thought. However, due to what Kristeva considers to be an ongoing crisis of Christian discourses and metaphysics in modern Western culture, literature and art have emerged as the primary means of responding to abjection – reaching all the way back to its most 'archaic', pre-Christian manifestations. The most extreme example of this is arguably Sade, whose name has become synonymous with modern transgression as a radical defilement of the Law, particularly insofar as this transgression serves to affirm, in a violently perverse manner, the death of (the Christian conception of) God and the end of the moral, social and metaphysical order this death entails. Beyond the violence of Sade's literary ventures, modern literature has nonetheless succeeded in offering linguistically, psychologically and culturally diverse sublimations of abjection and, as such, Kristeva regards it as the most revolutionary attempt to give meaning to the experience of 'non-being' formerly addressed within discourses on the sacred.

By the same token, Kristeva's theory of abjection echoes her theory of revolution in poetic language, with psychoanalysis now joining the revolutionary effort in a more prominent manner, both as a clinical practice and as a theoretical and critical discourse, returning us – individually and collectively – and returning *to us*, what had been excluded, rejected or repressed at the limits of our corporeal, psychic and social being. The concept of abjection, in other words, allows Kristeva to reconsider the task of analysis around giving a name to the unnameable: no longer the unnameable object of desire but also the unnameable abject at the core of one's troubled being, presenting a permanent challenge to subjectivity and symbolization. Crucially, this task does not allow for a clear separation between subjective and social crises; indeed, its aim is to bear witness, both practically and critically, to the fact that, on the one hand, abjection 'is a universal phenomenon: one encounters it as soon as the symbolic and/or social dimension of man is constituted, and this throughout the course of civilization', and, on the other hand, that 'abjection assumes specific shapes and different codings according to the various "symbolic systems"' (PH 68). The implications of the latter point are particularly easy to miss. Kristeva's argument is that abjection is not simply an objective threat to the human subject and the symbolic order that supports it but rather a threat that, to a considerable extent, is constructed and sustained by the process of its physical, psychological and/or symbolic exclusion. This becomes apparent, for instance, when we consider seemingly irrational religious taboos related to food, clothes, language, social interaction, gender or sexuality. One of the most significant aspects of psychoanalysis, in this respect, is its capacity to explore, alongside and beyond their literary sublimations, both subjective and social sources of abjection in a manner that helps, on the one hand, disentangle the real, imaginary and symbolic powers of its horror, and, on the other hand, allows for a meaningful, honest reconsideration of the real, imaginary and symbolic origins of the Law to which we remain subject.

> The border between abjection and the sacred, between desire and knowledge, between death and society, can be faced squarely, uttered without sham innocence or modest self-effacement, provided one sees in it an incidence of man's particularity as *mortal and speaking*. 'There is an abject' is henceforth stated as, 'I am abject, that is, mortal and speaking.'
> (PH 88)

As Kristeva is quick to emphasize, in this regard, the concepts of 'abjection' and the 'abject' emerged in the course of her early clinical experience in response to symptoms she considered as unique to late modern culture, 'in which the distinction between "subject" and "object" is not clear, and in which these two pseudo-entities exhaust themselves in a dialectic of attraction and repulsion' (HF 12). Such 'new maladies of the soul', as she calls them, manifest themselves in borderline personalities, as well as in certain forms of depression, anxiety, phobia or paranoia that haunt modern subjects. Beyond individual afflictions, modern abjection also manifests itself in certain kinds of social and political phenomena, such as extreme, irrational hatred aimed at people or concepts whose real, imaginary or symbolic foreignness is seen as a danger to the stability of the boundaries that are presumed to guarantee collective purity, safety or merely familiarity. It is on account of these concerns that, since the late 1970s, Kristeva's work has come to privilege psychoanalysis as the signifying practice best equipped to address the problem of abjection in the experience of the modern subject both within and beyond clinical practice. 'Psychoanalysis – as the locus of extreme abjection, the refuge of private horror that can be lifted only by an infinite-indefinite displacement in speech and its effects – represents for me today the logical consequence of my initial questioning, which it still allows me to pursue' (PK 10). This does not mean, to be sure, that psychoanalysis is a replacement for religious and poetic language; rather, it constitutes a clinical/critical practice that must remain at a radical proximity to certain kinds of religious and literary concerns in a manner that is neither merely conventional nor merely deconstructive in its treatment of the symbolic resources embodied within the social, cultural, moral and political order.

15

Avant-garde

Christos Hadjiyiannis

The 'avant-garde' features centrally in Julia Kristeva's writings. Kristeva invokes the term frequently and uses it in its customary double sense: to refer to art that is experimental and unconventional, and to art that seeks to be political through erasing boundaries between art and life praxis. Though she does not offer a unified theory of the avant-garde, and despite appearing at times hesitant about its capacity for fundamental political change, Kristeva finds in the avant-garde a practice and a process invested with possibilities for creative instability, radical rupture and change. Most crucial of all, Kristeva sees the avant-garde as a dynamic process representing the dialectical condition of the subject in language, 'a subject in process/on trial' (RPL 23, 37, 111).

Understood as a general aesthetic category, 'avant-garde' indicates radical experimentation with literary or artistic norms. As a historical term, the 'avant-garde' refers to the practices of writers and artists at work in the late nineteenth and early twentieth centuries who challenged existing conventions, whether through revolutionizing form or through radically redefining what counts as legitimate artistic content. This is what is often called the 'historical avant-garde' and, within the context of modernism, it includes such movements as Futurism, Vorticism, *Der Blaue Reiter*, Cubism, Dada and Surrealism. Though aware that the avant-garde undoes any strict distinctions between artistic media, Kristeva focuses chiefly on the literary avant-garde and has in mind specifically Lautréamont, Mallarmé, Artaud, Joyce and Aragon. But applying the term in its broader sense, too, she uses it to describe later innovative approaches to literature by Philippe Sollers and the writers in the *Tel Quel* circle, who were experimenting in the 1960s and

1970s with the *nouveau roman*. In keeping with other genealogies of the avant-garde that trace its roots back to the German Romanticism of the Jena group, Kristeva finds literature's earliest 'encounter with the impossible' in the genre-bending writing published in the *Athenaeum* (the journal set up by the Schlegel brothers in 1798).[1] That was the time when, Kristeva explains, literature 'renounced its role as purveyor of beautiful language and seductive beauty', stopped being 'religion's little sister' and began to ask difficult questions, including questions about its own conditions of possibility. From then onwards, literature 'first entered a radical debate... with religion and philosophy'; then 'it explored the impasses of consciousness and associated itself with madness'; until, finally, 'it came up against the resistance of social reality in order not to disavow it but to reflect it no longer and, more, to disavow the imaginary, and thus literature, in favor of social reality' (SNS 107). According to the timeline presented in *The Sense and Non-Sense of Revolt* (1996), literature's encounter with the impossible in French literature can be divided into three periods: 'the first is that of Rimbaud, Lautréamont, and Mallarmé; the second is surrealism; the third, *Tel Quel*' (SNS 107).

What has traditionally distinguished the 'avant-garde' from other experimental forms of writing is its distinct social and political intention – its promise and ambition to challenge and disrupt prevailing political, social and even economic orders. To give one well-known example: Marcel Duchamp's 1917 readymade urinal, *Fountain*, attacked bourgeois notions of what art is, challenging not only viewers' expectations but also the institution of art and the market machinations that underpin it. For Peter Bürger, herein precisely lies the success – and inevitable limit – of the historical avant-garde: while the avant-garde artwork attacks the idea of art as autonomous by denaturalizing artistic genius as the source of aesthetic value, in the end it is subsumed and co-opted by institutions that always and necessarily mediate between art and life.[2] In this reading, later avant-gardes can only be seen as inauthentic postures lacking the insurrectionary powers that the historical avant-garde promised. Kristeva holds at times on to a similar 'melancholic' attitude towards the avant-garde's potential to subvert the political as Bürger did. Yet approaching the avant-garde from within a much broader, sociocultural, subjective context, she has continued to look to its power to disrupt the conventional in creative and emancipatory ways.

A common thread running between various manifestations of the historical avant-garde is the idea that literature and art more broadly can – and ought to – break through conventional discourse. Within writers, this conviction has often been cast as an opposition between 'prose' and 'poetry'. The antithesis is not to be taken in its literal sense: 'prose' is the language of mundane communication, whereas 'poetry' is the advance guard of language. 'Poetry', the domain of the *avant-gardiste*, contains the new, the original, the cutting edge and the intuitive; it is a means of communication that has an intensity and directness lacking in 'prose', which is the used, commodified language of the marketplace and of dated social and philosophical systems. We find a version of this distinction in the writings of *avant-gardistes* from Mallarmé and Hofmannsthal through to Apollinaire, Shklovsky, Stramm, de Gourmont, Hulme and Pound.[3] We also find a version of this distinction (though reconfigured) in Kristeva's theorization of the avant-garde. To be clear, none of Kristeva's distinctions – between the symbolic and the semiotic, phenotext and genotext, or stasis and rejection – can be mapped on to the antithesis between 'prose' and 'poetry' postulated by these earlier thinkers. However, her understanding of poetic language as language that is transrational, trans-subjective and trans-syntactic does follow in a not-too-dissimilar vein.

Key to understanding Kristeva's discussion of the avant-garde is her distinction between the symbolic (associated with syntax, grammar, position and judgement) and the semiotic (referring to the instinctual processes and energies she associates with Freudian 'drives'). Both are essential to signification. The symbolic provides stability, keeping signification structured, while the semiotic provides movement or what Kristeva names 'negativity'. The symbolic is a signifying modality operating through rules and codes that help us communicate shared or established meanings. The semiotic is transversal to meaning: it embraces the less visible role of tone, gesture and rhythm and the non-discursive aspects of meaning and subjectivity, those related to embodied experience, material and biological processes, and to affect and emotion. The semiotic, to put it another way, affects language by disrupting it and by multiplying meaning. In *Powers of Horror* (1980), Kristeva connected the semiotic force of instinctual drives to abject or revolting aspects of the maternal, her idea in this book being that the revolting becomes revolutionary through the return of the repressed maternal within paternally-connoted symbolic systems (PH 409). In *Revolution in Poetic Language* (1974), she focused instead on the semiotic *chora*: the space in which drives enter language. The semiotic *chora* is a place of perpetual renewal in the signifying process, and a space associated with the maternal body and the sounds and rhythms connected with it – though we should not identify it too closely with the mother's body. It is, Kristeva writes, a 'nonexpressive totality formed by the drives and their stases in a motility that is as full of movement as it is regulated' (RPL 25). These drives do not have their source in the naturalized body of the mother, nor in the naturalized organs of the infant; rather, they emerge as preverbal marks full of capacities not yet inscribed in the symbolic.[4] The symbolic and the semiotic yield in turn two different types of text: the *phenotext*, the signifying dimension of language; and the *genotext*, the poetic aspects of language which open signification to a process of crisis and renewal. The phenotext is structured and grammatical, making communication possible, whereas the genotext has a capacity for play and pleasure and reveals an underlying drive force in language that cannot be calculated. Invoking an analogy used by several historical *avant-gardistes*, Kristeva describes the phenotext as static and as calculated in algebra (RPL 87). Crucially for understanding the central function of the avant-garde in Kristeva's thinking, genotexts are actualized in poetic language – in texts that convey the crises within the signifying process.

In Kristeva's reading, the historical avant-garde's shattering of conventional discourse was a result of changing social structures in the nineteenth century. The idea is one shared by other theorists of the avant-garde, who, like Kristeva, trace its roots in modernity's many contradictions.[5] Gaps between social practices and their representation in the dominant ideology, loss of meaning and of value from institutional discourses and language, and the effacement of lived experience always cause a great amount of frustration and a deep repression of human capacities. Abandoning narrow sociological explanations of the avant-garde in favour of a psychoanalytic angle, and bringing into discussion Freud's theory of the death drive, Kristeva maintains that the frustration and repression felt by many in the nineteenth century produced negativity and rejection drives.[6] These are drives that avant-garde literature has always tried to channel – as Kristeva puts it, the avant-garde always brings 'into play the speaking body's complex relationship with society' (I 97). The key word here is 'complex', for Kristeva is keen to make clear that the avant-garde embraces many different and overlapping crises: of language, of subjectivity, of politics among them.[7] In this broad sense, the works of Lautréamont, Mallarmé, Artaud and Joyce represent a signifying practice that 'attests to a "crisis" of social structures' (RPL 15).[8]

In *Revolution in Poetic Language* and elsewhere in her work, Kristeva details the different ways in which the avant-garde pulverizes linguistic structures and meanings, shattering the syntactic stability and the constructions of identity that belong to the symbolic – whether it's the way Lautréamont 'shatters conceptual unity into rhythms [and] logical distortions' or how Mallarmé employs 'paragrams and syntactic inventions' in order to disrupt any sense of unity (RPL 185). Not that the avant-garde text is equal to the semiotic; as literature it is, after all, part symbolic language. What an avant-garde text does, according to Kristeva, is reactivate the contradiction between the symbolic and the semiotic, and so reveal the process of signification. Kristeva compares it to a Hegelian experience, which, however, does not lead to resolution. The Hegelian dialectic has three sides or moments: the moment of understanding or fixity, the 'dialectical' or 'negative' moment of instability, and the 'speculative' or 'positive' moment when contraries are dissolved. Kristeva makes Hegel's second moment – the negative moment of dissolution – the organizing principle of the signifying process. She is interested in that which dissolves unity (as opposed to contradictions), that which multiplies meaning – that which is governed by what she calls a 'productive dissolution' (SP 138). This is the possibility Kristeva finds in the literary avant-garde: avant-garde literature, she writes, 'combines rejection, its signifying reversal, *and* its "knowledge"', and, further, it 'constitutes a process, but one that analyzes itself endlessly' (RPL 188).

The literary avant-garde in Kristeva's understanding is therefore at once a dynamic process representing a crisis, a process that disrupts the symbolic moment and a process that never ceases to harness its own disruptive negativity.[9] This is ultimately how heterogeneous, 'incomprehensible' texts – whether those of Lautréamont, Mallarmé, Artaud, Joyce, the Surrealists, Aragon or Sollers – operate. They are engaged in an unresolved, open dialogue with themselves. They make transparent the process through which signification is possible and reactivate the inherent contradiction between the symbolic and the semiotic. In so doing, they bring negativity and rejection to the foreground of signification. Semiotic negativity is important because it is a necessary element of the signifying process that cannot be incorporated into symbolic stasis. Deliberately playing with negativity, poetic language fragments the signifying unity of ordinary language and challenges its logic. Thinking specifically of Lautréamont and Mallarmé, Kristeva explains that their poetic language has remodelled traditional and historical expectations 'through the proposition of the representation of a different relation to natural objects, to social apparatuses, and to the body itself' (SP 142).

The key question for Kristeva – and the one that sets her apart from those scholars of the avant-garde who approach it from a social and political perspective – is how the dynamics of avant-garde poetic language relate to subjectivity. In short, Kristeva maintains that, by unsettling fixity and identity and subverting the symbolic, avant-garde writing represents the dialectical condition of the subject in language. When a text disrupts the inertia of language habits, it invites us to study the becoming of the significations of signs and, in doing so, to free ourselves from linguistic, psychic and social networks. Further, insofar as an avant-garde text manifests a semiotic dimension (is genotext), it channels and reveals drives connected to the semiotic: the pre/trans-symbolic, the pre/trans-verbal, the abject maternal. It may do so by paying attention to devices such as alliteration, consonance and rhyme (what Kristeva calls 'phonematic devices') or intonation and rhythm ('melodic devices'). It may be a nineteenth-century text by Mallarmé, an early twentieth-century work by Joyce or a *nouveau roman* by Sollers, in whose 1973 novel *H*, for instance, Kristeva saw 'my own negation erected as representation' (DL 163). What matters is that, whether inside or outside the text, the subject-in-process is caught up in radical heterogeneity. Just as the subject-in-process of writing is a subjectivity in revolt against the signifier, so the subject-in-process outside literature is engaged in a struggle between the social and the singular, a struggle, in short, between the symbolic and the semiotic.

Early on in *Revolution in Poetic Language*, Kristeva writes that 'The text is a practice that could be compared to political revolution: the one brings about in the subject what the other introduces into society' (RPL 17). She makes a similar point in *The Sense and Non-Sense of Revolt* (2000), where she rescues 'revolt' from its strictly political meaning, drawing instead links between political and formal revolts (SNS 3, 7). Reconfiguring the terms of the *avant-gardiste* desire to merge politics and art, Kristeva makes it clear that the literary practice she favours is one that treats literature as inseparable from politics. She calls this literary practice *signifiance*, a signifying process that capitalist society represses, and which Kristeva describes as 'this unceasing operation of the drives towards, in, and through the exchange system and its protagonists – the subject and his institutions' (RPL 17). In various places in her work, however, she appears sceptical about the avant-garde's ability actually to impact the political. In fact, in some ways, she says, the historical avant-garde is actually a symptom of this failure, born as it was in a moment when social dissatisfactions (the ones that gave birth to revolutions across Europe in the mid-nineteenth century) were dispersed and absorbed by capitalism. As she puts it, 'Capitalism leaves the subject the right to revolt, preserving for itself the right to suppress that revolt' (RPL 210). That is to say, by inscribing negativity in its formation, the avant-garde actually provided a site of confrontation with the repression through which capitalism sustains itself. Further, while only the avant-garde text is able to inscribe 'the negativity that (capitalist) society and its official ideology represses', the avant-garde text 'also plays into its hands: through the text, the system provides itself with what it lacks – rejection – but keeps it in a domain apart, confining it to the ego, to the "inner experience" of an elite, and to esotericism'. And she adds: 'The text becomes the agent of a new religion that is no longer universal but elitist and esoteric'. This is the most serious accusation that Kristeva levels at the historical avant-garde: that it lacks sociohistorical content and that it 'seeks only to be for itself' (RPL 186–7).

What she envisages instead is an avant-garde practice that combines heterogeneous contradiction with revolutionary critique of the established social order: for 'this is precisely what the dominant ideology and its various mechanisms of liberalism, oppression, and defense find intolerable'. Elaborating on this desire in *Revolution in Poetic Language*, she draws a distinction between experience and practice. While experience can only lead to 'a strictly individual, naturalist, or esoteric representation', the imperative for practice demands that 'the system of representation that binds the text is also rooted in social practice, or even its revolutionary phase' (RPL 191, 195–6). In the 1960s she found this promise best articulated in the avant-gardism of the *Tel Quel* group and in Soller's belief that 'only the socialist Revolution could provide a social setting propitious to avant-garde writing' (PK 13). That was then, however, and the socialist revolution would anyway never happen in France. And so the world moved on to what Kristeva described in 1991 as our 'mediatic society', in which any aesthetic revolt can only be 'clouded and confused' (I 216). In this 'individualistic' world, it has become so much more difficult for avant-garde collectives to exist, so much harder for art to carry a unified political cause – let alone to alter the political order.

Perhaps this awareness of the inevitable political limitations of the avant-garde made Kristeva prioritize its power to reveal societal mechanisms and symbolic processes over its political efficacy. More than any other critic, Kristeva has shown how powerful the poetic language of the avant-garde can be in disrupting established modes of thought and also how, ultimately, what matters in the avant-garde is not efficacy but the effect that an avant-garde text can have on the reader as a subject-in-process. That said, however, Kristeva, remaining 'committed to a possibility of change' (I 217), could never possibly accept that the historical avant-garde is a failed project, nor that there is no longer a necessity for a culture of revolt. She explained her reasoning for that in *The Sense and Non-Sense of Revolt*, from 1996:

> what is the necessity of the culture of revolt? Why relentlessly attempt to resuscitate forms of cultures whose antecedents lie in… the avant-garde? Aren't they simply lost forever? Why should we want to find modern responses to these past experiences? After the death of ideologies, shouldn't we just be content with entertainment culture, show culture, and complacent commentary?
> We shouldn't!
>
> (SNS 7)

As she proceeds to argue in this text, the fact that 'Our modern world has reached a point in its development where a certain type of culture and art, if not all culture and all art, is threatened, indeed, impossible' simply means that the responsibility 'to be interpreters, givers of meaning' has fallen on critics (SNS 8). And so in *The Sense and Non-Sense of Revolt* Kristeva issues the following clarion call to critics: 'Rather than falling asleep in the new normalizing order, let us try to rekindle the flame (easily extinguishable) of revolt' (SNS 9). The historical avant-garde may be long dead, but its promise, Kristeva maintains, has survived in the practice of critics like Roland Barthes, in whose criticism she finds 'a search for dialectical laws of *signifiance*' and 'a negativity that works against the transparency of language and the symbolic function in general' (SNS 210–11). This is what Kristeva has also sought to do. In a career spanning several decades, and through a practice that crosses literary criticism, semiotics, psychoanalysis and creative writing, she has continued to carry the mantle of the avant-garde forward, remaining committed to its project of disrupting and of subverting the symbolic.

Notes

1. For a discussion of Jena Romanticism as the first avant-garde, see Lacoue-Labarthe and Nancy (1988: 8, 133 n.2). See also Phelan (2009: 42).
2. See Bürger (1984: 47–53).
3. See, for example, Mallarmé (2007: 205–11); Apollinaire (2000: 39); Shklovsky (1998: 218); de Gourmont (1907: 37, 142); Hulme, 'Notes on Language and Style', 'A Lecture on Modern Poetry' and 'Romanticism and Classicism', in Csengeri (1994: 24–7, 55, 69–70); Pound, 'The Wisdom of Poetry' and 'The Serious Artist', in Nadel (2005: 192, 242, 244). On the distinction as manifested in Stramm and Hofmannsthal, see Butler (1994: 9–10, 244–5).
4. See Beardsworth (2004: 45).
5. See, for example, Poggioli (1968: 37), and Horkheimer and Adorno (1973: 83–4).
6. On Kristeva's debt to Freud, see Beardsworth (2004: 41); Oliver (1993: 42); and Gambaudo (2016: 18–34).
7. Kristeva treats the avant-garde as the crossing point of various relationships including also sexuality, religion, history, theory of the state. See Hill (1990: 145).
8. The list includes Louis Aragon. See PK 430, where Kristeva explains how Aragon's writing broaches the linguistic, the sexual and the ideological.
9. On this point, see again Hill (1990: 146).

References

Apollinaire, G. (2000), 'Zone', in G. Rees (ed.), *Guillaume Apollinaire: Alcools*, 39–44, London: Athlone.
Beardsworth, S. (2004), *Julia Kristeva: Psychoanalysis and Modernity*, Albany, NY: State University of New York Press.
Bürger, P. (1984), *Theory of the Avant-Garde*, trans. M. Shaw, Minneapolis, MN: University of Minnesota Press.
Butler, C. (1994), *Early Modernism: Literature, Music, and Painting in Europe, 1900–1916*, Oxford: Clarendon Press.
Csengeri, K., ed. (1994), *The Collected Writings of T. E. Hulme*, Oxford: Oxford University Press.
de Gourmont, R. (1907), *Le problème du style*, Paris: Mercure de France.
Gambaudo, S. (2016), *Kristeva, Psychoanalysis and Culture: Subjectivity in Crisis*, London: Routledge.
Hill, L. (1990), 'Julia Kristeva: Theorising the Avant-Garde?', in J. Fletcher and A. Benjamin (eds), *Abjection, Melancholia and Love: The Work of Julia Kristeva*, 137–56, London: Routledge.
Horkheimer, M. and T. Adorno (1973), *Negative Dialectics*, trans. E. B. Ashton, New York: Continuum.

Lacoue-Labarthe, P. and J.-L. Nancy (1988), *The Literary Absolute: The Theory of Literature in German Romanticism*, trans. P. Barnard and C. Lester, Albany, NY: State University of New York Press.
Mallarmé, S. (2007), 'Crisis of Verse', in B. Johnson (trans.), *Divagations*, 201–11, Cambridge, MA: Belknap Press of Harvard University Press.
Nadel, I. B., ed. (2005), *Ezra Pound: Early Writings*, London: Penguin.
Oliver, K. (1993), *Reading Kristeva: Unraveling the Double-bind*, Bloomington, IN: Indiana University Press.
Phelan, A. (2009), 'Prose Fiction of the German Romantics', in N. Saul (ed.), *The Cambridge Companion to German Romanticism*, 41–66, Cambridge: Cambridge University Press.
Poggioli, R. (1968), *The Theory of the Avant-Garde*, trans. G. Fitzgerald, Cambridge, MA: Belknap Press of Harvard University Press.
Shklovsky, V. (1998), 'Art as Technique', in V. Kolocotroni, J. Goldman and O. Taxidou (eds), *Modernism: An Anthology of Sources and Documents*, 217–21, Edinburgh: Edinburgh University Press.

16

Female genius

Elisabetta Convento

Julia Kristeva's three intellectual biographies of Hannah Arendt, Melanie Klein and Sidonie-Gabrielle Colette, published in French under the collective title *Le Génie féminin* (1999, 2000, 2002) and translated into English respectively as *Hannah Arendt* (2001), *Melanie Klein* (2002) and *Colette* (2004), can be considered as the climax of Kristeva's investigation of feminine specificity. These three female figures, all linked to each other because of their ideas, are selected among others for their remarkable accomplishments, but also because of the affinities that Kristeva has with them; in fact, by analysing the life-work of her geniuses, the transferential connections with them emerge, and Kristeva, whether unconsciously or not, discloses aspects of her own genius. In the volume *Hannah Arendt*, Kristeva defines her geniuses as 'those who force us to discuss their story because it is so closely bound up with their creations, in the innovations that support the development of thought and beings, and in the onslaught of questions, discoveries, and pleasures that their creations have inspired' (HA xi). For all three geniuses, and for Kristeva as well, we can speak of 'Life not as *zōē* but as *bios*' (Kristeva 2004: 499). Hannah Arendt imagines a political space that can guarantee the singularity of each person in the plurality of spaces of relation. Kristeva is indebted to Arendt for this definition which distinguishes *zōē*, or biological life, and *bios*, or narrated life, and affirms that all great actions pertain to *bios* and open to the individual the doors of the genius.

Kristeva's interest in the feminine has occupied most of her career, from the writing of theoretical works, such as *Revolution in Poetic Language* (1974), to psychoanalytical texts, such as *Black Sun* (1987), which focuses on melancholia and depression, and from her inquiry into the sacredness of the feminine with *The Feminine and the Sacred* (1998) to the reflections on mysticism and pleasure in *Teresa, My Love* (2008), just to mention some of her most prominent engagements with the psychic specificity of the feminine. The *Female Genius* is to date Kristeva's most detailed, multifaceted and, perhaps, most controversial exploration of the feminine. It is dedicated to Simone de Beauvoir, who, with *The Second Sex* (1949), made an important contribution to women's advancement, but, according to Kristeva, left partially unanswered some questions related to the realization of women's potential and freedom. For de Beauvoir, the condition of deprivation, repression and renunciation to which women are subjected should be a stimulus to overcome their limits and dedicate themselves to great enterprises. De Beauvoir highlights the ability of the female subject to take control of the universe, arguing that this implies first of all to take possession of oneself. In this position we can find a proximity with the ideas expressed by Kristeva in her own works. However, while acknowledging de Beauvoir's merit in fighting for the liberation of the female subject, until then considered as the *other* of man, Kristeva argues that 'Beauvoir never lost her rage against metaphysics because it imprisons woman in her status of the Other, consigning her to the realm of facticity and of immanence' (2004: 495). She notes that de Beauvoir's struggle to improve women's conditions in general did not fully comprise the realization of the female subject in its singularity, which is precisely what Kristeva aims for with her development of the concept of a female genius.

Therefore, the trilogy works as a demonstration of the thesis posed in the introductory chapter of the first volume, titled 'Female Genius', which presents the subject of the three biographies, while the last chapter of the third volume, devoted to Colette, attempts a response to the question on the existence of a female genius. For Kristeva, the key issue is not to define womankind but to appreciate the peculiarity of the feminine which is present with some differences in women as well as in men, and which consists primarily in a creative force providing a source of resistance to the evils of history, as well as to the awareness of the inevitability of death. One may think of Hannah Arendt's work and its contribution to the fight against totalitarianism, or to Colette's novels emphasizing birth and renaissance. The idea of genius is the guiding principle that enables Kristeva to discuss how the extraordinary women, who are the protagonists of the three volumes, could excel in the fields of political philosophy, psychoanalysis and literature, but it is also the driving force that encourages the readers to push themselves to match the achievements of the three geniuses.

Starting from Plato and moving on to the medieval philosophy of Duns Scotus, from Thomas Aquinas to Voltaire, passing through German Romanticism and Kant and culminating with Hannah Arendt, the idea of genius has always been debated, praised or condemned. The supposed spontaneity of genius and of poetic creation is strongly denied, for example, by Kristeva's master Roland Barthes in *Mythologies* (1957) or by Jean-Paul Sartre, whose philosophical writing Kristeva analysed in depth in various works, such as *Intimate Revolt: The Powers and Limits of Psychoanalysis* (1997).

Kristeva's idea of genius is presented as an overcoming of the traditional concept of *ingenium* as innate gift or talent, to embrace instead the genius as expression of *techne*, the human ability to convert creativity into action. Kristeva brings back into vogue, under a new angle, an idea of genius that draws from Duns Scotus' concept of *hæcceitas*, according to which a person's greatness lies mainly in her or his singularity. The trilogy is therefore conceived as an appeal to the individual right to singularity and creativity. According to the philosopher, the sphere of application of the genius in the contemporary world is enormous, as it gives each one the possibility to be unique, exceed and become the *qui* theorized by Hannah Arendt, someone and not just anyone. The genius, therefore, represents the hope of salvation from the uniformity of a globalized life.

Kristeva's three-volume work unveils to the reader a composite picture of female genius by offering a kaleidoscopic view of the feminine which disseminates in various fields, such as literature, history, philosophy and psychoanalysis. The ideological-philosophical structure of the *Female Genius* is mainly the one that Kristeva borrows from Arendt, hence the emphasis on singularity; the analytical method derives from the Kleinian psychoanalysis centred on the maternal, the feminine and sexuality; lastly, the field of application and the meeting point of her two theoretical frames is Colette's life-work. It does not appear unjustified to venture the hypothesis that with the triptych of the *Female Genius* Kristeva wants to propose a secular and feminine version of the Trinity. As an alternative to the Father, the Son and the Holy Spirit, Kristeva's feminine trinity is formed by the mother, which is at the centre of Melanie Klein's production, the word made flesh in the writings by Colette and life as this is reclaimed in Hannah Arendt's philosophy. As in the Christian Trinity, each of the three geniuses expresses her singularity in a different way, but is part of a same common essence. In fact, Kristeva's emphasis is certainly on the singular element of the triptych, but with continuous reminders to the sacrality of the bond that joins them, which, altogether, seems to be the most complete expression of female genius.

Overall, the main features of the female genius can be summarized in three central ideas: the importance of relationships, the coincidence between life and thought and, ultimately, a peculiar temporality of birth and renewal. All of these ideas intertwine in the trilogy which, as Kristeva herself states, is structured as an exploration of the feminine guided by the three protagonists: 'I began this study with the hypothesis that I knew nothing, that "woman" is an unknown, or at least that I preferred not to "define" what a woman is so that an answer might emerge out of a careful accumulation of examples' (HA xx). Through the complex interweaving of personal reflections, quotations from their works and a vast critical apparatus from which she draws, Kristeva is able to revive her three authors, disclose memory and meaning as well as lay the ground for the possibility of change.

As we have seen, broadly speaking, the discourse on genius is largely rooted in tradition, and this is precisely where Kristeva's innovation stands; from the very title of the trilogy, the reader is made aware that the author's main interest is for an original and gendered concept of genius which abandons conventional, male-dominated forms to embrace the feminine.

Kristeva's idea of female genius has been explored by the author well before writing the trilogy. In the 1979 essay 'Women's Time', for example, Kristeva discusses types and features of feminine-connoted temporalities, cyclical time and monumental time, and distinguishes them from linear time, often associated with masculinity. In defining cyclical time, Kristeva draws from Hannah Arendt's *The Human Condition* (1958), in which Arendt refers to a temporality of organic living, of the cycles of the seasons or the rotation of the earth around the sun. This idea of a cosmic temporality can also be observed in many works by Colette, especially in *Sido* (1929) and *La Naissance du jour* (1928). Monumental temporality is described by Kristeva as eternal time. 'All-encompassing and infinite like imaginary space, this temporality reminds one of Kronos in Hesiod's mythology' (Kristeva 1981: 16). Both cyclical and monumental concepts of time, while not 'fundamentally incompatible with "masculine" values' (Kristeva 1981: 17), show a problematic relation to linear time, which is also that of history, with its logical succession from beginning to end. The concept of female temporality reappears also in *The Sense and Non-Sense of Revolt: The Powers and Limits of Psychoanalysis* (1996), and then in the *Female Genius*, where a nonlinear temporality of blossoming and rebirth is indicated as most appropriate for a discussion of the feminine and the maternal. Arendt, for example, establishes her philosophical reflections on an idea of freedom which is based on forgiveness and promise, where every birth is a new beginning. Likewise, Klein invites us to consider psychoanalytic treatment as a new beginning. But it is Colette who exemplifies at its best the poetics of blossoming. By writing about the most complex and distressing affective and material difficulties, Colette is able to reconstruct herself and sublimate sufferance with joy of life which is often symbolized by flowers in bloom. For the French writer, the temporality of transformation and renewal becomes a way of life.

Kristeva gives a passionate and at the same time accurate reading of the 'life-work' of her three geniuses. She presents the distinctness of each one and traces a picture of the complexity of their contribution to the culture of the twentieth century. What these atypical geniuses share, explains Kristeva, is a harmony made of singularities, dissonances and counterpoints. Kristeva's approach to the authors has numerous similarities with a psychoanalytic treatment during which the female geniuses disclose themselves by narrating aspects of their thought and life. As we have mentioned before, at times, Kristeva's voice and her reflections mingle with those of her geniuses, so that we are unable to fully distinguish who is who. In a sense, by writing on her three female protagonists, Kristeva rewrites herself as well. Therefore, the merit of the trilogy is to establish a lively dialogue between its author, the three geniuses who are the object of reflection and the many others who are caught at the heart of the transference/counter-transference, an experience that involves the reader as well.

The appeal to the genius of everyone consists in an attempt to set women free from the limits of biology and from their social destiny, targeting various types of determinism. By highlighting the importance of creativity, which can take the shape of artistic creation, of love or social engagement, Kristeva shows the possibilities of the imaginary, which is an essential component of the female genius. The possibility of contesting, the 'intimate revolt' which enables human beings to upturn language and ideas, can bring about important changes in social customs and an individual's mindset.

It is no coincidence, then, that the climax of the trilogy is reached in the volume devoted to Colette, who challenges moral and social norms not only by disregarding interdictions and taboos but by making them the subject of her writing. The author was able to let her creativity flow in a triumph of sexual and linguistic *jouissance* so as to overcome the neuroses that Freud attributed to women. Kristeva has often stated that the French author is a writer in 'osmosis' with writing, which is approached with a feverish voracity because for Colette it is a physical act, a gesture not just of the hand but of the whole body. The writer is a genius in using each and all tools provided by the language; she is an engineer of lexicon, alliterations and assonances, and pushes paradoxes and metaphors to their extreme. In Kristeva's book on Colette we are caught by the writer's ability to reconcile life and work by conceiving a new alphabet that captures the intimacy of the subject. This alphabet shows some similitudes with the pre-language, as defined by Klein and elaborated by Kristeva in *Revolution in Poetic Language*. According to Kristeva, Colette's alphabet reveals one of the writer's most brilliant intuitions, namely that language allows us to reconcile ourselves with our identity whatever it is, allowing for new definitions of the self and of sexuality.

Even though all three geniuses highlight in their works the importance of relationships, Melanie Klein's elaboration of the mother–child relation is truly revolutionary. Female sexuality is described by Klein as very complicated, as it first involves a rejection of the mother figure, followed by a process of identification with the father, which is the one to whom the subject owes the ability to think, speak and integrate in society. This process implies a primary and then a secondary Oedipus complex. Klein is capable of moving from a Freudian male-focused Oedipus theory, to a version that provides an account of the specificities of the girl's development and of the complexity of the mother–daughter relation. This relation must culminate in a symbolic matricide in order for personal growth to take place and for the creativity and uniqueness of the genius to unfold.

If twentieth-century feminism gave women the opportunity to proclaim their own sexual, linguistic and political difference, Kristeva takes the argument further by claiming that motherhood, which was previously considered as an obstacle to female genius, is now placed into its very core. She states, 'Mothers can be geniuses… of a certain approach to living the life of the mind. That approach to being a mother and a woman… bestows upon mothers a genius all of their own' (HA xv). As far as she is concerned, Colette focuses on the reparation of the relationship with the mother by creating the mythical figure of Sido, and in her narrative works she achieves the sublimation of the *[père]-version* into *mère-version*. Thanks to Melanie Klein's innovations and to the non-traditional examples of motherhood presented in Colette's works, Kristeva makes of the maternal experience the cornerstone of the female genius. Motherhood is not simple biology but the first elaboration of a relationship with another creature considered in her/his singularity; it is the first attempt at recognizing the singularity of another being, the first true encounter with a total other. The dialectic exchange with de Beauvoir, whose concern with the liberation of women from biology leads her to a refusal of motherhood, determines Kristeva's resolution to show with the *Female Genius* how motherhood can be a free choice and can contribute to the realization of the subject: 'The work of a genius culminates in the birth of a subject' (HA x).

Undoubtedly, as we saw above, the reader of the trilogy faces a complex intertwining of various disciplines with psychoanalysis and their application to an investigation of the female genius. The result of the polyphonic fusion of different methods consists in a distinctive approach that does not lack risks and contradictions. Kristeva's atypical biography does not always completely translate the voices of the three geniuses, neither does she devote full attention to the historical context, but she is rather focused on letting her female protagonists come to light by narrating their experiences. As noted by Schippers, 'For Kristeva, experience is not an epistemological category, linked to knowledge, but an ethical one that allows the subject of experience to engage in a more meaningful relationship with the other' (Schippers 2011: 122). This is the reason why Kristeva is able to include the experience of maternity as part of the creative process of the genius. Yet the insertion of motherhood in a definition of the genius is seen as ambivalent, especially by some feminist critics,[1] as the extension of the idea of genius beyond its exceptionality, which is mostly related to artistic creation, makes the genius more accessible and, therefore, less extraordinary. Apparently, there is some inconsistency in highlighting the singularity of the genius and at the same time allowing everyone to be a genius.

Despite Kristeva's contribution to an important interrogation of the feminine and motherhood, her reluctance to align herself with a straightforward feminist agenda in the trilogy has been most controversial. Starting from her personal experience of the Bulgarian regime, which posed limitations to thought and personal freedom,[2] and from the observation that in the contemporary world the challenge of the Augustinian retrospective question *quaestio mihi factus sum* has been suspended in favour of new reassuring dogmas, Kristeva takes a stand against multiple and emerging -isms: racism, fundamentalism but also feminism, which she reproaches for not being able to grasp the specificity of the feminine in the singularity of every woman. Kristeva's position, as well as her concept of the female genius, which aims at overcoming sexual difference by proposing a notion of the feminine that can be claimed by men as well, is quite different from that of Luce Irigaray, who proposes a concept of female subjectivity based on sexual difference.[3] Even though Kristeva recognizes the '*radical strangeness*, constitutive exclusion, irreparable solitude' (C 416) of the feminine subject, her books on Melanie Klein and Colette clarify that this '*strangeness*' is a component of both female and male subjectivity. Additionally, Birgit Schippers sees some contradictions in Kristeva's praise for the singularity of Simone de Beauvoir in the *Female Genius*, while in previous works, such as 'Women's Time', for example, de Beauvoir was an object of criticism as part of that first-generation existential feminism that rejected motherhood.[4]

Nevertheless, Kristeva's volumes on Hannah Arendt, Melanie Klein and Colette are able to seduce and solicit the reader, providing us with a better understanding of our contemporary world, as the questions of equality and difference, the development of a global consciousness and the respect for singularity are central for the twenty-first century. Kristeva's *Female Genius* dives into these subjects with a level of depth that we welcome and need, particularly because the three geniuses are able to follow original trajectories without bending to the pre-established symbolic order. Kristeva's female genius is in the end the creative singularity of authors whose life-work is disseminated in the experience of the maternal, in the crossing (through therapy or language) of the dark sides of history as well as of the psyche or sex, but above all in the elaboration of a concept of the feminine which is openness to others, renewal and hope for the future, or 'mental hermaphroditism' (Colette 2000: 62), to use Colette's expression.

Genius, as Roland Barthes argues, consists in changing places, in being reborn, in surprising others by being where it is not expected to be.[5] With the trilogy, Kristeva puts her own genius into play, opening a path that leads to a peculiar, dynamic and heterogeneous approach to the feminine which, due to its structure, cannot become the ground for a rigid theorization of the female genius, but rather allows for a possibility of uniqueness for women and men.

Notes

1. The idea that Kristeva's concept of the female genius can be viewed as an anticlimax, because Kristeva seems to make it accessible to all, can be found in Ann Jefferson (2015: 212–18). In *Because of Beauvoir: Christianity and the Cultivation of Female Genius*, Alison Jasper considers both the ambiguity of female difference as radical strangeness and Kristeva's complex reference to maternity (2012: 45–69). Finally, Cecilia Sjöholm discusses the cult of natality in Kristeva's theory of the female genius (2005: 46–8).

2. Kristeva explains: 'I have long mistrusted the liberation movements of our democratic societies. I always fear that they may have hidden totalitarian aims… It is out of this mistrust that I have tried to dissociate myself even from mass feminism, while at the same time paying tribute to feminine creativity' (Kristeva 2008: 353).

3. Luce Irigaray's perspective on sexual difference, 'The natural is at least two: male and female… we should make reality the point of departure: it is *two*' (1996: 35), sets her quite far from Kristeva's concept of the female genius. Some specificities of the difference between the sexes contribute to making the separation of the two authors even bigger. According to the Belgian philosopher, the departure from the mother is more painful for boys because of their sexual difference: 'Woman is not at all in the same type of subjective identity as man. If fact she does not have to distance herself from her mother as he does… She must be or become a woman like her mother and, at the same time, be capable of differentiating herself from her' (Irigaray 1994: 18). Melanie Klein's crucial stages that shape a girl's development and the mother–daughter relation, which are an essential constituent of Kristeva's female genius, are radically different from the developmental process Irigaray describes.

4. Schippers notes that 'it is from her critique of feminism, which she reaffirms in her conclusion to the genius trilogy, that she turns to the figure of Simone de Beauvoir, who is embraced, in the same text, as another example of genius and singularity… This is rather surprising, as it is de Beauvoir who is the, unnamed, object of criticism in Kristeva's earlier attempts to distance herself from a conception of feminism that, she claims, rejects motherhood' (2011: 139–40).

5. Roland Barthes states that 'Être immortel, c'est naître absolument de nouveau; l'œuvre à faire est médiatrice de cette immortalité-là' (2003: 284).

References

Barthes, R. (2003), *La préparation du roman I et II. Cours et séminaires au Collège de France (1978–1979 et 1979–1980)*, ed. N. Léger, Paris: Seuil.

Colette, G. S. (2000), *The Pure and the Impure*, trans. H. Briffault, New York: New York Review Books.

Irigaray, L. (1994), *Thinking the Difference: For a Peaceful Revolution*, trans. K. Montin, London: Athlone.
Irigaray, L. (1996), *I Love to You: Sketch for a Possible Felicity in History*, trans. A. Martin, London: Routledge.
Jasper, A. E. (2012), *Because of Beauvoir: Christianity and the Cultivation of Female Genius*, Waco, TX: Baylor University Press.
Jefferson, A. (2015), *Genius in France: An Idea and Its Uses*, Princeton, NJ: Princeton University Press.
Kristeva, J. (1981), 'Women's Time', *Signs*, 7 (1): 13–35.
Kristeva, J. (2004), 'Is There a Feminine Genius?', *Critical Inquiry*, 30 (3): 493–504.
Kristeva, J. (2008), 'Refoundation as Survival: An Interrogation of Hannah Arendt', *Common Knowledge*, 14 (3): 353–64.
Schippers, B. (2011), *Julia Kristeva and Feminist Thought*, Edinburgh: Edinburgh University Press.
Sjöholm, C. (2005), *Kristeva and the Political*, London: Routledge.

17

Intertextuality

Gertrude Postl

Kristeva is credited with introducing the term 'intertextuality' into the intellectual discourse of the late 1960s. Combining Saussurean structuralism with the work of Mikhail Bakhtin and eventually with Roland Barthes' theory of the text and Freudian psychoanalysis, she contributed to the transition from structuralism to what was to become post-structuralism, originally closely associated with the *Tel Quel* group in Paris. *Tel Quel*'s appeal for Kristeva – apart from personal affiliations – was its focus on the intersection of literature, politics and philosophy which she expanded with the areas of linguistics and semiotics. Critical of the dominant linguistic theories of the time, most importantly structuralism and Russian formalism, she developed her own brand of semiotics, *semanalysis*, which 'conceives of meaning not as a sign-system but as a *signifying process*' (KR 28). This notion of language as a 'signifying process' also entered Kristeva's understanding of intertextuality, which she elaborated predominantly in her early work, most importantly in the texts collected or reprinted in *Séméiotiké* (1969) and *Polylogue* (1977),[1] but also in her 1974 *La révolution du langage poétique* (*Revolution in Poetic Language*, 1984). Overall, her approach to the process of signification at this stage could be best described in terms of a deconstructive move that investigates linguistic phenomena while at the same time criticizing and lastly overcoming key elements of meaning production: '*Semanalysis*, as I tried to define it... [is] to describe... signifying phenomena, while analyzing, criticizing, and dissolving "phenomenon," "meaning," and "signifier"' (DL vii).

Literary criticism during the 1960s and 1970s popularized a form of textual interconnectedness understood as 'study of sources'. But Kristeva eventually came to reject this meaning so much so that – after having originally introduced the term 'intertextuality' – she substituted it in *Revolution in Poetic Language* with 'transposition': 'The term *inter-textuality* denotes this transposition of one (or several) sign system(s) into another; but since this term has often been understood in the banal sense of "study of sources," we prefer the term *transposition*' (RPL 59–60). Kristeva's original use of intertextuality – before her turn towards psychoanalysis and the resulting replacement of the term with 'transposition' – has strong affinities with the currently popular notion of the term, as found in literary criticism, cultural theory, but also certain brands of philosophy. Going beyond a mere 'study of sources', the term intertextuality now refers to a general interconnectedness and mutual influence among texts, challenging the assumption of a text as unified, independent, self-enclosed entity. In the words of Graham Allen: 'Meaning becomes something which exists between a text and all the other texts to which it refers and relates, moving out from the independent text into a network of textual relations. The text becomes the intertext' (2011: 1).

Kristeva's original conception of intertextuality is indebted to the work of Mikhail Bakhtin, especially his insistence on the importance of history and social context for the meaning production of the sign, both of no concern for Saussure's structuralist account of language: 'studying the text as intertextuality, considers it… within (the text of) society and history' (DL 37). This focus on the social and historical dimensions of language has necessarily to let go of the concept of the speaking/writing subject as originator of utterances/texts and of the idea that the text is a self-enclosed and coherent unity. In 'Word, Dialogue, and Novel' (her most elaborate encounter with the work of Bakhtin) Kristeva offers the notion of intertextuality as substitute for intersubjectivity: 'any text is constructed as a mosaic of quotations; any text is the absorption and transformation of another. The notion of *intertextuality* replaces that of intersubjectivity' (DL 66). In Kristeva's view, the subject – which is always already a subject in process – is a textual subject; it cannot be distinguished from the (spoken or written) texts it produces. Or, in the words of Allen: 'Whenever subjects enter language they enter into situations in which their personal subjectivity is lost' (2011: 40). Thus, the linguistic relations between subjects (intersubjectivity) can be conceived in terms of a relationship between texts, called intertextuality at that point and directly traceable to Bakhtin's notion of dialogue.

For Bakhtin, all language is dialogical, or, as Kristeva puts it, 'dialogism is inherent in language itself' (DL 67–8). However, this use of 'dialogue' has very little to do with speakers or protagonists in a novel simply talking to each other; rather, it refers to the tension inherent in language between the meaning a word has as such and the meaning it acquires through the historical and social context of its use, including past texts or utterances. Every time we speak/write some 'other' is present, some 'double', some outside that shapes the meaning of what is said or written: previous texts, the specific relationship between the speaker and the addressee, the circumstances of the speech situation, possible linguistic transgressions, etc. The tension between linguistic forces pulling in different directions is present in every utterance and Bakhtin described this in terms of the distinction between monological and dialogical utterances, whereby 'dialogue can be monological, and what is called monologue can be dialogical' (DL 67). While the monological aspect is associated with established forms of socially sanctioned conventions, thus with a form of linguistic 'truth' or fixed meaning, the dialogical utterance refers to those aspects of the speech situation (or of writing) that undermine any linguistic stability in that they allow outside or past layers of meaning to enter the scene – what Bakhtin referred to as 'heteroglossia', 'double voice', or 'ambivalence'. Historical examples for the dialogical structure of language offered by Bakhtin and appropriated by Kristeva are the Menippean satire and, in particular, the carnivalesque. 'The scene of the carnival ... is ... both stage and life, game and dream, discourse and spectacle ... language escapes linearity (law) to live as drama in three dimensions ... On the omnified stage of carnival, language parodies and relativizes itself' (DL 79).

Kristeva's interest in Bakhtin's account of dialogism, understood as that which reaches beyond codified language or outside of the actual utterance or text, foreshadows her later distinctions between genotext and phenotext,[2] and, to some extent, the distinction between the semiotic and the symbolic – attempts to account for something outside the actual speech act but nevertheless entering it and thereby contributing to its meaning. '[A] text cannot be grasped through linguistics alone. Bakhtin postulates the necessity for what he calls a *translinguistic* science, which, developed on the basis of language's dialogism, would enable us to understand intertextual *relationships*', which she explains, referring to Lautréamont, as 'a constant dialogue with the preceding literary corpus, a perpetual challenge of past writing', something 'that permits the writer to enter history' (DL 69). Intertextual relationships go beyond the intersubjective exchange in that the encounter with another speaking/writing subject always already takes place along the lines of interrelating historical trajectories. Yet as Kristeva explains in one of her interviews, her understanding of intertextuality differs from Bakhtin's dialogism in 'that a textual segment, sentence, utterance, or paragraph is not simply the intersection of two voices ... rather, the segment is the result of the intersection of a number of voices, of a number of textual interventions' (I 189).

According to Kristeva, the dialogical structure of language, as proposed by Bakhtin, manifests itself via two crossing axes of meaning production. 'The word's status is ... defined *horizontally* (the word in the text belongs to both writing subject and addressee) as well as *vertically* (the word in the text is oriented toward an anterior or synchronic literary corpus' (DL 66).

This crossing of an intersubjective and an intertextual (or historical) axis for the generation of meaning is an adaptation of Saussure's distinction between synchrony and diachrony – understood by Kristeva as an ongoing dialogical process between the utterances of textual subjects and outside influences on these very utterances.

Bakhtin's dialogism and the notion of intertextuality that Kristeva derives from it imply a reconfiguring of the processes of writing and reading. 'Bakhtin ... does not see dialogue only as language assumed by a subject; he sees it, rather, as a *writing* where one reads the *other* ... Bakhtinian dialogism identifies writing as both subjectivity and communication, or better, as intertextuality' (DL 68). Through the activities of reading, a text's history can gain influence over a newly written text. 'Bakhtin situates the text within history and society, which are then seen as texts read by the writer, and into which he inserts himself by rewriting them' (DL 65). Subsequently, a text is no longer viewed as the expression of the authoritative voice of the author but as 'an *intersection of textual surfaces* ... a dialogue among several writings: that of the writer, the addressee (or the character), and the contemporary or earlier cultural context' (DL 65). This is to say that Kristeva challenges not only the concept of the author as the self-identical creator and sole origin of a text (the 'authoritative voice') but also the subject position of the reader. 'If we are readers of intertextuality, we must be capable of the same putting-into-process of our identities', since reading a text as an intertext requires that we are able to identify with 'different types of texts, voices, and semantic, syntactic, and phonic systems at play in a given text' (I 190).

The meaning of texts or utterances that are situated within a historical process and which allow the 'other' to enter the signifying unit is necessarily ambivalent – yet another term that Kristeva appropriates from Bakhtin. 'The term "ambivalence" implies the insertion of history (society) into a text and of this text into history' (DL 68). Kristeva calls this type of ambivalent language poetic language (indicating the centrepiece of her later work) and claims that 'the minimal unit of poetic language is at least *double*, not in the sense of the signifier/signified dyad, but rather, in terms of *one and other*... where each "unit"... acts as a multidetermined *peak*' (DL 69). The use of the term 'poetic language' is not limited to poetry. It is, rather, a reference to a type of language which signifies not in terms of identity and homogeneity (monologism in Bakhtin's sense) but within the parameters of multilayered and multidimensional meaning production that escapes the established modes of signification. 'Poetic language appears as a dialogue of texts: every sequence is made in relation to another sequence deriving from another corpus, such that every sequence has a double orientation: toward the act of reminiscence... and toward the act of summation' (TSP 30). Kristeva characterizes this language in terms of a '0–2 interval, a continuity where 0 denotes and 1 is implicitly transgressed', whereby 1 stands for 'the linguistic, psychic, and social "prohibition"… (God, Law, Definition)' (DL70). This 'poetic logic' or 'dream logic' is in opposition to the '0–1 sequence' of modern logic which she also associates (in accordance with Bakhtin) with the realist narrative, considered as dogmatic in that it follows a thinking of determination, definition and the value of equation (DL 69).

Kristeva's use of intertextuality in her early texts is thus more than just placing texts within a historical context and emphasizing their mutual interdependence. She wants to escape the 'signifier/signified dyad', central for a structuralist account of the sign, in favour of ambivalence, multiplicity of meaning, and, most importantly, she wants to situate language within the context of laws of prohibition and the possible means to circumvent these laws on the level of language. While intertextuality per se is not equivalent with poetic language, what Kristeva means by poetic language can be thought only within the framework of her notion of intertextuality. Intertextuality fully came to the fore with the break that occurred in the form of the novel with the onset of modernism (she mentions Joyce, Proust and Kafka). 'Beginning with this break – not only literary but also social, political, and philosophical in nature – the problem of intertextuality (intertextual dialogue) appears as such' (DL 71).

While Bakhtin clearly was the dominant influence for Kristeva's early work on intertextuality, her most important contemporary with regard to this topic was, without a doubt, Roland Barthes. 'My concept of intertextuality… goes back to Bakhtin's dialogism and Barthes' text theory' (ND 8). Barthes' claim of the death of the author, the resulting focus on the reader and thus the importance of the writing/reading process, his distinction between readerly and writerly texts, his insistence on the open-ended structure and the citational character of texts or his inclusion of non-linguistic signifying systems (e.g. the fashion system) into his analysis of signification – all these are themes that rendered him the perfect interlocutor for Kristeva. To quote Kristeva, Barthes 'located literary practice at the intersection of subject and history', so he could study 'this practice as symptom of the ideological tearings in the social fabric' (DL 93). Barthes' connecting 'the pleasure of the text' or 'a jouissance of meaning' (SNS 188) with a concern for history (against accusations of being a mere structuralist) and his definition of writing (*écriture*) 'as a negativity, a movement that questions all "identity" (whether linguistic, corporeal, or historical)' (SNS 193) resonated with Kristeva's interest in meaning production as a combined effort between affects and drives on one side (the semiotic) and the symbolic law on the other (society, history). All these theoretical affinities between Kristeva's and Barthes' work are held together by his challenge of meaning itself which he relates to a conception of the subject as non-unified, shifting and dispersed. Questioning 'a unity – an "I," a "we" – that can have meaning or seek meaning', Barthes encounters the limits of '*the possibility of meaning itself*' and offers instead 'the abyss of a polyvalence of meaning, as well as a polyphony internal to subjects investigating meaning' (SNS 189). Kristeva's own texts about Barthes, including his role as one of the key figures of her revolt project, confirm the overall impact he had on her thinking.[3]

As stated already, Kristeva's early account of intertextuality gave way to the notion of transposition in *Revolution in Poetic Language*. '[W]e prefer the term *transposition* because it specifies that the passage from one signifying system to another demands a new articulation of the thetic – of enunciative and denotative positionality' (RPL 60). The theoretical context for this shift is to be seen in Kristeva's growing commitment to Freudian psychoanalysis and her subsequent distinction between the semiotic and symbolic, understood as two radically different modes of meaning production (pre-linguistic primary processes entering and interrupting the established linguistic codes with the thetic phase marking 'the threshold of language' [RPL 45]). The shift from 'intertextuality' to 'transposition' can best be described as a shift from a network of texts to a network of signifying systems. As examples for 'different sign systems', Kristeva mentions 'carnival, courtly poetry, scholastic discourse' (RPL 59). Signifying systems are, for example, literary genres or established types of discourse, but could also include non-linguistic signifying configurations, such as Barthes' fashion system. How this transposition from one system to the other unfolds depends on 'the articulation of the thetic', on the way the transition from the semiotic to the symbolic is organized. What distinguishes different signifying systems is how they allow or prohibit the ways the semiotic forces itself on to the symbolic, or to put it differently, how the ongoing conflict between the energy drives of the primary processes and the regulated linguistic codes of the established symbolic law (grammar, syntax, etc.) are articulated. This, in turn, determines the position of the thetic, understood as 'a break in the signifying process', the first separation of an object from the subject, 'a positing of identity or difference… that… represents the nucleus of judgment or proposition' (RPL 43).

While Kristeva's replacement of the term 'intertextuality' with 'transposition' received a lot of attention, it seems worth noting that she continued to use the term 'intertextuality' in its original meaning in a number of texts, interviews and lectures even after the publication of *Revolution in Poetic Language*.[4] As she states in *Hatred and Forgiveness* (2010), the main purpose for employing the term was to invite 'the reader to interpret a text as a crossing of texts', and 'a way of introducing history into structuralism' so as to 'reveal the inauthenticity of the writing subject' (HF 10).

If one were to turn this use of the term 'intertextuality' into a blueprint for a style of writing, Kristeva's own texts would qualify. Her numerous works on other authors can be considered as perfect examples of how to orchestrate a 'crossing of texts' in writing and how to connect the subject to history – all this without exercising the traditionally assumed authority of a preconceived author-position. Presenting herself not so much as author but as writer/reader (reader/writer), she allows other texts to speak on their own terms, constructing dialogues or conversations rather than pursuing a streamlined argument from above that subordinates other voices. This practice of what might be called 'intertextual writing' succeeds in unearthing in other texts that which has not been explicitly said, producing yet additional layers of meaning. By interconnecting other texts with her own, Kristeva creates a multiplicity of intersecting voices that reflect any given political and historical currents as well as the reading/writing experience of their 'author'. Understanding 'creative subjectivity as a kaleidoscope, a "polyphony"', Kristeva views the 'creator' as 'the one who produces a text by placing himself or herself at the intersection of this plurality of texts on their very different levels… semantic, syntactic, or phonic' (I 190). She herself is a prime example of this type of creator.

Notes

1 Some of which were translated into English and included in *Desire in Language* (1980), most importantly 'The Bounded Text' (DL 36–63) and 'Word, Dialogue, and Novel' (DL 64–91).
2 'The presence of the *genotext* within the *phenotext* is indicated by what I have called a *semiotic disposition*… the *semiotic disposition* will be the various deviations from the grammatical rules of the language… These variations may be partly described by way of what are called the *primary* processes (displacement, condensation – or metonymy, metaphor), transversal to the logico-symbolic processes that function in the predicative synthesis towards establishing the language system' (KR 28–9).
3 See 'How Does One Speak to Literature?' (DL 92–123; first published in French in *Tel Quel* in 1971), SNS 187–215, and IR 81–122. As for Barthes' writing on Kristeva, see 'Kristeva's *Semeiotike*', (Barthes 1986: 168–71).
4 See, among others, I 189–95, IR 258, ND and HF 10–11.

References

Allen, G. (2011), *Intertextuality*, London: Routledge.
Barthes, R. (1986), *The Rustle of Language,* trans. R. Howard, New York: Hill and Wang.

18

Intimate revolt

Gertrude Postl

Kristeva initially developed the concept of 'revolt', understood as 'intimate revolt', in her 1996 *Sens and non-sens de la révolte* (*The Sense and Non-Sense of Revolt*, 2000), followed by *La révolte intime* (1997, *Intimate Revolt*, 2002). From then onwards the notion of revolt appears in a number of other texts, including 'New Forms of Revolt' (2014), where she discusses the need for revolt in light of contemporary political developments and the problem of the adolescent's desire to believe. Kristeva's interest in revolt is a continuation of her earlier work on revolution in *La révolution du langage poétique* from 1974 (*Revolution in Poetic Language*, 1984), but it also marks a shift in perspective. *Revolution in Poetic Language*, with its focus on the relationship of the semiotic and the symbolic within the individual speaking subject, addressed the political dimension only indirectly by offering a discussion of the revolutionary potential of avant-garde literature. With the introduction of the concept of 'revolt' the individual speaking subject becomes located within the historically specific circumstances of the West at the end of the twentieth century and the psychoanalytic concern for individual psychic life is now related to broader cultural and political developments. Kristeva aims to explore the contributions psychoanalysis can make to the question of 'What Revolt Today?' – a question prominently placed at the beginning of both *The Sense and Non-Sense of Revolt* and *Intimate Revolt* (SNS 1; IR 1), the subtitle of both being *The Powers and Limits of Psychoanalysis*.

In Kristeva's account, we live in a new world order or a society of the spectacle (borrowing Guy Debord's famous phrase) which is dominated by media images, entertainment, and commodity exchange. In this new world order, clearly recognizable structures of political authority have given way to a dissemination of power or a power vacuum, and human beings have been turned into commodified configurations of body-parts or patrimonial individuals. As a result, revolt becomes impossible: 'who can revolt if man has become a simple conglomerate of organs, no longer a subject but a patrimonial person... a person barely free enough to use a remote control to choose his channel' (IR 4). In times of the perpetual reign of the pleasure principle, the encroachment of the entertainment industry, and the disappearance of a recognizable political power, 'who can revolt, and against what?' (SNS 8). Traditional cultural forms of revolt – inherent in European modernism – are being sidelined and eliminated by the superficiality of the spectacles contemporary culture has to offer: 'an essential aspect of the European culture of revolt and art is in peril... the very notion of culture as revolt and of art as revolt is in peril, submerged as we are in the culture of entertainment, the culture of performance, the culture of the show' (SNS 6). The only way to resurrect this disappearing culture of revolt is to turn to an intimate sphere beyond the influences of the spectral manifestations of commodities and images. But even this intimate realm is in danger of being colonized. As Kristeva stated already in *New Maladies of the Soul* (1995), 'today's men and women – who are stress-ridden and eager to achieve, to spend money, have fun, and die – dispense with the representation of their experience that we call psychic life' (NMS 7). Exploring one's psychic life is sacrificed for the artificial ease and consumption mentality of mainstream culture. 'Modern man is losing his soul, but he does not know it' (NMS 8), he is too caught up finding satisfaction in the superficiality of the show. But without this inner psychic life, no revolt is possible because 'the intimate is what is most profound and most singular in the human experience' (IR 44).

In order to explain her understanding of 'revolt', Kristeva turns to etymology. She locates the origin of the term 'revolt' in the Latin verb *volvere* which – free from any political connotations – means 'curve', 'entourage', 'turn' and 'return'. The term's meaning in Old French included 'to envelop', 'curvature', 'vault' but also 'to roll' and 'to roll oneself in'. Finally, the Italian meaning of *volta* and *voltare* adds the dimension of circular movement, a turning back and temporal return (SNS 1–2). The current, explicitly political meaning of 'revolt' was acquired only at the time of the French Revolution (IR 3). Overall, Kristeva points out 'the "plasticity" of the term throughout its history' and 'the richness of its polyvalence' (SNS 3). The most important dimension of this wide range of meanings discussed by Kristeva is 'turn', 'return' and 'turning back' which she connects to a 'questioning and displacement of the past' (IR 5). It is not sufficient just to revisit the past, the tradition that is in danger of being lost also has to be questioned so as to revise and adapt it to the challenges of the present. 'There is an urgent need to develop the culture of revolt starting with our aesthetic heritage and to find new variants of it' (SNS 7). Insisting on finding 'new variants' of an aesthetic tradition of contestation reveals that the project of 'revolt' is a project that concerns issues of representation – the 'retrospective return' of revolt leads to 'the limits of the representable/thinkable/tenable' (IR 7).

This plea to bring back to life – through questioning – a cultural history of revolt evokes the achievements of European modern thought (Descartes' doubt, the Enlightenment, Hegelian negativity, Marx and Freud), as well as those of twentieth-century avant-garde artists (the Bauhaus, Surrealism, Artaud, Stockhausen, Picasso, Pollock and Francis Bacon). 'Europeans are cultured in the sense that culture is their critical conscience.... The great moments of twentieth-century art and culture are moments of formal and metaphysical revolt' (SNS 6–7). The examples Kristeva chooses to discuss for these 'great moments' of revolt in modernism are Jean-Paul Sartre, Roland Barthes and Louis Aragon – different manifestations of revolt in terms of thought as well as style (SNS 29). More recently, responding to a general crisis of humanity and human identity, Kristeva ties her concept of revolt to European humanism, understood 'in the Nietzschean sense of a "transvaluation of values"' (2017: 17).[1]

This understanding of revolt as retrospective return and questioning of the cultural history of modernism, Kristeva wants 'to anchor... firmly in Freudian thought' (SNS 12), in particular in Freud's account of the Oedipal revolt and in his notion of the unconscious as a return to the archaic. The first meaning of revolt, found in Freud, is the story of the murder of the father by the brothers which leads to establishing binding sacrificial rituals or laws. Freud's second account of revolt – the unconscious as the ground underneath consciousness, as expressed by Freud in a letter to Ludwig Binswanger – 'signifies the possibility that psychoanalysis has to access the archaic, to overturn conscious meaning' (SNS 15), thereby gaining 'access to a timeless temporality' (the German *zeitlos*) which renders Freud 'a revolutionary in search of lost time' (SNS 16). Resulting from the Freudian contribution, Kristeva proposes three figures of revolt: (1) revolt as transgression of prohibition, understood as rebellion against the law; (2) revolt as repetition, in the sense of working through – addressing both the psychoanalytic situation and 'a certain literature', which attempt to retrieve lost memories, for example Proust's 'search for a lost time'; and (3) revolt as displacement and game – exemplified by Aragon, Sartre and Barthes, whose 'style and thought' she analyses in terms of 'the *combinatory* or the *game*' (SNS 28–9).

Considering the Freudian approach for her conception of revolt – violence, the archaic, timeless temporality but also the sacred and the sacrificial ritual – allows Kristeva to establish a link to her previous work in *Revolution in Poetic Language*. Both the violence of the patricide and the archaic timelessness encountered in the unconscious can be related to the destructive force of the semiotic which threatens, disrupts and irritates the order of the symbolic. While, on the other hand, the sacred, the sacrifice and the ritual resonate with a social law established to maintain order and keep the onslaught of the semiotic forces at bay. Art and literature all along have been trying to navigate a path between those tensions: 'art and literature are in fact a continuation of the sacred by other means' (SNS 13). But they are also a continuation of or substitute for bodily drives and sense experience. For this reason, Kristeva invests in (especially modernist) art and literature as manifestations of intimate revolt, in that there we find privileged examples for the transgression of the symbolic law through semiotic forces.

Crucial to the concept of intimate revolt is, furthermore, 'the arrival of women at the forefront of the social and ethical scene' (IR 5). Evoking the connection between the semiotic *chora* and the body of the mother, made in *Revolution in Poetic Language*, Kristeva relates women to 'sensory intimacy' and views the 'rehabilitation of the sensory' as 'alternative to the robotizing and spectacular society' (IR 5). Thus, the revival and questioning of a (masculine) cultural past has to allow for the expression of bodily states (the semiotic) and 'sensory experience', thereby highlighting the specific contribution of women to intimate revolt.

Revolt, however, is not to be confused with nihilism and its commitment to 'the stability of new values' at the price of a 'suspension of retrospective return, which amounts to a suspension of thought' (IR 6). Here in agreement with Arendt, Kristeva views this nihilistic dismissal of questioning (thus thinking) in favour of seeming new certainties as a form of totalitarianism. Instead, her approach to revolt – far from being a simple denial or refusal of established meaning – involves a kind of *jouissance* that results from the tension between 'unity, being, or the authority of the law' and the 'centrifugal forces of dissolution and dispersion' (IR 7). This tension between 'the law' and the dissolution and dispersion thereof, again can be cast in terms of meaning or representation. 'Thought or writing in revolt... attempt to find a representation (a language, a thought, a style) for this confrontation with the unity of law, being and the self... the bringing to the fore of everything that puts the very possibility of unitary meaning to the test' (IR 10). This is to say that 'intimate revolt' as a questioning and retrospective return has to be viewed as a form of expression – be it in literature, art or the psychoanalytic process – that at the same time adheres to the standards of the law but is also open to a destructive potential which is closely tied to the body and the sensory. Discussing Hegel, Heidegger and Sartre as examples for the negativity involved in a retrospective return, Kristeva claims that they all 'come up against a psychical reality that endangers consciousness... Erasure of subject/object borders, assault of the drive: language becomes tonality (*Stimmung*), memory of being, music of the body and of matter' (IR 9).

The artificiality and emptiness of the image world generated in the society of the spectacle turns the struggle for representation and meaning into the central problem of contemporary man: 'all these symptomatologies share a common denominator – the inability to represent... such a deficiency of psychic representation hinders sensory, sexual, and intellectual life' (NMS 9). The only chance to regain the ability to represent is to find this intimate psychic realm in which the rich tradition of art and literature as revolt can be revived against the reality of the spectacle and the bombardment of images. Fixed and frozen modes of representation have to give way to the *jouissance* – the negativity and violence – that results from negotiating the law and its undoing at the same time. Artists, writers, critics, but also psychoanalysts serve as model for this very negotiation: 'it is our responsibility to be interpreters, givers of meaning' – givers of meaning of 'a certain type of culture and art... [that] is threatened, indeed, impossible... the art and culture of revolt' (SNS 8). Giving meaning on the personal level through a retrospective return, a questioning and a sensory intimacy will revive those elements of cultural history that always had a critical potential and thus made possible the insertion of the semiotic into the symbolic. This is, according to Kristeva, the only way to prevent a life of death, of unhappiness, of bondage. If a culture of revolt 'did not exist, life would become a life of death' (SNS 7). A commitment to life requires revolt: 'happiness exists only at the price of a revolt. None of us has pleasure without confronting an obstacle, prohibition, authority, or law that allows us to realize ourselves as autonomous and free' (SNS 7). The goals of an 'intimate revolt' are thus ultimately political in that they involve issues of authority, autonomy and freedom. '[T]his cultural revolt intrinsically concerns public life and consequently has profoundly political implications... it poses the question of another politics, that of permanent conflictuality' (IR 11).

While the contemporary world certainly does not lack conflicts and conflict-solving has always been of concern for politics, this other politics of 'permanent conflictuality' Kristeva is talking about differs significantly from a traditional understanding of politics in terms of action. Here clearly distinguishing herself from Arendt's account of the political, Kristeva states that 'it is not exclusively in the world of action that this revolt is realized but in that of psychical life and its social manifestations (writing, thought, art)' (IR 11). It is on the level of language, or taken more broadly, on the level of representation and signs, that this politics of 'permanent conflictuality' is enacted. 'Intimate revolt' is a form of politics precisely because it allows, through the ongoing questioning of the retrospective return, an opening up of the realm of representation to the sensory and thus it enables the semiotic to break through the established laws of the symbolic order. Why else the detour through Freud, the urgency to unearth the unconscious, the access to the archaic, the role of the psychoanalyst as interpreter, translator and giver of meaning? Allowing for a particular form of (linguistic) expression, one that does do justice to the tension between the law and its dispersion and which does not repress the body and its drives is, for Kristeva, an ultimate political 'act'. But it is a political act that starts on the individual personal level – in the process of writing, the creation of works of art or in the exchange between analyst and analysand within the psychoanalytic process. An act of 'intimate revolt' counters the streamlined modes of expression generated by the society of the spectacle. A politics of 'permanent conflictuality' allows for the dissemination of meaning, for the representation of what cannot be represented, for cracks, disruptions, irritations of the identity and unity of the symbolic order, for a negativity to unfold and for the body itself to speak. All this undermines and threatens the pseudo-certainties of a commodity and entertainment culture and is thus a form of political intervention.

Whether Kristeva's emphasis on the psychoanalytic process, on the individual experience of the speaking subject and on an affect-guided transgression of modes of representation is, in fact, a form of politics or not, has generated an ongoing and creative debate on the meaning of politics and the political in Kristeva. Charges brought against Kristeva, including her alleged downplaying of the importance of action and political organization or her insensitivity towards issues of racism and colonialism,[2] have been counteracted by numerous attempts that critically evaluate but also defend a notion of politics that starts from the intimacy of psychic life and the ongoing renegotiation of meaning.[3]

To summarize: Kristeva's concept of intimate revolt responds to some of the most pressing challenges of our times, such as religious fundamentalism, populist movements, a culture of the image and a weakening of traditional democratic structures. When the entertainment industry and the market rule the world, when politics itself has become a spectacle and when the modes of representation have been reduced to meaningless sound bites and catchy images, insisting on the importance of the individual inner life and on forms of representation that allow for tensions and contradictions becomes an act of resistance or revolt. In Kristeva's own words: 'The permanence of contradiction, the temporariness of reconciliation, the bringing to the fore of everything that puts the very possibility of unified meaning to the test... this is what the culture of revolt explores' (2014: 9). What, however, remains an open question which needs to be addressed is whether this course of political intervention can exclusively rely on the history of *Western* art and literature.

Notes

1 This text is a shorter version of Kristeva (2014).
2 See Ahmed (2005), Gratton (2007) and Miller (2014).
3 See, among others, McAfee (2004), Sjöholm (2005), Chanter and Ziarek (2005), Margaroni (2007), Oliver and Keltner (2009) and Hansen and Tuvel (2017).

References

Ahmed, S. (2005), 'The Skin of the Community: Affect and Boundary Formation', in T. Chanter and E. P. Ziarek (eds), *Revolt, Affect, Collectivity. The Unstable Boundaries of Kristeva's Polis*, 95–111, Albany: State University of New York Press.

Chanter, T. and E. P. Ziarek, eds (2005), *Revolt, Affect, Collectivity. The Unstable Boundaries of Kristeva's Polis*, Albany, NY: State University of New York Press.

Gratton, P. (2007), 'What Are Psychoanalysts for in a Destitute Time? Kristeva and the Community in Revolt', *Journal for Cultural Research*, 11 (1): 1–13.

Hansen, S. and R. Tuvel, eds (2017), *New Forms of Revolt. Essays on Kristeva's Intimate Politics*, Albany, NY: State University of New York Press.

Kristeva, J. (2014), 'New Forms of Revolt', *Journal of French and Francophone Philosophy*, 22 (2): 1–19.

Kristeva, J. (2017), 'New Forms of Revolt', in S. Hansen and R. Tuvel (eds), *New Forms of Revolt. Essays on Kristeva's Intimate Politics*, 17–21, Albany: State University of New York Press.

Margaroni, M. (2007), 'Recent Work on and by Julia Kristeva: Towards a Psychoanalytic Social Theory', *Signs: Journal of Women in Culture and Society*, 32 (3): 794–808.

McAfee, N. (2004), *Julia Kristeva*, London: Routledge.

Miller, E. (2014), 'Investing in a Third: Colonization, Religious Fundamentalism, and Adolescence', *Journal of French and Francophone Philosophy*, 22 (2): 36–45.

Oliver, K. and S. K. Keltner, eds (2009), *Psychoanalysis, Aesthetics, and Politics in the Work of Julia Kristeva*, Albany, NY: State University of New York Press.

Sjöholm, C. (2005), *Kristeva and the Political*, London: Routledge.

19

Spirituality

Alison Jasper

References to religion are manifold in Kristeva's work. They draw, to a considerable extent, on her knowledge and experience of Christianity, which is significant. Her use of the term 'religion' also reveals certain assumptions about a 'world religions' paradigm. To critique this in the simplest terms, we could say that it has developed out of a predominantly Western context. From that perspective, it has promoted Christianity as template for a universal category. Comparisons and contrasts can thus be made more easily between 'religions'. Incommensurabilities, which trouble the assumption we are actually talking about 'a something' ('religion') at all, tend to be ignored. 'Religion' is assumed to exist in all human societies, although individual examples are variable and thus the discussion of greater or lesser value and sophistication has also tended to creep in. Given the body of work now challenging this paradigm (Masuzawa 2005; Asad 2003; Fitzgerald 2007; Cavanaugh 2009), it seems more appropriate, here, to set aside Kristeva's references to 'other religions' and concentrate on her more substantive engagements with Christianity. It is perhaps particularly important to avoid confusing Kristeva's interweaving of psychoanalysis and the history of European Christianity, with her sometimes controversial references to Islam. This controversy may be, in part, a consequence of her being a public intellectual living in France, where the separation of 'secular' state and 'religion' is a matter of, we might say, sacred principle. However, although Kristeva herself may talk about Islam as another 'religion' to be contrasted with Christianity, that aspect of her work is not the focus of this short piece.[1]

Giving this section the title of 'spirituality' is, then, a way to consider Kristeva's knowledge and understanding of Christianity in more detail without compounding issues surrounding her use of the term 'religion'. And in terms of what we might call Christian spirituality, she certainly draws extensively on notable writings – Loyola's *Spiritual Exercises*, John of the Cross' *Ascent of Mount Carmel* and Teresa of Avila's *Way of Perfection* and her *Interior Castle* are all referenced in detail in her work. What is also clear, however, is that these texts do not appear in her work as her personal guides for a journey towards the Christian God they invoke. In this sense, they do not appear 'on their own terms'.

More broadly, Christian doctrinal and spiritual works and Christian scriptures in particular are frequent and significant intertexts. In her early work, *Powers of Horror* (1980), she makes reference to a reading of the Levitical prohibitions to develop her notion of abjection. In *In the Beginning Was Love* (1985) she compares psychoanalysis with the foundational relationship of love within Christianity. In *The Feminine and the Sacred* (1998) she discusses with novelist and critic Catherine Clément whether or not Christianity has fostered the feminine. And since 2006, she has published two further works in which Christian ideas and writers, figure seriously. First *This Incredible Need to Believe* (2006) returns to the theme of how Christianity and psychoanalysis are, in some ways, parallel discourses, here coalescing around a fundamental wager on belief (INB vii). Her novelistic study of identity formation, *Teresa, My Love* (2008), knits historical records and the writings of the sixteenth-century Spanish saint Teresa of Avila in a form of extended analytical interpretation. It is unsurprising to learn that, in spite of growing up in Bulgaria in the former communist USSR, Kristeva's family were Orthodox Christians. She describes her continuing fascination with Christianity, as necessarily oedipal (*'forcément oedipiens'*),[2] both passionate and critical, fostered in lively debate with her father (HP 413), whose Christianity she repudiated but to whom (posthumously) she dedicated *Teresa, My Love*, a discussion of the saint's remarkable oedipal wrestlings and of her equally remarkable achievements.

But of course, Kristeva remains an 'atheist', 'non-believer' or 'humanist' (PSF 23; Kearney 2016: 97). Her treatment of the saint in *Teresa, My Love*, is indicative. An author should not be identified with a book's narrator, but there is a close enough resemblance between the narrator, Sylvia Leclerq, a French psychoanalyst, and Julia Kristeva, the author, to make the point tenable. In all her extensive researches, the narrator never concedes the slightest ground to Teresa's Christian convictions or beliefs. Some discussion and curiosity about Christian theology occurs but not as a means to her own salvation. At the same time, Leclerq fully acknowledges that Teresa's beliefs are fundamental, enabling her to work through the unpropitious circumstances of her time and family romances. Kristeva shares with a wide range of scholars of an atheistic – and feminist – bent, the desire to ask questions and to encourage people to think critically rather than simply to accept what they are told. So she sees the positive side of the Christian imagery of the Virgin Mary, in which the feminine and maternal have clearly been able to play some role in Western tradition (FS 60), however conflicted. But she is also conscious of the problem that remains. Maternal *réliance* (for Kristeva, the unavoidably fundamental role of the maternal, Kearney 2016: 114–15) may be the 'dawn of the psyche', preceding in importance, even the kickstart of our need to believe,[3] but it remains true that for the most part '[r]eligions either forget [a woman] or make her a goddess, a queen' (Kearney 2016: 104). In this way, her atheism is justified on feminist grounds but also in the sense in which this critique itself bears the mark of the speaking and 'revolting' as well as believing subject (INB 1) who questions the nature of (the Christian) God. Catherine Clément suggests that Kristeva is 'a Christian atheist' (FS 105), drawing, as she does, on such a richness of European Christian language, symbols and sources. Her 'sober and modest' atheism is 'the resorption of th[at] sacred into the tenderness of the connection to the other' (FS 60). But though Kristeva admires, she is sure she is not swayed. The Christian passion narrative is 'superb storytelling' (INB 59) but no doubt exists in her mind that however beneficial it has been in the past, this storytelling produces an undertow that makes it dangerous in the twenty-first century. Not the least of the problems is that it obstructs a woman's choice of whether or not to be a mother (Kearney 2016: 115). But if Kristeva is a (Christian) atheist, she is also a discriminating one. She has no interest in the sort of 'battle against religion' (INB 60) that we might associate with Richard Dawkins and some of the New Atheists who are also somewhat guilty of identifying 'religion' within a world religions paradigm.[4] More significantly perhaps, she remains adamantly opposed to the nihilistic atheism of ideological socialism, which, in the case of the former Soviet Union, she accuses of a massive failure of human compassion, not the least towards her own father (HP 413). This is, for Kristeva, the deathly nihilism of those in the modern world who 'hope to go without an ethics' and, often at the same time, 'use God for political ends' (Kearney 2016: 99–100).

'Spirituality' is not a word to be carelessly associated with Kristeva. Nonetheless, it can perhaps serve as a way to highlight or signpost some aspects of what 'inspires' Kristeva's work, and to open up a little further, her anti-nihilistic, post-Christian perspective. First of all, we need to remind ourselves that although Kristeva began her academic career within the context of poststructuralism and literary analysis, bringing Russian formalism to bear in her relationship with French intellectuals such as Roland Barthes (McAfee 2004: 4–9), Lacanian and Freudian psychoanalysis represents the ruling discourse in Kristeva's writing since the 1960s. And as an analyst in clinical practice, the one thing that clearly 'inspires' her is the hope of addressing human suffering and assuaging psychic pain. With this purpose in mind, she has continued to explore parallels between psychoanalytical and Christian modes of believing, however much she has resisted any investment in its theological premises. And in psychoanalytical terms, she is very clear that belief – aligned to understandings of (Christian) 'faith' – is fundamental in the development of the human psyche. Freud is well known for his strictures on Christianity as a (somewhat helpful) illusion, and Kristeva does not disagree with him. But she puts more emphasis on the fact that Freud himself needed to risk believing in something. Freud's God, logos, supports his faith in the possibility of rational thought, albeit employed in relation to an aspect of the human that is not itself ruled by reason (INB 6). Today, however, Kristeva thinks our global human culture is undergoing a quite unprecedented, existential crisis concerning the definition and value of the human (Kearney 2016: 93). The challenges we are facing overwhelm not only the capacities of Christian narratives but even the erstwhile capable framework in respect of logos on which Freud relied. We are struggling to find new, sufficiently provocative idealizations that can engage the unconscious as well as the conscious processes of the subject. We cannot seem to find structures or narratives sufficiently seductive and yet flexible, both to assure us of love and value and to support us when these idealizations – of parents, teachers, political leaders, messiahs and causes – inevitably fail or disappoint. Kristeva frequently suggests that Christianity was capable of doing this in the past. Now, she fears, we become entangled in these disillusionments, turning instead to the self-destructions of self-medication or suicide. In what she characterizes, after Guy Debord, as a 'society of the spectacle' (1967), she believes that the symbols and representations available for dealing with these shattering fluctuations in our psychic lives have become too banal and accessible. They have little power to generate the transmutational magic of a psychic process that grasps and then works through successive idealizations before they can inflict too much damage on individuals or the societies in which they live. The characteristic process of ongoing revolt as questioning, re-presenting and reflecting – generated and expressed in analysis or, optimally, in writing – is, for Kristeva, the only way to address the challenges we face. But to do this, we need a culture that encourages such rebellious questioning and fertile imagining, rather than one that subordinates them to values of uniformity and modes of efficiency. If the well of Christianity has run dry, however, she is clear that the process of encouraging rebellious questioning was once its proper mission.

And so, in the face of this intensifying threat, Kristeva proposes a 'post-Christian humanism' (Kearney 2016: 93). The post 'Christian' seems significant. She speaks of developing an ethics of solidarity with the weak and contesting any 'overemphasise on the cult of man [sic]' (Kearney 2016: 99). It should pay proper attention to a concept of singularity owing something to the notion of *haecceitas* in the work of philosopher-theologian Duns Scotus (1266–1308). We need to focus on the uniqueness and truth of human beings in this one or that one woman or man, rather than in some universal notion of humankind (Kearney 2016: 95). At the same time, she acknowledges her project must still provide enough coherence to generate the questioning and reimaging that engenders new idealizations to work with and through. In this sense, she claims her work is concerned with the greater question mark 'concerning that which is most serious'. This is a question mark that has long been associated with use of the (Christian) term 'God' (Kearney 2016: 99), but now needs a new trajectory. The humanism she advocates is associated with fostering tenderness and compassion, in relation both to self and to the other, within and outside ourselves. It must welcome strangers to ourselves. It must recognize humanity's embeddedness in the world, not just as men but also as women, as mothers, as adolescents grappling, often unsupported, with their initiation into adulthood, and always incarnated as bodies. Interestingly, however, she does not favour 'revolutionizing the city before revolutionizing ourselves' (Kearney 2016: 110). She does not follow the lead of liberation theology's moves to address the discontents of our contemporary civilization by prioritizing the communal and collective (Kearney 2016: 105). Instead:

> For the first time in history, we realize that it is not enough to replace old values with new ones. This is not a solution for us in the West because every solution ... in its turn, congeals into dogmas and dead ends that are potentially totalitarian... we forget that the speaking being is actually living, provided that one has a mental life. And yet this life only exists if it is a perpetual questioning of its norms and powers; of its own sexual, national, linguistic identity; of its desires, its sufferings, its loves and its hates. It is rebellious men and women who are threatened by the misfortunes in civilization, not political systems.
> (Kearney 2016: 109)

Of course, there are long-standing criticisms of her work, some of which will still apply to her new humanism for the twenty-first century, while others undoubtedly reference this Christian sensibility. The very largely European palette of influences within her work will still be seen as a weakness. The postcolonial scholar Gayatri Spivak notoriously found herself repelled by what she saw as Kristeva's 'Christianising psychoanalysis' (Spivak 1993: 17), which she felt expressed universalizing or essentializing moves Kristeva had no basis for making in her analysis of Chinese women. And Kristeva's preoccupations with Christianity and psychoanalysis have always hit a nerve for feminist theorists concerned that she strikes an altogether too patriarchal or 'dutiful' tone (Grosz 1990: 150) in respect of dominating influences, past and present. To be fair to Kristeva, in this humanistic project, she does seem to be listening to her critics. Speaking with Richard Kearney, she certainly addresses feminist concerns about motherhood, fully acknowledging that we need to encourage new – rebellious – theorizations that can allow for the erotic as well as for maternal *réliance*, keeping women linked to conventions (Kearney 2016: 114–15). She does recognize – at least in theory – that she cannot universalize her own perspective. Her new overtures towards Chinese cultures must begin with the fundamental recognition of heterogeneity. She wishes for further communication, but acknowledges 'gaps' it is better not to rush to fill:

> the best knowledge of Chinese male and female analysands invites us to better learn these 'gaps' and to keep count of them, in order to avoid the temptations for normativism and reductionism that can tempt psychoanalysis, and to diversify this listening to human singularities that specifies the ethic of psychoanalysis.
>
> (Kearney 2016: 121)

At the end of a conversation in which she has talked at some length about this new humanism, Kristeva comes back to the writing of Marcel Proust, and particularly to *À la recherche du temps perdu* (1913–27), which exemplifies her claims for the integrative power of writing. This is, for her, an outstanding narrative, characterized by questioning rebelliousness sufficient to address the maladies of Proust's soul, and perhaps, of some of his readers. So saying, it is interesting, in the light of what one might almost describe as Kristeva's '*Christian réliance*', to note the language she uses. It is, she says, an imaginative incorporation of the world – the transmutation of a body into literature (Kearney 2016: 125). Proust joins, she ventures, a Christlike ambition with Greek sensualism; 'the passion become man, sacrifices himself to the last cult – that of literature – which seems to him the only thing capable of closing the loop, of leading the Word to flesh' (Kearney 2016: 126). Perhaps, at the end, Kristeva would have to allow that her own work remains, in some sense, haunted by a Christian presence that refuses finally to be entombed.

Of course, when the classics of Christian spirituality make appearances in Kristeva's work, their theological claims are discounted. While keenly appreciative of their subtle power and deep complexity, Kristeva uses this spiritual work and her many references to Christianity, more as a measure of the current risks to our psychic well-being. As a practising psychoanalyst, she is evidently concerned for the human psyche or whatever constitutes the human soul.[5] Yes, she seems to say, Christian ontologies and ecclesial powers, no matter how impressive, have had their day. But in a world now overwhelmed with choices, she conjures up a troubling picture of '[w]eb-surfers' rushing towards 'supermarkets of spirituality' (Kearney 2016: 101), under the impression that it is easy to pick up reliable substitutes. Against the background of her well-rehearsed arguments about the challenges necessary to the subject in process or on trial (*en procès*) or to the speaking subject, the consequence of this headlong slide is becoming prey to disillusionment or sick with the malaise of ideality (INB 13, 16, 19), without the means to work through destructive idealizations towards a better, a more joyous, accommodation with the realities of our lives. In this sense, Kristeva suggests that stepping away from the past – from these now outmoded, but for millennia, capable forms of European Christianity – is not that straightforward. She is poised, inspired to move forward, encouraging serious and rebellious questioners to take up their pens, spray-cans or cameras, but not, definitely not, without a backward glance.

Notes

1. For those interested in exploring Kristeva's references to Islam, occurring for the most part in discussions of what Ian Almond calls 'the European subject and its symbolic discourse', many excellent studies are available, for example, McAfee (2000), Almond (2007) and Ibrahim (2018).
2. Perhaps this is something that Kristeva has come to understand about herself over the course of her career. In 1985 she traced her interest in Christianity back, not to any 'matter of oedipal rebellion', but to her own strong attraction to the Orthodox sensibilities of her childhood (PSF 23).
3. See Jasper (2013: 284–6).
4. In this vein, in recent years, she has participated in some international 'interreligious' meetings (Kearney 2016: 97–8).
5. See NMS.

References

Almond, I. (2007), *The New Orientalists: Postmodern Representations of Islam from Foucault to Baudrillard*, London: I.B. Tauris.
Asad, T. (2003), *Formations of the Secular: Christianity, Islam, Modernity*, Stanford, CA: Stanford University Press.
Cavanaugh, W. T. (2009), *The Myth of Religious Violence: Secular Ideology and the Roots of Modern Conflict*, Oxford: Oxford University Press.
Debord, G. (1967), *La Société du Spectacle*, Paris: Buchet/Chastel.
Fitzgerald, T. (2007), *Discourse on Civility and Barbarism: A Critical History of Religion and Related Categories*, Oxford: Oxford University Press.
Grosz, E. (1990), *Jacques Lacan: A Feminist Introduction*, London: Routledge.
Ibrahim, H. M. (2018), 'Foreigners to Kristeva: Refashioning Orientalism and the Limits of Love', *Journal of Commonwealth Literature*, 8 (2): 1–12, doi/10.1177/2158244018785700.
Ignatius of Loyola, St (1996), *Personal Writings*, trans. J. A. Munitiz and P. Endean, London: Penguin.

Jasper, A. (2013), 'Feminism, Religion and *This Incredible Need to Believe*: Working with Julia Kristeva Again', *Feminist Theology*, 21 (3): 279–94.

John of the Cross, St (1973), *The Collected Works of St John of the Cross*, trans. K. Kavanaugh and O. Rodriquez, Washington, DC: Institute of Carmelite Studies.

Kearney, R. and J. Zimmerman, eds (2016), *Reimagining the Sacred: Richard Kearney Debates God*, New York: Columbia University Press.

McAfee, N. (2000), *Habermas, Kristeva and Citizenship*, New York: Cornell University Press.

McAfee, N. (2004), *Julia Kristeva*, London: Routledge.

Masuzawa, T. (2005), *The Invention of World Religions*, Chicago: University of Chicago Press.

Proust, M. (1913–27), *À la recherche du temps perdu*, Paris: Gallimard.

Spivak, G. C. (1993), *Outside in the Teaching Machine*, London: Routledge.

Teresa of Avila, St (1976–85), *The Collected Works of St. Teresa of Avila*, trans. K. Kavanaugh and O. Rodriquez, Washington, DC: Institute of Carmelite Studies.

Teresa of Avila, St (2001–07), *The Collected Letters of St. Teresa of Avila*, trans. K. Kavanaugh, Washington, DC: Institute of Carmelite Studies.

20

Subject in process/on trial

Esther Hutfless and Elisabeth Schäfer

The *subject in process/on trial* represents one of the key concepts of Julia Kristeva's thinking. Developed already in her early works 'Le sujet en procès' (1973), *La révolution du langage* poétique (1974) and in the essay-collection *Polylogue* (1977)[1] and later further specified with regard to the subject of the intimate revolt, it is essentially connected with her thinking of the semiotic as a specific trans-linguistic, drive-related, bodily source within the signifying process and with her notion of poetic language. Based on her perception of the signifying process as consisting of both semiotic and symbolic modalities, Kristeva develops a theory of language and a correlative theory of the subject – both perceived as in process or on trial (Keltner 2009: 3).

With her notion of the subject in process/on trial, Kristeva takes into account the multiplicity of processes of signification, as well as the ever-ambivalent character of these processes, located on the edge of subversion, transgression, revolution and creativity on the one hand and the destruction or dissolution of meaning and subjectivity on the other hand. In this respect, the subject in process always carries this precarious character. As Patrick ffrench explains, Kristeva's use of the French word *procès* suggests 'elements of violence and struggle involved in the passage of subjectivity' (SP 173). Kristeva's subject in process therefore questions the paradigms and limits of modernity, focusing on a radical otherness that shatters the assumed safe ground of the Cartesian cogito, which sustains the sciences, liberal politics and all established forms of representation. Kristeva's subject in process does not mark a fixed position, it is no identity, no essence. It is a movement – the in-between of the semiotic and the symbolic, the materiality of the body and of language. It is thus the 'fragile border that conditions the speaking being' (Keltner 2009: 3). Situated between the semiotic and the symbolic, it is also the exceptional hinge of an open contact between the singular, the intimate – which is not the private – and the social and symbolic. Meaning is constituted, shattered, shifted and deconstructed in an open, relational and reciprocal contact among bodies, materiality, and the social.

From Jacques Lacan's split subject to Julia Kristeva's subject in process/on trial

For Kristeva, as for Lacan, subject formation goes hand in hand with language acquisition and is made possible and structured after the subject enters the symbolic that creates it as split. An important phase in Lacan's theory of subject formation is the mirror-stage, in the course of which the child recognizes itself as a whole through identification with its mirror image. Through this identification with its image, the child leaves behind the experience of a fragmented body, a body that eludes control, that suffers from unmet needs and that is perceived as unseparated from the maternal body and develops a compensatory perception of the body as separate, unified and whole, a perception Lacan calls illusionary. In Lacan's theory the subject finally turns to the paternal law, to the phallus and begins to speak in an attempt to overcome its constitutive lack, trying to satisfy its needs via language and the symbolic. The subject in Lacan's theory is split because it is structured based on this constitutive lack, alienated and divided through its entry into language and the symbolic (Lechte and Margaroni 2004: 26). In contrast, for Kristeva, the subject is split *not* because the fragmented body has to be left behind as the other of signification or as lack but because the bodily drives – Kristeva speaks of the semiotic – as an important aspect in the process of signification break in and interrupt the symbolic time and again (Lechte and Margaroni 2004: 26). This permanent semiotic interruption constitutes the symbolic as well as the subject *in process/on trial*.

In her text 'The Subject in Process' ('Le sujet en procès'), Kristeva refers to the fact that the subject of Lacanian psychoanalysis, which is marked by a lack and constituted as an imaginary unity, cannot grasp other economies of signification that annihilate, liquefy or exceed the unified process of signification marked by the phallus, which for Lacan functions as the empty signifier that structures the symbolic (SP 134). Kristeva, on the contrary, describes this seemingly unified subject of psychoanalysis as 'only one moment, a time of arrest, a stasis, exceeded and threatened by this movement [of the drives and the semiotic operations]' (SP 134). While in Lacan the body becomes the remainder, that which falls apart from signification and remains outside of the symbolic but causes and enables it, Kristeva attributes important aspects of signification to the effects of bodily drives, the semiotic and to the maternal function[2] that mediates the symbolic for the child (RPL 27). Signifying processes are based on and are the result of bodily processes and via the semiotic, the drives find their way into language and into the symbolic, but not in terms of representation or a simple transformation of the drives into language but in terms of discharges (PK xvi). The drives which articulate what Kristeva calls a semiotic *chora* are meaningful, but do not signify or represent something (PK xiv; RPL 26). Adopted from Plato, the *chora* in Kristeva's thinking cannot be perceived as an inner space within the subject, but is located in the intersubjective space initially created between mother and child and, similar to Plato's *chora*, it is related to processes of becoming and change that keep the subject in suspense and functions as an infinite source of signifying processes (RPL 26).

Through her approach, Kristeva brings the drives, the body, back into structural psychoanalysis and builds a bridge from Lacanian theory back to Freud's drive theory. But her approach goes far beyond that. With her notion of the subject in process/on trial Kristeva refuses to think of the relationship between body and language, materiality and the symbolic as a simple representational relationship. Neither does she think of this relationship in terms of a simple rejection of the material in favour of the symbolic. Instead, she further enhances psychoanalytic approaches in important aspects. Signification for Kristeva is a dialectic process between the semiotic and the symbolic, between moments of negativity, dissolution, transgression and moments of identity and stasis: 'Without the symbolic element of signification, we have only sounds or delirious babble. But without the semiotic element of signification, signification would be empty and we would not speak' (PK xv). Unlike in Lacan's phallus-based theory of signification, in Kristeva it is the semiotic *chora* that infuses meaning with significance and content.

Mobilized by the continuous irruption of the semiotic that threatens its identity, Kristeva's subject is always in motion, in a drift of change, a subject in process/on trial. In this process in which the unitary subject is annihilated by the semiotic drives, 'the Unconscious/Conscious division, the Signifier/Signified division, that is, even the very censoring through which the subject and the social order are constituted' (SP 134) get rejected. The subject in process is determined by a negativity running through it, which constitutes this subject as 'a mobile, non-subjectal and free subject' (SP 137). Kristeva's use of the concept of negativity differs significantly from its development within Hegel's framework. The idea that Hegel presents and unfolds in *The Phenomenology of Spirit* lies in the discovery of the meaning of negativity as a term that characterizes everything that exists. The subject, also characterized by negativity, returns to itself through its opposite and thus always becomes other and non-identical with itself. Contrary to Hegel, for Kristeva there is no synthesis, no *Aufhebung* of the two dialectic elements;

the contradiction between the semiotic and the symbolic will never be neutralized (PK xv). Negativity for Kristeva appears as the potentiality for restructuring the processes of the semiotic and the symbolic. Negativity here is not to be confused with negation, since it precedes symbol formation and can be understood as a deconstructing force. The intimate structure of the subject in process reveals itself in touching the frontier of absolute negativity as a permanent element of thought. Being is revealed not through insight into its abiding truth but in the form of conflict and contradiction. By contrast, in Hegel the negativity of being gives birth to the dialectic.

Kristeva turns towards a materialistic understanding of Hegel. As she states, 'a materialist reading of Hegel allows a thinking of this negativity as the trans-subjective and trans-semiotic moment of the separation of matter which is constitutive of the conditions of symbolicity, without confusing it with this symbolicity itself or with the negations internal to it' (SP 139; see also RPL 117). Thus, negativity must not be confused with negation which remains within the framework of logic. Rather, it is the essential moment that integrates rupture in Hegelian becoming. Negativity therefore is already a concept in process and in a state of deconstruction. As such, it produces effects. For Kristeva, a comprehensive understanding of the effects of negativity can only be gained through a connection with Freud's drive theory. This includes the idea of the lasting heterogeneity of the symbolic, which can never be purified from its physical-material origin or needs and desires, although the subject always strives for such purification. Similarly, the subject in process/on trial remains heterogeneous. Kristeva assumes it can never be completely derived from the activity of matter, even if it is related to it. The negativity that is constitutive of the subject in process appears as '*expenditure* or *expulsion*' (SP 139) and sets up an object separate from the body, fixing it as absent at the moment of separation: that is, as a sign.

The subject in process and poetic language

Kristeva's subject in process is constitutive of what she calls poetic language. Poetic language is shaped by specific forms of signification, shattering and unsettling the identity of meaning as much as of the speaking subject and 'consequently, of transcendence' (DL 125). Poetic language in Kristeva's understanding is situated on a precarious and ambivalent edge: it may accompany and mirror crisis within social, political and institutional structures. The mutations of such structures may be inscribed into poetic language. Yet due to its distinct economy, poetic language is close to psychosis.

> In certain schizoid phenomena and in the 'poetic language' of the modern text, negation and syntactic structure will have their status transformed,

or their normativity disturbed. These textual phenomena bear witness to a specific pulsional economy, an expenditure or a freeing up of the 'pulsional vector', and thus to a modification of the relation of the subject to the outside.

(SP 141–2)

While in psychosis the forces of negativity can lead to the loss of reality and destroy every syntactic linkage, the poetic text is in Kristeva's understanding an 'experience of limits' which translates and transforms the struggle of the psychotic with symbolicity (a struggle between stasis and expulsion) into a new organization of reality and into new forms of signification (SP 142). Thus *poeisis*, this form of creation which allows the heterogeneity of the drives to become productive, can be understood as a 'subversive strategy of displacement, one which dislodges the hegemony of the paternal law by releasing the repressed multiplicity interior to language itself' (Butler 1993: 170).

For Kristeva a subject that speaks always finds itself in the space of 'the gap opened up between signifier and signified' (DL 128) and is thus situated in a space that always already exceeds linear and unequivocal structures of meaning. With the subject in process, Kristeva attempts to describe processes of signification as they can be found in avant-garde literature, processes characterized above all by the incompleteness, the interminability of both subject and meaning. Here, language does not serve simply to describe or depict something that lies outside of itself. Poetic language as employed in avant-garde literature is more concerned with the structure of language itself. The focus is on material forces that are always at work in processes of the constitution of meaning – like, for example, writing poetry – and which are normally obscured by conventional grammar. These material forces are connected to the drives and Kristeva's understanding of how the drives work in the semiotic and therefore push the semiotic into the symbolic. In Freud's view, the drive is to be understood as a borderline concept, located between body and the psyche. Poetry neither depicts nor describes drives but makes the processes of signification itself visible (Oliver 1993: 3). In poetry language tends to be detached from its symbolic function and opened towards a semiotic articulation. With a material carrier like the body and its voice, this semiotic network gives literature rhythm and musicality.

Kristeva thinks not merely of subjectivity but also of the body, of materiality as processual. Thus, the body in Kristeva's work does not represent a unity but a plurality of separate parts that form a diverse site where the drives are applied. This 'dismembered body' cannot be put together – according to a unity assumed to be original. It sets itself in motion, unless it is contained in a practice that attempts to fix the process of signification.

The subject in process, therefore, is not simply the Lacanian subject of the symbolic. It is itself located on the edges of symbolicity: 'The subject of expenditure is... not a punctual site, a subject of enunciation; it acts across the organization (the structure or finitude) of the text in which the *chora* of the process is figured' (SP 142). As poetry is the paradigmatic topos for the subject in process, the site where the heterogeneity and plurality of meaning become productive, Kelly Oliver suggests that for Kristeva 'the openness to poetry is the openness to difference' (1993: 2). While the symbolic needs identity and unity, the semiotic always questions and disrupts this unity, a fact that lends the dialectic between the two an ethical and political significance.

The subject in process and its ethico-political stakes

Kristeva's subject in process has repeatedly been approached as an important source for thinking both the ethical and the political, because it is associated with a radical otherness that is inscribed into every meaning and leads to permanent challenges, deconstructions and reconstructions of subjectivity as much as of the symbolic. The subject in process describes a subject that is capable of putting itself as well as meaning at risk again and again. It constitutes a specific form of ethical practice, traced by Kristeva in the '*ethical function* of the text':

> 'Ethics' should be understood here to mean the negativizing of narcissism within a practice; in other words, a practice is ethical when it dissolves those narcissistic fixations (ones that are narrowly confined to the subject) to which the signifying process succumbs in its socio-symbolic realization. Practice, such as we have defined it, positing and dissolving meaning and the unity of the subject, therefore encompasses the ethical.
> (RPL 233)

Kristeva's subject in process is a subject that does not exclude and suppress the radical otherness within itself but makes it productive. 'It thus attacks closed ideological systems', as well as 'the structures of social domination (the state)' (SP 137). Kristeva considers the subject in process not only as questioning its own identity along with the truth of every meaning but also as the productive source against all forms of norms and ideology, the critical source within revolution itself. Therefore, it is the consistent precursor of the subject of the intimate revolt in her later work. 'The subject of intimate revolt is continuing the work of the subject-in-process', Cecilia Sjöholm argues (2005: 101). Kristeva understands intimate revolt as a return of the subject to itself, which leads to an unfinished process of searching for truth. The subject of intimate revolt, for example, rebels against a technocratic world and constantly questions its institutions anew. Like the subject in process introduced in the 1970s, it is determined by the situation of our bodily being in the world, that is, by the semiotic *chora*, and calls for new perspectives on corporeality to be explored in philosophy, art, literature and the practice of psychoanalysis. In both its earlier and more recent theorizations, Kristeva's subject in process is a subject that never reaches totality, unity or identity but is structured by crisis and difference. As such, it is the source of a productive and not violent relation to the other, because the subject itself is always the place of the other.

Notes

1 Eight of the essays in this collection were translated in English and included in the anthology *Desire in Language*.
2 Kristeva's thinking of the maternal is based more on Melanie Klein's works than on those of Jacques Lacan. Of course, for Kristeva it is important that the child separates from the maternal body, but she perceives the maternal as an important mediating force that precedes the law of the father. For the process of the constitution of meaning, the movement of detachment from the mother's body – what Kristeva describes as a movement from a corps-à-corps to a face-à-face avec la mère – is therefore central (HDA 321, 325).

References

Butler, J. (1993), 'The Body Politics of Julia Kristeva', in K. Oliver (ed.), *Ethics, Politics, and Difference in Julia Kristeva's Writing*, 164–78, New York: Routledge.
Keltner, S. K. (2009), 'Introduction', in K. Oliver and S. K. Keltner (eds), *Psychoanalysis, Aesthetics, and Politics in the Work of Kristeva*, 1–15, Albany: State University of New York Press.
Lechte, J. and M. Margaroni (2004), *Julia Kristeva: Live Theory*, London: Continuum.
Oliver, K. (1993), 'Introduction', in K. Oliver (ed.), *Ethics, Politics, and Difference in Julia Kristeva's Writing*, 1–22, New York: Routledge.
Sjöholm, C. (2005), *Kristeva and the Political*, New York: Routledge.

21

The semiotic/The symbolic

Dawid Kołoszyc

The terms 'semiotic' (*le sémiotique*) and 'symbolic' (*le symbolique*) designate two distinct, yet inseparable, modalities of the signifying process in Kristeva's theory of meaning. The question of their relationship remains essential throughout Kristeva's thought, even as her concerns move away from semiotic and literary theory to psychoanalytic explorations of the limits and possibilities of subjective experience in a late modern, Western culture afflicted by a crisis of meaning.

The earliest version of the distinction may be found in Kristeva's semanalysis, developed in the late 1960s and early 1970s in response to formalist, structuralist and poststructuralist approaches to text interpretation. Semanalysis distinguishes between 'phenotext', or the manifest text organized according to formal rules of presentation and communication, and 'genotext', or the productivity involved in the generation of textual meaning and inscribed within the text. Combining Hegelian and Marxist dialectics with the linguistic/semiotic theories of Hjemslev, Benveniste and Jakobson, as well as with Freud's psychoanalytic exploration of dreamwork and subjectivity, Kristeva's aim was to chart out a meaningful critique of three dominant, interrelated tendencies in contemporary theories of meaning: (1) the tendency to describe *systems* of meaning while neglecting meaning as a *process*; (2) the tendency to emphasize formal aspects of meaning as a product while neglecting what cannot be signified, symbolized and organized according to formal logic; and (3) the tendency to exclude the embodied, speaking subject in favour of radically impersonal notions of 'text' and 'discourse'. In short, the distinction between genotext and phenotext allowed Kristeva to challenge linguistic and semiotic theories that treated meaning as a *product* by proposing a dialectical approach that treated meaning as a *productivity*, taking into account 'the production of meaning prior to meaning' (KR 84) without reducing it to an endless slippage (or deferral) of a textual signification detached from human experience. As Kristeva explains in 'My Memory's Hyperbole', the purpose of her semiotic theory was to *dynamize* structuralist thought by considering human subjectivity at the crossroads of *soma* and *psyche*, biology and society, unconscious and conscious meaning, rather than to engage in yet another kind of textual deconstruction (PK 9).

The intimate connection between the earlier and the later terms of Kristeva's distinction becomes explicit in 'The System and the Speaking Subject' (1973), where semanalysis constitutes an attempt to reconsider the problem of meaning dialectically by bringing into play a material (bodily/ unconscious) *heterogeneity* that had been excluded as much from Derrida's deconstruction, which focuses on the infinite play of the (textual) signifier, as from Hegelian and Marxist dialectics, both of which end up privileging a final reconciliation of antagonisms. The symbolic, as described in this essay, echoes the phenotext, constituting the order of language, which is also the order of social rules and conventions involved in the maintenance of meaning; and the genotext is clearly identified with the semiotic: 'The presence of the *genotext* within the *phenotext* is indicated by what I have called a *semiotic disposition*' (KR 28). In 'Politique de la littérature' (1973), 'symbolic' and 'semiotic' figure as the preferred terms. The symbolic is described here as belonging 'to the order of the sign, so to speak, and at the same time of nomination, syntax, signification and denotation of an object', and, consequently, to 'a scientific "truth"'.[1] The semiotic is said to be 'chronologically anterior and synchronically transverse to the sign, to syntax, to denotation and signification. Made of frays [*frayages*] and their marking, it is a provisory articulation, a non-expressive rhythm' (PL 14). The semiotic therefore names an experience that, while meaningful in itself, marks the limits of language as a formal system of signifiers. A cry or a laughter, for instance, may be called 'non-sensical', though only insofar as we identify meaning with the symbolic; without such experiences, however, the symbolic would remain radically superficial, if not altogether inhuman.

Strictly speaking, then, meaning exists only as an ongoing, dynamic process between the two modalities; Kristeva calls this the 'materialist' version of Hegelian 'negativity'. 'The process of signification, in its dialectical materialist complexity, consists of the contradiction of the two modes. To say that language is a practice is to grasp precisely how the symbolic, and with it meaning, is displaced under pressure from the semiotic' (PL 14). The symbolic names aspects of meaning that can be posited and shared via conventional discourse: the realm of communicative discourse and representation, the realm of signs, objects and ideas that can be grasped by consciousness. The semiotic names the process through which meaning is disrupted by something heterogeneous inherent in it, bearing witness to the irreducibility of human experience – particularly its life and death drives – to any fixed or final thesis. 'The symbolic (and language) is thetic [*thétique*]: language is thesis par excellence. However, far from being a point of origin (idealistic conception), this symbolic is a rupture and a displacement of the semiotic process' (PL 14). In the absence of the semiotic, the symbolic would be reduced to 'simple repetitive systems'. Through its eruptions, the semiotic 'displaces, infinitely and indefinitely, the thesis' that language is and hence functions as a 'mechanism of renewal'. Nevertheless, '[t]he semiotic is the revolutionary factor of a [signifying] practice only on the condition that it confront its symbolic thesis (from meaning to structure)' (PL 14–15).

The 'revolutionary' character of the constructive/destructive dialectic between the semiotic and the symbolic constitutes the central concern of Kristeva's *Revolution in Poetic Language*, published in French in 1974. The text offers the most complex elaboration of Kristeva's theory of meaning (or *signifiance*, a term that resists translation) while focusing on what cannot be fully contained within formal articulations of meaning: a materiality always already infused with a mentality, an alterity within language that is essential to the very existence of language and that, insofar as it is excluded from any social, political, religious or philosophical system, haunts it from within. Here Kristeva defines the semiotic etymologically (from Greek, *sémeion*) as a 'distinctive mark, trace, index, precursory sign, proof, engraved or written sign, imprint, trace, figuration' (RPL 25; see also DL 133). This definition is meant to emphasize that the semiotic articulates something that is neither meaningless nor reducible to grammar, syntax and logic; and that the symbolic, while necessary for the maintenance of the possibility of shared meaning, would feel like a hollow script or jargon without it. All discourses may be described in terms of the particular kind of dialectical interaction between the semiotic and the symbolic: from the linguistic formalism of theory to the semiotically inclined language of certain kinds of modern poetry or song. In any case, *signifiance* as a dynamic process involving a dialectical interplay between the two realms of meaning can never arrive at any kind of final synthesis, any kind of absolute Meaning.

Kristeva's discussions of the semiotic and the symbolic in *Revolution in Poetic Language* confirm the central role of psychoanalytic concerns in her thought, enabling her to pursue a dialectical process that is not only historical or economic but also subjective – biological, psychological *and* social – in order to establish 'a theory of signification based on the subject, his formation, and his corporeal, linguistic, and social dialectic' (RLP 14–15). The point of this work was to explore, in her own manner, Freud's affirmation of unconscious (bodily and psychic) inscriptions that are meaningful even before being systematically articulated. The challenge, in this respect, was to develop a coherent alternative to Lacan's own move beyond Freud in his theory of the three psychic registers: real, imaginary and symbolic.

Kristeva's notion of the semiotic, borrowing aspects of Hjemslev's theory of a fundamental, 'amorphous' meaning, accomplishes this by indicating that the 'real' is not merely a 'blank' or an 'emptiness' but rather is already infused with expressible 'imaginary' traces despite the absence of 'symbolic' thought (I 23). This, in effect, embodies Kristeva's own 'return to Freud', one that rejects Lacan's understanding of the unconscious as structured according to the logic of language. In Kristeva's view, Lacan's approach echoes Derrida's assertion that it is impossible to think anything, including the body 'in itself', that is not already a text or a metaphor. Kristeva acknowledges that her notion of the semiotic may resemble, in some respects, Derrida's notions of 'trace' and 'gramme', yet insists on the logical and chronological priority of the semiotic. There is something unnameable within subjective experience – and within every signifying process – which is nonetheless never simply an 'absence', a 'lack' or a 'void' but a psychosomatic process that persists in the subject of meaning even when repressed or excluded from conscious and/or social signification.

The effort to describe the dialectic between the semiotic and the symbolic is, within this scheme, a means of thinking not only the emergence and dynamics of meaning but also the emergence and dynamics of subjective experience as already meaningful prior to entry into language. 'The genesis of the *functions* organizing the semiotic process can be accurately elucidated only within a theory of the subject that does not reduce the subject to one of understanding, but instead opens up within the subject this other scene of pre-symbolic functions' (RPL 27). Kristeva's effort to describe the origins of subjective experience closest to the realm of pure biology or materiality, and prior to any form of subjective unity or identity, is most explicit in her elaboration of Plato's concept of *chora* – a formless receptacle of all becoming – as the semiotic *chora*. Kristeva describes this as 'a nonexpressive totality formed by the drives and their stases in a motility that is as full of movement as it is regulated' (RPL 25). Elsewhere in her early work, Kristeva refers to the semiotic *chora* as 'unnameable' and 'hybrid', 'definitely heterogeneous to meaning but always in sight of it or in either a negative or surplus relationship to it' (DL 133). While subject to certain kinds of natural and sociohistorical constraints, which Kristeva refers to as an 'ordering' [*ordonnancement*] (RPL 26), 'the semiotic chora is no more than the place where the subject is both generated and negated, the place where his unity succumbs before the process of charges and stases that produce him' (RPL 28). Within the *chora*, bodily drives discover the possibility of metaphor and metonymy, laying the foundation for the acquisition of language in general, and poetic language in particular. The *chora* can never be fully left behind or absorbed into the symbolic, manifesting its presence in the former through pulsations, pressures or disruptions.

Once the semiotic *chora* encounters the possibility of signification defined through *positioning* and the play of differences, subjective experience informed by propositions and judgements is first established. Echoing Hegel's concept of *thesis*, Kristeva describes the break that leads to signification as the *thetic* phase: the inexplicable, 'qualitative leap' (RPL 66) from the semiotic to the symbolic, 'that crucial place on the basis of which the human being constitutes himself as signifying and/or as social' (RPL 67). The thetic phase thus names a 'threshold' (RPL 48) between the semiotic and the symbolic: a process of unification that simultaneously entails a rupture, putting 'a heterogeneous functioning in the position of signifier' (RPL 49). The semiotic *chora* figures as the precondition of the thetic phase, rather than its failure; indeed, the very transgression or tearing open of the thetic by the semiotic is the condition for the possibility of *poetic language* – a designation which names any signifying practice capable of infusing the symbolic with an influx of the semiotic in a 'creative' manner, challenging the symbolic order with a new experience of signification.

The renewal of the heterogeneous, mobile possibilities of the semiotic within the symbolic is what enables the revolutionary potential of any signifying practice whose aim is new meaning, and what distinguishes it from the (neurotic or conventional) fixation on superficial meaning as well as from the (psychotic or nihilistic) rejection of meaning in favour of non-sense. Kristeva describes the *revolutionary* activity of the semiotic as 'articulated by flow and marks: facilitation, energy transfers, the cutting up of the corporeal and social continuum as well as that of signifying material' (RPL 40). This, therefore, is first and foremost a revolution in meaning and subjectivity: a revolution in the relationship between the embodied and ruptured human subject and the symbolic order in all of its distinct yet inseparable manifestations, whether cultural, historical, political, religious, economic, literary, artistic, scientific, or critical. Echoing Lévi-Strauss' structuralist anthropology, Kristeva asserts that, within the terms of this dynamic, the thetic embodies a certain experience of sacrifice along with the emergence of logos, and therefore tends to be theologized as the site of the sacred – differently, depending on culture, but always accompanied by the establishment of a limit to *jouissance*. Art and literature, on the other hand, transcend the logic of sacrifice, demonstrating that the emergence of the thetic phase is possible beyond sacrifice, beyond prohibition, and beyond any fetishization of the thetic. Defined as the 'semiotization of the symbolic' (RPL 79), revolutionary art, poetry, literature, theatre, music and dance transform the socio-symbolic order by splitting it open and enabling the experience of *jouissance* within the limits and opportunities offered by this order – but also, in certain cases, transgressing them. Kristeva effectively argues that the revolution in poetic language is a permanent affair: both unavoidable and necessary. At stake is the possibility of a constant renewal of the experience of the semiotic within the symbolic order so as to infuse the latter with the promise of a *beyond* that is no longer a metaphysical or onto-theological absolute, yet not a mere descent into irrationalism, nonsense or madness either. In 'From One Identity to Another', poetic language is defined as 'the very place where social code is destroyed and renewed' (DL 132). In a later interview, Kristeva speaks of the importance of inclusion of the semiotic within the symbolic in order to 'reach a moment of distortion, a moment of rhetorical figures, rhythms, and alliterations, what is in fact poetic language in all its particularities' (I 212). Poetic language is revolutionary insofar as it embodies both a renewal of the symbolic and an affirmation of the psychosomatic origins of any signifying process.

As in her earlier work, the distinction between the semiotic and the symbolic remains, strictly speaking, theoretical in this context; in reality, neither modality can be entirely isolated, just as neither refers to a singular phenomenon. Regardless of the emphasis on revolution here, Kristeva's terminology conceals a double paradox: The semiotic must be understood, at once, as the precondition of the symbolic *and* its transgression; and the symbolic constitutes, at once, the order of the repression of the semiotic *and* the condition of its meaningful manifestation. Kristeva never ceases to insist on this paradox:

> By symbolic, I mean the tributary signification of language, all the effects of meaning that appear from the moment linguistic signs are articulated into grammar, not only chronologically but logically as well ... By semiotic, on the other hand, I mean the effects of meaning that are not reducible to language or that can operate outside language, even if language is necessary as an immediate context or as a final referent.
>
> (I 21)

The paradox is enhanced by the fact that, within this scheme, both the *chora* and the *thetic* describe something radically indistinct, so that it may be appropriate to consider them as naming otherwise unnameable events or experiences within the ongoing dialectic between the semiotic and the symbolic. The former thus figures as a formless yet bounded 'space' associated with pre-oedipal maternality, where the subject first experiences himself or herself as a meaningful body in relation to a meaningful other prior to any symbolic meaning, and the latter as a 'moment' of rupture that is neither semiotic nor symbolic, neither pure productivity nor (yet) a product, but 'where positions and their syntheses (i.e. their relations) are set up' (RPL 72). In the end, the semiotic *chora* serves as a necessary reminder of the 'otherness' inherent in every subject – of the fact that the speaking being, as a productivity of drives and affects, can never be fully realized within a play of signifiers, even if, without the symbolic, there is no human 'subject' to consider.

While the use of the terms 'semiotic' and 'symbolic' becomes increasingly less prominent in Kristeva's later work, particularly after 1990, their relationship remains significant as much in her psychoanalytic studies as in her critical reflections on politics, culture and religion. Indeed, Kristeva returns to them in her essays and interviews in a manner that clearly indicates their continuing importance across many of her clinical and critical concerns. The discussions of language and melancholia in *Black Sun*, for instance, rely heavily on the assumption that a meaningful relationship between the semiotic and the symbolic is crucial to a healthy psychic life. While shifting Kristeva's earlier emphasis on the revolutionary potential of the semiotic towards an emphasis on symbolic resources in the face of a total collapse of meaning, these discussions continue to affirm the crucial role of the 'heterogenous dimensions of language that are liable to different psychic imprints' (BS 40) for a symbolic constitution that feels genuine and embedded with possibilities. The psychoanalyst's task, in this respect, is to pay special attention to the depressive subject's incapacity to experience a (physically and psychically) meaningful life due to the *double* 'rejection of the signifier as well as semiotic representatives of drives and affects' (BS 44). More than a decade and a half later, in 'Thinking about Liberty in Dark Times' (2004), Kristeva still speaks of the relationship between the semiotic and the symbolic as an ongoing concern that resists any particular 'program', political or otherwise, and in terms that explicitly resonate with her earliest theoretical formulations:

> It is simply an attempt to think of 'meaning' not only as a 'structure' but also as a 'process' or 'trial'... by looking at the same time at syntax, logic, and what transgresses them, or the trans-verbal... The semiotic is not independent of language, but underpins language and, under the control of language, it articulates other aspects of 'meaning' which are more than mere 'significations,' such as rhythmical and melodic inflections. Under the influence of Freudian distinctions between the representations of things and the representations of words, I try to take into consideration this dual nature of the human mind, and especially the constraints of biology and the instinctual drives that sustain and influence meaning and signification.
>
> (HF 11)

Kristeva's attempt to respond to what she increasingly came to consider a crisis of meaning and subjectivity in late modernity is the key reason for her growing emphasis on a meaningful balance between the semiotization of the symbolic and the symbolization of the semiotic. In the psychoanalytic studies of the 1980s, art and literature are no longer regarded predominantly as a means to challenge the symbolic order but, along with psychoanalytic and even religious discourses, as a symbolic support for the modern subject: increasingly anxious and depressed, increasingly fragmented within a growing diversity of symbolic demands and possibilities, and increasingly deprived of – or incapable of assuming – any kind of stable, symbolic existence in a culture engaged in an ongoing process of self-deconstruction. In this respect, Kristeva's early, semiotic theory of meaning, along with its psychoanalytic applications, gradually assumes the form of an extensive, critical analysis of what may be described as the two faces of late modern nihilism: on the one hand, nihilism as a superficial, cynical or merely desperate affirmation of nonsense or 'asymbolia', unwilling or unable to produce anything meaningful; on the other hand, nihilism as an uncritical or totalitarian effort – techno-scientific, political, economic or cultural – to reduce all meaning to calculation; to put an end, once and for all, to the risk of ambiguity, uncertainty and disorder; and to repress or reject as useless, untrue or meaningless anything that cannot be absorbed into some kind of fixed logic or constituted as a universal product. Arguably, the continuing relevance of Kristeva's theory of the relationship between the semiotic and the symbolic has much to do precisely with its capacity to challenge any attempt to offer a definite diagnosis for this so-called 'postmodern condition', while offering ever new ways of thinking the meaning of the crisis that characterizes it and affirming both the possibility and the necessity of an endless process of meaningful (semiotic *and* symbolic) revolts across a variety of signifying practices.

Note

1   All translations from this text are mine.

INDEX

abjection/abject 5, 8–9, 63–4, 75–6, 84–7, 111–18, 149–69, 180–90, 240, 247, 261, 269–76
   abysmal abjection 160
   civilization 208
   definition of 198–201, 272
   fascist fantasies 114
   modernism/modernity 6
   on modernist art 9, 197–209
   Nordic abjection 159
   political abjection 8, 150
   and powers of abstraction 156–63
   in *Powers of Horror* 5, 63, 159, 181, 197, 200, 269, 314
   pragmatism to 75–7, 89–90
   psychic formations of 82
   to resist 88–9
   subject-object relationship 115–16
   symbolic and semiotic 117–18
abstracting treatment 163
academics and Communist intellectuals 25
Action Poétique (journal) 27
Ades, Dawn 204
Ahmed, Sara 119, 125–7
Algra, Keimpe 40, 43
ALP. *See* Anna Livia Plurabelle (ALP)
Althusser, Louis 17, 22, 25
androgyny/androgynous 216, 222, 225, 227 n.2
animal condition 197, 204, 208–9
Anna Livia Plurabelle (ALP) 153
Anthropocene 8, 150, 162, 168, 174
antisemitism 141, 166, 168, 182
Aragon, Louis 4, 19, 23, 307
   Irene's Cunt 64, 67

Arendt, Hannah 8, 145 n.3, 150–63, 287–93
   abjection 164–7
   communicational function 132
   dissertation on Augustine 135–6
   The Human Condition 134, 138, 140
   natality 130, 134–40
   The Origins of Totalitarianism 134
   plurality 140–4
   in political 131, 133–4, 136, 138–40
   Rahel Varnhagen: The Life of a Jewess 140–1
   reflective judgment 135, 145 n.7
   On Revolution 138
   on space age 150
   subject 131
   transpolitical effect 169
art 58, 111, 117, 233
   abject 184, 197–8, 201
   anamnesis 118
   avant-garde 47, 277–8
   and literature 29, 118, 246, 274, 308–10, 333, 335
   modernist art 9, 58, 69, 179–80
   with psychoanalysis 125
   veiling in 111–12, 125
Art Press (magazine) 28
atheism 220, 315
atomic age 150
autotextuality 66
avant-garde 277–84. *See also* European avant-gardes
   artists 67–9
   feminine and 57–72
   French 63

historical 277–8, 280
literary/artistic 277
and modernism 59
psychoanalysis 63
subject in process (*see* subject/
  subjectivity)
symbolic and semiotic 280

Bacon, Francis 201
  *Diptych: Study of the Human
    Body – From a Drawing by
    Ingres* 204–5
  fluid bodies 203–5
  Fragment of a Crucifixion 204
  *Three Studies for Figures at the
    Base of a Crucifixion* 204
  *Triptych – Studies of the Human
    Body* 204
Badiou, Alain, 'La subversion
  infinitésimale' 66, 70–1, 163
Bakhtin, Mikhail 18, 20–1, 59,
  297–301
Bannerman, Henrietta 253–6, 259
Barthes, Roland 5, 16–18, 24, 168,
  289, 293, 294 n.5, 297,
  301–2, 307, 315
  Criticism and Truth 20
  Mythologies 289
Bataille, Georges, *My mother* 58, 204,
  210 n.1, 274
Baudelaire, Charles
  Les Chats 58, 60–1
  Les Fleurs du mal 231
  poetry of 244
Baudrillard, Jean 168–9
Baudry, Jean Louis 25–6
Beardsworth, Sara 71 n.2, 184, 236
Beckettian not-I 115
Bellmer, Hans 201–6
Benjamin, Walter 9, 232, 244–7
Benveniste, Émile 59–61
Berlinguer, Enrico 31–2
Bernard of Clairvaux, St. 173, 175
Bernstein, Richard J. 134–5
biological sex 112
bisexuality 214–16, 220, 223
Blamey, Norman 186
Bloom, Leopold 150–2

body
  body-awareness painting 205–8
  body fragment 9, 198, 200, 204–5,
    208–9, 322
  embodiment 9, 105, 206
  poetic language 5
Boehm, Gottfried 206
Breton, André, *Nadja* 67
Brodsky, Joseph 29–30
Butler, Judith 111–13, 115, 127 n.1,
  135
Butts, Mary 179–80

Camus, Albert 29
Canovan, Margaret 133–4, 138
Cantor, Georg, infinity concept 37–8,
  46, 49–50, 53 n.20
capitalist culture 77, 80, 82–3, 85, 89
castration 114–15, 119, 122, 202,
  213–14
Cavanagh, Clare 3
Céline, Louis-Ferdinand 4, 114, 132,
  145 n.1, 150–63, 181–4
Change (journal) 27
Chare, Nicholas 118–19
Chinese Cultural Revolution 28
chora 37–9, 52 n.12–14, 334
  axioms of set theory 45–6
  definition of 40–3
  as Freudian maternal thing 44–5
  maternal 112
  mathematical aspect of 39–41
  as receptacle 40–6
  relation to Plato's *Timaeus* 40–4,
    50–1
  semiotic 37–8, 47, 68, 70–1, 110,
    279, 323, 332–3
choreography 264–5
Christian/Christianity 77–8, 98–9,
  102–3, 313
  fundamentalism 80, 83, 94–9,
    105 n.2
  hypocrisy of church 95
  Orthodox East 172–6
  post-Christian humanism 316
  Roman West 170–4
  secular disillusionment with 95
  spirituality 313–19

Clément, Catherine 315
Colette, Sidonie-Gabrielle 57, 65, 71, 133, 288–93
colonization/colonialism 7, 120, 122–3, 167, 310
communities 109–10, 119
consumerism 81–3
Corey, Frederick 257
cosmic temporality 290
creative resistance theory 85, 89
Critique (journal) 18

Daix, Pierre 21, 24
Daniel, Yuli 29
de Beauvoir, Simone, *The Second Sex* 288, 292–3
Debord, Guy 316
Dedalus, Stephen 150
defilement 202, 270, 274
de Mille, Agnes 252–3
DeNiro, Robert 251
Derrida, Jacques 42, 51 n.6, 330, 332
    'Dissemination' 66, 70
de-Stalinization 17, 22, 24
detective fiction 82
dialogism 18, 37, 298–301
Diderot, Denis, *The Nun* 94–6
Die Puppe 201
Diprose, Rosalyn 136–7
discursive retrieval 111
dissemination 306, 310
dissidence 28–31
    Biennale of Dissent 1977 29–32
    dissident writer 29–32
Douglas, Mary 180, 199, 274
drapery 9, 181, 185–6, 189–90, 192 n.26
dual personalities/psychical splits 122

écriture textuelle 19
ego identification 113–14
Eichmann trial 134–5
emotional intelligence 75
Eurocentrism 6
Eurocommunism 30–1
European avant-gardes
    impasses and risks of 4
    Kristeva's contribution to 1–7
    legacy of 3–4, 10 n.5
    myths of 2–3
    Tel Quel and 17, 22–3, 26
    value of writings 3
experimentation 1, 11 n.10, 277

false mysticism 94, 99–103
fanaticism/scepticism 96, 98–9, 102–4
Fanon, Frantz 122
fascism 114, 144, 167–8, 171
    transpolitical 167–8
Faulkner, William 76
Faye, Jean-Pierre 21, 27
female genius 287–94
The Feminine and the Sacred 288, 314
feminine/femininity 5, 9
    concepts of woman and 237
    conceptualization of 57, 65–7
    double negativity 225
    irony 213–20
    jouissance 255, 262
    psychic depth 61
    sacredness of 288
    semiotic and 61
    subjectivation 221, 293
    transformative aspect of 65
fetishism 77, 185, 216
fictitious unity 112
Figure at a Washbasin 204
filioque/per filium 172–3
foreigner/stranger 103–5, 136
    estrangement 103, 198, 272
fort/da game 256
Foucault, M. 20, 112
Franko, Mark 257
Fraser, Nancy 139–40
French Communist Party 17, 19, 22
Freud, Sigmund 64, 105 n.1
    fort/da game 256
    Freudian *Zeitlos* 252, 254, 257, 265
    neo-Freudian framework 77
    uncanny 269, 272
fundamentalism 80, 83, 94–9, 105 n.2

gender normativity 201
genius 133
genotext 59, 279–81, 299, 303 n.2, 329–30

Girard, René 95
God 171–6, 317
Goldmann, Lucien 18
gothic 179–93
Graham, Martha
  Cave of the Heart 251
  dance and mirroring 264–5
  Freud's *fort/da* game 256–7
  Hérodiade 251–65
  and Kristeva's semiotic 254–7
  Mallarmé's poem 251–4, 258–9, 261–2
  Martha Graham Dance Company 252
  maternal body 261–4
  maternal subjectivity 260–4
  mirror stage 252–4, 256, 260, 264–5, 272
  semiotic and symbolic modalities 255–6
  Zeitlos and 257–60

Hamlyn, Anne 185–6
Hawthorne, Nathaniel, *The Scarlet Letter* 77
Haynes, John 184–5
hejab/hijab 94–5, 103, 121
Henric, Jacques 28–9
heterogeneity 140–4, 330
  heterogeneous matter 3, 333
Hilbert, David 46
Hindemith, Paul 251–2
history of science 79–80, 82, 87–90
Hope, Alexander 41
Houdebine, Jean-Louis 23, 27, 38
Huguenin, Jean-René 19
human sciences 21, 25, 82
hupodochê (receptacle) 43–4. *See also* receptacle, *chora*
Huxley, Aldous 179

imaginary father 61, 64
imperialism 8, 18, 79, 134, 162–72, 221
  imperialist nostalgia 175
indifference 72 n.11
  indifferent feminine
    conceptualization of feminine 57, 65–7

linguistics to psychoanalysis 57–8
male artists 62–3
maternal function 61
mère-version 63–5
preliminaries 58–62
psychoanalytic perspective 65–7
woman-effect (*see* feminine/femininity)
individuality. *See* singularity
infinity 7, 37–9, 48–50, 59, 66
  infinity point 70–1
ingenium 289
inner life 310
International Association for Semiotic Studies 59
interpersonal and socio-symbolic 118
intersectionality 18, 84, 134, 227, 234, 271, 297, 299–301, 303
intertextuality 59, 297–303
intimacy 97–8
Irigaray, Luce 293, 294 n.3
irony 9, 213–20, 226
Islam 106 n.6, 313, 319 n.1. *See also* Muslim
  beliefs and practices 106 n.4
  cultures of 120–2
  fundamentalism 96, 99
Ivanov, Vyacheslav 21

Jakobson, Roman 21, 31, 48
  'On a Generation That Squandered its Poets' 30
  structuralism 58
James, M. R. 179–93
  abjection 183
  antisemitic sentiments 182
  boundary breakdown 182
  'Canon Alberic's Scrap-Book' 185
  'The Diary of Mr. Poynter' 185
  fabric of fear 184–6
  ghost stories 9, 179–80, 183, 185, 187–91
  Judith 191 n.10
  manuscript apocalypses 183–4
  'Oh, Whistle, and I'll Come to You, My Lad' 187–91

'The Stalls of Barchester Cathedral' 184
strangeness 180
'The Uncommon Prayer-Book' 182
Jardine, Alice 18, 21, 59, 64
Jasper, Alison 111
Jean, Raymond 24
Jones, Allen 186
Joyce, James 150–63, 179
  Dubliners 151
  Finnegan's Wake 153
  Ulysses 150–3
Judaism 98–9
Judt, Tony, *Past Imperfect* 30
Juin, Hubert 19

Keltner, Stacy 110
Klein, Melanie 131, 133, 142–3, 287–94
Konrad, Gyorky 29–30
Kristeva, Julia. See also Sollers, Philippe
  analyses of avant-gardes 1–7 (*see also* avant-garde)
  'A New Type of Intellectual: The Dissident' 28
  on Arendt's work 129–45, 157–67
  Black Sun 5, 287–8, 335
  chora (*see* chora)
  concept of political 164–7
  Crisis of the European Subject 77
  'Dissident Literature as the Refutation of Left Discourse' 30
  'Distance and anti-representation' 20
  The Enchanted Clock 75–90
  'Engendering the Formula' 66–7, 69–70
  'Europhilia, Europhobia' 78, 85
  Female Genius: Life, Madness, Words – Hannah Arendt, Melanie Klein, Colette 88–9
  'For a semiology of paragrams' 18
  Graham and 254–7
  Hatred and Forgiveness 272, 302
  'The Ideology of Discourse on Literature' 27–8
  Klein's studies and theories 143
  La révolution du langage poétique (Revolution in Poetic Language) 1–2, 5, 38, 40, 46–7, 50, 60, 63, 68, 136–7, 163–4, 255, 274, 279–80, 282, 287, 291, 297–8, 302, 305, 307–8, 321, 331
  Le Génie féminin 287
  'Le Langage poétique comme infinité' ('Poetic Language as Infinity') 38
  'Le mot, le dialogue et le roman' 37
  and Martha Graham's *Hérodiade* 251–65
  Mémoire (My Memory's Hyperbole) 16–17, 28, 330
  'Motherhood According to Bellini' 78
  Nations without Nationalism 86
  New Maladies of the Soul 23, 239, 275, 306
  'The Novel as Polylogue' 4
  on number (*see* number)
  The Old Man and the Wolves 76–7, 80, 82–3, 85, 88
  Polylogue 297, 321
  'Pour une sémiologie des paragrammes' ('Towards a Semiology of Paragrams') 38
  Powers of Horror: An Essay on Abjection 5, 63, 111, 159–60, 163–4, 200, 255, 271, 279, 314
  'Prelude to an Ethics of the Feminine' 65
  presentation at Biennale 30–1
  'The Problems of the Structuration of the Text' 25–6
  reconceptualization of God 171–6
  relationship to PCF 22–4
  The Samurai 81, 86
  Séméiotiké, Recherches pour un sémanalyse 18, 60, 297
  'Semiology Today in the Soviet Union' 20
  'Semiotics: A Critical Science and/or a Critique of Science' 25–6

semiotics transition 5, 18–19, 21, 26, 37–8, 62–3
The Sense and Non-Sense of Revolt 4, 5, 64, 67, 85, 192 n.26, 278, 282–3, 290, 305
The Severed Head: Capital Visions 111, 119
'Stabat Mater' 262
Stalinism 17, 22–5
Strangers to Ourselves 103–5
study on Céline 149–67, 181–4
Tales of Love 57, 173
Teresa, My Love: An Imagined Life of the Saint of Avila 64, 66, 78, 93–4, 99–100, 103–5, 288, 314
as terrorist aesthetics 2–3
'Thinking about Liberty in Dark Times' 335
This Incredible Need to Believe 314
and Todorov 17–18, 22
'What's the Use of Politics in Times of Distress' 22
'Women's Time' 139
'Word, Dialogue, Novel' 18
work on Bakhtin 18, 20–1, 59
works with *Tel Quel* 15–32, 297 (see also Tel Quel)

Lacan, Jacques
  mirror stage 252–4, 256, 260, 264–5, 272
  Name-of-the-Father 114
  object petit a 123
  Other 271
  phallic monism 213–14
  psychoanalysis 130, 224
  Real 219
  Seminar XX 240
  split subject 322–4
  symbolic order 112, 242, 246
La Nouvelle Critique 23–5, 27
Lassnig, Maria 205–8
  'Body-awareness-painting' 207
  korperbilder (body awareness) 206
LeClercq, Sylvia 78, 94–106, 314
Le Fanu, Sheridan 180
lesbianism 215–16

le sémiotique (the semiotic) 5, 37–40, 46–51, 52 n.12, 53 n.16, 60–4, 68–71, 83, 110–13, 117–19, 126, 127 n.1, 153, 181, 190, 200, 214, 216, 234–9, 242–3, 246, 248, 254–7, 260, 263, 279–81, 299–302, 305–9, 321–7, 329–36
Les Lettres Françaises 19, 23–5
Levinas, Emmanuel 112, 116–17
Lévy, Bernard-Henri 31
liberalism 77–8, 85
liminal/liminality 4, 9, 126, 185, 232, 234–5
  experience of limits 3, 325
L'Infini (magazine) 16
linguistics 18, 26–7
  and psychoanalysis 57–8, 60, 64
  supremacist 114
Litauer, Emilia 59
literary criticism 297–8
literary realism 20
literary semiology. *See* semiotics/semiology
The London Mercury 179
Lorey, Eric 183–4
Lotman, Juri 21, 59
love 9, 89, 97, 135–6, 173, 232–48, 314
Luxemburg, Rosa 166

MacCannell, Juliet Flower 112–15, 127 n.3
Macciocchi, Maria-Antonietta 30
Maddy, Penelope 39
Madison Avenue tactics 170–1
male artists, indifferent feminine 62–3
Mallarmé, Stéphane
  'Hérodiade' 258–9
  'La Musique et les lettres' 53 n.24
  poetics 47–51, 251–4, 261–2
  '*Un coup de dés*' 37, 40, 48–9
Map, Walter, *De Nugis Curialum* 186
Maria Agnese Firrao 101
Maria Luisa 100–3, 107 n.7–8

INDEX

Marty, Martin 105 n.2
Marxism 16–17, 22–3, 26–7, 29, 31, 105 n.1, 138
mass culture 28
materialism 3, 59, 77–8, 83, 204, 330
mathematical concept 7, 18–19, 37–40, 66, 70, 186. *See also* infinity
May 1968 20, 26–7, 168
McGinn, Colin 199
Meillassoux, Quentin 37, 47–51, 53 n.18, 53 n.20
melancholic modernism 6, 231–48. *See also* modernism
melancholy 232, 237–8, 244–5, 262
mère-version 63–5
metaphor/metamorphosis 96–7
mirror stage 252–4, 256, 260, 264–5, 272
Mitterand, Henri 25
modern dance 251–65
    choreography 264–5
    Hérodiade 251
    Mallarmé's poem 251–2
    and mirroring 264–5
    poetic language of movement 255
modernism 1, 4–6, 37, 93
    abject modernism 6
    avant-garde and 57–9, 63, 277
    fundamentalism and 80, 83, 94–9, 105 n.2
    Gothic modernism 179–93
    late modernism 208
    melancholic modernism 6, 231–48
    pragmatism and 81
    Proustian moments 81–2
    psychoanalytic 151
    revolutionary modernism 6
    sublimatory modernism 6
    in visual arts 197
    zerological 156–63
modernity/modernist
    in Enlightenment 93, 95, 102–3
    fallen public space 150
    lyricism 84–5
    metaphysics of motion 149–55
    poetry 58–9
    re-oedipalizing 171–6
    in Roman Catholicism 100, 107 n.7

    transpolitical of 167–71
    zero-hour 156–7
monotheism 77
monumental temporality 290
motherhood/maternity
    double agent 114
    maternal body 112, 136, 261
    maternal *chora* 112
    maternal function 61
    maternal *reliance* 263–4, 315, 318
    maternal subjectivity 260–4
    maternal support 131
    and Virgin Mary 100–3, 154–5, 261–2
Mulvey, Laura 186, 192 n.16–17
Muslim 94–6, 98–9, 103–4, 106 n.4, 106 n.6, 120
myths 2–3, 124, 255

nationalism 2, 78–9, 86, 90, 124
Negri, Antonio 145 n.6
neoliberalism 8, 134, 139–40, 143
The New Yorker (magazine) 24
nihilism 95, 151, 156, 162, 308, 315, 336
Nikolchina, Miglena 83
Noguchi, Isamu 251–2, 256–7
nombrant 68–71. *See also* infinity
nonlinear temporality 290
number 7, 37, 48–9, 69–70
    le nombrant 7, 66–7

Obrist, Hans Ulrich 207
O'Donnell, May 261, 265
Oedipus complex
    Oedipal phase 214, 261–2
    Oedipal triangle 113–14
    two-sided Oedipus 61, 65, 213
Oliver, Kelly 97, 254
orientalism 111–13, 118–19, 122–3

paradigm 144, 209, 213, 224, 313, 315, 321
Pasolini, Pier Paolo 29–30
phallus 124–5, 193 n.26, 214–19, 322
    illusionary nature of 215
phenomenology of sensation 116–17, 206–9

phenotext 26, 59, 279–80, 299, 303 n.2, 329–30
phonematic devices 281
Plato, *Timaeus*
  chora 40–7, 51 n.7, 68, 332
play 223, 227, 258, 263, 330, 332, 334. *See also fort/da* game
plurality/pluralism 140–4
  pluralization 49–50
poetic language 2, 5, 37–43, 48, 255, 300, 334
  subject in process and 324–6
politics/political 3–9, 16, 19, 23–5, 27–9, 62, 65, 83, 90, 93, 109, 112–13, 120–2, 126, 129–44, 149–73, 248, 275–83, 287, 305–6, 309–10, 326–7
Pope Leo XII 101
Pope Pius IX 101
post-Christian humanism 316–17
postmodern condition 336
poststructuralism 297, 315
pragmatism 75–84, 87–90
  to abjection 75–7, 89–90
  and resistance 85, 89
  technology and science 87–8
precarity 8, 131–2, 144
primary processes 43–4, 48, 53 n.25
productivity 38, 59–60, 329–30, 334
prohibition/transgression 125, 204, 233, 238, 243, 245, 274, 301, 307, 333–4
Protestantism 77, 102–3, 174
Proust, Marcel 64, 81–2, 88–9, 132, 141, 165–7, 181, 301, 307, 318
psychic depth 61
psychoanalysis 57–8, 60, 63–8, 218, 274–6
  art and 125
  and astrophysics 77, 79–81, 87, 89
  and ethics 87
  heteronormativity of 115
  hostility to 130, 171
  politics and history 93
Pythagoreanism 40–1

racism 119, 221, 310
radical strangeness 293
receptacle, *chora* 40–6, 50–1, 52 n.12
reflective judgment 135, 145 n.7
religious fundamentalism 93–5, 310
revolt 132, 238, 305–8
  culture 3–4
  in exquisite gesture 125
  intimate revolt 305–10
  Oedipal/anti-Oedipal 172, 307
  Orlando's 213–27
  violence 307
revolutionary modernism 6. *See also* modernism
Rhys, Jean 9, 231–48
Richard, Claude 77
Richer, Paul, *Études cliniques sur la grande hystérie ou hystéro-épilepsie* 80
Risset, Jacqueline 32 n.1
robotization 61
Roman Catholic revision 171–6
Ronat, Mitsou 27
Rose, Jacqueline 110–11
Roudinesco, Elisabeth 27
Russian formalism 21, 23, 26, 30, 58–9, 297, 315

Saint Augustine 96, 103, 135–6
Sallis, John 41–4
salon culture 158
Samoyault, Tiphaine 16
Sartre, Jean-Paul 2, 29, 307
Saussure, Ferdinand de 297–8
  'Anagrammes' 18
  concept of sign 58–9, 66, 69–70, 110
Scalia, Gianni 32
scandal 95, 102–3, 105, 258–9
Scarpetta, Guy 29
Schippers, Birgit 292–3, 294 n.4
Scorcese, Martin, *Taxi Driver* 251
Scotus, Duns 218, 289, 316
Scullion, Rosemarie 182
secularism 8
  and fundamentalism 94–9
sémanalyse 37

semiotics/semiology 18–21, 329–36.
    See also *le sémiotique* (the semiotic)
  avant-garde art 47
  and *chora* 61, 68
  critical semiotics 19
  disposition 330
  feminine identity 61–3
  materialist 46
  and mathematics 37–41
  as science 18, 26, 60
  signification 60, 117
  symbolization of 47–51, 52 n.12, 53 n.16, 60, 110, 112–13, 117–18, 254–7
  and *Zeitlos* 254
set theory 37–40
  chora as 45–6
Seurat, Georges, *Veil* 124
Sheth, Falguni 119–27
sign 26, 58–9, 69–70, 110
  communities 109–10, 119
signifiance 2, 5, 59–60, 63–4, 69, 117, 282–3, 297, 302, 321, 323, 329, 332, 334
singularity 97, 134–40
Sinyavsky, Andrei 29–30
Sjöholm, Cecilia 124
social conformism 151, 169
socialist realism 23–4, 29
Söderbäck, Fanny 262
Sollers, Philippe 15–17, 29, 277, 281
  claimed PCF 25
  H 4, 281
  hyper-modernist novels 37
  Kristeva and 16–17
  Numbers 58, 66–7, 69–70
  Tel Quel 15
spectacle, society of the 83, 305, 308, 310, 316
Spillers, Hortense 111
spirituality 94, 101, 313–19
  sacred 96
Spivak, Gayatri 317
Stalinism 17, 22–5
Stodelle, E. 253, 258

strangeness 103–5, 180, 293. *See also* foreigner/stranger
structuralism 18–19, 21, 26, 58–60, 297
subject/subjectivity 63–4
  ego identification 113–14
  and object relationship 110–18
  phenomenological subject 115
  politics and 129–34
  semiotic and 110–11
  subject-formation 9
  subject in process/on trial *(le sujet-en-procès)* 3, 5, 137, 161–2, 173, 223, 248 n.2, 252, 281, 283, 298, 318–27
    and ethico-political stakes 326–7
    Lacan's split subject 322–4
    and poetic language 324–6
  subjective crisis 1
sublimatory modernism 6. *See also* modernism
symbolic 110–27, 136–8, 143–4, 201, 254–7, 261–2, 329–36

The Tales of Hoffmann 201
technology 79–80, 131
Tel Quel (magazine) 2, 15–17
  avant-garde venture 17
  Communist Party and 17, 19, 22–4
  Kristeva's works in 16–20, 297
  La Nouvelle Critique and 23, 26–7
  literary semiotics 18–20
  with PCF intellectuals 23–4, 26–8
  political positions 19–20
  'The revolution here and now' 26
  Sollers' literary journal 15–17, 277
  Soviet semiotics and 21–2
  structuralism 18–19, 21, 26, 58–60
  'Theoretical Studies Group' 27
  Todorov and 17–18, 20
  workings of language 17
temporality 252, 264, 290
  female temporality 290
  timeless 307
Teresa of Avila 78, 101, 314
  divine 97
  faith 94, 96

intimacy 97–8
metaphors/metamorphosis 96–7
singularity 97
spirituality 94, 96, 101
The Way of Perfection 97, 314
terrorist aesthetics 2–3
textiles 185–6
text/textuality 18–20, 49, 69, 140–1, 150, 279–83, 326, 329, 331. *See also* genotext; phenotext
thesis 331, 333
thetic break/phase 104, 333
timbre rythmé (rhythmical timbre) 47–8
Todorov, Tzvetan 17–18
  'Formalists and Futurists' 20
  Théorie de la littérature 18, 20–1
totalitarianism 134
transfinite 37
translinguistic process 59–60
transpolitical conformism 167–71
transposition 11 n.8, 48, 163, 298, 302
transubstantiation 5, 6, 64, 71
traumatic real 109–27
tropism 207

uncanny 104–5, 269, 272
unrepresentable 115
untorelli (plague carriers) 31–2
uprootedness 131, 158–60, 163, 167, 219–20

Vaneigem, Raoul 149–50
veil/veiling
  aesthetic strategy 7
  of art 111–12, 125
  castration anxiety 119
  colonialist logic 122
  dual personalities/psychical splits 122

Enlightenment thinking 124
fluid veils 124
of phallus 192 n.26
prohibition on wearing of 125
realm of art 125
subject of 111
symbolism of 120–3
Western imaginaries 123
violence 4, 53 n.23, 75, 89, 134, 142–3, 156, 173, 274, 307, 309
visual arts 208–9
von Reisach, Karl 101

Watkin, William 71 n.2
Weber, Max, *The Protestant Ethic and the Spirit of Capitalism* 77
Wolf, Hubert, *The Nuns of Sant'Ambrogio: The True Story of a Convent in Scandal* 99–100, 107 n.8
woman-effect 61. *See also* feminine/femininity
Woolf, Virginia 76
  Mrs Dalloway 81
  Orlando 9, 213–28
world-religions 105 n.2, 313, 315
writer/writing 2–10, 16–25, 28–30, 57–9, 64–7, 69–70, 75, 85, 156–8, 163, 180, 183–6, 216–18, 232–40, 243–4, 277–9, 281–3, 290–1, 298–9, 301–3, 309, 318
  choreography 262, 264
  structuralism 19, 21

Yannakakis, Ilios 29–30
Yeğenoğlu, M. 122

Ziarek, Ewa Plonowska 136–7

www.ingramcontent.com/pod-product-compliance
Lightning Source LLC
LaVergne TN
LVHW021559201224
799625LV00001B/44